A

HISTORY *of* PSYCHOLOGY

in AUTOBIOGRAPHY

Volume IV

By

Walter Van Dyke Bingham

Edwin Garrigues Boring

Cyril Burt

Richard M. Elliott

Agostino Gemelli

Arnold Gesell

Clark L. Hull

Walter S. Hunter

David Katz

Albert Michotte

Jean Piaget

Henri Piéron

Godfrey Thomson

L. L. Thurstone

Edward Chace Tolman

Edited by

Edwin G. Boring

Herbert S. Langfeld

Heinz Werner

Robert M. Yerkes

CLARK UNIVERSITY PRESS

Worcester, Massachusetts

Printed in the United States of America
by Commonwealth Press
Worcester, Massachusetts

PREFACE

It is now fifteen years since the third volume of *History of Psychology in Autobiography* appeared. These preceding volumes, modelled after the German series *Die Philosophie der Gegenwart in Selbstdarstellungen* and edited by Carl Murchison, consist of short autobiographies of prominent psychologists who had been asked by the editors to write their "intellectual histories."

Since we felt that this series ought not to be allowed to lapse, especially now that a new generation has reached the age from which looking backward becomes profitable, the American Psychological Association appointed us as a committee to arrange for the publication of a fourth volume and to edit it.

We sought and found eight Americans and seven Europeans, all distinguished psychologists and all over sixty years of age (with one exception), who had not already contributed to this series of volumes and who might be expected to have acquired a sufficient past to make an account of it worth while. We note how arbitrary our choice of authors has been. Some choice was necessary. Every choice was bound to be invidious.

The reader of this volume will see how much our autobiographers differ from one another in the nature of their efforts. Perhaps they differ most in the degree with which they find unity in their lives. Presumably every one of them would like to see his intellectual history as the evolution of a single purpose, for integrity is good and simplicity is elegant. No one, of course, fully succeeds in this undertaking, for the story of every life is constrained by the exigencies of its owner's environment.

Some of these accounts are more intellectualistic than others, and it may be that they show the greater unity, either because some irrelevancies are omitted from the life history or because irrelevancies are actually, at least to a certain degree, omitted from the actual living. Other accounts are more environmentalistic, because social and institutional events and accidents have figured so largely in them. The environmentalistic autobiographer may have had a chief long-term goal, have pursued it, have achieved it with some fair degree of success, yet he may feel that the unforeseeable accidents of living have determined much of his life and have perhaps even altered his

v

goal. The intellectualist, if such we may call him, may, on the other hand, have suffered disruption of plans less than his colleague, but it is probable that he has also been less interested in the effect of external forces upon himself.

No one, not even the members of this group of distinguished psychologists, can hope to deal adequately with the springs of his motivation. What he tells about himself and what he shows about his values can, however, go far toward instructing the reader as to how human motive moves to make science progress. The accidents of living do not always seem irrelevant to progress when they operate in the manner which the pages of this book show. Psychology in autobiography cannot be complete, but it can make a contribution to the history of psychology which is unique.

We are grateful for the hearty cooperation of our fifteen authors. We are grateful to the American Psychological Association, who, at our request, sponsored this project. We acknowledge a debt of gratitude to Helen S. Orr of Princeton University for her invaluable assistance in editing the manuscript. We must also express our appreciation of the Clark University Press which has risen from recent inactivity for the express purpose of continuing this series which it initiated so happily in 1932.

Edwin G. Boring
Heinz Werner
Robert M. Yerkes
Herbert S. Langfeld, *Chairman*

TABLE OF CONTENTS

Walter Van Dyke Bingham

Edwin Garrigues Boring

Cyril Burt

Richard M. Elliott

Agostino Gemelli

Arnold Gesell

Clark L. Hull

Walter S. Hunter

David Katz   Albert Michotte

Jean Piaget   Henri Piéron

Godfrey Thomson

L. L. Thurstone

Edward Chace Tolman

A HISTORY OF PSYCHOLOGY
IN AUTOBIOGRAPHY

VOLUME IV

WALTER VAN DYKE BINGHAM

IN the history of psychology the epoch I have seen in the making spans roughly the first half of the twentieth century. I have watched an astonishingly rapid growth in psychological science and in the infant profession of the practicing psychologist. When elected Secretary-Treasurer of the American Psychological Association at the nineteenth meeting held at the University of Minnesota in 1910, I found in the record book the names of 222 members. More than three-quarters of these were teaching psychology to college students. Scarcely a handful were earning a livelihood off campus, practicing clinical psychology in homes for the feeble-minded, or in mental hospitals — then still called insane asylums. I recall but one member in private practice without institutional affiliation.

Only 32 members came to that Minneapolis meeting. Forty years later, at Pennsylvania State College, attendance was a hundred times as large. The Association then had 7,250 members, of whom *a majority were practitioners* in industries, business offices, railways, hospitals, schools, clinics, welfare agencies, employment services, and government bureaus. Psychology was approaching maturity, not only as a science but also as a technology and a profession.

My part in facilitating this transformation is here to be told. What have I done, in peace and in wartime, to advance psychotechnology and to open doors of opportunity for psychologists by finding the talented, encouraging their advancement, making known their potentialities in non-academic circles, and so speeding the emergence of a psychological profession? These questions the editors of this volume have asked me to answer.

Here, then, is a sketch of my family background and the circumstances that shaped my development, told so as to portray the combination of interests, abilities and opportunities which led me toward a career in psychology rather than in Latin or mathematics, or in merchandising, my father's occupation. The narrative also makes clear, I think, how it was that my activities came to a focus on the psychology of work, educational and occupational

1

counseling, and industrial personnel management, the areas in which my efforts to augment our knowledge and to make it of use have been most fruitful.

I. Family Background

Much younger than my four sisters and my brother, Lewis, I was born in 1880, in Swan Lake City, Iowa. This frontier village, then the county seat of Emmet County, seemed destined for speedy growth upon construction of a projected railroad; but the road went elsewhere, so my birthplace vanished from the map.

My father, Lemuel Rothwell Bingham, grew up on a farm near Ellsworth in eastern Ohio. He was a retail clerk in Youngstown when, aged 20, he yielded to the call of adventure at the height of the Gold Rush and went to California. After four years he brought back gold enough to buy a well stocked farm in southwestern Wisconsin, but hog cholera invaded his pens and robbed him of his properties. Farming was not for him; so he headed west, to begin again, this time as a merchant.

Meanwhile he had married my mother, Martha Evarts Tracy, daughter of Deacon Samuel Tracy of Platteville, Wisconsin. Born and brought up on a farm in Hartford, Vermont, close to White River Junction, when sixteen she had migrated with her parents to Wisconsin, and was not to see New England again for fifty years. A graduate of Platteville Academy, now a state teachers college, she was eager, vivid and deeply religious. Her intellectual interests led her throughout an arduous life of child-rearing and housekeeping to set aside in each busy day a time for serious reading, which made our dining table a center of discussion about books.

Both the Tracy and the Bingham lines reach back to colonial times. The first Thomas Bingham came from England when he was 17, settling in Norwich, Connecticut, in 1650. The first Stephen Tracy had preceded him, arriving in 1623. Both strains were prolific, and pious. Among the Tracys were several Congregational ministers, deacons, and missionaries to the Orient. On the Bingham side, piety did not so often become a profession; but Presbyterian elders were common, and my two oldest sisters married Presbyterian ministers. My father adhered strictly to the Mosaic ratio and gave a tenth of his net income to church and charities. No matter what the provocation, he never uttered a word of profanity. Nor could he be persuaded to do any business on Sunday. I respected his strict integrity, but could not admire all his rigidities. His fondness for exploration never left him. Knowing that the earth conceals buried treasure, he spent a good deal of time looking into and investing in mining projects: lead and zinc in Missouri, and coal in our northern Iowa. If this spirit of the pioneer cropped out in his younger son, it is in his efforts to open up new areas in applied psychology. But my intellectual interests as well as my interest in people and my enjoyment in helping them, came straight from my mother.

There were not many pupils in the Swan Lake school which I entered at the age of six, and each of us was permitted to push ahead at his own pace. When I was eight, we moved a few miles west, to Estherville, a town of nearly two thousand which had become the county seat and a division point on the railway. The kindly principal of schools, with long black side-whiskers and deep-set eyes, examined me by asking a few questions in mental arithmetic and then handing me one reader after another to see how readily I made my way through pages of increasing difficulty. Then he put me into the fifth grade instead of the third. That is why I entered college at the age of sixteen, pretty immature as well as ill-prepared.

In the unfolding drama of self-discovery the occupational tryout played a leading role. Sampling varied employments while still a schoolboy, I learned about my own capacities and preferences.[1] In reviewing these first-hand work experiences, it is easy to discern the origins of later interests in occupational psychology, vocational guidance, industrial safety, personnel management, motion study and work simplification. Moreover, while in high school, I tasted the pleasure of explaining to fellow students puzzling propositions in geometry and obscure constructions in Cicero. These samples of what a teacher does made me think that I might like to be a teacher.

II. INTERESTS

When E. K. Strong first made available a scoring stencil for ascertaining the resemblance of one's interests to those of psychologists, I was taken aback to find that my letter rating was C. My likes and dislikes corresponded to those of his normative group no more closely than those of "men in general" did. But I was relieved on learning that Donald G. Paterson also rated C. Both of us have always been keenly interested, not only in books, statistics, and psychological experiments, but even more in persons. We have relished close contacts with all sorts of people, and have particularly enjoyed helping those who showed promise. At present, using the current form of Strong's vocational interest blank and Kreidt's scoring stencil, Paterson and I find ourselves no longer out in the cold. We score B+. Possibly our social interests and attitudes have become more like those of members of our profession who provided Strong with his first norms, but I think it is the other way around. Are not a majority of psychologists of today genuinely interested in persons, more socially inclined and less frequently introverted than was the typical psychologist twenty years ago?

[1] W. V. Bingham, Try-out experiences of a small-town boy, *Voc Guid Mag*, March, 1940, 1–4.

I confess to a liking for editorial work. A disproportionate fraction of my hours and years has been spent in facilitating communication by puzzling out ways of saying things more crisply, interestingly, and informingly. Such duties have fascinated me no matter whether the drafts to be polished have been written by myself or by my helpers, or by would-be contributors to journals on whose editorial boards I have too frequently consented to serve.[2] Reluctant to reject outright an unsatisfactory manuscript, I have tried to show in detail how it might be made acceptable by rearrangement, condensation, or clarification.

Add now to these interests a fondness for looking ahead, planning, and *initiating a cooperative enterprise* in the common good. There emerges a pattern of motivations that in restrospect helps to account for several turns in the road I have traversed.

Music has been a hobby always. It is said that in the kilt skirt epoch before I can remember, I enjoyed standing in the church pew between my parents and singing lustily the familiar hymns. From the time I was ten I experimented with all sorts of musical instruments, from harmonium to French horn, to find out what kinds of sounds, rhythmical and harmonious or otherwise, each instrument could be made to produce. The cello had unsurpassed acoustical resources. With it one could not fail to learn a good deal about vibration ratios, upper partials, changes in timbre or tonal quality, consonance, harmonics, difference tones and their numerical relationships. This fondness for musical activities has been associated with my curiosity about musical ethnology and also about auditory and acoustical phenomena, and speech.

In our parlor was an old reed organ on which as a boy I found out many things about consonances and dissonances, chords and scales. When ten years old I had a chance to learn to play an alto horn in the village band then in need of a performer on that humble instrument. Many were the evenings we spent rehearsing *The Poet and Peasant Overture* in the back room of the State Bank. Later I tried to manage a reed instrument, the clarinet. My sisters offered to get me something they thought more refined, a flute; but a few attempts to play the scale on a borrowed instrument proved most discouraging. Instead, I bought for $12 a violoncello which became my intimate companion for a dozen years. As a college sophomore I attacked a piano which stood helpless in the common room of the dormitory. Another instrument I ventured to try was the French horn, a devilishly tricky contraption which, nevertheless, helped me to earn a part of my tuition in

---

[2] My name has appeared on the mastheads of the *Journal of Educational Psychology, Journal of Consulting Psychology, Annalen der Betriebswirtschaft und Arbeitsforschung,* and notably on Vol. 1, No 1 of the *Journal of Applied Psychology,* 1917; *Personnel,* 1918, *Journal of Personnel Research,* 1922; and *Personnel Psychology,* 1948.

the graduate school at the University of Chicago by playing in the university band.

I made repeated attempts to learn to sing. I liked to rehearse in the college glee club with Ding Darling, in a church choir led by a masterful organist, and in the community choral society. I even organized a mixed quartet to sing the commonly preferred hymns, unaccompanied, at home funerals. For these services the leading undertakers willingly paid each of us two dollars. My voice unfortunately has an extremely narrow range and I never quite learned how to manage a tense throat. Even a half hour of singing made me so hoarse that I was likely to catch a cold. Eventually I had to give up all singing, but not until I had achieved some familiarity with the great oratorios, masses, cantatas and ballads from Handel to Percy Grainger.

A related interest was management of musical enterprises. I was elected manager of the Beloit Choral Society and was responsible for making the business arrangements, handling publicity, and collecting dues; and to this day I cherish a presentation volume bound in sumptuous leather, containing a copy of each of the oratorios and cantatas sung by that Society during the period of my managership.

Another fling at musical management was at the University of Chicago Settlement back of the stockyards, where as a graduate student I spent an evening each week rehearsing a boys' orchestra. The prime requisite for membership was not a high average in tests of musical aptitude; it was a note from the head resident advising me that the applicant was on probation from the juvenile court. But I had no disciplinary problems.

III. Two Colleges

In the late nineties Kansas University was famed for the productivity of its scientists. The town of Lawrence, originally settled by New Englanders who stampeded there in the fifties to save the state for freedom, was still predominantly a Yankee community in the finest Congregational traditions of goodwill, piety, neighborliness and tolerance – a good place in which to go to college.

But my main reasons for going to Lawrence were economic. Except for a few hundred dollars earned and saved during six years of working after school, Saturdays, and summers, I expected to earn my way. The tuition was only $10 a year for non-residents. (No charge at all for Kansans.) And I had a chance to work for my board. Yet another weighty reason was that this university was willing to admit me in spite of a heavy load of conditions. These I managed to work off during the first semester.

Mathematics was my easiest course, and neither introductory chemistry nor German gave me much trouble; but Latin was my favorite. How I relished the lilt and rhythm of scanning Horace's odes and the illumination of finding in Livy's crisp prose the precise shades of meaning of the roots of words long familiar!

Looking back on that year I realize how few acquaintances I made. Of college life I saw nothing. That explains why I, the youngest freshman, was the only one to come through the year with grades of A in all courses, and why in July, at home in northern Iowa, I did not want to go back to Kansas University. I transferred to Beloit. But here my interest in Latin waned. If I were to teach, it would be mathematics and physics, or perhaps a biological science.

In psychology we had a brilliant young teacher, Guy Alan Tawney, who had earned his doctorate under Wundt with a dissertation on tactile discrimination of two points. He was equally at home in the history of philosophy from Thales to Herbert Spencer, a mind-stretching route that we traced with him throughout senior year. He almost won our adherence to each philosophical system he described before taking up its successor.

It was not until after graduation that I found out what it was like to work with Tawney and Stetson in the laboratory, taking part as subject or as experimenter in psychological research.

IV. GRADUATE STUDY

After four years of teaching in secondary schools, I entered the University of Chicago. There, in 1905, the campus seethed with intellectual ferment. Angell, Mead, Tufts, and their disciples were campaigning for a functional psychology rather than for a purely descriptive structural science. Of any specific mental activity they asked, what does this process do? What is it for? What good is it? What does it accomplish in facilitating adjustment between the organism and its surroundings? In this atmosphere John Dewey and his associates were developing a school of thought[a] and a method which William James, following Charles Peirce, was to baptize pragmatism.

In those days a student preparing for his doctoral examination was sure to consult the *Psychological Review*, 1896, volume 3. The book would open itself to the well-thumbed pages of Dewey's epoch-making paper on "The reflex arc concept in psychology." That article was misnamed. It should have been called "The organic circuit concept," or "The reflex arc concept — its absurdity in psychology." In it Dewey made clear how fallacious it is to carry over into psychology the neurological picture of a sensori-motor apparatus, with sensation antedating action. The ocular act of looking at the candle precedes the sensation of light. When a specific stimulus occurs,

[a] See *Psychol Bull*, 1904, 1, 1, where James enthusiastically welcomes the "Chicago School."

the organism, he pointed out, is already responding to a situation, making an adjustment. The ongoing response defines, or ignores, the stimulus. The activity is not merely a response to, but into, the stimulus. Sensation and movement lie inside, not outside, the act of coordination. That article of Dewey's provided a cornerstone for the Chicago variety of functional psychology.

In Angell's overcrowded laboratory I found John B. Watson in charge not only of the animal laboratory in the cellar, but also of the experimental course which followed closely the four volumes of Titchener's *Manual.* I became his student assistant, and during one Winter Quarter took charge of the course while he went to the Dry Tortugas off the west coast of Florida to initiate his famous observations on the behavior of the noddy and sooty terns. Watson, by the way, used to have difficulty in making consistent introspective reports, *e.g.,* when experimenting on visual after images and color contrast; and some of us speculated in later years as to whether this fact may not have supplied part of the urge which eventually drove him toward a purely objective behavioristic system.

My first published paper[4] described an exciting opportunity that came my way to examine a woman teacher who could hear fairly well without benefit of mechanical hearing aids although an infection had deprived her in childhood of the drum membranes and larger ossicles of both ears. What a stroke of good fortune! I was able to demonstrate that she could hear difference tones, including the so-called subjective combination tones which were said by Helmholtz to originate in the tympanic membrane. What I found also emphasized the fact that the chief function of eardrum and ossicles is not to amplify sound vibrations but to protect the delicate membranes of the inner ear and prevent injuries induced by intense sudden noises.

When deciding on the topic for a doctoral dissertation, what was more natural than to select a problem at the point of intersection between my interest in psychological experimentation and my nonvocational interest in music? I chose the nature of melody.[5]

Learning to Teach Psychology

Teaching is an art. Teaching psychology is a very special art. I early observed that feeding facts by textbook and lecture accomplished little unless the students' appetites were whetted to the point of eager interest and questioning. To this end a favorite device of Angell's at the beginning of a class period was to ask a few questions until two of the students suddenly realized

[4] Bingham, The role of the tympanic mechanism in audition, *Psychol. Rev.*, 1907, 14, 229–243.
[5] Bingham, Studies in melody, *Psychol. Monogr.*, 1910, 12, No. 50.

that they had committed themselves to opposite sides of a controversy. Then he required them to argue the point, and soon everyone in the room was thinking the issues through for himself.

Watson lectured. He would present both sides of a controversial matter vividly, describe a scientific approach to the problem involved, and wind up with a compact summary of conclusions and of issues remaining to be re-solved. He avoided class discussion. The results in terms of final examina-tion marks were excellent, somewhat to Angell's astonishment.

One day two of us from the graduate laboratory dropped in to observe Watson's way of handling a class in introductory psychology. On the stroke of nine in came the brisk instructor, placed his manuscript on the reading desk, and began to speak; but at the end of the first sentence, he paused. His hand went to his forehead. Then, grasping the table, he apologized for not feeling well. Catching sight of me, he asked, "Mr. Bingham, will you take charge?" and off he went. I followed Angell's pattern and promptly got up a lively argument among the students.

Word of the incident got back to the laboratory. Two days later Pro-fessor Angell asked about my plans for the following year. I explained that I was arranging to work off a minor in philosophy at Harvard with Royce, Santayana, and young Ralph Barton Perry, while continuing, in Münster-berg's laboratory, to gather data for my dissertation. "Would you consider postponing that for a year?" Angell asked. "We must have another instruc-tor who will give his entire time to the teaching of sections of the intro-ductory course. I should like you to take that assignment" — adding with emphasis, "for one year only." I did as he wished. A year later I had under my belt the content of the general course from the point of view of the teacher.

On the way to Harvard I spent the summer of 1907 in Berlin where I learned little about teaching but made friendships that long endured: Kurt Koffka, Wolfgang Kohler, Hans Rupp, and of course the great Carl Stumpf. I found there two American students. One was Abraham Flexner; the other was Herbert S. Langfeld, who introduced me to Nagel's laboratory where his own researches were at the time under way. I also renewed contacts with the musicologist, Erich von Hornbostel, whom I had first met in 1905 in Chicago where he had been brought by the Field Museum to study their phonographic recordings of Pawnee Indian music.

On my way back to America I stopped in London long enough to visit Charles Spearman in his laboratory; to make the acquaintance of a congenial spirit, Cyril Burt; and in Cambridge to visit Charles S. Myers in his relatively new psychological laboratory which the University had built with a generous gift from the venerable society of drapers.

At Harvard I was assigned a laboratory room on the third floor of Emerson

Hall. From Munsterberg I learned little about the teaching of psychology. His own seminar that year was in ethics, the theory of values, and I did not attend. His assistant, E. B. Holt, ran the laboratory, and from him I found out how much can be taught during casual conversation in the shop, and after hours.

Back at the University of Chicago for the summer, I completed my dissertation and took the doctoral examination. The examiners wrangled so long before announcing the verdict that I decided I had failed. It turned out that the dispute was whether the degree should be awarded with great praise, or with highest praise. I was happy to have it *magna*.

At Columbia where I spent the years 1908–10 as instructor in Teachers College and assistant to E. L. Thorndike, I observed some remarkably skillful teaching by Naomi Norsworthy, and compared her ways with those of Cattell, Woodworth, and Boas. Unlike any of them were the unique clinical demonstrations on Welfare Island by Adolf Meyer. Each of these teachers had his own way of stimulating thought and sending his listeners off to the library, to the laboratory, or to their own introspections and meditations for more light.

While carrying my share of the instruction in elementary and educational psychology, I was allowed to initiate an advanced course in experimental educational psychology. The students did not repeat classical experiments in learning. They worked on problems faced by teachers in the Speyer School, an experimental school, or in Horace Mann, the model school.

My rolltop desk was next to Thorndike's. What a dynamo he was! One day just before noon he glanced at the clock and remarked, "I must give a lecture in five minutes. It would be fifty per cent better if I spent this time in preparation. But let's compute another coefficient of correlation!" The lecture was nevertheless compact and vivid as usual; and the men in his advanced courses ground away furiously.

During this period I clarified my notions about "intelligence." I liked Woodworth's way of reminding us that intelligence is really an adverb, not the name of a thing. It refers to the *way* in which an organism behaves — intelligently, or not so intelligently. As to the determiners of this way of behaving — alertly, brightly, dully, stupidly — I agreed with Thorndike that a great many factors of more or less importance are operative, not just one general factor, "g," with several factors specific to each situation, as Spearman had maintained since 1904. When characterizing and differentiating the abilities of different people to act intelligently, it struck me as highly appropriate to think in terms of Thorndike's three dimensions: speed, difficulty, and range. The connectionism he advocated seemed oversimplified, but I recognized that as an explanatory principle it served a useful purpose.

V. At Dartmouth

One day in the spring of 1910 I was surprised to receive a letter from E. F. Nichols, President of Dartmouth College, asking whether I would be interested in an opportunity to take the chair of psychology there. The suggestion did not appeal to me, but surely it would do no harm to show the letter to my chief. Thorndike read it at a glance and remarked, "This is really interesting. You know Dartmouth is the least decadent of any of the New England colleges," — a remark not too impudent, coming as it did from an alumnus of Wesleyan and of Harvard.

I accepted a five-year appointment, with responsibility for instruction in both psychology and education. The schedule was not heavy. The classes were small, but they grew steadily so that when I left in 1915, the chair had become a settee to be filled by an instructor and two full professors whom I selected. Before long the professors were made college presidents: Moore at Skidmore and McConoughy at Knox.

There was no laboratory until I was given space in a corner of the physics building and a modest appropriation for apparatus. While the getting was good, I insisted that the library procure a complete set of the *Biometrika* folios. This investment paid off, if only in what one undergraduate, Beardsley Ruml, dug out of them.

My first student assistant was Harold Burtt, the ablest scholar in his class. Nearly all his courses had been in Latin, Greek, and mathematics, but that did not prevent him from undertaking graduate work with Munsterberg and becoming one of America's leading specialists in applied psychology.

For counseling about choice of courses each student had a faculty adviser who followed him pretty closely. To provide information about certain measurable abilities, in 1912 I introduced a program of testing. The tests included Woodworth and Wells's cancellation test, color naming test, and ten logical relations tests; also Osborn's perception of form test, and the tests of logical memory, memory span, discrimination of lifted weights, endurance of grip, and tapping, then included in the Columbia battery. Most of these tests were given to the freshmen individually, by psychology students.

In December of 1914 President Nichols announced my election to a permanent professorship. What a happy prospect, always to teach psychology in a congenial atmosphere in the midst of such natural beauty! But those years had been in many ways an apprenticeship for a different, a more varied career, pioneering in an emergent profession.

VI. Applying Psychology at Carnegie Institute of Technology

These pages tell of the first formal establishment in America of a department of applied psychology, a development for which the times were ripe.

I made the acquaintance of the institution which was to foster this novel enterprise on New Year's Day, 1915. Three days earlier, after presiding at a session of the American Psychological Association then meeting in Philadelphia, I had been approached by a short businesslike man with a somewhat abrupt manner. His card bore the legend "A. A. Hamerschlag, Carnegie Institute of Technology." "We have a flourishing young institution in Pittsburgh," he began. "What are you doing this weekend, after the meetings? Won't you come and look us over, and then tell us what in your opinion psychology could do for such a technical institution?" I had indeed heard of Carnegie Institute of Technology, then ten years old; but it was confused in my mind with its parent institution across the ravine — Carnegie Institute.

I accepted the invitation. The Institute of Technology was a revelation. I found not only a typical college of engineering, but also a woman's vocational college resembling Simmons, a college of industries which taught the processes basic to machine production, building construction, and the printing industry; and a college of fine arts which offered instruction in architecture, music, and dramatic art, as well as in painting and illustration, interior decoration, and sculpture. For such an institution, what should I recommend?

My first suggestion grew out of the observation that a majority of the 2300 day students were looking toward careers in industrial management, social work, teaching, dramatic art, or some other field in which their success would in a measure depend upon their *ability to understand and influence people*. They would surely profit by instruction in those facts and principles of psychology which would help them better to understand and control the activities of learners and of workers.

Students with such a variety of educational opportunities faced lively problems of occupational choice. Was it not high time to challenge psychology to help these students to identify their special talents and their limitations? This possibility was the second mentioned in my memorandum, mailed to President Hamerschlag after my return to New Hampshire. I pointed out that patient research would have to precede any considerable usefulness of aptitude tests. But where could this research be carried forward to better advantage than in a young institution offering on a single campus such varied types of vocational education?

The task of selecting students was my third topic. I recommended no immediate reliance on psychological examinations, but instead a period of trial during which test scores and personal interview ratings of all freshmen should be accumulated in order to ascertain their predictive value in combination with high school marks, principals' estimates, and standings in ordinary entrance examinations.

Other uses for psychological techniques were mentioned. Data regarding traits and difference in ability should be of interest to deans and class officers when talking with students about their methods of work and their personal development, and serviceable also to the placement bureau in attempting to find the right positions for seniors and alumni. The courses in educational psychology offered to prospective teachers of the manual, industrial and domestic arts, should, I thought, be enriched with experimental studies of learning, habit formation and the acquisition of skills. The Fine Arts College should have a psychologist familiar with experimental methods, to discover and teach principles underlying both art production and art appreciation. I also urged employment of a psychologist specializing in motion studies and fatigue in relation to industrial efficiency. In a closing paragraph I named the psychologist who seemed to me best able to develop such a program, and glowingly described his qualifications.

A few weeks later I was astonished to be invited to undertake that role myself. With characteristic forthrightness, President Hamerschlag told me, "The professor you nominated came here at my invitation. It will take you two years to learn as much about this field as he knows already. But our people seem to think that they can work with you." Within a year and a half that nominee was a member of our staff.

On accepting the directorship, I arranged at once for the appointment of three consultants: F. L. Wells, G. M. Whipple, and Raymond Dodge. For their wise advice at that juncture my indebtedness is great.

In this young institution psychology was not an unknown discipline before 1915. Those students who planned to teach their specialties took one or two semesters of general and educational psychology. The new arrangement established a central department serving the students, faculty, and administration of all four colleges. Advanced graduate training in applied psychology and service to business and industry, soon to become outstanding features of the new Division, were not yet in the picture.

When the Division began to function in September, 1915, I had four associates: J. B. Miner from the University of Minnesota; J. L. Zerbe and Katherine Murdock, who had been instructors in the Industries school and the Margaret Morrison Carnegie College for Women, and L. L. Thurstone, whom I had found studying in Angell's laboratory. Thurstone took the learning process as his province, and soon initiated experiments in cooperation with the linotype instructors in the printing department. Miss Murdock prepared a scale for measuring merit in sewing, a step preliminary to research on the relative worth of rival methods of instruction in domestic art. Zerbe continued some studies he had been making on the distribution of grades given in classroom and shop courses. Miner took the problem of getting for the Placement Bureau dependable ratings of seniors in nonintellectual traits. He broke new ground by devising his Analysis of Work

Interests blank. He also examined students individually, and devoted some time to diagnosis and training of a few who had remediable handicaps of personality. All of us shared in the development and standardization of group tests, for several of which we accumulated norms. Among these were tests newly devised by Thurstone for measuring ability to deal with ideas of space relations, an ability without which it seemed to be difficult for a student to succeed in descriptive geometry, pattern-making, sheet-metal work, costume design or architecture. The following autumn Kate Gordon came from Bryn Mawr to develop tests of taste in color and in design, and also tests of dramatic insight.

Some equipment was installed, including a Seashore tonoscope for vocational examining in music, an Einthoven galvanometer for research in fatigue, and several tachistoscopes.

Cooperative Research in Selecting Salesmen

After a few weeks in Pittsburgh I met Edward A. Woods, who owned a large agency of the Equitable Life Assurance Society. He suggested that we should give courses in salesmanship! "What is the matter with the courses now offered by the various institutes of salesmanship?" I asked. "They are all right, but they don't get very far." "You wouldn't want us, then, to duplicate such courses?" "No." "Well, then, before entering this field we ought to find out more than is now known about selling and salesmen. We should have to learn what the differences are between successful and relatively unsuccessful salesmen, by studying their duties, personal histories, talents, aptitudes, and traits."

I prepared a five-year plan for a research bureau to be supported by thirty cooperating firms, each to pay $500 a year. This budget was underwritten by Mr. Woods and his friends, H. J. Heinz, the manufacturer of food products, and Norval A. Hawkins, then manager of sales for Henry Ford. They in turn secured the cooperation of other concerns such as American Rolling Mill, Burroughs Adding Machine, Carnegie Steel, Westinghouse Electric, Armstrong Cork, American Multigraph, Packard Automobile, Goodrich Rubber, Eli Lilly, and several life insurance companies.

This Bureau of Salesmanship Research illustrates a form of cooperation between college and business which had been originated by industrial chemists at Kansas University (soon transferred to Pittsburgh where it became the Mellon Institute) but which had not then been tried in our field.

There was a dearth of psychologists familiar with business operations. I finally persuaded Northwestern University to loan us Walter Dill Scott, who took up his duties in Pittsburgh on June 1, 1916, as the first American

Professor of Applied Psychology.[6] His personal leadership coupled with his scientific preoccupations and his shrewd insight into business affairs were invaluable in this movement to study live problems of management by the methods of psychology.

In that first year Scott had six assistants, "fellows" we called them. Conferences with sales managers of the cooperating concerns helped to define a line of attack. Their methods were analyzed and compared, their experience pooled. Experiments were tried. Scott's seminar soon produced a volume of *Aids in Selecting Salesmen* which included a model application form or personal history blank, an ingenious letter of reference to former employers, a set of aids in personal interview which focused attention on essential points and, by means of a man-to-man comparison rating scale, quantified the interviewer's judgments. It provided also a battery of mental tests, among them a range-of-interest test devised by E. S. Robinson as well as a paper-and-pencil adult intelligence test, one of the forerunners of Army Alpha. These *Aids* were issued to the member companies to use while accumulating data for checking against the criterion of relative sales success.

Then came World War I. Practically the entire staff of the Bureau of Salesmanship Research and several other members of our Division of Applied Psychology found their best opportunity for usefulness in army personnel work under The Adjutant General or in psychological examining and clinical diagnosis under The Surgeon General.

In the spring of 1917, Whipple, Wells, and I served on Yerkes' committee of seven which prepared the first psychological examination methods for army use. The best elements of our intelligence tests were incorporated with similar materials of Otis, Terman, Yerkes, and others to make up Army A.[7] With that examination and its successor, Alpha, 1,700,000 men were tested and the data found to be of special value in balancing the distribution of personnel to military units and in selecting soldiers for special training.

In midsummer Scott became director and I the executive secretary of the Committee on Classification of Personnel in the Army, and, under Secretary Baker's direction, assembled the group of psychologists and industrial employment executives who devised and administered the army personnel system.

Our interviewer's score sheets became the "Scott Rating Scale" for use in selecting officer candidates and rating officers. Our personal history record, greatly metamorphosed, became the CCP Qualification Card, by aid of which three million men were classified for military purposes according to

---

[6] J. P. Porter's appointment to the faculty of Clark College with this title occurred that same year.

[7] R. M. Yerkes, Psychological examining in the U. S. Army, *Mem. Nat Acad Sci*, 1921, 15, 7–10, 299–311.

their occupational, educational, and personal traits.[8] My first years in Pittsburgh proved to have been a rehearsal for the enormous task of military classification and assignment.

If peace had been a preparation for war, war prepared no less for peace. There was demand for improvement in selecting, classifying, and developing clerical and executive personnel as well as salesmen. I had brought Whipple from Illinois to pilot the Bureau in Scott's absence. He initiated investigations of the training and supervision of salesmen while continuing the studies of selection. Scott returned from Washington in the spring of 1919, but shortly incorporated the Scott Company and relinquished to C. S. Yoakum the direction of the Bureau which then took the name "Bureau of Personnel Research" because its problems and activities had far outrun the original definition of scope. Some of the cooperating firms withdrew support; others doubled their fees, so that the total budget was increased; and still other firms interested in specific problems, notably Thomas A. Edison, Inc., entered into contracts for more research and consultation than a membership fee could provide.

During 1919–20 a Division of Anthropology and Psychology was being established in the National Research Council, and Angell, then Chairman of the Council, insisted that I act as chairman of the new division, giving it half time. So I oscillated between Pittsburgh and Washington. Memories of that hectic year are too complicated to be disentangled here.

The readiness of businessmen to join in cooperative research undertakings was expressed in terms of what they were willing to pay toward their maintenance. Little did I think when first we talked in 1916 about support for a research bureau that within six years the Division of Applied Psychology would have received from such sources $237,000 for operating expenses. Nor could I then picture clearly the succession of fine, loyal men and women whose industry and talent multiplied the value of that sum for science, for commerce and for society.

Cooperation in personnel research had indeed proved to be a fertile idea. The first bureau soon had a lusty offspring, the Research Bureau for Retail Training. Edgar J. Kaufmann, a department store executive, secured the cooperation of six other stores, and with them undertook, in 1917, to provide $32,000 annually for a five-year period for the support of a bureau devoted to problems of employment, supervision, and training in the retail field. The detailed plans were worked out by Miner, who directed the enterprise during its first critical year. Then, in 1918, I persuaded W. W. Charters to come from Illinois to take charge. This Bureau prepared employment tests, training manuals, merchandise manuals, and specific procedures for correct-

[8] Committee on Classification of Personnel in the Army, *History of the Personnel System*, Vol. 1 of *The Personnel System of the U. S. Army*, 1919.

ing defects of sales personality and of supervision. It developed retail sales-manship courses for high school use. It annually trained a small group of graduate students to become research workers or educational directors in stores. Its publications, extensively distributed, modified for the better the retail sales service of the nation.

The initiation of a department of educational research in the Division of Applied Psychology dates from 1918. After Whipple had served one term as acting director of the Bureau of Salesmanship Research in Scott's absence, he became our Professor of Educational Research. But his function was not that of studying public school problems. Instead he concentrated on our own problems of admission, of curricula, of methods of instruction, of admin-istration. He assembled for the benefit of the entire faculty an exhibit of new objective examination methods and other teaching aids designed to lighten the instructor's load. The rest of us helped. I worked mainly on administrative problems; Thurstone took the admissions problem, Miner, the marking system; Charters worked on curriculum research, and also con-ducted, during the first half of each year, a seminar for inexperienced in-structors in methods of college teaching. E. K. Strong, Jr., coming in 1919 to succeed Whipple who went to the University of Michigan, made job analyses of the manager's functions in machine production, building con-struction, and printing concerns, in order to get light on problems of curricula in the Industries College. He also investigated the study methods of fresh-men. But I needed his help particularly in preparing a three-months course of training for life insurance salesmen, the demand for which had grown insistently. So I teamed him with John A. Stevenson, from the University of Illinois, whose doctorate was in educational psychology, and with G. M. Lovelace, a life insurance executive from Hartford, Connecticut. My own contribution to this enterprise was insistence that field practice in actual soliciting, under direction, be an integral part of the training, dovetailed day by day with the lecture and textbook materials of instruction.

This experiment in adult vocational education established a pattern which was soon widely adopted. For what it accomplished toward raising the standard of competence and of ethical attitude among salesmen who offer to prospective customers their counsel on the purchase of the kind and amount of life insurance they really need, the American public should indeed be grateful.

My own researches during this period included experiments to ascertain the psychological effects produced by different sorts of music heard by vari-ous kinds of listeners engaged in specified activities such as routine work, creative thinking, artistic design, or sheer relaxation.

The Dispersal

In 1924 the Carnegie Institute of Technology discontinued graduate instruction in psychology and education and the several bureaus were scattered far and wide. Before that year, Stevenson and Lovelace had already gone east to become vice presidents of the Equitable Life and the New York Life, respectively. Kate Gordon had transferred to the University of California at Los Angeles. Miner had been drawn to the University of Kentucky to head the department of psychology. Thurstone in 1923 headed the staff of the Bureau of Public Personnel Administration in Washington, moving the next year to the University of Chicago. Strong went to Stanford to carry forward the research on interest inventories for which the studies of Miner, B. V. Moore, Ream, Freyd, and Grace Manson provided a foundation. C. F. Hansen became assistant to W. T. Grant. Marion Bills built up a practice as consultant in office management. Yoakum took Miss Manson with him when he went to Ann Arbor as professor of personnel management. Satisfactory openings were found for the younger staff members.

Why this dispersal? The reasons for so drastic a change in institutional policy were complex. Some of them were sound. Advanced graduate instruction in psychology and much of the research were more appropriate to the graduate school of a university than to an essentially undergraduate institute of technology — a consideration which would not have outweighed the obvious benefits to Carnegie Institute of Technology had it not been for two other considerations, one of them relevant.

The Carnegie Corporation had initiated in 1921 a searching inquiry into the relations between Carnegie Institute of Technology and the community it served, since it was clear that in the long run funds to provide for the institution's normal growth must come from that community, not from the Corporation in New York. Chancellor Samuel P. Capen of the University of Buffalo was chairman of the survey commission. He and his four associates submitted a substantial report which was not, however, designed for publication. One of its sections, I understand, vigorously urged elimination of all unnecessary duplication of activities which competed with the University of Pittsburgh. Another section spoke most favorably of what had been accomplished by the Division of Applied Psychology to develop and to deserve the support of the local community and indeed of that whole geographic region, thus leading the way toward the very cooperation which the corporation deemed essential. Later, when the time came for the Institute of Technology to negotiate with the University regarding elimination of duplication, Chancellor Bowman was most hospitable to the suggestion that the University abandon its curricula in certain lines of engineering and architecture while accepting full responsibility for the training of teachers of

vocational subjects. He also welcomed the Research Bureau for Retail Training and the School of Life Insurance Salesmanship, neither of which would
put any burden on the University's budget.[9] But the Life Insurance Sales
Research Bureau moved to New York to be nearer the home offices, and
eventually to Hartford, Connecticut. Professors Schoen and Cleeton alone
remained at Carnegie Institute of Technology to take care of undergraduate
instruction in psychology and to help the administration with its work of
student selection, guidance, and placement.

The irrelevant consideration that may have weighed with the trustees in
their decision to discontinue what had first been called the Division of Applied Psychology harked back to personal antagonisms of long standing
between President Hamerschlag and Samuel Harden Church, President of
Carnegie Institute, who finally succeeded in 1923 in having Mr. Hamerschlag
replaced by an administrator whose merits included an ability to avoid doing
anything that looked different from what was customary in institutions of
higher learning. The Division of Applied Psychology was different. And
it was President Hamerschlag's pride and joy. These considerations doubtless had some influence in bringing about the great dispersal, but I think
they were of less moment than the determination to eliminate unnecessary
duplication and to effect good working relations with the University.

After all staff members of the Division had been suitably placed, I consented to take up in New York the direction of the Personnel Research Federation, editorship of its *Journal*, and part-time private practice of industrial
psychology.

It was not easy to say goodbye to so many superb collaborators, but I knew
that each, transplanted to favorable soil, would in due course help to multi-
ply the number of practicing psychologists and add steadily to our store of
psychotechnical knowledge.

VII. Spokesman for Psychology

During the twenties and thirties our profession flourished numerically, and
greatly expanded the range of its contacts. One of my principal functions
from 1924 to 1940 seems to have been that of emissary of psychology to the
heathen — the heathen being experts in various aspects of human behavior
who claimed little familiarity with the science of psychology. Among them
could be found outstanding economists, engineers, business executives, and
social work administrators, as well as employment managers, occupational
counselors, labor leaders, safety specialists, college registrars and university
presidents. The record shows a never-ending round of committee meetings,

[9] Since 1924 the stores of Pittsburgh have given the University $700,000 to cover current
expenses of the Research Bureau and $500,000 for its endowment.

conventions, and conferences both informal and formal, at which psychologists were a small but welcome minority. A complementary function was to tell my own profession what I saw beyond our borders.

Liaison among these groups was conspicuously required because each was involved in the relatively new specialty, personnel management. The personnel movement in industry had three roots, antedating the first world war: employment management, which concentrated on hiring and placement; corporation schools, responsible for indoctrination and initial training; and medical services for employees. During the twenties the oversight of these and related activities such as foreman training, establishment of wage rates and incentives, employee publications, safety engineering, recreation, and plant morale, needed to be consolidated. Gradually these functions came to be recognized as concerns of the personnel manager, or, for policy determination, of a vice president for personnel. Research on problems of concern to such an executive might be primarily psychological. On the other hand it might require competence in a nonpsychological discipline like accounting, or public health. A personnel investigator was likely to be on safer ground if he was not wholly unfamiliar with several of these specialties. Let me mention one surprise among the many I encountered.

In a new Western Electric plant at Kearny, New Jersey, where I spent each Monday for a couple of years, more than twenty thousand employees were at work; but, to my amazement, specialization of their duties was so extreme that in that large population I could find only three jobs at which as many as twenty employees were doing the same work under the same conditions. One of these was the jack-solderer's job. Ninety young men were soldering the ends of varicolored wires to strips of jacks which go into telephone switchboards. All were working with the same sorts of materials and tools under similar conditions of supervision, illumination, and wage incentive. Here was one job where it was possible to carry out controlled experiments contrasting the effectiveness of two ways of training, or two kinds of wage incentive. Among the wires in a cable the proper one to solder to each jack had to be identified partly by the color of its insulation; so I asked my helper (who knew his academic psychology but unhappily had not yet learned one of the first principles of good employee supervision) to find out whether any of the slow workers was handicapped by color weakness. Sure enough, he shortly marched up the aisle bringing in triumph a slow operator who had difficulty in sorting the reddish skeins of Holmgren worsteds from the greens. But from that moment this young psychologist's usefulness for work in this particular shop was at an end. Those 90 jack-solderers had seen him "show up" one of their buddies. Such asinine impudence they could not pardon.

Significant aspects of working conditions and job requirements cropped up in each situation in which I served as a consultant. Some of the more spectacular came to light while reducing traffic accidents among the 2900 streetcar and bus operators employed by the Boston Elevated Railway. With the help of the late C. S. Slocombe, then a recent arrival from Australia via Spearman's laboratory in London, I chose for diagnosis and treatment about twenty per cent of the operators, namely, those whose record over a period of years put them in what I called the accident-prone class. Then with the help of supervisors, company physicians, and my psychologists, an effort was made to cure the accident susceptibility of each of these employees. Several required retraining; others, discipline, appeal to pride, a more nourishing diet, a change of spectacles, or just a friendly personal interest. During three years of such concentrated individual attention to the most susceptible of the accident-prone, a forty-seven per cent reduction in traffic accidents was achieved without resort to discharge and without introducing changes in standards of employment. A few psychologists hearing about these achievements have incorrectly attributed them to improved methods of personnel selection, but the accident-prone were not fired and replaced. They were cured — a good many of them.

For several years I undertook to facilitate collaboration among organizations concerned with educational and vocational guidance by helping to shape the programs of their annual meetings and arranging joint sessions on topics of common interest. This strategy of facilitating acquaintance and joint action gave rise to the Council of Guidance and Personnel Associations in which were represented the American College Personnel Association, Personnel Research Federation, National Vocational Guidance Association, National Association of Deans of Women, and four smaller organizations. We failed to bring in the Deans of Men who insisted that they came to their annual gatherings to enjoy a jovial reunion unhindered by serious discussions. The Collegiate Registrars, although their programs were solid and technical, also chose to keep to themselves.

During the thirties the rapid growth in clinical, industrial, and vocational psychology was not fully reflected in the transactions of the American Psychological Association. Responsibility for psychology as a profession was left to the Association of Consulting Psychologists, to its successor, the American Association for Applied Psychology, and to state associations like the one in New York of which I was president in 1939.

The AAAP dates from 1937. With lively annual meetings and an excellent journal, it burgeoned in four short years to an active membership of 615. I served as its president in 1942. Fortunately statesmen of psychology like Robert M. Yerkes saw clearly the trend of the times. On their initiative the Emergency Committee of the Division of Anthropology and Psychology of the National Research Council appointed a subcommittee on Survey and

Planning. Its deliberations under the leadership of Yerkes produced a plan for reorientation and reorganization of the APA and its consolidation with the AAAP. Ample provision was made for professional as well as scientific interests by establishing no less than nineteen divisions, ten of which repreent technical specialties in areas of professional practice. At an inter-society constitutional convention, the intransigent AAAP willingly came home, bringing its journal and other assets, and ending a revolution symptomatic of an approach to maturity after the adolescent period in the history of psychology. In this reorganization I took little part because I was preoccupied, not to say overwhelmed, by military duties.

The first of four books I published during this period was *Procedures in Employment Psychology* (1926). Written jointly with Max Freyd, it was ahead of its time and did not enjoy a wide distribution.

How to Interview (1931), written with B. V. Moore after we had carried through two pioneer studies in interviewing industrial workers, has been twice revised. Another product of those years was *Psychology Today* (1932). It contains thirty study manuals which accompanied a program of Saturday evening radio lectures by leading specialists. I had enjoined each speaker to include in his address new material on his topic, not yet published, so that any psychologist listening in would learn something important; and to put what he had to tell in such clear language that listeners who had never been to high school might follow him with keen interest. Not an easy assignment, but after repeated revisions each script met specifications.

Aptitudes and Aptitude Testing (1937) has been read by many counselors of students and of veterans, but has long needed revision. It will not, however, be necessary to alter my essentially conservative position regarding the uses and limitations of tests in industry and in education.

VIII. MILITARY PSYCHOLOGY

In the years following demobilization in 1919 I watched with pride the advances our little army made in its staff schools and training methods. Contrary to common impression, there were also improvements in trade testing, psychological examining, and ways of sifting applicants for training as mechanics, radio operators, and airplane pilots, thanks to the initiative of O'Rourke, Toops, Thurstone, C. R. Mann, J. A. Randall, Colonel Mashburn of the Medical Corps, and others. In the thirties it was good to find able officers like Major Lewis B. Hershey and Major John Dahlquist on duty in the personnel branch of the General Staff, revising plans for mobilization to avoid wasteful personnel practices to which we had drawn attention when writing our *History* in 1919. But by 1937, like many others, I was complacent in the belief that never again in our time would America have to mobilize for war.

So I thought until 1939. In the spring of that year I arranged a celebration of the twentieth anniversary of the demobilization of the Committee on Classification of Personnel in the Army. Our commander, Colonel Walter Dill Scott, came to New York for the occasion. Angell, Thorndike, Yerkes, Clothier, Ruml, Kelley, Thurstone, Frazier, and forty other survivors joined in jovial reminiscence until Colonel William C. Rose, speaking for The Adjutant General, drew attention to the cloud discernible on the European horizon. Within a few short months Hitler marched into Poland.

Anticipating what might come to pass, several of us then brushed the dust from contacts with the Army and Navy; and on April 2, 1940, Major General Emory S. Adams, The Adjutant General, asked the National Research Council to designate a committee of psychologists to advise him on the classification of military personnel. The appointees were C. C. Brigham,[10] H. E. Garrett, L. J. O'Rourke, M. W. Richardson, C. L. Shartle, L. L. Thurstone, and the writer, who acted as chairman. For seven years we met when summoned, to consider questions related to the work of the Personnel Research and Procedures Branch of The Adjutant General's Office, which was responsible for developing aids in classifying officers and men with respect to their abilities and skills, educational background, civilian and military experience, intellectual capacity, personal qualifications, special aptitudes, and indicated best Army usefulness.

We were asked first to review the War Department's plans for what came to be called the Army General Classification Test, to be used at reception centers for sorting recruits into a few broad groupings with respect to their ability to learn quickly the duties of a soldier.[11] This test made no pretense of measuring *native* intelligence. We were well aware that many of the abilities it sampled had been learned, in school or out. We did not even label it a test of intelligence. And yet it was found to correlate with Army Alpha, the National Intelligence Test, the Otis Higher, and the Terman Group Test more closely than those intelligence tests did with each other. The AGCT was eventually taken by ten million men. The records of their scores were particularly valuable to commanders of combat troops who wanted to insure a balanced distribution of capacity among the units of a command so that no one platoon, battery, or wing would be burdened with an excessive load of slow learners, or a serious shortage of bright pace-setters.

The Committee's suggestions were soon sought as to methods of selecting men for training as officers, securing better officer-efficiency reports, improving occupational interviews, standardizing tests of proficiency in a trade, and developing more valid tests of aptitude for work which calls for mechanical ingenuity or other special talent.

[10] After his untimely death, January 23, 1943, Dr. Brigham's place was filled by C. F. Hansen.
[11] Bingham, How the army sorts its man power, *Harpers Mag.*, 1942, 185, 432–440; Personnel classification testing in the army, *Science*, 1944, 100, 275–280, Inequalities in adult capacity —from military data, *Science*, 1946, 104, 147–152.

By August 6, 1940, I was in the War Department full time, with the title of Chief Psychologist, a capacity in which I served until June 30, 1947. My first duties were to supervise a very small staff, civilian and military, and to speak for The Adjutant General when psychologists and pseudopsychologists descended on him with fluent proposals and offers of service, some of which were of great help. I drafted the order which established the Personnel Research Section, defined its responsibilities, and announced to all commanders the availability of its services.

This is no place to record in detail the accomplishments and shortcomings of the enterprises with which I was connected during the war. The most significant of these have been summarized elsewhere.[12] Here may be mentioned a few of the opportunities that came my way to facilitate liaison and communication between army officers and leaders of my profession.[13]

Our welcome was in sharp contrast to experiences of World War I, since personnel management and scientific psychology were subjects no longer unfamiliar to officers of the regular army. I kept the Chief of Staff as well as The Adjutant General advised of our activities, and on two memorable occasions General Marshall, joining the Committee on Classification of Military Personnel at lunch, shared with us some of his own purposes and anxieties.

Certain contacts with other agencies were formalized. I was named a representative of The Adjutant General on the National Research Council's Committee on Service Personnel — Selection and Training; and as his liaison with the Applied Psychology Panel of the National Defense Research Committee; also as chairman of a board advisory to The Surgeon General and to Colonel William C. Menninger during a period when clinical psychologists were much in demand. It was our responsibility to endorse and encourage plans that gave promise of helping the army toward early victory while putting the brakes on projects that dealt with fundamental questions of great scientific interest but which seemed unlikely to yield usable information without hampering the rapid training of troops.

Proposals to experiment with the stress interview fell midway between these categories. Again and again officers and psychologists eager to learn more about the personal characteristics of leaders and to improve the screening of candidates for training as officers urged adoption of the stress interview and also of group tests of leadership similar to those employed by the Germans, the British, and our own Office of Strategic Services. Voluminous

[12] Bingham, Lessons from the Second World War, in *Progrès de la Psychotechnique, 1939–1945*, Berne (Ed., Franziska Baumgarten), 1949, pp. 139–146.
[13] Due to the fact that the Department of Defense has not yet published a volume narrating the history of the Personnel Research and Procedures Branch, written by many hands in 1946–7, the best description of our work is, strange to say, an 86-page well-illustrated volume in Portuguese: Murilo Braga, *A mobilização do pessoal nos Estados Unidos*, Rio de Janeiro, 1943.

reports from overseas were digested. Preliminary experiments in three training centers were carried out. Garrett gave several weeks to an evaluation
of those projects and of all evidence available regarding the validity of the
methods in question. His conservative report left its readers skeptical as to
the worth of such methods in the army. Two or three days devoted to observation and performance testing of a number of candidates, carefully
scrutinized as to their self-control and social behavior under specified conditions of group activity and of extreme stress, were not found to add much
if any validity to the estimates of leadership potential already available,
namely, the appraisals made by the applicant's immediate superiors based
on his personal history record, his scores in paper-and-pencil tests, and their
knowledge of him after watching his rise through the noncommissioned
ratings and observing for several months his performance in actually leading
the privates he was helping to train. Further experimentation with the
German and British techniques was called off, I think wisely.

One notable achievement was the demonstration of how much can be accomplished in a few weeks to train illiterate adults to read. Our working
definition of literacy was "ability to read English as well as the average man
who has had only four years of schooling." The regular basic training was
beyond the capacity of nearly all illiterates. But when, late in 1943, the
nation had to face the necessity of scraping the bottom of the manpower
barrel, an experiment was tried — that of accepting illiterates and giving them
six or eight weeks of special training before allowing them to attempt the
basic training course. "Special training" included indoctrination and drill
to familiarize them with army ways, as well as a good deal of skillfully devised instruction in reading road signs, labels, diagrams, and bulletins.
Everyone was astonished to see what a large fraction of those illiterates
(eighty-five per cent) was in this way enabled then to assimilate basic training. Such special instruction, costly in dollars, should long since have been
provided by the civilian economy instead of being left to the armed forces
at a time of national emergency. American educators and statesmen would,
we hoped, not be permitted to forget this lesson learned in World War II,
namely, that we need not have so many illiterates in this country.

My preoccupation with the psychology of occupational adjustment, civilian as well as military, continued all through the war, and after. As early
as 1940–41 I noted that soldiers whose terms of service were nearly over,
and drafted recruits approaching the end of their year of training, had to
make decisions as to employment, schooling, or re-enlistment. A well-
rounded army personnel system, I was convinced, must supply these men
with up-to-date information about educational opportunities and employment conditions, and encourage them to re-define their goals in the light of
what they and the army had learned about their capacities. No less than

200,000 men were to be separated that fall. Commanders were expected
to make provision for counseling and for an impressive separation ceremony.
Some of them prepared "report cards" to show to former employers. That
was in September 1941. Nine short weeks later the Pearl Harbor attack
plunged us headlong into global war. Most of the men already separated
were called again to active duty and not until 1943 was much attention paid
to the need for counseling those who were discharged because they were
incapacitated, or for other reasons. This kept me awake nights, trying to
think how to create opportunities for psychologists like Brotemarkle, Clyde
Coombs, Wilson Bender, Hugh Bell and Esco Obermann to establish a
working organization of officers well prepared to direct a sound program of
pre-separation counseling. Unexpected encouragement came from the
Reeves Committee of the National Resources Planning Board, Lieutenant
General Somervell of the Army Service Forces, and Brigadier General W. F.
Tompkins, who headed a demobilization planning division of the General
Staff. After the necessary manuals had been compiled, a six-weeks trial run
at Fort Slocum prepared the way for a series of schools at Fort Dix to train
officers in separation counseling. At suitable locations separation centers
were established, manned, and put to work before cessation of hostilities in
Europe loosed the avalanche.

What had to be done in those hectic days taught us lessons the armed
forces shared with collaborating agencies: the Public Employment Service,
corporations employing many workers, the schools and colleges of the nation, and particularly the advisement and guidance service of the Veterans'
Administration on whose shoulders Congress had placed a tremendous responsibility. During these postwar years it has been my privilege to keep
in touch with these developments in an advisory capacity, free of administrative burdens.

I have claimed to be a modest person, but these closing paragraphs reveal
an unblushing willingness to accept applause. One round was started by
Fryer[14] who pointed out that my favorite activity is "the discovery and encouragement of professional talent." This predilection is but one manifestation of a dominant purpose, namely, to invest my energies in helping the
well-adjusted to achieve their fullest usefulness. I have preferred to give a
hand to the promising rather than to the third rate; to the emotionally stable,
the strong and vigorous, the very bright, rather than to the weak, the unhappy, the unadjusted, whom we psychologists may wisely leave, whenever
we can, to the ministrations of our friends, the psychiatrists and the social
workers. We should thank them for their willingness to relieve us of all
responsibility for therapy, thereby freeing the psychological profession for

[14] D. Fryer, *J consult Psychol*, 1942, 6, 53–54.

the more congenial and, I sincerely believe, more socially useful task of augmenting the productivity and the happiness of the mentally well.

———

In July, 1948, Walter Dill Scott and his wife celebrated their Golden Wedding Anniversary. He acknowledged my note of congratulation in these words: "In 1916 you picked me up, took me out of a small local community, and placed me down in a national environment. The three years we worked together were in many ways the most significant of our lives." Assurances of this kind, volunteered from time to time by fellow workers, make me grateful for the opportunities I have had to help them, and through them to help a thousand others.

EDWIN GARRIGUES BORING

HERE am I, a psychologist, born in Philadelphia on October 23, 1886, now sixty-four years old, and asked to write my professional autobiography, to tell what I think I have accomplished, wherein I believe I have failed and *why* — in so far as the question *why* can ever be answered for the individual personality — why these things were as they were.   A man's life in almost every detail is a joint function of his heredity and his environment, but inevitably the biographer writes as an environmentalist because he knows so little about the genes.   So it is to my environment that I turn for an incomplete answer to my question *why*.

FIRST MATURATION 1886–1904

Let me first say a word about the family into which I was born, for some of my attitudes and values were certainly social effects of the small matriarchy of ten other persons which I joined on that October morning in 1886.

On the corner of 10th Street and Fairmount Avenue in Philadelphia was the drug store of my great grandfather, Edward B. Garrigues, an Orthodox Quaker.   He lived in the house next door with his sister, the great great aunt who at that time dominated the family, and with his unmarried daughter, the great-aunt who was always kind to children.   These were the old people — the very old people.   Over the store lived my grandmother who was another daughter of Edward B. Garrigues, my blind grandfather who was a Hicksite Quaker, my mother, my father who had come to Philadelphia from Lancaster, Pa., after fighting all through the Civil War, to learn the drug business from my great grandfather and who had presently married his boss' granddaughter and had then become his partner, my three older sisters, and now I.[1]   We were a large family for the houses were connected and

[1] The Garrigues genealogy, from Jean Garrigues (French Huguenot, fled France in 1685, arriving later in Philadelphia), has been compiled by Edmund Garrigues, and his manuscript of 1054 pages in six volumes was deposited in 1939 with the Historical Society of Pennsylvania in Philadelphia.   The Borings were not so ancestor-conscious as the Garrigueses, but the Boring line from John Boreing (emigrated from England to Maryland in 1670), has now been brought together by R. S. Hecklinger and E. G. Boring, *The Descendants of John Boreing, Maryland Planter*, 1950, in a 42-page mimeographed pamphlet of which copies have been deposited in certain historical societies and in the Library of Congress.

we all had our meals together. After the three very old people had died and when I was four, we moved from over the store into the big house, and now it was my grandmother who dominated the household. I have called this large family a matriarchy because in my lifetime women dominated it and the men had inferior status. Not only had my Hicksite grandfather gone blind, he was also a business failure. My father, a member of the Moravian church, counted as an outsider in this Quaker family, which thought he lacked the cultural background of the Garrigueses, a lack for which he fully compensated by his insistence on a college education for his children. I, a boy, had turned up as an unwelcome surprise, for girls were taken for granted, whereas a boy created strange problems. My grandmother, moreover, disapproved of my mother's having even daughters and now put down an extra black mark against my father.

Religion was important in this family but the religious affiliations were mixed. My grandmother had been disowned from Orthodox Quaker meeting for marrying a Hicksite Quaker (the Hicksites were the liberal branch) and my father was a Moravian. My parents were married in the Moravian Church, and after my grandfather died we all attended that church. My sisters went to a Hicksite Quaker school, but I went to an Orthodox Quaker school. We all used the "plain language" (*thee*, not *thou*) and my wife and I still use it to each other and to our children. There was, as I grew into childhood, much going to church, and a pervasive sense of duty and right whenever decisions were being made.

The family had too little social life. My parents felt that they were not well off and, when they married, they decided they could not afford to entertain. So we had few guests and seldom went out. Nor had I any playmates, for the neighborhood, which had been good when my great grandfather founded the drug business in 1843, had deteriorated and I was not allowed to play outdoors with the tough little gangs which I would so dearly have loved to join. I did have for many years an imaginary playmate named "Mamie," and I had other fantasies, as might be expected in so isolated a child.

As I look back on my childhood it seems to me that there were three family attitudes which assumed especial importance in my life. (a) One was the religious background for action, that ever-present sense of right and duty. It certainly got into my superego. (b) Another was my father's strong belief in education, which, as I have suggested, may have been compensation for some of his own frustrations. This Boring family is academic. Among us four children there are two college teachers, one high-school teacher, one wife to a college president, and our children tend toward the academic too. (c) The third attitude had to do with money. Father felt poor, worried and talked constantly about money. There never seemed to be enough to do what he or we wanted, though it is clear now that he always got his family away to summer vacations, that he sent his children to private schools and then to college. Still this money worry got into me and I have always had my feeling of insecurity reinforced by my sense of being unable to do or have the things that seemed to go properly with my professional success. Now my children have been growing up too thrifty. A money complex has run through three generations.

My parents found me a tough problem. They thought me too "excitable" to send to school until I was nine. This excitability showed up especially on those rare occasions when a visiting relative would bring along a son as an afternoon's playmate for me. Then I would rush around the room and play violently. They thought me better off without playmates, but I really needed them — playmates of any kind. My enuresis, clearly an infantile regression, was another sign that I wanted something that I did not have.

At school, entering the first grade at an over-sized nine when I should have been but six, I soon made up the three missing years, yet I remained isolated at first because I was not athletic. I was simply no good at sports, perhaps in part because I was too shy to face the failures that a learner inevitably meets. On the other hand, I was good at my studies, but scholastic skill combined with athletic incompetence tended at first to make me into a "teacher's pet." Later in the high-school years so many of the boys tended to drop out of this private Quaker school that other values came to predominate — as they would in a class that was four-fifths girls. I was then, at long last, important, not only being near the top of the class in most studies, but also finding success in the debating club and the school magazine.

In my lonely play at home the magic of electricity had caught my imagination. It was then that I made up my mind that I wanted to be an electrical engineer, and I chose Cornell for a place to go because I had heard how excellent was its engineering. My father supported this wish of mine, which was formed without advice and turned out later to have been in error, since what I really wanted was physics, not engineering. At school, however, I prepared for Cornell's engineering by taking science and advanced mathematics; yet I did well in English too. Already I liked to write.

It seems to me that my personality, if not predictable from these childhood data, is at least psychologically consistent with them. What sort of a person, I ask myself, was being matured then? Let me set down what I think are my principal psychological attributes.

In the first place there is my persistent sense of *inferiority*, my readiness to expect the worst, to believe in my failures and mistrust my successes. That could get started by a frustrated childhood, could it not?

Then there are my *compulsions* which control my life. I set them up nowadays and turn myself over to them, and each works, for years if necessary, until its goal is achieved. They drive me, torture me and are the principal reason for whatever success I have had. They might indeed be regarded as compensations for the inferiority. They enslave me, but I have gotten fond of them.

The outstanding characteristic of my personality seems to me, however, to be this eternal conflict between my need for *power and success,* my ambition, and my need for *approval and affection.* It is plausible to regard each of these needs as a compensation for a lack of security and love in childhood.

There are also other conventional ways of specifying my personality pattern. In W. H. Sheldon's terms I am a 4-5-2 in both body type and temperament — an affection-needing 4, which fights a power-wielding 5, with only a 2 of self-assured intellection in the background.[2] A new book on personality in peptic ulcers seems almost to describe me exactly, and indeed I have had a duodenal ulcer since the Clark controversy in 1922.[3] I suspect it was these nearly incompatible needs of mine that produced the ulcer by their conflict. At any rate I think the following pages show how my successes, whenever they have occurred, have all been of the sort that resolves the conflict inherent in finding personal affection without surrendering power.

VOCATIONAL TRIAL AND ERROR 1904–1910

It was in the autumn of 1904 that I went to Cornell to study electrical engineering. My father supported me in college with an allowance of fifty dollars a month, out of which I paid all expenses including tuition. The engineering course was stiff and I had to study very hard to achieve but average grades. Though I failed in no courses, I did brilliantly in none and worked long hours getting the many laboratory reports complete. I never really liked engineering, but it took me five years to find that out. What I wanted was some kind of science. Engineering puts successful operation ahead of the understanding of general principles and it aims at low costs, whereas the more interesting scientific principles may be the expensive ones. I received my M.E. degree in 1908 and moved on to an engineering job with the Bethlehem Steel Company, in Bethlehem, Pa., in 1908.

My undergraduate social life was meager. I was not asked to join a fraternity and could not have afforded to live in one. I tried distance-running as a Freshman but was not good enough. I made the class debating club but not any important team. I knew almost no girls all through the four years. I had advanced beyond felt inferiority and mediocrity in childhood

---

[2] On Sheldon's somatotypy, see W. H. Sheldon, S. S. Stevens and W. B. Tucker, *The Varieties of Human Physique,* 1940, esp. 1–9; Sheldon and Stevens, *The Varieties of Human Temperament,* 1942, esp. 1–11, 24–95.

[3] On the ulcer personality, see A. J. Sullivan and T. E. McKell, *Personality in Peptic Ulcer,* 1950, esp. 23–50, 73–77.

to success and importance in high school; now I was back in mediocrity again.

In the rigid engineering schedule there were just a few electives. For two of them I made queer choices. I chose English composition and elementary psychology. When I asked to register for the latter the professor of mechanical engineering, a great big burly 4-6-1 of a man, looked me up and down in astonishment and then shouted across the room to the professor of electrical engineering: "Hell, here's a damned engineer wants to take psychology!"

So it came about that I turned up in E. B. Titchener's course in elementary psychology in the fall of 1905 when Titchener as a lecturer was still in the prime of his showmanship. The room, in the old laboratory at the top of Morrill Hall, was crowded with students and the long desk was jammed with apparatus for demonstration. Titchener lectured in his Master's gown. "It gives me," he said, "the right to be dogmatic," fitting his discourse to the gown. The lectures were magic, so potent that my roommates on each lecture day demanded to be told what had been said. And what had been said? I do not know now. I remember being excited by the lecture on tonal beats and by Titchener's sermon after our first written test, a discourse on the one free gift for which we do not have to work — the English language! In this test I, however, had done well, and Titchener himself handed me my paper with a 90-something on it, and said, "*You* have the psychological point of view!" That remark was an accolade. It was still fresh in my mind five years later when I turned to psychology, the profession where at last I found permanent satisfaction.

After college I had my year with the Bethlehem Steel Company. As a college graduate I was given eighteen cents an hour for work which paid others only sixteen cents, so already college was worth two cents more an hour in an eighty-four hour week. Yes, it was an eighty-four hour week, for this was the old system of the steel plants in which a man and his "buddy" kept a job going continuously, each working seven nights one week and seven days the next. Eighteen cents an hour came to $65 a month, all my own money. I bought a standard typewriter, and presently a canoe.

This after-college year was fun, for I found a social life in Bethlehem in a group of young people and was at last independent of my father. Still I did not like engineering, and finally I resigned my job entirely rather than accept a promotion to be assistant night foreman of a steel mill. I left with a letter which read: "This is to certify that Mr. E. G. Boring has been in my employ for the past year and take great pleasure in recommending him to anyone in need of a first class electrician. I have found him to be sober, industrious and attentive to his work at all times." I was not flattered by being reduced to these primitive virtues.

The next year I stayed on in Bethlehem to teach science and mathematics at the Moravian Parochial School. I taught six subjects, and I ran into disciplinary troubles. The principal urged me not to quit, warning me that my leaving after a single year would not look well on my record, but I wanted to get back to college. My desire was probably an escape from difficulty by regression, but I rationalized it as the need for an A.M. (I had no A.B.) if I were to become a teacher. So back I went, regressing, to Cornell, intending to try for an A.M. in physics, but being caught by Madison Bentley for animal psychology. He captured me with earthworms, paramecia and finally flatworms, and then in February 1911 he got me an assistantship at $500 a year. I saw that I was now fixed for life, independent of my father and able to do what I wanted, for a man could live on $500 a year. So I struck out for the Ph.D.

CORNELL AND PSYCHOLOGY 1910–1918

Psychology at Cornell — at least the orthodox psychology that centered in the laboratory — revolved around and was kept in its orbit by the personality of E. B. Titchener. What a man! To me he has always seemed the nearest approach to genius of anyone with whom I have been closely associated. I used to watch my conversations with him, hoping I might gain some insight into why his thinking was so much better than mine. I decided presently that his superiority lay in his easy command of memory traces, his ready entertainment of novel relationships, his equally ready abandonment of unprofitable hypotheses, and his avidity in the pursuit of goals. His mind seemed never to gather wool, never to try the same blind alley twice. Titchener loved to solve puzzles, and his skill in numismatics was developed over the problems posed by Mohammedan coins. He was always ready with unexpected advice. If you had mushrooms, he would tell you how to cook them. If you were buying oak for a new floor, he would at once come forward with all the advantages of ash. If you were engaged to be married, he would have his certain and insistent advice about the most unexpected aspects of your problems, and, if you were honeymooning, he would write to remind you, as he did me, on what day you ought to be back at work. Seldom did he distinguish between his wisdom and his convictions and he never hid either.

The stories about Titchener are legion but this is not his biography.[4] Most of the stories centered upon his personality — his dominance or his magnetism, depending on how you regarded his contact with your life. Many of

[4] The description of Titchener and the publication of some of the Titcheneriana I essayed many years ago. E. G. Boring, Edward Bradford Titchener 1867–1927, *Amer. J Psychol*, 1927, 38, 489–506.

his more able graduate students came to resent his interference and control and eventually rebelled, to find themselves suddenly on the outside, excommunicated, bitter, with return impossible. Quite early in our married life my wife and I decided that we would accept "insults" and arbitrary control from Titchener in order to retain the stimulus and charm of his sometimes paternal and sometimes patronizing friendship. I never broke with the master and I still feel that the credit balance remained on my side. After Titchener's death I went over the two hundred twelve letters I had had from him since I left Ithaca to see what worth publishing was in them, and there was a little but not much.[5] All the rest of this personalized magnetism was Titchener's interest in my affairs, or his plan that "we" should support an appointment because it would add another laboratory to "our" group of loyal institutions. Titchener's friendships (like Freud's) were authoritarian and paternal. Each needed to play the father-role, dispensing much real kindness to those disciples who avoided transgression.[6]

Although I never broke with Titchener, I did not follow him blindly. On systematic issues I differed from him vehemently in the privacy of the laboratory, recognizing the importance of Titchener's views by calling myself a heretic. In my research I spread too far afield to have Titchener's complete approval, but Cornell's requirement of two minor subjects for a Ph.D. constituted a partial defense for me. Actually I had the equivalent of four minor subjects, and I published in each. With Madison Bentley I worked in animal psychology, publishing on the behavior of flatworms.[7] With Sutherland Simpson I studied physiology, and it was with him that I conducted my four-year-long experiment on protopathic and epicritic sensibility during nerve-regeneration.[8] With G. M. Whipple in educational psychology I completed a study of the fidelity of report on moving-picture incidents.[9] Then in the summer of 1912 I went to work with S. I. Franz at the Government Hospital for the Insane in Washington and got out a monograph on learning in schizophrenics.[10] That was an invaluable summer in broadening my experience and in establishing a close personal friendship with Franz, but

[5] E. G. Boring, Titchener and the existential, *ibid.*, 1937, 50, 470–483; Titchener on meaning, *Psychol. Rev.*, 1938, 45, 92–96.
[6] The intimate personal account of Freud, the one that makes me see resemblances between him and Titchener, is the one by Hanns Sachs, *Freud, Master and Friend,* 1944. In assessing my judgment about the similarities of Freud and Titchener, the reader will do well to note that Sachs was the disciple who never broke with the stern master, a relationship which resembles mine to Titchener.
[7] Boring, Note on the negative reaction under light-adaptation in the planarian, *J. animal Behav*, 1912, 2, 229–248.
[8] Boring, Cutaneous sensation after nerve-division, *Quart J. exp. Physiol*, 1916, 10, 1–95. It was a whole number of Schaefer's Journal and I was proud.
[9] Boring, Capacity to report upon moving pictures as conditioned by sex and age, *J. crim. Law & Criminol*, 1916, 6, 820–834.
[10] Boring, Learning in dementia precox, *Psychol Monogr.*, 1913, 15, no. 2; Introspection in dementia precox, *Amer. J. Psychol.* 1913, 24, 145–170.

Titchener looked solemn as he perceived me straying from the straight and narrow path.

In the laboratory I became a member of Titchener's in-group. There were many of us, men and women, and we lived in the laboratory from 8 a.m. to midnight. Presently I was falling in love with Lucy M. Day, who got her start in psychology with S. P. Hayes at Mt. Holyoke. We became engaged in October 1911, to be married two and a half years later, the day after I got my Ph.D.

In 1912, when Bentley went to Illinois, Titchener undertook to reestablish the old courses in systematic psychology, the courses he once gave himself and which covered the entire range of orthodox psychology in three lectures a week spread over two years — a 200-lecture course. The instructors and assistants, Titchener decided, were to give this top-level graduate course — to each other and to the other graduate students. Titchener's personal assistant delivered this decree to us, and how we worked to turn the German literature on experimental psychology into creditable lectures! There were no good secondary sources then, except Schaefer's *Physiology* and Nagel's *Handbuch* in the field of sensation. It was wonderful training in acquisition of erudition, and also the beginning of my knowledge of the history of experimental psychology, for the spell of Titchener compelled us to present the topics historically.

It was late in 1911 that Titchener set me a thesis on visceral sensibility, telling me to read Meumann in the *Archiv* and Becher in the *Zeitschrift* and to go on from there. My next conference with him about this thesis was early in 1914 when he told me to hurry up to take the degree in June. I did. In the two-year interval I had learned the stomach-tube technique so as to get at a part of my own insides and had found greater sensitivity of the esophagus and stomach to warmth, cold and the pressures and pains of distension than had been supposed to exist.[11]

Lucy Day, my fiancée, had taken her doctorate in 1912 and then had a year of teaching in psychology at Vassar under Miss Washburn. In 1914 I got my doctorate and married on a salary just increased to $1000. We left the word *obey* out of the marriage service, but my wife promised me privately never to be jealous of my devotion to psychology and she has always kept her word. During our first year of marriage she taught at Wells College, twenty-five miles down Lake Cayuga, but then we decided we wanted a family. My son was born on January 11, 1916, Titchener's birthday. We could hardly, my wife and I, have paid Titchener a greater tribute, nor one that would more certainly have secured the necessary forgiveness for my being late to his all-male birthday party.

[11] Boring, The sensations of the alimentary canal, *ibid*, 1915, 26, 1–57, The thermal sensitivity of the stomach, *ibid*, 485–494; Processes referred to the alimentary tract a qualitative analysis, *Psychol Rev*, 1915, 22, 306–331.

Graduate work expanded imperceptibly into an instructor's job. I kept on with research in both the psychological and physiological laboratories. I found other papers to publish and began to have students who took on minor problems under my direction and who got their papers written up for publication by me. There was no future ahead for me at Cornell, but the First World War settled that problem.

THE FIRST WORLD WAR 1918–1919

The war and the draft for men under thirty-one made all young psychologists restless. The birth of my second son caused the draft to pass over me at age 30.8, but still I wanted to serve. Yerkes had said that he wanted me in the Army work on intelligence testing, so I volunteered and was appointed, because of my age and status, a Captain in the Medical Department of the Army. In February 1918 I reported to Camp Greenleaf, Georgia, for training. Here we psychologists lived a healthy barracks life with plenty of good exercise mixed in with the study and drill on testing procedures. Many lasting friendships were formed under these intimate conditions of living.

Then I went to Camp Upton on Long Island where Joseph W. Hayes was Chief Psychological Examiner and I was second in command, succeeding him when he was later ordered away. I liked this experience too, of testing the New York City draft, and I was impressed with how little education and intelligence were to be found in that segment of the population of the United States.

When the Armistice came in November 1918, Yerkes wanted me in Washington to work on the big report of the Army testing program. I have profited immensely by Yerkes' faith in me, just as I did earlier by Franz's. Yerkes made me his first assistant but left me free to plan and organize the section on results in this mammoth report, which has in it 439 tables and fifteen chapters by nine psychologist-authors, in addition to five other scanty chapters which I wrote because no good author was available.[12] I gained by this experience too, for I learned about testing and about theory of probabilities, and I discovered also that the mental testers among the psychologists were, like the experimentalists, honest, sincere, intelligent, 80-hour-a-week psychologists.

My learning about theory of probabilities at this time was still another special service that the war did me. In 1919 I found the statisticians employing the normal law of error as an *a priori* hypothesis to predict frequencies in the face of ignorance. In the Library of Congress I read up on the

[12] R. M. Yerkes, ed , Psychological examining in the United States Army, *Mem Nat. Acad., Sci.,* 1921, no. 15. It is a huge report of 890 quarter pages with lines 36 picas long.

history of the theory of probabilities and on its logic, and I have been troubled for thirty years now by the contradictions involved in using probability theory as a scientific model. I published on this matter in 1920 and again in 1941, but my voice has cried in a wilderness where accepted usage persists without possibility of validation.[13] (I have thought that it was this first paper which impressed R. B. Perry with the desirability of calling me to Harvard.)

CLARK 1919–1922

Yerkes, my chief in Washington, had agreed to go to Minnesota to develop psychology there with a group of psychologists, most of whom were already associated with him in Washington. He wanted me to join this group. Later he withdrew from this undertaking to work for the new National Research Council, designating R. M. Elliott as his substitute — a very wise choice as three decades of Elliott's success at Minnesota have shown.[14] Elliott also wanted me for Minnesota, but Harvard had invited me to become a Lecturer for a year, while William McDougall, due at Harvard from England in the fall of 1920, looked me over and decided whether to keep me or to get somebody better. Harvard commanded my imagination. I do not fully know why. Titchener had always said that Harvard was the strongest university in America, that Hugo Münsterberg had debased psychology there, that Harvard psychology needed to be brought clearly into the scientific circle and rescued from the philosophers who still dominated it. To me Harvard was opportunity, challenge, insecurity and probable loneliness. Minnesota was security, promise, facilities and friendliness. Which does one choose in such a case, difficulties or security? Obviously difficulties. Yerkes forgave me but I think he never understood my choice.

In the summer of 1919 my family and I moved into an apartment in Cambridge. No sooner were we in it than there came a letter from G. Stanley Hall, then psychologist-president of Clark University, inviting me to become Professor of Experimental Psychology at Clark for three years and adding that my appointment would be made permanent at the end of my term *if* my work had been satisfactory. What a decision! Baird had died in 1917 and I was being offered his post. I was not so charmed by Harvard that I did not believe that the two best positions in psychology in America were Baird's and Titchener's, both graduate-school research appointments. Was I committed to Harvard to wait for McDougall's inspection while the Clark post went to someone else? President Lowell said No and I accepted Clark.

[13] Boring, The logic of the normal law of error in mental measurement, *Amer. J Psychol*, 1920, 31, 1–33; Statistical frequencies as dynamic equilibria, *Psychol. Rev.*, 1941, 48, 279–300.
[14] On the history of the Department of Psychology at Minnesota, see the autobiography of R. M. Elliott in this volume.

At Clark I found a laboratory of a few big rooms. It had been Sanford's from 1892 to 1909, and then Baird's until 1917. S. W. Fernberger was there as assistant professor, so I had been put "over" him by Hall's whim, as it were. That he supported me enthusiastically and that our life-long friendship grew out of this relation is a tribute to his generous nature which all his friends know so well. Carroll C. Pratt was there as a graduate student, and Marjorie Bates, whom he married later, and M. Yokoyama from Japan. Those three persons were my three Clark Ph.D.s. Fernberger went back to his beloved Pennsylvania in 1920 and Pratt became instructor in 1921.

I tried to form an in-group on the Titchener model, meaning that Clark should become satellite to Cornell. We were a busy little band during the next three years. There were never more than eight of us, staff and graduate students, but we were all doing research and I was teaching vigorously. I got up and gave by myself a 200-lecture course in systematic psychology, built on the Cornell model. At the end of the triennium we had almost two score of published papers to show for our enthusiasm.

In 1920 Wallace Walter Atwood, a Harvard geographer, replaced Hall as president. Then I knew why Hall would not defer his offer to me a year earlier to let me first fulfill my Harvard obligation. He wanted to make Clark safe for psychology, but it turned out to be Atwood's business largely to displace psychology by geography, and that fact, which could not be publicly announced, or at any rate was not announced, doubtless explains why Atwood was so cool and seemingly unfriendly to me in my first contacts with him. Many of the changes which the new president introduced were directed toward making the university less important in relation to Clark College, which had hitherto been independent. The chemist, Charles A. Kraus, and I fought those changes, so Atwood soon had real ground to dislike me.

The Clark controversy, as it came to be called, did not begin until 1921–1922. The *casus belli* was a lecture by the radical, Scott Nearing, given with Faculty permission under the auspices of the Liberal Club of Clark College. Atwood stopped this lecture in the middle, starting a storm of protest among the students. There was much newspaper publicity and I have a 160-page book of clippings on this early phase of the controversy and other books on its later phases. There were five of us on the University faculty who figured prominently in the controversy and came later to be called "the disaffected professors": Charles A. Kraus, the chemist, who presently went to Brown; Frank H. Hankins, the sociologist, and Harry Elmer Barnes, the historian, both of whom soon were asked to Smith by President Nielsen; and Pratt and I, who went together to Harvard in the fall of 1922.[15]

[15] For a discussion of the whole Clark controversy, see A. O. Lovejoy, Chmn., Report on Clark University, *Bull Amer. Assoc Univ Prof*, 1924, 10, 412–479.

At that time my three-year term of appointment was running out and I tried to invoke Hall's letter which had said my appointment would be made permanent, *if* my work had been satisfactory. I doubted that it would be judged unsatisfactory. No reappointment was made in the spring, however, and meanwhile Harvard had come back to me with an offer and Stanford also wanted me. I did not really wish to stay at the changed Clark, but I sought the justification of reappointment and resignation. I never had that satisfaction.

Harvard offered me only an associate professorship, whereas I had been full professor at Clark. Stanford offered a full professorship and more money than Harvard. Still I inclined toward Harvard. The difficulties attracted me or else I was ashamed to retreat from them. There may have been other inaccessible motives in my unconscious. Stanford had won my admiration and loyalty when I taught there in the summer of 1921, and the choice was hard. Stanford's President Wilbur, however, soon decided the matter by withdrawing the offer when I raised questions about conditions instead of accepting. So Harvard it was. There I found both the opportunity and difficulty that I wanted and expected.

HARVARD 1922–1929

In the fall of 1922 I came to Harvard and began my new life by letting a strange automobile on a misty night fracture my skull and land me for six weeks in the hospital with a concussion. This event was tough on H. S. Langfeld who took over all my work, distressing to my wife who had all the worrying to do, and alarming to Harvard which now wondered whether it might have given a precious professorship to a future idiot. I have no proof that the accident did not make me brighter. Medical science lacks controls. But the consequences were interesting, for I had a retroactive and a progressive amnesia. I chatted with everyone from the first but immediately forgot what I had said or that I had talked. In 1933 this experience led me to doubt that a man is ever conscious in the sense of being *immediately* aware of his awareness; awareness seems always to involve memory.[16] The accident, moreover, removed my fear of death, for I had, like Lazarus, been dead and then alive again with no great discomfort. It is those who are left who suffer from death.

After Christmas I went back to life, Langfeld and the philosophers. The philosophers had not arranged life too well for Langfeld and me. They now had on their hands two vigorous egoistic youngish psychologists, each

[16] E. G. Boring, *The Physical Dimensions of Consciousness*, 1933, 221–238, esp 227–229. For my first insight on the relation of awareness to memory, see Boring, Attribute and sensation, *Amer. J. Psychol*, 1924, 35, 301–304.

with ideas about what should be done in the same laboratory. Langfeld had been director. They asked him to forego that title, did not give it to me, gave him the rank of associate professor which they had given me, and then left the irresistible force and the immovable body to get going. We did indeed get along but each of us was thwarted.

So in 1924, when Howard C. Warren asked me on Titchener's advice to come to Princeton for more rank and less money, I wondered whether I should go. I wanted to stay to work at my mission of rescuing psychology from the philosophers, and I asked myself the question: Had not Warren and Titchener tossed a coin in deciding between Langfeld and me, and would not Langfeld be asked if I refused? I had to trust to my intuition, for Titchener and Warren were sphinxes on this matter; but I took a chance, refused Warren, stuck to my Harvard mission, and, sure enough, Langfeld was asked and accepted. They must have used the coin. It is pleasant to think back now on this difficulty because it makes so clear my feeling of warm affection for Langfeld that has persisted for nearly thirty years. He has shared so much thought and endeavor with me in a never stagnant correspondence, but we could not have managed it sitting in the same chair, as the philosophers thought we might.

In the summer of 1923 my wife and I went abroad to the VIIth International Congress of Psychology at Oxford. That was fun, to meet and talk with the persons who had the great names, and especially with Kohler and Koffka, who represented the new Gestalt psychology which Americans were excited about and did not as yet understand.

I have never been in Germany. That lack in my education was a matter of some shame and some bitterness before Hitler destroyed German science, but I could not afford much travel with our children needing support and education. What I did about this deficiency was to compensate. I wrote my *History of Experimental Psychology* largely about German psychology with a map of German universities as a cover-lining and when, after G. E. Müller's death, German psychologists wrote me to ask questions about their own compatriot, I felt that I had triumphed over space and budget.

In 1925 Titchener withdrew as editor of the *American Journal of Psychology*, which K. M. Dallenbach had bought from Stanley Hall in 1920 and had set up at Cornell as practically Titchener's journal. Dallenbach, who assumed all the financial risk of the journal, was ultimately obliged to refuse some change in policy which Titchener wanted, and Titchener, unwilling to accept Dallenbach's proper fiscal control, resigned in defense of what was to him his dignity. Who was now to rescue the oldest English-language journal of the new psychology from this sudden catastrophe? Dallenbach asked Madison Bentley, Margaret Washburn and me to become joint editors with him, and after a conference we consented, beginning with the 1926 volume. It was a dangerous arrangement, but it worked well because of Dallenbach's skill in maintaining for each of us sovereignty in the acceptance and rejection of papers. For twenty-three years I kept on at this increasingly unpleasant task of making other people's papers readable. Then I resigned, hoping that younger heads and hands might take over. Although I disapprove of the private ownership of scientific journals in general, this ownership has worked splendidly, and my long association with the AJP strengthened what was already a close friendship with Dallenbach.

Titchener's death in 1927 brought me the offer to succeed him at Cornell. Think of that! Had difficulties been the only assets that a job has, I ought to have accepted, for Cornell presented more difficulties than Harvard. But Cornell was poor, there seemed to be little prospect of my later advancement there, and my mission to rescue Harvard psychology from the philosophers was still unfulfilled. So I stayed in Cambridge. This call was my last important offer elsewhere. I was forty-one and getting too old to move. I had come through a period of difficult decisions, but never for a moment have I regretted any one of them. Is it that my choices were wise, or is it that I was pliant and adjustable?

In 1926 Morton Prince appeared bearing $75,000 from an anonymous donor (the sum was later increased to $125,000) to use in establishing a "department of abnormal psychology" under a faculty of arts and sciences. His purpose was to bring abnormal and normal psychology closer together, just as Janet, a friend of Prince's, had been trying to do since 1895. My contribution here was to suggest that the word *dynamic* be added to *abnormal psychology* in the deed of gift to protect the University in case abnormal psychology should cease to exist as a separate field in the next century or two. Thus the new Harvard Psychological Clinic was founded to give instruction and conduct research "in abnormal and dynamic psychology."

A little later Edgar Pierce, an 1895 Ph.D. of Münsterberg's, died, leaving his estate to Harvard for "additional instruction in philosophy and psychology and the development of the Psychological Laboratory." The estate amounted, after Mrs. Pierce's death, to $872,802. The word *additional* created much discussion in the councils of the University. Did it mean that our budget of 1928, when the gift was accepted, must be guaranteed forever, so that the Pierce increment would be truly an addition? The Harvard Corporation finally granted that view in modified substance, but no problem has as yet come up because the total departmental budget has continued to expand along with the total funds of the University.

Pierce's phrase "and the development of the Psychological Laboratory" threw responsibility on me. How much should the Laboratory have? That decision had to be made by the six permanent professors — five philosophers and I, who was the youngest. Our annual budget for the Laboratory was then, I think, $2500. We hired out the mechanician to get money for materials and tools. I paid the secretary from my pocket. We needed money desperately and I figured what seemed to me a proper Laboratory budget of $6100, about one-fifth of the expected initial income. The philosophers would hardly have spent so much on their laboratory-child, which they regarded with enthusiastic ambivalence, but I, the expert, stood firm and they were an intelligent honorable majority, too wise to vote a competent minority down. So we got our needed $6100.

The 1920s I spent in teaching, administration, writing and the direction of research. I was Director of the Laboratory *de jure* and chairman of a non-existent department *de facto* — for we were linked with philosophy in departmental organization and a philosopher was always chairman. The constant demands of correspondence and conferences took most of my time and I did no important research of my own. That might have been because I was turning out to be more of a book-writer than an experimentalist, but the fact remains that even the book-writing had to be done almost entirely in the summers because I could find no free time for such work between September and June. In those days most of the graduate students carried on their experimental work under my direction, but they chose their own problems and I was never very successful in getting them to work on mine.

The 200-lecture systematic course I brought with me from Clark and kept up for ten years until 1932. By that time I felt that no one man could any longer cover the whole field of experimental psychology. Besides there were by then such good texts and handbooks at the graduate level, that the task of the instructor changed from abstracting German research papers to assessing fields of research in which papers in English came more and more to predominate. As I was obsessed with the idea that we ought somehow to weld our psychologists, all of them Harvard individualists, together into an understanding unity, I conceived the idea of having different members of the staff take on different parts of the systematic course and of all of us attending each others' lectures. The staff agreed but this plan for mutual comprehension failed, for I was the only one of us to attend all the lectures for the first two years. Now we have substituted a Proseminar for the big course, with J. G. Beebe-Center and me taking the heavy part of the work and others coming in for brief contact with the new graduate students. That plan works, but not as a means of unifying the staff.

The Wednesday afternoon Colloquium for graduate students and staff was begun at my instance in 1924 and it helped us to gain community of thought within the Department. The early colloquia led to real discussion among the staff, and it was there that we got from Kohler the insight into what kind of analysis Gestalt psychology allows and what kind it eschews, and from

McDougall the insight that what he was calling freedom of the human mind was the same item as the experimentalist's probable error of observation. Now that the Department has become so large, discussion in the colloquia is no longer intimate nor productive of important new insights for the staff.

The most successful device for bringing unity to the staff were the Laboratory luncheons. These were begun in the early 1930s when I brought my lunch to the Laboratory and offered free coffee to anyone who would lunch with me. Later these staff luncheons became an institution, organized on the principle that no one on an academic salary could afford to pay more than twenty cents (after inflation, twenty-five cents) for a lunch. So most of us came together nearly every day, though later the Psychological Clinic formed its own in-group lunch and Lashley ate with us only on occasion. The conversation has always been good, and the luncheons still provide understanding and communication among the persons with very different basic values who are added from time to time to our staff.

It was during the 1920s that I wrote my *A History of Experimental Psychology*, which was published in 1929. I have already said how the systematic course at Cornell gave me the historical slant toward the understanding of psychological problems. I worked hard at this book, especially in summers, wondering what Titchener would say to my presumption in aiming at a goal which seemed to need his own erudition. Then Titchener died in 1927 and I felt as released as must have John Stuart Mill when his dominating father died. I had to take my first sabbatical half-year to finish the writing in the spring of 1929 and the book appeared in the fall. It was successful, selling 1316 copies in 1930, 2843 in 1947, and 16,765 in the twenty-one years before it was revised. It is a stiff book and it is hard for me to see how so many persons can have needed to buy it, but it is a thorough secondary source on the history of experimental psychology and gets used as a text in many courses. I wanted to make American psychologists history-conscious. I think I have succeeded as well as I had any right to hope to do.

There were many other events in the 1920s which represent my participation in the professional scene. In 1919–1922 I was secretary of the American Psychological Association, thus making many valuable and satisfying contacts with colleagues. In 1924 I became Director of the Harvard Psychological Laboratory, a post which I held for twenty-five years. In 1925 Margery, the Boston medium, introduced to Harvard by McDougall, took some of my attention. My hair was pulled in the dark in the Laboratory one night. Did Margery do it with her toes, or was it done by Walter, her deceased brother? I never knew for sure about the first hypothesis, but the second seemed to me to state only a pseudoproblem. McDougall resigned in 1927 to go to Duke and we filled in for a long time with visiting professors — Wolfgang Kohler, Karl Bühler, Leonard Carmichael and E. S. Robinson. I chafed at not being a full professor when my equivalents elsewhere held the top rank, but my promotion came through in 1928 after I had refused the Cornell offer. In 1928 I was president of the American Psychological Association and gave my presidential address in New York at the banquet — the last meeting at which the address was given at the banquet. I took as my subject the paradox between psychologists' insight into personal motives and the aggression of their egoistic productive drives. I have kept at that theme all my life and have got it into the 1950 revision of my *History*. The truth transcends the individual scientist and is given ultimately only to posterity. In large measure the living scientist is the unwitting agent of the *Zeitgeist*.

At the end of the 1920s there was at last an American International Congress of Psychology — at New Haven in 1929. Cattell was president. I was secretary, and we clashed so often that I once remarked to him that I thought we were too different to be on the same committee. "No," Cattell replied, "we are too much alike" — alike, he meant, in aggressive insistence.

The 1920s were a decade of hard work for me. Having a compulsive temperament, I drove ahead on an eighty-hour week with the firm conviction that I might not be so bright as many of my colleagues but that I might make up for this deficiency by working harder. Unfortunately eighty hours is so near the physiological limit that I found myself thwarted and baffled for lack of time or brains, since more of either would have sufficed to make me discontent at some higher level of production. Being caught in many activities, I contributed no important research of my very own. On the other hand, my activities were mixed in with the *Zeitgeist* of American psychology, and I became its agent in the various ways I have just described.

All in all, I believed thoroughly in *tout comprendre c'est tout pardonner,* and my personal paradox has been that I have the will to promote the doctrine of valueless phenomenology without weakening my own compulsive drives. I accept compulsions and let them work. I like having them though they make me sweat. And I mistrust them always as possible grounds for prejudice and blindness. It may be that the truth has to transcend the individual, but I was inconsistent enough to hope that I could fix things so that it would not transcend me.[17]

HARVARD 1930–1941

The 1930s started off with my writing of *The Physical Dimensions of Consciousness*. Why I became a monist and a physicalist, reacting against

[17] On the relation of the *Zeitgeist* to scientific creativity, see E. G. Boring, *A History of Experimental Psychology*, 2 ed., 1950, 7–9, 22f., 743–745, Great men and scientific progress, *Proc Amer. Philos Soc*, 1950, 94, 339–351. On the relation of ego-involvement to scientific objectivity, see Boring, *Sensation and Perception in the History of Experimental Psychology*, 1942, 608–613.

Titchener's dualism and mentalism, is not entirely clear. Dualism seemed unsatisfactory to me, to represent a discontinuous causal relation, action at a distance. And physicalism seemed to me to solve the meaning problem as mentalism could not. Even Titchener in his context theory of meaning had been forced unwittingly into behaviorism, I thought, for the unconscious meanings of familiar perceptions can be known only through discriminative behavior. E. B. Holt and E. C. Tolman saw that point earlier than I, but I was not influenced by them. In general, dualism seemed insecure and all my life I have been reacting against felt insecurity. My faith in monism was thus one of my heresies against Titchener, a negative item in my ambivalence toward him. There was, however, a positive item, too, for *The Physical Dimensions* was my attempt to explicate Titchener's inchoate doctrine of dimensionalism, as far as I understood it. Tucked away in my little book there was this basic faith in operationism, a faith which in my thinking goes back at least to my paper on the stimulus-error in 1921[18] and which was founded, of course, on Titchener's positivism of the Ernst Mach kind (not modern logical positivism). Because the book was not clear about the operationistic logic inherent in it, I have always called it "my immature book," but some people have liked it and 105 copies of it were sold in the seventeenth year of its existence.

When I had finished with *The Physical Dimensions*, I went into psychoanalysis with Hanns Sachs, Freud's loyal adjutant, recently come to Boston from Berlin. Why? To know why you wish to be analyzed is almost equivalent to not needing to be analyzed. I was insecure, unhappy, frustrated, afraid. I was afraid mostly of not being successful. My compulsions were still with me but they were not getting enough work out of me nor was I sure of the quality of what they were achieving. So I asked Sachs to rescue me to competent and effective productivity, and he, kindly *gemutlich* soul, took me on for one hundred sixty-eight sessions. Although he was somewhat of a Titchener-substitute to me, I felt that I never got the degree of transfer, positive or negative, that would have been desirable. After the analysis was over — over, though perhaps not completed — Sachs and I discussed in print, at my suggestion, the question of whether it had been successful, whether you could ever tell when analysis is successful since it can not have an experimental control.[19] Altogether I am glad to have had this experience. I now know a little about analysis from the inside. I know also something of what it does not do. I learned to my surprise that it does not guarantee emotional maturity — not even in the analyzed analysts, although Sachs himself was, I think, the most emotionally mature person I have ever known.

[18] Boring, The stimulus-error, *Amer. J. Psychol*, 1921, 32, 449–471.
[19] Boring, Was this analysis a success?, *J. abn soc Psychol*, 1940, 35, 4–10; Hanns Sachs, Was this analysis a success? — comment, *ibid.*, 11–16; Franz Alexander, A jury trial of psychoanalysis, *ibid.*, 305–323, esp. 317.

In 1933 President Conant succeeded President Lowell at Harvard. Lowell had not cared much about psychology, but Conant did. He remarked to me during the first year of his presidency that he thought that the day of the physical sciences was passing and the day of psychology dawning, a prediction borne out for psychology and not for physics. One of his early acts was to appoint his first *ad hoc* committee to find "the best psychologist in the world" to elect to a chair at Harvard. I was on that committee, which was chosen to favor biotropic psychology, not the philosophical kind. Conant was shocked to discover how generally psychologists contradicted one another about who was the best psychologist, but eventually the committee decided that the best was K. S. Lashley, whom I had been backing all along and who had almost accepted a Harvard offer in 1929 when Chicago suddenly intervened and took him. The appointment was made with maximal dignity. Lashley was first elected Professor of Psychology and then informed and asked whether he would accept. He did accept and was given space in the Biological Laboratories. Thus psychology at Harvard grew, becoming scattered geographically.

After twelve years my mission at Harvard was still unfulfilled. We were still tied up with philosophy. Lowell would have kept us thus, but Conant was ready for change. It was I in 1934 who made the motion that the Department of Philosophy and Psychology be divided into two separate departments under a Division of Philosophy and Psychology, and again it was I in 1936 who made the motion that the Faculty abolish all divisions as obsolete. Both motions were carried, and now at long last we had access to the Dean without a philosopher intermediary. My mission was accomplished. I was the first chairman of the new Department of Psychology, but I resigned in favor of G. W. Allport two years later. How simple this change, once accomplished, seemed, and how silly! It amounted merely to a *de jure* recognition of a *de facto* independence already nearly achieved, and I am confident now that it would have come about had I never come to Harvard. The *Zeitgeist* had this event up its sleeve all along. Thus I had another lesson as to how the free action of a personal will in a naturalistic world is a delusion.

The next thing after my analysis that took time and attention was the first of the BLW textbooks. I had thought that I would never write a textbook, that there were too many of them, that the effort spent on them was taken away from research. Most authors of textbooks, however, hope to achieve the perfect text that will end all other texts, and H. P. Weld of Cornell came forward with the suggestion that Langfeld and I cooperate with him in getting out an authoritative text, one in which the various chapters would be written each by an expert, and in which psychology would assert its coming of age by showing that it could give facts to students without discussion of controversy and without limiting the facts to the methods by which they were observed. Dubious truths were to be omitted. So were the names of researchers except the names of such great as every student should know. Facts were to be exhibited as independent both of method of investigation and of the investigator. The first volume was called *Psychology: a Factual Textbook* and came out in 1935. In 1939 we issued a revision, so much revised, with sensation and perception put last instead of first, that we gave it a new name; and in 1948, after the Second World War, we got out a third greatly enlarged edition, with new chapters, new authors, new organization, and new format. These books have been successful as texts in the elementary course in some of the large universities and for advanced courses in many colleges, though they may indeed be too full of fact for the comfort of the average college freshman.

Along about 1939 I got into problems of apparent visual size — the size-constancy problem and the moon illusion. A. H. Holway was my exceptionally able assistant and he brought L. M. Hurvich along as his assistant. Later D. W. Taylor took over from Holway. Holway and I published jointly, and later Taylor and I, but eventually I got most of the credit because I was better known and because I published interpretative summary articles under my own name. We showed that size-constancy holds in free binocular vision up to 200 feet and that it is reduced toward the proportionality of apparent size to retinal size by successively eliminating clues to perceived distance.[20] We showed that the moon illusion depends on the shrinkage of apparent size with elevated regard (as others had shown), that the phenomenon depends on the elevation of the eyes in the head and not on movement of the head, and that it depends on the use of two eyes.[21] Astronomers hailed our discovery as settling this moon problem and taking it out of astronomy into psychology,[22] but others noted that we had not solved the fundamental psychophysiological problem of why apparent size is changed in this manner by movement of the eyes.

My most important work at the end of the 1930s and before the naval disaster at Pearl Harbor was the writing of a second volume of history, the book that appeared in 1942 as *Sensation and Perception in the History of*

[20] A. H. Holway and Boring, Determinants of apparent visual size with distance variant, *Amer. J Psychol*, 1941, 54, 21–37, D. W. Taylor and Boring, Apparent visual size as a function of distance for monocular observers, *ibid*, 1942, 55, 102–105, Boring, Perception of objects, *Amer. J. Phys*, 1946, 14, 99–107. We got only partial reduction of apparent size to retinal size, complete reduction was obtained later by W. Lichten and S. Lurie, A new technique for the study of perceived size, *Amer J Psychol*, 1950, 63, 280–282.

[21] A. H. Holway and Boring, The moon illusion and the angle of regard, *Amer. J. Psychol.*, 1940, 53, 109–116, The apparent size of the moon as a function of the angle of regard. further experiments, *ibid*, 537–553; D. W. Taylor and Boring, The moon illusion as a function of binocular regard, *ibid*, 1942, 55, 189–201, Boring, The moon illusion, *Amer. J. Phys.*, 1943, 11, 55–60.

[22] F. L. Whipple, *Earth, Moon and Planets*, 1941, 101f.; Clyde Fisher, *The Story of the Moon*, 1943, 65–70.

Experimental Psychology. The first volume of 1929 had been only the introduction to the history of experimental psychology, and its title has been criticized because it dealt so largely with theoretical systems and the men who made them. I published it when it got too large to be carried further but forgot to change its title to something like "Men and Systems in Modern Scientific Psychology." Now I was getting into the material in which I had soaked since Titchener put me up to giving the Cornell systematic lectures in 1912. I tried out vision first, for I feared that that huge field could be handled only by an expert, but when its chapters seemed not too bad I finished the book, dating the preface December 6, 1941, as the day before the attack on Pearl Harbor and thus the last day when pure scholarship could be undertaken with a clear conscience. On the whole, I am inclined to think that the book is about as good a job as could have been done by any ordinary author in so broad a field. Some specialists have criticized the parts in which they were expert, and I keep wondering whether the book's failure to get more criticism is due to the profundity of its author's erudition or to the dearth of competent critics. It is a sobering responsibility, to decide as you write what hundreds of graduate students will thereafter learn as the truth. ("No one," Titchener once said, "has the right to use an encyclopedia, unless he knows enough to tell when it is wrong!")

HARVARD 1942–1950

Emotionally the Second World War was harder on me than the First, for I had no prescribed job and had to hunt around for essential service, leaving the more obvious needs to be met by younger men. I began by taking on more teaching, and my first real sacrifice was to contribute the services of my efficient secretary, Jane Morgan, to the firing line in the National Research Council in Washington. In 1940 The National Research Council's Emergency Committee on Psychology had been organized under the chairmanship of K. M. Dallenbach to promote the contribution of American psychology to the war effort, and, although I was not on that committee, I knew seven of its original nine members well and followed its work.[23]

Ever since the First World War there had been talk about the need for a textbook of military psychology and now that talk was revived in the Emergency Committee. With BLW experience behind me, I was sure that the chapters could be written by experts and edited into a unity. I made that proposal to the Emergency Committee in May 1942 and was appointed chairman of a subcommittee authorized to get the book written and pub-

[23] K. M. Dallenbach, The Emergency Committee in Psychology, National Research Council, *Amer. J. Psychol.*, 1946, 59, 496–582.

lished. On the committee with me were Colonel E. L. Munson, Jr., and Colonel Joseph I. Greene, the editor of the *Infantry Journal*, a wise academic in the Army, who presently, because of his wisdom and humanity, became my friend.[24]

Colonels Greene and Munson were both sure that the Army needed a sound popular book on the use of psychology by the common GI soldier more than a text at officer level, so we changed our first objective and relied on Marjorie Van de Water of Science Service as our instructor in popular scientific writing. Fifty-two authors contributed to the book, but Miss Van de Water and I wrote and rewrote their material, shuffling their parts around to get the final whole. She knew how to write at this level and I learned from her. It was fun. Never before had I undertaken to manipulate my English style voluntarily, but, with repeated criticism from both Miss Van de Water and Colonel Greene, I learned. When the book was completed, academic circles viewed it with shocked astonishment, for academics do not write to the man in the street or in the front line, but what we had done was right. The little volume appeared in the summer of 1943 under the title *Psychology for the Fighting Man*, a twenty-five cent book with the imprint of the Penguin Series and the Infantry Journal. It sold eventually about 380,000 copies and brought the National Research Council about $10,000 in royalties which, since the services of the committee and the contributors had been free, left about $6000 above the actual expenses to use in other services of psychology to national welfare.

As soon as *Psychology for the Fighting Man* was done, I was supposed to turn to writing the long-discussed textbook of military psychology, employing the contributions that had been sent us for the popular book and that were mostly too technical for use without rewriting. An ulcer attack held up this job but eventually the book was written and appeared in the summer of 1945 under the title *Psychology for the Armed Services*. The volume was not severely criticized, but it had no phenomenal success. I came to think that its level of difficulty had not been pitched high enough, but it is also true that the Army wanted from psychologists texts on leadership more than texts on the whole range of the psychology which is useful in war.

In May 1942, Yerkes organized, under the Emergency Committee, his Survey and Planning Committee, whose purpose it was to bring a group of psychologists together for deliberation of the war's psychological needs, to provide more time for discussion than was available in the meetings of the Emergency Committee. Yerkes asked five others and me to make up his first committee and we met for a week at Vineland, New Jersey,

---

[24] On the Subcommittee on a Textbook in Military Psychology, *ibid.*, 526–530.

in June as guests of The Training School. During the next three years, this committee met nine times at Vineland, never for less than four days. We worked hard, morning, afternoon and evening, and we made many recommendations to the Emergency Committee.[25] One of our major achievements, a success that was realized after the war was over, was the planning of the amalgamation of the important psychological societies into one large body which could represent all of American psychology to America. That meant getting the American Psychological Association and the Association for Applied Psychology to merge and to take in such other societies as were willing. I became chairman of an Intersociety Constitutional Convention which met in May 1943, but after that the councils of the associations took over and I dropped out. Everyone knows how the reorganized American Psychological Association has grown in size, in range of activities and in responsibilities.[26] It has in it a Policy and Planning Board, modelled on the old Survey and Planning Committee, and I was its first chairman.

The war had one great effect upon psychology at Harvard. It taught the social psychologists that they had a common mission with the cultural anthropologists and the empirical sociologists, since they were all trying to study human nature in its social setting. Now at Harvard they proposed a fusion of these three fields to form a new department, which would also take in clinical psychology. Let the peace, they said, not dissipate the wisdom learned in war. Fusion, however, means fission. It takes an out-group to make an in-group. The new arrangement would split psychology down the middle, leaving experimental and physiological psychology outside the new unity. I was doubtful, but these human naturalists were sure, and I gave in when Jerome S. Bruner, like Edward VIII before Stanley Baldwin, pleaded for the right of the social psychologists to marry for love. It was I who suggested that the Psychological Laboratory ought, after forty years, to get out of Emerson Hall into more suitable environs. Our new Dean, Paul H. Buck, showed his statesmanship by lending vigorous support to both sides of this fission. So it came about that in 1945 a new Department of Social Relations and Laboratory of Social Relations got the top of Emerson Hall with decent outside funds for development,[27] while biotropic psychology got expansion in a splendid new 108-room Laboratory created in the basement of Memorial Hall by S. S. Stevens out of the dirty cellar and the old commons kitchen.[28]

We were very happy in our new quarters, and the immediate accessibility

[25] On the Subcommittee on Survey and Planning, *ibid*, 530–536.
[26] Dael Wolfle, The reorganized American Psychological Association, *Amer. Psychologist*, 1946, 1, 3–6.
[27] G. W. Allport and E. G. Boring, Psychology and Social Relations at Harvard University, *Amer Psychologist*, 1946, 1, 119–122.
[28] S. S. Stevens and E G. Boring, The new Harvard Psychological Laboratories, *ibid*, 1947, 2, 239–243.

of books and journals gave me an expanded sense of power. I, now the patriarch, was given a huge office supplied with Münsterberg's refinished desk, for at first we thought we had plenty of space. Soon, however, Lowell's bon mot, "These professors follow the gas law," became clear again. We were jammed full when B. F. Skinner had joined the staff and we regretted our earlier expansiveness.

It is proper to say here just a word about Stevens. Of all the graduate students who have worked with me, he is the one in whose ultimate success I had the most certain belief, in whose future I made the largest investment of identification. Outsiders have thought of him as my favorite, and indeed he was, but with good reason, as the outsiders kept finding out when they learned what he could do. In the early days I taught Stevens some of his knowledge, and even how to write well. Now he instructs me. This relationship has been, on the whole, very rewarding for it has been genuinely paternal. I count every success of Stevens' as my own, not publicly, of course, but in my secret thought. It is in such relations that an older man gets through a younger one of the most satisfying reimbursements that the academic profession has to offer and also, by identification, a little grasp on immortality.

When the fission with Social Relations occurred, I found myself landed in the chairmanship of the Department again. I had tried without success to follow the rule of E. P. Cubberley at Stanford that a chairman should resign at the age of forty-five, leaving power to younger men. The alternative is that the chairman should be a person appointed specifically for this administrative job. His work should not be carried on as an incidental addition to a teaching or research appointment. With this thought in mind we succeeded in 1948 in getting E. B. Newman appointed both as Associate Director of the Laboratories and as Chairman of the Department, a kind of executive secretary of our outfit, and the plan has worked splendidly.

When the Second World War was safely over and there was time to return to scholarship, I undertook the revision of my 1929 *A History of Experimental Psychology*. I expanded the volume by a quarter (the publisher prayed I would not make it unmanageably large), I rewrote about half of the old material and radically revised the rest, and I brought the book up to date with all the progress that had occurred in the twenty-one years since the first edition. What pleased me most about the revision was that I felt it was more mature, that the discussion was structured about a wiser conception of what is going on when science advances. I had also solved to my own satisfaction the problem of why American psychology, while attempting to copy German *Inhaltspsychologie*, nevertheless went functional. That matter had troubled me in 1929. Also I got into the text the paradox of the *Zeitgeist* which controls the Great Men and yet is controlled by them. If the book does not last another twenty years, it ought at least to last ten.

Perspective 1886–1950

Now would be the time for me to attempt a perspective of myself. Limits of space, however, hold me to an outline of the systems of values and the traits and abilities which seem to me to have determined my life.

What *values* have become fixed with me to compel my actions and rule my decisions? I list them as four dichotomies.

(1) *Physicalism vs. dualism.* I feel more secure as a physicalist and that view of nature seems to me the more satisfying.

(2) *Determinism vs. freedom.* My determinism follows from my physicalism. Freedom (personal and hence political) seems to me a negative concept and unworthy of intelligent espousal. Free choice is, nevertheless, man's most useful and important delusion, a delusion required by his culture even when repudiated by his intelligence.

(3) *Altruism vs. egoism.* I have already said how I have feared ego-involvement as the enemy of truth. I am for altruism in science, politics and human affairs, but I know that egoism is still man's most useful and important prejudice, a *sine qua non* of his basic nature.

(4) *Description vs. evaluation.* I fear value judgments because psychologically they are prejudices. *Tout comprendre, c'est tout pardonner* is my recipe for maturity. Immaturity and egoistic hysteria seem to me to be the world's troubles now and throughout historical time.

Now what am I like?

(a) I am a *compulsive* person, whose compulsions drive him on inexorably to goals. These compulsions work for minutes and also for years and only achievement satisfies them. I believe in the importance of the unconscious in motivation, and in no place is it more evident than in my writing. Then it is that my unconscious cerebration operates my typewriter and puts down there wiser thoughts and more apt expressions than I ever anticipated when I began. Thus I have learned to turn myself over to my unconscious motivations and to let them work through me.

(b) Am I *intelligent?* I do not know. I think I am at least the average of the run of graduate students in the Harvard Laboratory. It is these irresistible compulsions and thus my capacity for hard work on an eighty-hour week and a fifty-week year that have made the most of my brains.

(c) The outstanding feature of my personality seems to me, however, to have been the conflict between my *need for power and achievement* and my *need for approval and affection.* Everything I have done well has been an activity which operates to resolve this conflict and to give me both of these two near-incompatibles at once. Thus I find myself in (i) *administration,* identifying myself with my department and regarding its history as my own history, seeking always to become the "commanding servant" of my group, trying to win loyalty by the beneficent exercise of authority. My other solution has been my (ii) *writing*, for there I command the attention of a much larger group than ever sit before me in a lecture, and I am always vividly aware of them as I write, soliciting their assent and approval. This faith that my post-publication audience is already listening as I write sustains me and is reënforced by occasional evidence that what I have already published has really been read and approved by other persons.

(d) To all this I ought to add my persistent sense of *insecurity*, which was established at age five and which dominated me on through the fifties. Rarely have I been sure of the quality of my work. I have needed repeated approbation and often mistrusted its validity. This feeling, however, has diminished in my sixties, perhaps because I feel that I have arrived, which is to say I feel that I have reached the peak of my achievement and am no longer set for a future which could be made to transcend the past.

(e) Have I finally attained that *maturity* for which I have so long striven, the maturity in which the drives to action continue undiminished while the emotions of frustration and the constant desire to dispense blame to others disappear? No. I can still get angry, but I am nearer my ideal of substituting comprehension for recrimination than I ever was. Hormonal change might have something to do with such late maturity but I tend also to connect my growing tolerance with what we adults call "experience." *Tout comprendre* remains, if not my rule of living, at least my constant aspiration and my protection against censoriousness. At age sixty-four, through the incidence of six decades, I like to imagine that I have been admitted to the company of those wise human beings who understand, however imperfectly, the nature and purpose of living. They form indeed a select society and perhaps they would not recognize my membership in their club; yet my secret vanity is that I did, somehow or other, get elected and that I am going to stay elected if it takes my last ounce of compulsion to maintain my hard-won serenity!

CYRIL BURT

I HAVE always thought that every psychologist should regard himself as a kind of problem child, brought to his own psychological laboratory to be studied by the self-same methods and along much the same lines that he would adopt with anyone else.[1] In his case there would be an added gain. Trained in habits of impartial introspection and perhaps already psychoanalyzed, the psychologist would be able to supply much further information, such as might throw a revealing light on the development and the behavior of persons like himself.

Were I to apply my own methods of case study to myself, I should follow my favorite scheme: to start with my family history, and to look first for evidences of heredity to account for my numerous oddities and foibles, and then to turn to environmental influences — life at home, at school, and with my early companions in the world outside. With regard to my own mental development, however, the questions commonly put to me refer, not to the reasons for my delinquent or neurotic lapses nor for my intellectual defects, numerous as they are, but to the grounds for my choice of a vocation. "Fifty years ago," the questioner explains, "psychologists were scarcely heard of; so what made you take up psychology?" It is a question I have often asked myself. During my own lifetime perhaps the most remarkable event has been what Mr. H. G. Wells has called "the advent and the impact of the new science of psychology." And younger readers, I imagine, will be far more interested in the development of the science than the development of one humble scientist. So I shall keep mainly to the problem of "vocational selection."

On my father's side my family, as the surname will suggest, were country

[1] Many years ago I was asked by Professor Carl Murchison to contribute an autobiography for his well-known series. Much of what follows was drafted at that time. But eventually I decided that a life story should be written (if at all) towards the end of one's career rather than in the middle. Some time ago, however, the Editor of *Occupational Psychology* invited me to supply an autobiographical sketch. Hence some of the earlier part of what follows here has already appeared in that journal. I am indebted to the Editor for permission to make use of it if I wished.

folk from Wessex. According to a genealogical tree, which some enthusiast compiled many years ago, my grandfather owned a farm and a quarry at a place called Montacute — land which had been granted to a remoter ancestor in Tudor days, so the story went, for services as Warden of that portion of the New Forest. The legend is partly borne out by a coat of arms bearing three bugles, to which a few more distant relatives lay claim. Not long ago, in correspondence with Professor Harold Burtt (Chairman of the Department of Psychology at Ohio State University), I learned that he too possessed a shield with a similar coat of arms, belonging to his ancestors, who apparently left the same part of England a couple of centuries ago. He guesses that he and I must be "seventeenth cousins or thereabouts." As for occupation, the last six generations have included six surgeons or physicians, three ministers of the church on the male side, and three school teachers on the female side. Of my grandfather's six children, all except my father emigrated to the United States, Australia, or Canada; and, as a result, I have one first cousin who was until recently Professor of Chemistry in Toronto.

My parents were firm believers in heredity. Apart from the usual references to similarities in physical appearance, I was constantly told that I had tricks of gesture and behavior that were strikingly reminiscent of relatives I had never seen or who had gone abroad before I had met them. Racially, I was reminded, I was a mixture of Angle, Saxon, and Celt, and from the earliest years was warned to avoid the well-known defects of each, and to cultivate their redeeming qualities.

To commemorate the Saxon strain, my father gave me an out-of-the-way Christian name which pursued me as a nickname through my earlier years; and my mother, in playful reference to some ill-founded claims of my paternal relatives, would dub me Ethel-bert the Unready. My father's mother was a Miss Barrow. Her family belonged to Norfolk and she traced her descent from Newton's mathematical tutor at Cambridge, Sir Isaac Barrow. Like so many other Cambridge mathematicians, Barrow was an East Anglian. The only other thing my grandmother knew about him was that Charles the Second had said of his sermons: "Once he has started a theme he never leaves it until he has exhausted both the subject and his listeners." I sometimes fear this trait may have rested on a transmissible gene.

On my mother's side the genealogy is less complete. She was an Evans from Monmouth, proud of her Welsh descent. Nevertheless she always feared that I might develop the failings of the Celt, particularly the "irresponsible artistic temperament" of her brother. He was an erratic landscape painter, who taught me water colors and who ended a long bohemian life in a solitary hut at the top of the Kymin. At home there were large paintings by my uncle hanging on the walls. On the bookshelves there were ancient medical tomes belonging to my great-grandfather. And, if I showed an early interest in painting or in medicine, I suspect it was due as much to these and other reminders as to any direct inheritance.

At the time I was born, March 3rd, 1883, my father was a house-physician at Westminster Hospital. He paid his fees by keeping a chemist's shop, with my mother in charge when he was away at the hospital. For eight years I enjoyed the advantages and the handicaps of an only child. My parents were then living in Petty France, a small street near St. James's Park. Their house was only a stone's throw from No. 19, the site of the "pretty garden house" belonging to John Milton and later occupied by Bentham, Hazlitt, and the Mills. (It had been demolished three or four years before I was born.) Gladstone lived close by, at Buckingham Gate, and my parents' proud allusions to these celebrated personages drove home a number of simple ideas on politics, theology, and morals.

It was generally assumed that I should eventually follow one of the callings that predominated in my father's family, and become either a parson or a doctor. My mother, I fancy, secretly hoped I should enter the Church. When I dressed up in surplice and hood, and preached her a sermon, she entered into the game; and she has treasured a notebook containing numerous sermons which I wrote, or rather commenced, at the age of seven, and from which I once rashly computed my own IQ. My father, however, with most of my male relatives, was a Congregationalist, not an Anglican, and in his eyes I was, like my sister, unquestionably destined from birth to follow him as a doctor. The idea of achieving success in sport, politics, or money-making was curiously remote from my family's ideals. In part this limited outlook was fostered by the fact that all the members of my family who have been brought up in towns have developed a weakly physique. Oddly enough, no one seems to have thought of me as a teacher, although the inclination to teach other people seems to have been strong on both sides of the family.

My father was himself a keen classical scholar, an admirer of the Romans rather than the Greeks. He taught me the Latin declensions morning by morning while I was still in my cot, with stories from Livy or Nepos as a reward. A few years later my grandfather, who was a great admirer of German science and philosophy, made me learn the German declensions, and recite the song from *Wilhelm Tell*. I constructed a toy theater in which Schiller's play was performed with cardboard figures and lycopodium lightning. Painting toy scenery became a great hobby, in which my father, grandfather, and my disreputable uncle all helped on various occasions; this, I fancy, was the real beginning of my interest in art. From my grandfather, who was far more talkative than my father, I also picked up all sorts of out-of-the-way scientific information which he, I think, gleaned mainly from his weekly copy of *Nature* or from the queer German publications that he picked up for a few coppers at the open-air book stalls in Farringdon Market.

My mother, who was new to London, was shocked by the condition of the barefoot urchins in the Pimlico slums, and used to give informal help at the "ragged school," with which my grandfather was connected. *Oliver Twist* was the novel she most frequently quoted. She cherished an ill-concealed dread lest some day I should be kidnapped and brought up in a thieves' kitchen. However, though her stories of Fagin and the Artful Dodger alarmed me at the time, they left a lurking curiosity to learn more of the adventurous life that seemed to be found in the London slums. Her own ideal was the seventh Earl of Shaftesbury, "the rescuer of little chimney sweeps and tiny factory hands"; and I remember sobbing whenever she sang: "Please give me a penny, Sir, my mother dear is dead." Apart from a box of bricks and my home-made theaters, I cannot recollect receiving any toys of the usual childish type, nor of playing the commoner indoor games in which most children indulge; by far the most frequent birthday or Christmas gifts were books or paint boxes. Both my parents were interested in music, and I learned to strum as soon as I could safely perch on a rotating piano stool. Here again was the germ of another major interest that has remained with me all through life.

The interests and outlook of my paternal and maternal relatives sometimes conflicted, but more often tended to balance each other. My father's tastes and temperament were classical; he admired Milton, Raphael, Mozart, Christopher Wien, and modelled his prose style, even in his letters to me at school, on that of Dr. Johnson. The interests of my mother and her artist-brother were frankly romantic, from them I learned to love Scott, Shelley, Turner, Mendelssohn (who later gave way to Wagner), Virginia Water by moonlight, and the Gothic cathedrals. I fancy this was not wholly a question of Teuton versus Celt; it was rather the effect of a long-standing tradition in their two families.

When I was ten, my father, on account of his health, took a country practice in Snitterfield, a tiny Warwickshire village where the Shakespeare family had its original home. The Trevelyans, who owned the land, had refused to allow the railway to pass through. Accordingly, day by day I trundled six miles to school at Warwick on a tricycle. As the examinations drew near, my mother regularly related how my father had once won so many prizes at St. Saviour's Grammar School that a cab was necessary to cart them home, and I felt I should be disgraced if I did not bring back at least one prize. To make quite sure, I generally aimed at the Scripture prize, which nobody else seemed to covet.

My games, or rather my hobbies, now took a more scientific turn. My sister and I started a "Vatican Museum," which housed collections of fossils, old coins, birds' eggs, postage stamps, botanical specimens, and prehistoric implements that we gathered on our walks or cycling expeditions. When my father started a series of popular lectures on chemistry, I transformed a disused fowl-house into a laboratory, in which I manufactured nitrous oxide, and turned salts of iron now blue, now red — to the joyful astonishment of my sister — chiefly with the assistance of my father's drugs. Hitherto I had been a solitary youngster. But the son of the village schoolmaster had strong scientific interests, and together we went botanizing, collecting fossils, or cycling round to all the rural churches to study Gothic architecture. Partly, perhaps, because our school was so far away, we never became members of any cricket or football team; and, though my aunts and cousins thought this deplorable, it meant that I was acquiring a good many interests or bits of information that made up for a lack of any scientific teaching in a Victorian grammar school.

At the age of eleven, thanks chiefly to the queer assortment of "general knowledge" I had acquired at home, I managed to win a scholarship[2] to Christ's Hospital, the "bluecoat school," founded by Edward VI in what was left of the Grey Friars Monastery, and famous as the school of Coleridge, Leigh Hunt, and Charles Lamb. The headmaster, "Dicky" Lee, sought, and sought successfully, to exercise the same influence on his boys as Arnold at Rugby. We copied his ideals, his mannerisms, his turns of speech, while affectionately making fun of his stout and stately little person. Alike in his lessons and his sermons it was his deep interest in human character and in problems of philosophy that attracted me. In this, I fancy, I was almost alone. When those of my year became "Grecians," as the members of the top form were called, I claimed the Head as my favorite master, the others mainly put their faith in the two younger classical masters, who, while taking Greats at Oxford, had both concentrated on the historical rather than the philosophical side.

But there can be no question that for me the most powerful influences at this time were those of the other boys with whom I came in contact, especially those who were, mentally if not chronologically, a little older than myself. Of these the earliest was Sir Cyril Fox (as he now is), Director of the National Museum at Wales. He was a year older, and I remember modelling my handwriting on his; but, though I did not realize it at the time, his interest in the archaeological aspects of the Classics influenced me still more. Two others were Sir John Forsdyke, until a year or two ago Director

[2] I cannot miss this opportunity of recording my gratitude to those who assisted me (and many other boys of my time) to achieve an education which would otherwise have been financially impossible — first, to the Governors of the Warwick Grammar School, later to Christ's Hospital, and my own College at Oxford; also to the Grocers' Company at whose examination I won an exhibition, and finally to Mr. W. J. Thomson, a generous Governor of "Housey," who added a private donation to both my friend and myself when we won our scholarships at the University. My mother claimed that, from the age of nine, my education "never cost my parents a penny." Scholarships have thus played so indispensable a part in my life that, not unnaturally, one of my chief interests has been to widen, and if possible improve, the scholarship system and allied methods of examination and selection

of the British Museum, and Sir John Beazley, Professor of Classical Archaeology at Oxford. Beazley had the reputation of being the most brilliant boy that the school had produced for many years, I got my first inkling of the meaning of mental age when the Headmaster told us, "Intellectually that babe is a good year older than any of you" (he was then fifteen and we were seventeen). But my closest friend was a lanky lad named Bradford, with hair *en brosse*, who was for this and other reasons regarded by the rest as a decided freak. He still further encouraged my peculiar tastes: we made a point of studying anything that was not in the curriculum — Egyptian hieroglyphics at the British Museum, fossils at South Kensington, the Italian primitives at the National Gallery, and the history of London at the Abbey and the Tower. Wherever we went, our long blue coats and yellow stockings attracted a friendly custodian or guide. When we became prefects together, our pet game was to guess the characters and dispositions of the other boys in our House or Form — a procedure which we held was essential to justice and order, and we imitated the Headmaster by giving the promising youngsters an intellectual age.

Every Wednesday afternoon, with or without my companion, I used to visit my grandfather for tea. One wet day I remember coming across Ward's article on "Psychology" in a copy of the *Encyclopaedia Britannica*, which he kept in his study. I still have the loose-leaf set of manuscript notes, started when I was about fifteen, based on this article, which proposed to cover the whole range of human character-qualities. On a neighboring shelf a pale blue volume of the *Strand Magazine* contained "The Adventures of Sherlock Holmes." This turned our attention to the study of crime and detection, and led us to haunt the more disreputable parts of Whitechapel and Limehouse in the hope of solving the mystery of Jack the Ripper.

During my holidays I delighted to act as coachman on my father's rounds. Occasionally he would persuade a passing youngster to "hold the horse," while I went up into the bedroom and "helped" him in his examination of the patient. This meant I was expected to note all the symptoms that I could — looking at the blacksmith's throat, listening through the stethoscope to the baker's chest, and percussing the farmer's wife to outline a duodenal tumor. Afterwards I received a lecture on the complaint, illustrated by diagrams from Quain or Michael Foster. The early training I thus obtained, starting at the age of twelve, has been of the utmost value to me in practical work.

There were a number of Victorian celebrities who had come to live in our part of Warwickshire: the Galtons, the Trevelyans, the Dugdales, Marie Corelli, and the Socialist Countess of Warwick. When my father had visited one of his more eminent patients, he would try to fire my ambition by describing their achievements or those of their relatives. Thus, when he had dosed Sir George Trevelyan for his rheumatism, I heard all about the famous uncle, Lord Macaulay, and devoured the celebrated essay on Milton, with disastrous effects on my literary style. Darwin Galton, an ailing old man of 80, lived three miles away at Claverdon, where Sir Francis Galton now lies buried. And since, as family physician, my father called there at least once a week, I heard more about Francis Galton than about anyone else. Next to Milton and Darwin, he was, I think, my father's supreme example of the Ideal Man; and as a model he had the further merit of being really alive. So it was that, on returning to school, I got from the library Galton's *Inquiries into Human Faculty,* and I still recollect a superstitious thrill when I noticed on the title-page that it first saw daylight in the same year that I was born.

At Christ's Hospital the only prizes I gained were for out-of-the-way subjects, like Scripture or Music, together with the Charles Lamb medal for an "Essay on the Victorian Epoch," a subject which afforded scope for the miscellaneous information I had picked up. The archaeological interests of the top form were due, I fancy, to S. E. Winbolt, who happened also to be my own Housemaster. In my last year but one he lent me the drafts of his book on *Pre-historic Britain,* and suggested anthropology as a possible vocation. The mathematical master considered I ought to drop my Latin and Greek, and aim at a scholarship in mathematics at Cambridge. This rather surprised me since, being afflicted all my life with a memory like a sieve, I had acquired a hearty dislike of Euclid and algebra, which in the lower classes were taught chiefly by rote. The Headmaster naturally favored the Classics, and that, together with memories of my father's enthusiasm, turned the scale.

After refusing an exhibition at Cambridge, I eventually chose Jesus College, Oxford, chiefly because I considered myself half Welsh, and was fortunate enough to win a scholarship there. At my father's suggestion, I then applied to read science, in the hope of becoming a medical student. As no science had been taught at my school, the answer was not surprising. "The College expects a *quid pro quo:* he who gains a scholarship in classics must take his examinations in classics."

Classics and *Litterae Humaniores* of course included philosophy, both ancient and modern. From Dean Inge, who was then a lecturer on philosophy at Oxford, I acquired an interest in both Neo-Platonist and mediaeval writers on psychology, and from Sir William Ross a profound admiration for Aristotle, if not as a metaphysician at least as a biologist. I still think that the best approach to psychology is from the angle of philosophy and the history of psychology working towards neurology and experiment, and not vice versa: In the latter case one picks up bad philosophy without knowing it, and takes as novelties time-honored doctrines that have been formulated, and sometimes exploded, centuries ago. My boyish interest in anthropology was at the same time encouraged by Sir John Rhys, the Principal of my College, and by Dr. Marett, whose lectures I also attended in Exeter College just opposite. Eventually it was agreed that I might go to Gotch and J. S. Haldane at the Physiological Laboratory. And there I encountered William McDougall.

I quickly resolved to take Psychology as a special subject for my final examination. For a while I was McDougall's only student. Later, Hocart, the anthropologist, Flugel (who has become a life-long friend and to whom I owe more than I can say), and afterwards May Smith, joined his little group. McDougall adopted what he called the German method of tuition. This consisted in requiring the student to attempt some small research of his own. As he was aware of my interest in Galton's work, he suggested as my topic the standardization of psychological tests for the anthropometric survey which a Committee of the British Association was planning at Galton's instigation. The scheme was to cover "all levels of the mental hierarchy," and would thus incidentally entail a broad acquaintance with the different aspects of psychology.

I had already purchased the first volume of *Biometrika*, a new periodical just founded by Galton. This number contained a fascinating article on "Anthropometry and the identification of criminals." Here Pearson suggested calculating from a table of correlations for bodily measurements (collected at Scotland Yard according to the Bertillon scheme) metrical assessments for a hypothetical set of "index-characters," or "factors" as they would now be called, from which the observable traits could more readily be predicted. It seemed to me that this kind of analysis might also be tried for psychological measurements. As it happened, at about this date Pearson himself came at McDougall's invitation to address a College society on the subject of "correlations and lines of closest fit," and I was invited to attend.

In this way I first met Karl Pearson. His own son was among the group of schoolboys I was testing, and that still further aroused his interest in the work we had undertaken. Spearman, who comparatively late in life had left the Army to study psychology at Leipzig, settled down for a while in a village near Oxford. He too had become interested in the Galton-McDougall scheme, and had started testing boys in the local school. On McDougall's lawn at Boar's Hill Spearman and I used to meet and submit tentative ideas to him for criticism and suggestion.

I do not think my younger Oxford companions influenced me so much as my companions at school. A small group of us founded a College club called the Delian Society, from a marble bust of the Delian Apollo, picked up second-hand for five shillings, which adorned my room. Our aim was to "educate ourselves eclectically." By way of showing how art, science, and Greek philosophy could be combined, I started the first meeting with a paper on the Psychology of Aesthetics (we were still under the influence of the wave of romantic aestheticism started by Pater and Oscar Wilde). My next effort was in "The calculation of index-characters for intellectual differences." Here I outlined a method of factorizing correlations (modified from Pearson's) which I subsequently used in my 1909 and 1917 articles, and described some home-made tests of ability based on a doctrine of logical analysis and synthesis I had learned from Cook Wilson (the tests of "Analogies," "Syllogisms," and "Relations" were perhaps the most original). Both papers were full of adolescent affectations, and the criticisms I received from fellow-members saved me from a good deal of foolishness when a few years afterwards I began to prepare articles for more serious purposes.

After I had taken my degree, a generous extension of my scholarship and later the award of the John Locke Scholarship, enabled me to continue my research and to spend some time at Wurzburg. There I became interested in Kulpe's work on aesthetics and the "higher thought processes," got fresh ideas for tests, met some of the forerunners of the Gestalt movement, and heard about the new investigation of Meumann, Stern, Wertheimer, Veraguth, and Freud. On the initiative of Keatinge, Reader in Education at Oxford, we started an informal child guidance center at his office, where backward and delinquent children were brought for testing and examination (on lines suggested by Galton's anthropometric laboratory in London); in this way we hoped to collect further data and to try out further tests.

In 1907 McDougall gave up his half-time post at University College, London, on condition that Spearman should follow him as Sully's assistant, and in the following year I was invited to accept a post in the Physiological Department at Liverpool under Sherrington. My predecessors were R. S. Woodworth and H. J. Watt. My own duties, however, were a little different: I was to teach psychology to medical students and to prospective teachers, and to supervise any research students who might present themselves. Sherrington, it was pointed out, had wisely coordinated all the researches in his department round a central topic. Accordingly I decided to supplement McDougall's work on social psychology by concentrating on the study of individual psychology. If Galton was right, the investigation of innate characteristics ought to come first. Hence our main topics were partly biological (mental inheritance, the mental differences between the sexes, and the assessment of instinctive differences), and partly educational and social (the study of backward and delinquent children). To get a better assessment of the social background of my cases, I lived at the Nile Street Settlement in a slum area close to the docks, where the Warden was Frederick Marquis (now Lord Woolton), and by this means I secured an informal but essential training in practical sociology. At the same time I also endeavored to give my home-taught smattering of physiology and medicine a more solid basis by attending as many of the medical courses as I could.

The introduction of psychology into the scientific curriculum of a University was a revolutionary step, and, with the vanity of youth, I felt it was up to me to make the most of the revolutionary views which I believed psychological studies would introduce. Liverpool was very tolerant of my heresies. When our tests showed that in intelligence women were on the average not discernibly inferior to men, it was indeed a little sceptical. McDougall's interest in emotions and the unconscious led me to study Freud, and to give what, I fancy, were the first lectures on psychoanalysis in any British course. There were demonstrations of hypnotized subjects, and criminals came to the laboratory to be tested. At no other University in those days would such innovations have been permitted.

My new duties delayed the publication of my work on mental tests. The original object had been to verify Galton's notion of "general" and "special" abilities, re-interpreted in the light of McDougall's doctrine of a hierarchy of intellectual levels, and investigated by the aid of a "hierarchical series of tests," some invented for the purpose, others devised by McDougall, and others adapted from Meumann. My own contribution lay chiefly in the idea of fitting the tables of inter-correlations with a set of hypothetical correlations deduced from the "highest common factor," and then testing the residuals for "specific abilities." This method was in effect a simplified substitute for Pearson's method of principal axes. Ward, the editor of the new *British Journal of Psychology*, was somewhat doubtful about printing "so lengthy an article based merely on an experimental or statistical research." I still have his letter in which he regretted that I had "devoted so much time and industry to a transient problem, like mental testing, which holds so little promise for the future." A long and suggestive correspondence ensued, first with Pearson and then with Spearman, to both of whom Ward sent my manuscript. They, however, criticized each other even more vigorously than they criticized me. In the end Ward tactfully suggested first that my questionable mathematics should be relegated to an appendix, and, a few weeks later, that the appendix should be filed for reference at the editor's office instead of appearing in print. Thus abridged, but still 80 pages in length, the article was finally published.

I had an encouraging note from Galton, and the scheme for a mental and physical survey to be carried out first through the schools led to a symposium on mental testing arranged by the Education Section of the British Association in the following year. Spearman championed the idea of a single general factor, and deprecated the idea of special factors. William Brown, who represented the Pearson standpoint, advocated special factors, and doubted the existence of the general factor. I incurred the criticism of each side in turn by maintaining the existence of both. Finally, Dr. Myers wound up with a paper on "The pitfalls of mental testing," in which he severely trounced us all. One obvious weakness arose from the fact that so far tests, which were all individuals tests, had been applied to exceedingly small groups. However, the Association voted a grant of £60 for further investigations of Mental and Physical Factors; and, as secretary of the investigating committee (with Professor J. A. Green), I was grateful to have this help towards the cost of duplicating test-material for a large-scale research on the possibility of group testing that I had already undertaken with Mr. R. C. Moore.

In all this the most active agent was Dr. C. W. Kimmins, who had been secretary of the Section during its earliest years. He was now Chief Inspector of the London Schools, and the most influential member of the Child Study Society. This body had been organized in 1893, at the suggestion of Galton, by James Sully, then Professor of Mental Philosophy at University College, in conjunction with several educationists. It was the only British society that published a journal on child psychology, and it very generously accepted several of my early efforts. The society's chief aim was to encourage the practising teacher to study the individual child along scientific lines and to seek expert guidance for the more difficult cases. As early as 1884 Galton had set up an anthropometric laboratory (later transferred to University College), and I still have a copy of the orange leaflet in which he invited parents and teachers to bring children for examination, at a fee of "ninepence for those on the register and one shilling for those not on the register." Later the educational side of the work was taken over by Sully and by psychologically-minded school inspectors like Ballard and Winch. This was, at any rate in Britain, the origin of the child guidance movement, and of the notion of a center or laboratory for the examination of special cases.

With the informal support of one of the officials of the Board of Education, of leading members of the teaching profession, and of eminent authorities like Galton, Sully, and Karl Pearson, Kimmins drew up a scheme, which was eventually accepted by the London County Council, for adding an educational psychologist to the inspectorate. The arguments that weighed most with the London education committee were the criticisms brought by teachers against the manner in which school medical officers were certifying mentally defective school children. The doctors held, not without justice, that every backward child would benefit by the small classes and individual methods of teaching prevalent in the special schools for the mentally defective. But the parents objected to the stigma which such certification and attendance entailed (the schools were familiarly known as the "dotty schools"); the finance committee objected to the expense; and the teachers' representatives, quoting Pearson on the fallacy of relying on anatomical stigmata and low cranial capacity, argued that the problem of school-allocation was not a medical matter at all.[3]

I was appointed on a half-time basis for a probationary period of three years only, on the understanding that if the scheme failed, it was to be dropped at the end of that time. At our first interview, Sir Robert Blair, the Chief Education Officer, promised his full support in whatever plans I put forward "no matter how ambitious," and he dismissed me with the declaration (in his strong Scottish accent): "Young man, ye're the fust official psychologist in the wurrld, and ye've all London at yer feet! Now come back in a week, and tell me what ye're going to do." My plan of work, which owed much to suggestions from McDougall and Keatinge, consisted in (1) broad periodical surveys of the schools, (2) more detailed surveys of a representative borough, (3) still more specialized studies of special groups — supernormal and subnormal, beginning with the mentally defective. At the same time it was agreed that individual cases should be referred by teachers, doctors, magistrates, or care committee officials "for psychological examination and report." No special paid assistants were appointed, but I was told that I might rely on the services of a medical assistant and of a social worker familiar with each area, and that in addition I might introduce honorary (*i.e.*, unpaid) assistants if I wished. The "Psychologist's Office" in the old education building on the Thames Embankment thus became the first official child guidance center in the country.

Galton had repeatedly argued that, just as hospitals were centers for research as well as for treatment, so schools might be used for purposes of psychological investigation as well as for the training of children. The permission to introduce honorary assistants meant that the schools and institutions of the London County Council were now thrown open to research students (many of them teachers of experience) who were planning investigations for higher degrees under Brown at King's College or Spearman at University College. A glance either at the Annual Reports of the Education Officer and the "Council's Psychologist," or at a book like Spearman's *Abilities of Man*, will show what a vast amount of research was carried out in this way. During the next fifteen years over thirty full-scale investigations and numerous minor inquiries were undertaken.

---

[3] Those whose memories do not go back so far may be interested to learn the methods adopted by school medical officers of those days. A common procedure was that described by Dr. Warner and used by him in his investigation of "mental conditions among 50,000 children." "The pupils are drawn up in ranks, a standard *i e.*, class or grade at a time. . . . The trained observer can then read off the physiognomy of the individual's features and other bodily parts, as quickly as a printed book." A "list of physical signs" is appended. (Frances Warner, *Mental Faculty*, Cambridge Univ. Press, 1890; cf. id., *J. Roy. Stat. Soc.*, 1893, 56, pp. 71f.) Warner, who was later Professor of Anatomy and Physiology at the Royal College of Surgeons, was for long one of the active opponents of "the new-fangled scheme of intelligence tests."

At the outset the most pressing problem in the schools was that of classification. The separation of the mentally defective from the rest was only part of the issue. Were there special disabilities as well as general, temperamental or moral defectives as well as intellectual defectives? What could be done for the emotional, the unstable, the neurotic, and the delinquent? In seeking to answer such questions, Pearson's methods of multivariate analysis proved invaluable, and I and my fellow workers were much indebted to his help and encouragement. I personally owed almost as much to Dr. W. F. Sheppard, one of His Majesty's Inspectors at the Board of Education, who is now perhaps best known for the tables of the "normal curve of error" that go by his name, and for what is still called "Sheppard's correction." The method of analysis that I adopted for my classificatory problems was based essentially on that suggested by Galton, Pearson, and Edgeworth; it consisted in attempting to reduce sets of correlated measurements to terms of uncorrelated variables. It differed from Pearson's procedure in substituting simple summation for determinantal calculations, and in seeking a minimum rather than a maximum number of components, it differed from Spearman's procedure in recognizing multiple factors rather than two types only, in proposing to calculate correlations between tests and certain internally determined criteria instead of external criteria only, and in working with the complete correlation table taken as a whole instead of with separate correlations. Although the methods thus evolved were somewhat severely criticized both by Pearson and by Spearman, they gained the approval and the assistance of Sheppard, who combined practical experience with high mathematical ability. It was also he who first suggested that the statistical problems involved might conveniently be treated by matrix algebra — a topic on which he himself was then writing a book.

In those days, however, editors of psychological journals were reluctant to inflict on their subscribers abstruse algebraic arguments or large tables of figures. I was repeatedly asked to contribute articles discussing our chief theoretical or practical conclusions, but statistical proofs or formulae and tables of figures were nearly always expunged. Fortunately the Education Officer of the Council appreciated statistics and thought others should, too. Accordingly I was allowed to submit the results of my work in the form of printed Annual Reports, which (until the war restricted paper and printing) appeared bound in the Council's vivid orange cover. From time to time the Council generously financed the publication of collections of special reports in book form. The first of these, on *The Distribution and Relations of Educational Abilities,* appeared in 1917. It contained 32 tables of figures, 15 diagrams, and nine plates printed in two colors, all for half a crown, and was an entirely new venture for a local education authority. Four years later *Mental and Scholastic Tests* (with 62 tables, more than a dozen photographed reproductions of children's drawing and handwriting, and a large collection of standardized tests) was also very generously subsidized by the Council.

It is the fashion nowadays to complain that older educational psychologists, in their eagerness to apply tests and measure innate abilities, overlooked the importance of social conditions and culture patterns. But I doubt whether any pupils either of McDougall at Oxford or of Rivers and Myers at Cambridge could have so far forgotten the teaching of their masters, who, in those early days, regarded themselves as anthropologists quite as much as psychologists. When I myself first returned to London to take up my new appointment under the Council, I made my quarters at a Settlement established near the Euston slums by the novelist, Mrs. Humphry Ward, granddaughter of Arnold of Rugby and a connection of the Trevelyans; and, in order to learn something of the differing home life of London pupils, I spent many a week end as the guest of a docker in Stepney, a coster in Kennington, or a burglar in a back street off the Seven Sisters Road. Later, when I determined to follow up my young delinquents in their after-school careers, I managed to get accepted as a presumable member of a criminal gang that planned its activities in a disreputable little Soho restaurant. As I am a born Londoner, I could drop into Cockney when circumstances required, and — what is much more difficult — understand both the idiom and the background. Nowadays it is so often forgotten that to appreciate the cultural outlook of the child you are studying you must yourself have shared it. The London teacher of today will relate many a story of the misunderstandings revealed in the reports of Harley Street psychiatrists or German-born psychologists who submit case histories of London delinquents without even realizing that the outlook of a slum youngster may be as different from their own as that of a Fiji Islander.

Soon after my appointment in London as half-time officer, Myers invited me to spend the other half of each term as his assistant at the new Psychological Laboratory at Cambridge. I found life in St. John's College, with a room near the Bridge of Sighs, a pleasant relief from the bustle of London. But as time went on I felt it impossible to return wholly to academic life at an older University, as Myers and Rivers desired. Of the senior students in the psychological department the most outstanding were F. C. Bartlett, who succeeded me as Assistant there, and W. R. Muscio, who was then becoming interested in industrial psychology. At the same time I gained much help and useful criticism in my statistical projects from Udny Yule, a former assistant of Karl Pearson at University College and then a Fellow of St. John's.

The outbreak of the first World War interrupted all our plans. Both Myers and Kimmins believed that the new methods which had been applied for testing and training children might be applied to select and train recruits. Largely at their instigation the British Association appointed a Psychological

Committee to deal with war-time problems, and I was asked to act as Secretary of the War Research Committee. Later Lord Leyton (as he now is) pressed me to join the Ministry of Munitions as a statistician. "Both guns and gunners," I was told, "can behave very much like children." This post also entailed submitting incidental reports on all kinds of out-of-the-way problems that one or two enterprising members of the War Office considered psychological. But most of all I valued the glimpses I was thus able to obtain into the psychology of the supernormal adult. My section had to draft a weekly progress report for the Minister — Mr. Lloyd George first of all, later Mr. Winston Churchill. One effort, in my usual exhaustive style, came back for filing with a note at the end in red ink: "The art of statistical reporting is that of picking out plums. W. S. C."

When the war was over, I resumed my work with the Council, and my first aim was to standardize a series of tests for children of school age. While at Liverpool I had been impressed both with the possibilities and with the defects of the Binet-Simon scale of intelligence tests, and had published a couple of papers on the subject. In 1910 I had already started to prepare an English revision of the scale, with the aid first of Binet and later of Simon, who were good enough to allow me the copyright of their tests for use in England. And now, assisted by a small group of psychologically trained teachers, I set about the task of standardizing the age-assignments, and of preparing a supplementary series of group and performance tests.

Towards the close of 1919, largely as a result of war-time experience, Dr. C. S. Myers decided to establish in London a National Institute of Industrial Psychology, and invited me to join him once again on a part-time basis as the first head of the Institute's vocational section. "Choice of employment" was a problem that was greatly exercising local education authorities at that time, and the officials of the London County Council welcomed the joint arrangement. The tests of cognitive and temperamental factors that I had first tried out with my students at Liverpool were now revived, and applied to a wider sample of young adults representing so far as possible not merely the academic but also the non-academic classes. With help from the Industrial Health Research Board a group of us were able to plan a follow-up study to demonstrate the value of vocational guidance, and to draw up rough norms for the common types of occupation. Perhaps our most exciting venture was the construction of psychological tests for post-war entrants to the Civil Service. Several thousand adults were tested in this way, and the data thus incidentally collected appeared strongly to confirm the view that many of the assumptions that had been verified in the case of children could also be confirmed in the case of adults.

McDougall's study of the primary emotions and instincts, regarded as innate conative tendencies, had from the first attracted my attention to what (in Aristotelian language) we called the orectic side of personality. Our earliest tests — apperception tests, inkblot tests, camouflaged questionnaires, Galton's test of free association, and the psychogalvanometer — had proved somewhat disappointing in the researches I had carried out in the laboratory at Liverpool, and we went on to devise some method of standardizing interviews and real-life situations. McDougall's doctrine of conative "forces" seemed to fit in with the idea that "factors" could be combined in accordance with the parallelogram of forces, and as early as 1915 Mr. Moore and I published studies which seemed to reveal the existence of temperamental "types" or rather temperamental tendencies. My own notions of methodology suggested that here as elsewhere the most fruitful method of attack would consist in combining a case-study approach with a statistical approach. The outcome was a series of investigations culminating in a volume on juvenile delinquency and another on the psychoneurotic child.

Before the outbreak of the war, a small group of psychologists, which included Ernest Jones (a former school medical officer of the London County Council), J. C. Flugel, Susan Isaacs, and myself, had started a British Psychoanalytic Society, this Society sought to arouse interest in a neglected group of children — the potentially neurotic. Here, as in the field of mental testing, the ideas and methods of psychologists had been strongly opposed by most members of the medical profession, who in those days believed that all disorders and defects were at bottom physical, and that they called for study along physical, and not along psychological, lines. The war had done little towards altering that attitude. Yet by about 1925 there was actually a demand for psychological instruction among some of those who were concerned with the training of medical students. Here Sherrington's support was invaluable. I and my assistants were asked by the Board of Education to assist in courses for school medical officers, and somewhat later the London School of Hygiene invited me to give lectures to medical audiences on the psychological approach to the "subnormal mind."

In 1926 I left the National Institute to accept, at the invitation of Sir Percy Nunn, the Chair of Educational Psychology at the London Day Training College, which was at that time under the London County Council but was subsequently transformed into an Institute of Education under the University. Nunn had recently become Principal of the College, and his idea was that degree students undertaking researches in the schools should have closer contact with the practising psychologist, and that prospective teachers and those training for work in child guidance should have a chance to watch case-demonstrations, attend case-conferences, undertake remedial work, and in fact enjoy some small apprenticeship to the job. My "psychological clinic" was consequently moved to the College. This had many incidental advantages. By exploiting the numerous workrooms, playrooms, and the like, we were able to improve many of our methods of assessing personality by using "standardized situations," and at the same time to investigate the value of systematic play as a means of investigation and treatment – a notion which seemed a natural corollary to our view of delinquency. Moreover, I now had passing through my hands a regular supply of trained research students to assist me in my work in schools.

Nunn and his staff had an active interest in the development of the emotional, moral, and aesthetic side of education. There was a strong interest both in art and in music, and for a while I was able, with the aid of interested specialists, to review an old hobby of mine – the psychology of aesthetic appreciation, particularly with reference to music, poetry, and painting. Another project was also resurrected – one that had attracted me ever since my Oxford days – namely, the idea of substituting a psychological investigation of personality for the ordinary scholarship and entrance examinations to Universities. With the help of other members of the staff, Nunn and I worked out an elaborate scheme for assessing candidates fresh from school. This project included not only reports and replies to a questionnaire from each applicant's teacher, but also a modified interview technique, a series of tests for intelligence, interests, and general knowledge, and what would now be called "projection tests." Though we were a postgraduate institution, we selected our future entrants as they left school. We were thus able to check our test-results later on by the students' academic careers, and by their after-histories when they had become teachers. This experience proved invaluable when later on I was consulted about schemes of personnel selection for recruits and officers in the fighting services and for post-war entrants to the civil service.

For three days a week I still worked in the Council's schools, but the work was becoming increasingly heavy. In 1927, however, after reading one of my Reports to the London County Council which happened to include a long memorandum on the need for more psychological centers or clinics (incorporated in *The Young Delinquent*, 1925), Mrs. St. Loe Strachey, wife of the editor of the *Spectator* and herself a magistrate of wide experience and influence, came to talk over the actual cost of setting up at least one well-equipped "laboratory for child guidance" (as it was called at first) along the lines I had laid down, and eventually suggested enlisting the sympathy of Mr. Harkness. Under the chairmanship of Sir Percy Nunn we called a meeting at the College of all the British psychologists and educationists we could muster. It was evident that we had the sympathy of the London County Council, the Board of Education and the Home Office. There and then a Child Guidance Council was formed with Mrs. Strachey as its first president, Dame Evelyn Fox as its first secretary, and myself as chairman of the executive committee. Eventually, thanks largely to the generosity of the American Commonwealth Fund, a model demonstration center, handsomely equipped, well financed, and with a capable staff, was established. It was our view that child guidance was primarily an educational not a medical problem. However, to allow children to attend during school hours, the sanction of the Ministry of Health was essential. The Minister of Health, Sir George Newman, invited me to become the Director. My first impulse was to accept, but both Nunn and Myers insisted that, owing to the shortage of psychologists in Britain, there was a greater need for persons to teach and study psychology than to practise it. Moreover, I had already accumulated far more research material than I could analyze. It was accordingly decided that the new director should be a medical man, chiefly on the ground that no medical man could be expected to work under a non-medical psychologist, whereas psychologists might readily be expected to work under a medical director. It now seemed likely that psychologists would be regularly excluded from appointment to the senior post at any psychological clinic. As Sir Percy Nunn predicted, this had, at any rate for a while, a disastrous effect on the recruitment of psychologists. "Their numbers," he said, "will be halved and their IQs drop by at least 10 points."

Shortly afterward I was invited to accept the Chair of Psychology at University College where, ever since my return to London, I had maintained close and friendly relations with the various departments. Now I became an official colleague of my old and valued friend, J. C. Flugel, with whom I had spent so many delightful vacations abroad, and of Karl Pearson, on whose support I was able to rely for many of my projects. Although I had now to deal with general rather than applied psychology, I did not entirely neglect my former interests. My "psychological clinic" was now moved to University College, but when the Tavistock Clinic took premises adjoining the College buildings, I was able to arrange that it should be recognized by the University, and our practical training in child psychology was mainly given there until its rooms were destroyed by bombing. Nor did I entirely abandon my links with social and industrial psychology. After Sir Henry Head's retirement I became Chairman of the Psychological Committee of the Industrial Health Research Board, a Committee which included Sir Charles Sherrington, Dr. C. S. Myers, Sir Frederic Bartlett, Professor Pear and Professor Vernon; and, as a member of the Board itself, I came once again into contact with Sir Frederick Marquis and with Mr. Ernest Bevin, both of whom were members at the same time. A number of fruitful researches were planned and published.

While Secretary of the British Association Psychological Committee during the first World War, I had developed an interest in military psychology, a subject which appeared to me to have been badly neglected in this country. One or two members of my staff at University College, notably Pryns

Hopkins, had endeavored, during their travels abroad, to collect what information was available, and now helped me to acquire the relevant American or Continental literature. As Chairman of the Psychological Committee of the Industrial Health Board I was once more brought into touch with various government departments, and revived old connections with the Admiralty and War Office. When war became imminent and ultimately broke out, the information we had already gathered and the tentative schemes we had crudely thought out proved extremely opportune. It was curious to see, within the span of a single adult life, how mental tests, which Ward had predicted would have no future, came to develop into a scheme of psychological assessment applied to men and women by the thousand in the Forces.

When I was invited to University College, I was reminded that its Department of Psychology had always been regarded as a research department, and was assured that, by being released from my other duties, I should have far more time and help for analyzing the data I had amassed, and far more leisure to resume my contacts with colleagues on the Continent and on the other side of the Atlantic. Unfortunately, however, in spite of Nunn's prediction, psychology started to become a popular subject. Whereas during my first two or three years at University College we had only about a dozen active research students (mostly from overseas) and less than half a dozen reading for a first degree, at the date of my retirement we had over 200 students on our class lists of whom nearly 80 are carrying out research in almost every conceivable branch — very large figures for a psychological department in England.

As regards undergraduate teaching, my innovations were few. During the first decade or so of the present century, psychological teaching in Great Britain was limited chiefly to introspective psychology, with the interest centering mainly on the traditional problems of the philosophers; Stout's *Manual* was the standard textbook. After 1911 the publication of Myers' *Textbook of Experimental Psychology* gave teaching an increasingly experimental turn. My own efforts, ever since my Liverpool days, have been to provide both branches with a more adequate physiological basis, including a knowledge of pathological phenomena. In this country the barrier between medical and non-medical subjects has always been extremely strong. Consequently I had myself to undertake the courses on physiological psychology, with dissections of the eye and brain, experiments on frogs, and the like. My connection with the London County Council facilitated students' visits to their medical institutions for the defective and insane. Some knowledge of child development, and still more of social psychology, seemed to me essential even at the undergraduate stage. Statistics I introduced chiefly as one branch of the methodology needed for any complex inductive science. Partly owing to lack of textbooks and publishing facilities, I made free use of roneo'd summaries for almost every lecture and of roneo'd memoranda for reporting new methods or statistical results.   This innovation was possible because, from the time of my first appointment at Liverpool, I had found it helpful to pay for a secretary of my own out of my salary. My tutorial groups were inevitably larger than those at Oxford or Cambridge; but, instead of making students read their essays aloud, I read their efforts beforehand and supplemented my corrections by a typed page or two of detailed comment or criticism on each one.   This double use of paper-work by the teacher, as well as by the class, was certainly a novelty when introduced, and has, I think, greatly improved the efficiency of our teaching.   Experimental work was made a feature of every course, although, owing to lack of funds, we had to eke out the apparatus bequeathed by Galton and McDougall with home-made materials of our own.

But during the twenty years that I have occupied the Chair of Psychology at University College, my main aim has been to preserve its original traditions, and to make it a focus for that branch of psychology which was founded and developed there by Galton — "individual" or, as Stern used to call it, "differential psychology" — the study of the mental differences between individuals, sexes, social classes and other groups.   No other psychology department in Britain has specialized in this particular sphere, whether for training or research.   As a result we have drawn research students, eager to study in this field, from almost every part of the British Commonwealth and from many other countries in all four continents.   London, with its government offices, its progressive Education Committee, its numerous firms and factories, and its countless social problems, has given rise to large demands for "applied psychologists," and provides a rich background for research workers and trainees.   This, too, is the line of work that has always attracted my ablest disciples whether at the National Institute, the London Day Training College, or University College: Raymond Cattell, William Stephenson, W. Line, F. J. Schonell, W. E. Field, A. H. El Koussy, E. L. McElwain, S. Brahmachari, Albert Marshall, Charles Wrigley, I. Cohen, H. J. Eysenck, and many others, who have since obtained chairs or readerships in various parts of the world.

Both before and since the war our great difficulty has been shortage of space, staff, and funds   For the greater part of my time at University College, I had only one (or at most two) full-time assistants, each largely tied to his own somewhat specialized field.   Further, until quite recently, other members of the University could not understand why we should need a separate department for psychology, still less a laboratory with instrumental equipment.   Psychology, they supposed, must be a branch either of philosophy or of medicine.   In this assumption they were strongly supported first by the philosophers and later by many of the medical faculty.   Several leading psychiatrists maintained that the study of individual personality was really a branch of medicine — a study for which the best training was that provided by the ordinary medical courses and by the personal experience picked up automatically as a result of clinical work. They have consequently been quite prepared to take over at their hospitals or elsewhere work in child guidance, personality testing, animal psychology, military psychology, personnel selection for the Civil Service, and even academic instruction for psychological degrees in Arts and Science, more recently still, having far larger funds than most departments of psychology, they have succeeded in attracting as junior members for their staff some of our ablest young psychologists. Finally, the war-time damage to our own College has gravely limited space and accommodation.

The war itself, however, has brought an increasing recognition of the claims of psychology to be regarded as a science in its own right. Happily, too, after a friendly but lively struggle, it has been possible to secure as my successor in the chair an American psychologist of high ability, one who is particularly aware of the need to develop psychology on its own basis, and keenly anxious to sustain "the Galtonian tradition of individual psychology for which University College is everywhere celebrated." At the same time we have succeeded in procuring for the laboratory, which he now takes over, a grant for apparatus and a staff that are several times as large as in preceding years, in addition to three secretarial assistants. In a British laboratory of psychology such aids have hitherto been the luxuries of the professor's pipe-dreams. It is therefore my confident hope that the tiny laboratory which McDougall first equipped will not only develop along the lines which it has followed since the days of Galton and Sully, but will also still further expand, both in size and in influence, during the coming years.

RICHARD M. ELLIOTT

IN the words of H. G. Wells, a biography — and I suppose he would include an autobiography — should be "a dissection and a demonstration of
how a particular human being was made and worked." Clear as this formula
seemingly is, everyone, and especially the psychologist, knows its application in the individual case is so complicated as to be inordinately difficult
and, within any scrupulous meaning of the term science, unachievable. Yet
about fourteen years ago at the University of Minnesota I conceived the idea
of an unorthodox sort of college course, calling it Biographical Psychology,
which assumed that an educationally worthwhile analysis of a human being
could be worked out, using psychological principles and drawing chiefly on
literary sources. My rash design, fashioned in the spirit of general education, was to let up more than a good bit on the usual standards of scientific
sobriety and offer to *undergraduates* only a course in the psychology of personality devoted to analyzing and interpreting life-histories and the factors
which determine their patterns and outcomes.

"Scientific" materials on life-histories are scanty and in part inappropriate
at this curricular level. So we eked them out by drawing unabashedly, but
with full recognition of their fallibility, upon suitable standard biographies
and autobiographies, published letters and personal journals. On the side,
healthy candid self-analysis was encouraged in the light of principles discussed
in class, and the instructor from first to last hammered on the hypothetical
role of numerous causal factors in the development of personality. It was
all fun for me, and the course has proved viable. As judged by the length
and quality of the term papers, a good many students "ate it up." Perhaps
for quite obvious reasons sometimes to their own detriment. Fortunately
for my conscience a check revealed that, with scarcely an exception, the
students enrolled in the course were also taking orthodox courses in psychology. And I obtained reinforcement when, in spite of my remonstrance, some
of my colleagues began to send graduate students to take the course.

I mention this course in order to disclaim at once any intention of undertaking here, where I must to some degree be autobiographical, a personal analysis of the kind which many of the students in the course prepared. Or even more what Santayana had in mind when he wrote that it requires courage for a man to see his equation written out. When one of my students does this with understanding, I feel an overwhelming respect for him, and get a sense of "that deep gravity which persists in every human being" (Matisse). In any event, a dissection of one's personality can neither be done in short compass nor would it be in keeping with the spirit of this series. The plain fact, well-known to the members of the committee who selected the contributors to this volume, is that I personally have created no psychology, have in truth advanced what is known in our science not one whit. Had I done so, believing as I do that psychological research is of tremendous importance at this juncture of human history, I should feel that it would be instructive and decidedly to the point to tell as precisely as space permitted how this particular researcher was made and worked. I hope that my colleagues are doing just that about themselves in their sections of this volume. Though what I write below must include some details, I want them to include many more. In the equivalent space I have elected to record something of my role in the history of a department of psychology.[1] For the committee of selection in exercising its unaccountably lenient and indulgent judgment knew very well that "R. M. Elliott" stands for administrator, teacher, and editor. And with all directness I assert that it could not be generally instructive to our profession to see how a person who has never pretended that he did research got made. The main theme of my story, then, begins with a January day in 1919 in Washington, D. C., when Robert M. Yerkes told Dean John B. Johnston of the College of Science, Literature, and the Arts at the University of Minnesota that despite his appointment two years earlier to head the department of psychology there he had decided, as he said to me "almost unwillingly," to remain in Washington as one of a small group of scientists whose responsibility it would be to shape the newly formed National Research Council. Everyone knows what Yerkes had been doing for the Army and indirectly for psychology during the war years in Washington. After delivering this blow to the stunned and sadly crestfallen dean, Yerkes proceeded to recommend that a slate of youngsters, with myself as chairman, should go to Minnesota to start the functioning of a Department of Psychology which was first created from the twin department Philosophy-Psychology in 1917 but which, with Yerkes on leave from the

---

[1] I am aware that the account of a department which has on the whole functioned as a team can be but illy told through the eyes of one person, especially perhaps those of its chairman. Bird, Paterson and Tinker, my colleagues for decades, have given me some suggestions for which I am grateful. It particularly pains me to think how selective I must be, how many able and cherished colleagues will receive no mention, and how much accomplishment must here be unsung When the reader has finished reading what I have to say, he might remind himself, for example, that Edna Heidbreder and Florence Goodenough were at Minnesota for many years

time of his appointment as chairman, had not been able to begin its full and separate existence during the war years. At a time when psychologists were in extraordinarily short supply, the University apparently decided it might not do better, and three of us were soon thereafter appointed.

Now I suppose I cannot refuse to tell anyone who cares to read this history something about the switches which had routed me so improbably to the point where, at thirty-one and without a record of research publication, I had been selected for this job. So, in all diffidence, to a thumbnail sketch of that "moving center of experience," me, and of the route that I had travelled up to the point in 1919 at which the Minnesota story properly begins. To conserve space I shall without further apology adopt a staccato style. No detail will be inserted which does not seem to have some relevance to the outcome, but I shall not always stop to point out just where and how.

Born in Lowell, Massachusetts, at the end of 1887. Two older brothers and two younger sisters. All our four grandparents, dissatisfied with the lack of opportunity in their native England, came to the thriving cotton-spinning milltown in Massachusetts in the 1830s. Our parents lived simply but were comfortably situated and were in a way influential in the community. At 12 father had left school to help support his widowed mother as a carpenter's apprentice. Later a builder and general real estate operator and a person whose sound judgment on all sorts of matters was often sought. Mother, a normal school graduate, had taught grade school briefly at Concord, Massachusetts, before early marriage. Our large household included two maiden aunts and one or more servants or nurses, as needed. Summers at our near-by farm where there was regular work as well as play for each child. While our family was inclined toward social self-sufficiency, the old eighteenth century farm house was often filled with the children's friends, sometimes for considerable visits. None of us ever needed discipline and we were a happy family. Our grandparents held orthodox religious views from which our parents broke away to liberal Unitarianism. Father highly religious and active in denominational affairs. RME a skinny puny kid, often laid up, though mildly. At a disadvantage in athletics and in expressing drive to be a leader of any kind. Inferiority feelings. Hypothesis of environmental influence: compensatory turning to books and interest in ideas. Marks in schools — elementary, grammar and high — and in college always near top. Rival, or supplementary, hypothesis of heredity: four out of the five sibs Phi Beta Kappa.

Entry from mother's journal *re* RME: "Can use many words at 16 months." No way of determining between hypotheses, probably in fact they are complementary, for both parents and one aunt fluent in speech with high vocabulary level. Further entries from mother's journal: At five "such a comical little chap! Good-natured from morning to night and always prying into boxes, closets and bureau drawers." ("Investigatory reflex?") At eight "a great reader and lover of books; he makes quite a study of his little Testament." At ten " 'I'd like to be a man of great learning.' "

Earliest and still persisting hobby interest in astronomy. Hypothetical origin in conditioning? At two had a quilt with what I called "moons" on it, and on seeing the moon rising said that one had come off and gone up into the sky. At three insisted on being shown planet Jupiter before being put to bed. Reported that if I happened to cry after dark would stop on being taken out to see the stars. No recollection when at a very early age I first learned the names of the brightest stars, probably from an aunt. Simple books on astronomy were given me early. A planisphere at age nine and at age 14 a refracting telescope which could show the polar caps of Mars and split the rings of Saturn were my most precious possessions. In early teens subscribed to the *Scientific American* and read every word of each issue.

Took college courses in astronomy (Dartmouth College, where my two brothers had preceded me). Reluctantly abandoned astronomy as life work only because mathematics and physics were my most difficult college subjects. Besides I lacked the necessary mechanical skill. Verbalism again. Initially at parents' urging, had total of four years of Latin and three years of Greek. Especially enjoyed Virgil, Horace, Homer, and simple selections from Greek philosophers. In general, a theoretical turn of mind. Majored in philosophy-psychology. Texts in beginning psychology course: James and Angell. In junior year as one of a team of three (others now a "starred" geneticist and a well-known painter) supported determinism in a classroom debate against three "Y.M.C.A.-ers" on the free-will side. Lost debate by close class vote, which we considered a moral victory because prof's views strongly on winners' side. H. H. Horne — who constituted the one-man "department" — a splendid teacher with a preacher's flair for the emotional appeal. He once read to the class a paper I had written on instinct. I recall that it bore the marks of my long-standing and now lifelong interest in nature-study (especially ornithology) and biology. Horne concluded the reading by commenting, with slow-drawn accent on the last word, and closing his fingers on an outstretched palm as he did so, "This paper shows grasp." I have since wondered if those fingers did not then and there pin me down to a particular career. Here was "reinforcement," and I had not been successful in any extra-curricular activities, was not even a member of a fraternity at that time.

Just before the beginning of my senior year Horne had resigned to go to New York University and Wilmon Henry Sheldon, later at Yale, replaced him. I was appointed his assistant with paper-reading duties. Upon graduation awarded a fellowship to go to graduate school and arrived at Harvard in the Department of Philosophy and Psychology in September 1910, most unhappily one month after William James' death.

My performance, that first year, was in no way distinguished. I must have been appallingly callow. According to the prevailing custom, the courses I took were at first about equally divided between philosophy and psychology. My teachers included the illustrious triumvirate of philosophers: Royce, whom we all loved but whose towering metaphysics left me unconvinced; Palmer, whose tidy and prim ethics I had already heard, though less expertly, from Unitarian preachers; and Santayana, whose exposition in unequalled diction of Greek philosophy taught me that science is the Greek way of thinking about the world and persuaded me that right conduct, right thinking, and the good life all depend upon discrimination, or knowledge. I also took a course under Ralph Barton Perry, whose neo-realism impressed me and whose assistant I became for one-half year. Münsterberg was then on leave as exchange professor in Berlin. After his return he directed my program, including the Ph.D. thesis on the subject "The psychophysics of handwriting."

To Munsterberg I owe the strong convictions in the future of applied psychology which automatically ignited later in the propitious Minnesota environment. Although "theory" was and is central in my interests, it was Munsterberg's influence which "set" me for enthusiastic participation in the work of the Army's psychologists in World War I and later led me at Minnesota to encourage both pure and applied psychology. It is amusing now to recall how statistically naive those forgotten early Munsterberg methods could be. To cite two examples: I was a member of his seminar where student-subjects were asked to estimate in writing the relative number of dots which occupied the four quadrants into which a large piece of cardboard was divided by black lines, the whole card briefly exposed to observation. A week later the experiment was repeated with a longer period of observation, and the subjects were given an opportunity to influence one another's judgment in discussion. We individually changed our minds and improved our judgments over the earlier ones so much more flexibly than did the students of his Radcliffe seminar under identical conditions that Münsterberg announced himself opposed to the service of women on juries! Again I recall the occasion when, lunching in Berlin, I found on the front page of the Berliner *Zeitung am Mittag* the scores that Henry T. Moore and I had made on a ten-minute card-sorting test which convinced Munsterberg that we would be the two best qualified of his subjects by virtue of quickness and accuracy of perception to be a ship's captain. Such methodological gropings notwithstanding, no one would deny that Münsterberg was a supremely ingenious pioneer and the only one at that time whose prognostication matched up to the accomplishments of applied psychology in the quarter century following his death. What he fortunately was spared knowing was that the first wholesale use of psychological tests took place in the

United States Army fighting against the Fatherland of which he always remained a subject.

My Ph.D. thesis, on the psychophysics of handwriting — which Munsterberg left me alone to work out after suggesting the use of carbon paper to measure writing pressure — was a fumbling attempt to use early correlational methods in tying differences in personality to characteristics of handwriting. It was not published for it did not deserve it, and it tells something of my limitations that I did not follow it up with any later experiments though I became convinced that graphology as a sub-area of gestural analysis, somewhat along the lines which Allport and Vernon have since explored, will eventually find a place in psycho-diagnostics.

To Munsterberg and all the members of his family I shall always be grateful for warm human kindness and for the hospitality of a home in which I had my first glimpse of cosmopolitan culture.

Great as Munsterberg's influence on me was, it was probably no more than that of two other psychologists then in the Harvard department, Holt and Yerkes. Holt I came in contact with at the time when he planned to rewrite James' briefer text to make it more suitable for contemporary class use. It is greatly to be regretted that he did not complete the project. We would then have had both the masterpiece and the revision, and however daring the idea may seem, in Holt's hands the latter would have triumphed over any possible charge of sacrilege. What Holt had been doing was to pick up the radical vein in the thought of William James which led James to conceive of consciousness as relation in "Does consciousness exist?" and develop from it the concepts of the behavioristic cross-section and the course of action which is a function of objects external to the responding organism. I remember one discussion in 1914 at Holt's house when he was reading the manuscript of *The Freudian Wish* to a few of his students. It lasted without bibulous support until sunrise. At that time I was already a convert to a strictly objectivist psychology. Holt had clinched the argument so far as I was concerned by expounding a broader and more sophisticated concept of response than Watson had in his early papers. Only Holt's students and a few of his colleagues knew the full sweep of his originality and his scholarly stature in wide areas of the history of psychology. He would come to seminars with a stack of musty classics in psychology and philosophy whose pages were interspersed with little slips of paper marking obscure quotations, which in his handling grew to something big and exciting. We delighted in the brilliance of his tongue and the bite of his wit.

At the same time Yerkes was impressing me greatly with the importance of the comparative method. From his achievements as an indefatigable researcher with animals he was then spreading over into the field of human differences (development of the Point Scale) and psychopathology. Through him I got a chance to work a little in the Boston Psychopathic Hospital and to know a great psychiatrist, Dr. E. E. Southard. I came most under Yerkes' influence when I was his assistant in the fall of 1914, and to *my* great benefit he entrusted his graduate students to my care when he went off to Santa Barbara in 1915 to do his first experimenting with apes.

Langfeld in general and experimental psychology and aesthetics, F. L. Wells in psychopathology, and G. H. Parker in comparative sensory physiology and neurology rounded out my psychological program. It was all intensely interesting, but evidently I did not have what it takes in motivation or in systematic inquisitiveness to make a research scientist. The same may be said of my opportunity during the year 1913–14, when after taking my Ph.D., I held a fellowship "for study and travel" in Europe. The terms of the fellowship required simply that I write a letter twice during the year to the Harvard dean telling him what I was doing. Though my wanderings took me from Edinburgh to Athens, I saved nine months of the year for psychology in Germany. At the University of Berlin during the fall and winter semesters I improved my German, attended lectures by men with great reputations, and got most out of Stumpf's colloquium and Bonhoeffer's psychiatric clinic.

In the spring semester I had a lark of a time, divided up between Gottingen where I attended the 6th Congress of the Society for Experimental Psychology (36 papers were presented, in good part by younger men who were already well-known), Giessen, where Koffka was working with fevered enthusiasm in the newborn field of Gestalt; Marburg, where I was invited to watch *Mensur* duelling between Junkerish students and was told by them that war with England was inevitable within two years, Frankfort, where I saw Schumann's bicycle wheel with which the Phi phenomenon was first demonstrated; Wurzburg, with Marbe, Peters and von Frey; and finally Munich, where Kulpe was head and where I could not force myself to help out Lillien J. Martin by serving as a subject daily and dully before a memory drum, when outside in the town during the rarest of Junes life was so wonderful.

Then one night the expression of people's faces suddenly changed. The Austrian archduke had been shot. A few weeks later in a remote Swiss valley in a railway carriage I learned from agitated German tourists that war had come. Soon at a railway junction they bundled out and I was alone in a compartment lit only by twilight. Then and there I prophesied. What has now happened, I predicted, will in all its consequences make my life one-third less worth living than it might have been in a world at peace. Except that I now know the quality of one's life is determined more from within than I then realized, I call the original estimate a good shot.

In September 1914 I was back at Harvard as instructor assisting Yerkes, Langfeld, and Münsterberg, the last in his big and popular introductory course. "Jshentlemen, yesterday I made a liddle ex-perrr-i-ment wiz a laydee." Response: Loud shuffling with the feet, which is the Harvard students' reaction to the unusual. Münsterberg's hand up in feigned protest: "But Jshentlemen, Jshentlemen, I said 'wiz a LAY-DEE.'" That *was* applied psychology!

From September 1915 until February 1918 I was instructor in general, experimental, and genetic psychology at Yale. There I worked fitfully on an experiment which might have anticipated Boring's work on the horizontal-vertical moon illusion. Having noticed how much greater the distance appears to be between two stars near the horizon and the same two stars at or near the zenith, I set up apparatus by which subjects in an adjustable reclining chair in a darkroom judged the distance between two movable pin points of light at different angles of elevation in comparison with a pair of pin points at the horizontal, or at some other angle. A great many data were collected, including some from the unmanipulatable and less quantifiable situation using the actual stars at night, but I simply did not have the experimental knack, or the drive, to work up a paper and to publish. One day a colleague, echoing President Wilson, stung me to attention with the uncomplimentary epithet "Too proud to write." Didn't he probably hit the truth? To the too exclusively theoretically oriented person the most simple little experiment may seem too trivial and a crucial worthwhile experiment seem, or be, beyond his powers. Hence the search for an *Umweg*. And the war helped me find mine.

In February 1918 I was commissioned First Lieutenant in the Sanitary Corps of the Army and ordered to the Medical officers training camp at Camp Greenleaf, Georgia, where a group of psychologists were to be trained as psychological examiners. What was accomplished at Camp Greenleaf has been officially described in the Memoirs of the National Academy of Science. Surely it was of far-reaching importance in the over-all training of our generation of American psychologists. The unofficial story of the psychologists' life and doings at Camp Greenleaf has never been told. To do it justice would have required the pens of a staff reporter and an artist from the *New Yorker*. Imagine a group of psychologists, many on a horse for the first time in their lives, careering and careening on retired old cavalry nags over Chickamauga battlefield. Picture a crestfallen company of zealous psychologists deprived of first honors at battalion inspection because the inspecting general, with an eye keener than our own major's, ordered an unmilitary psychologist to step one pace forward and pointed to his left leather puttee on his right leg and his right puttee on his left.

After Camp Greenleaf I was assigned for a month's duty under D. G. Paterson at Camp Wadsworth and then made chief psychological examiner at Camp Sevier in South Carolina. At first it was a time of effort without much to show for it. Then fortune favored the psychologists at Camp Sevier. A commanding officer who was not at all convinced that intelligence testing could be of service to him found himself the victim of the Army's theory that a well-trained division can without detriment absorb a small number of relatively raw men. In this instance the commanding general of a division just about to go overseas had been sent nearly 500 raw recruits whom he was supposed to take along, and they proved to be men who simply could not learn to drill. Hearing of the C.O.'s state of mind I proposed to him that we give those men intelligence tests. Sure enough, it was plain as day that somebody in another camp had been "dumping," perhaps using Army Alpha as a screening device! The facts and figures were wired to Washington, an order came back disposing of the incompetents mostly to labor battalions, and a new batch of trainable men was sent to take their places. "Psychology" thenceforth had a recognized role in Camp Sevier. (Was Captain R. M. Elliott also unwittingly getting a string on a ticket to Minneapolis?)

The armistice came. A fortnight later I received split orders. Three days a week I was to report to Major Yerkes in Washington, on the alternate days at the Rehabilitation Division in Walter Reed Hospital. Yerkes put me to work assembling materials for the report on what had been done by the Division of Psychology in the Surgeon General's office, and also for the report on the activities and history of the Psychology Committee of the National Research Council.[2] Within three months the episode already mentioned had occurred during which Yerkes recommended my appointment to Dean Johnston of the University of Minnesota. Later he recommended two others, William S. Foster (a stoutly Titchenerian psychologist from Cornell who taught experimental psychology and the history of psychology at Minnesota from 1919 till his untimely death in 1925), and Mabel R. Fernald (who represented the psychology of individual differences at Minnesota, 1919–1921).

It will be clear, then, since choice of personnel is the factor of prime importance, that the essential characteristics of the department had already been determined when, in early June, 1919, now a civilian again, I went to Minneapolis to make plans for the new academic year. On the morning of my arrival I answered an inquiry by Dean Johnston who asked which division of the Arts College I thought the new department of psy-

[2] R. M. Yerkes, Report of the Psychology Committee of the National Research Council, *Psychol Rev.*, 1919, 26, 83–149.

chology should belong to, now that it was no longer to be affiliated with philosophy, by replying that our status would be enhanced if we could join the division of natural science and we would try to prove our right to be there.   Lashley, representing animal and physiological psychology, had been appointed on Yerkes' recommendation in 1917 and he would find this appropriate; Woodrow, representing experimental psychology and testing, who had been at Minnesota since 1909, would not object; and I was speaking for the newcomers.   The Dean accepted the proposal and the faculty, meeting that night, voted approval.

My chief concerns on that initial visit to Minneapolis were to meet as many members of the faculty as possible, to plan alterations in the building vacated by the Department of Pathology which was destined to be our departmental home to this day, and to set in motion, with adaptations to the ideas of Lashley and Woodrow, whom I was meeting for the first time, the curriculum which Yerkes, Foster, Fernald and I had been blocking out during the spring in Washington.

I was eager to have the new department recognize at the outset the importance and strategic position of the introductory course.   I believed that if properly constructed and participated in by every member of the staff, at least while we were getting acquainted, it might be made a strong foundation for all the advanced work we planned to offer.   And one measure of our success would be the number and quality of the students who wanted more psychology.   I saw that until we were better known Minnesota would have to recruit most of its graduate students right at home.   Foster stood with me in these convictions, and through our combined urgings we raised the morale of the senior staff to a level where brave decisions could be made.

We set the length of the course at a full year and required that the students have at least sophomore standing.   In each week there was to be one lecture, one recitation period and two hours of laboratory work. Each senior staff member was to give a block of lectures, everybody would conduct recitation sections, and the over-all charge of the laboratory work was to go to Foster, an ardent dynamo of energy.

Practical reality immediately caught up with us in the shape of 669 students who enrolled the first year, but we stuck it out and laid a foundation which has in part endured.   Even now our policies continue in some measure to reflect our agreement with Seashore when he wrote: "Psychology is perhaps unequalled by other college subjects in its power to influence the life of the student; the introduction to this subject should, therefore, be taught by mature members of the department.   Young instructors can handle advanced work better than elementary."[3]

[3] C. E Seashore, Report of the committee of the American Psychological Association on the teaching of psychology, *Psychol Monogr*, 1910, 12, 91.

The first change in the general course was to shorten it, though offering the student alternative electives by which he could round out a full year of introductory orientation. The second step, taken because enrolments were overwhelming us, was to remove laboratory work from the first course and create an optional and supplementary elementary laboratory course which several hundred students have elected in every year since. The third step was to excuse some senior staff from the lecturing, as more advanced instruction was required. The fourth change, a Minnesota heresy, is one of several modifications in the content of the first course which I was especially responsible for. Here I felt I had to put my influence against Foster's. (In atonement I introduced him to golf! We remained close friends.) My strong behavioristic leanings made me, among other things, wish to get the topic of sensation, and all of structural psychology, out of the first course in order to make room for what I held to be more important material. Stepwise I succeeded, ineffectually concealing my pressures by sincerely terming sensation "the good that is the enemy of the better." I also used to urge that President Wilkins of Oberlin did not have structural psychology in mind when he called psychology the "key subject of the modern intellectual advance." By 1925 Foster was offering a course in the psychology of sensation as one of the optional supplements for those students who elected it to round out a full year of introductory psychology. There it has stayed, except for a short assignment of "outside" reading in the beginning course. No, I cannot persuade myself that sensation is of first importance when there are so many other topics dealing with the dynamics of behavior which are nearer to the lives of young men and women.

The fifth change came after 1927 and was adopted because the recitation sections had become as numerous as locusts and we had lost faith in their efficacy. A full statement of the case for abolishing them may be found in an article by H. P. Longstaff of our department.[4] Longstaff showed that *if we adopted certain criteria as evidence*, especially objective examinations prepared with great care, and students' ratings of the course, the reputed advantages of the small sections could not be demonstrated. Whatever the real facts may be, we have never been tempted in the slightest degree to reverse ourselves, a step which would either require seeking much new money or diverting support from other undertakings. Incidentally, advanced Minnesota graduate students must get their apprentice teaching in sections of the introductory laboratory course and in the summer in smaller sections of the first course.

I must beg permission to cite evidence that the course in introductory

---

[4] H P. Longstaff, Analysis of some factors conditioning learning in general psychology, *J appl. Psychol* , 1932, 16, 9–48 and 131–166.

psychology at Minnesota has flourished.[5] For years now it has been, by vote of the faculties of the respective professional schools, required of all students at Minnesota taking the pre-professional curricula for Education, Home Economics, Social Work, Nursing, Medicine, Law, for certain curricula in Journalism, and for many specialized curricula in Business Administration. Nearly 300 Engineering students elect it each year from among several "cultural" alternatives. The total registration in this sophomore course in the academic year (*i.e.*, summer school and extension courses not included) of peak registration (1946–47) reached 3,578. In addition there were 1,868 students who took the more elementary introductory psychology course (using Ruch as the text) in the two-year General College, which is a terminal college for most of its students. The grand total for an introductory psychology course, then, was 5,446.[6]

It would not be true to assert that in general the course is original in content.[7] Standard texts have been used, with one possible exception. While at Yale I had noted the students' warm approval of Bernard Hart's little book, unfortunately named *The Psychology of Insanity,* and for 30 years it has constituted the final reading in sophomore introductory psychology. If, speaking as just one of the lecturers, I venture to make one claim — in doing so I am almost crushingly aware of Seashore's hard-hitting admonition to lecturers not to attempt to appraise their own efforts — it would be that my first aim in lectures is to *motivate* the student, always with a forward thrust from the student's present to his possible future attitudes or activities. Conceived in these terms, all education in the broadest sense of the term is helping people first to *want* to know the right things and *then* to know them.

The best introductory text, it seems to me, is written with an eye to *teaching students,* not just to *what psychology is;* or to expand the formula, a text should teach young men and women what is or will be the most meaningful content within the purview of psychology, rather than expound to students what we professionals take our psychology to be.[8] It is the relative emphasis that counts. Clearly no one can deceive himself that a sententious formula like this can settle any issue in detail. Take the case, so much fought over, whether the nervous system should be included. Does it belong in the introductory course? I say it does. The human mind is a product (Lat. *producere:* to cause to appear) of protoplasm. I intro-

---

[5] Ninety-five per cent of the students rated the course above average in quality; 87 per cent as equal or more difficult compared to other college courses (*cf.* Longstaff, *loc cit.,* pp 11–22).

[6] In 1922 psychology's total student registration placed it tenth among Arts College departments; by 1938 it stood second.

[7] For an early statement of the aims of the course as I saw them *cf* Longstaff, *loc cit.,* pp. 5–7.

[8] I emphasized this idea in a seminar on the first course at Columbia in the summers of 1928 and 1929 which Floyd Ruch in the preface to the first edition of *Psychology and Life* credits with starting him on a new approach to the first course.

duce the functions of the nervous system and sweat blood in class trying to make them mean something by putting the nervous system in its place among big embracing ideas, especially its role in integrating the activities of an organism in relation to happenings that are spread out in both space and time. Unless I succeed, at least in part, I can entertain little hope of exorcising the ghostly agents whose wings and whims usurp the position rightly occupied by natural law in the thinking of an educated person groping to understand the sources of behavior.

If the foregoing account of our first course seems drawn out, it is only because my heart has long been very much in it. But I shall at least spare the reader what I think would be more tedious, an account of my multifarious committee and board connections through the years, for with two exceptions these have faded rapidly from memory. One of these exceptions was when I was chairman of the faculty committee to advise the regents of the University on the selection of a new president, and the second, during World War II when the National Research Council's subcommittee (of the Emergency Committee) on Survey and Planning in Psychology with Yerkes as chairman held nine meetings, sometimes for a whole week at Vineland. Our discussions ranged free from mandate over the whole universe of psychology, then in wartime ferment. It was a superlative example of what is called a "nice committee." We had time for banter and relaxation as well as work, and we believed enormously in some of our proposals, especially the plan for re-unification of psychology in a single federalized association which set the ball rolling toward our profession's present form of organization.

But what I have in general sharply preferred to committee work through the years has been the feel of personal administration, one of a small group in close contact with one another. Twice I sidestepped the offer of a deanship, because to my taste deaning would lack the *juice* of a field of learning, and besides I feared it might become a threat to my humanity. It may well be that merely administering a department does this. We have fewer department meetings than we once did, in part perhaps because we are driven at a harder pace.though also, I feel, because an older chairman is likely to be surer of himself and become less careful to see that consent is manufactured by democratic processes before throwing his influence around.

For the first fifteen years, in support of what I saw as the greatest need, I "identified" especially with Paterson in the development of personnel psychology. It won its place. Now at Minnesota as elsewhere what I interpret as the *Zeitgeist* calls for more clinical and social psychology and we are going along with it. In general I have been by turns planner, promoter, organizer, trouble-shooter and encourager. From first to last it has been my special aim to encourage the younger staff member with unusual research ability, not seldom rewarding him with a load of teaching and service lighter than that for some older colleagues. Summing up, I firmly hold that we have been a more than ordinarily cooperative department and without strong cliques for one that is so diverse in function and is blessed with a fair quota of strong personalities (of which the strongest is *not* the chairman; that *would* be bad!).

Turning to a review of Minnesota's chief areas of activity I shall name five, saying a little in detail about three where my role has been easier to identify. The five are: (1) behavioristics, animal and physiological psychology, (2) experimental psychology, (3) differential psychology and its flowering in various fields of applied psychology, (4) clinical psychology, and (5) social psychology, represented by three members of our staff in the interdepartmental Laboratory for Research in Social Relations.

In the behavioristic area we could shine almost at the start. Lashley was on a year's leave when the new staff arrived. He had held the rank of instructor when I first met him in the preceding June, and I insisted that he be promoted to assistant professor at once. After he had been back a year I urged even more violently that he be made associate professor, and two years after that full professor. I ought to say right here that we were blessed from the start in the kind of dean we worked under: John B. Johnston, a distinguished neurologist who in the course of his career as a dean became in good measure an educational psychologist. Deans at Minnesota, be it said, have power in appointments and in many other matters. Lashley's intellectual preeminence and the brilliant reports of study after study of brain function in rats and monkeys presented at our all-department seminar placed him in the prestige spot among us. I constituted myself guardian and protector outside his laboratory door, fending off official expectations of a usual teaching load and other threats to his research productivity, all the while shoving in to him and his students (how the good ones do flock around a good man!) whatever supplies and equipment they needed. We think those six years were the most productive period of Lashley's career.

Now I come back to the ordinary earthy run of things. Because it has been part of Minnesota's behavioristic trend since 1919, I venture to mention here an out-and-out maverick of a course given by myself. Too briefly described to make clear wherein its uniqueness lies, the course aims to synthesize a theoretical discussion of human behavior with a sketch of its genetic background in nature. Its order of topics runs about like this, when stripped of all embroidery and those idiosyncrasies which are just between the instructor and his students: Scientific method and its historical origins. Prediction and control through knowledge of causal dependencies. The hypothetical continuity of living and non-living phenomena. "If this isn't true, something with a *general* resemblance to it probably is" is the repeated refrain as astrophysics, biochemistry, genetics, cytology, morphogenesis and protozoology are drawn upon to bridge the gaps in the ancestry of the living organism. At this presumption I hear a critic snort: "Fools rush in where authorities fear to tread." As a pedagogue I remain unruffled by the taunt. My purpose is to stir the imagination of youth and to provide that kind of meaningfulness which comes from seeing links and discovering contexts, while insisting that often we are only sketching scaffolding, and in its final form no statement about the natural world can be stronger than its support in experiment. However provisional it may turn out to have been, I maintain, the acquiring of a general sense of direction in which empirical investigation will probably follow is an advance over preoccupation with *a priori* and anti-scientific entelechies or the vacuum of complete ignorance.

The course continues with the concept of adjustment as energy interchange between an organism and its environment whereby organic integrity is preserved, environmental insults withstood, and developmental activities promoted. Response, including growth, as activity preceded by stimulation and conduction. Modifiable behavior. Physiology vs. psychology. Purposive behavior a non-mystical complication of learned behavior. Language habits. The fiction of mind-body duality. The achievement of personal adjustment through integration and maturity.

All the references from which the students in this course choose their readings, according to capacity, are original sources: Among many others are books by Northrop, Oparin, Verworn, Sherrington, Loeb, Jennings, Child, Holt, Tolman, and Feigl. There are no textbooks bearing the brand of Moloch, pitched at a level which underestimates the capacity of good students. Wasn't it James who said — I cannot find his words — that the American textbook is a Moloch in whose belly living children are turned to ashes?

The students keep "logbooks" of their reactions and experiences in the course, guided by a full set of instructions and suggestions. Right-hand pages are for abstracting readings as a student wishes; left-hand pages are for recording ideas, queries, difficulties felt, objections, etc. These are read by the instructor or his assistant and returned with comments. The labor of doing this is shortened by code letters, translated for the student on mimeographed sheets, which cover the most frequent sorts of comment. A final summing up of the "log" — the outcome of the voyage, its meaning to the student — is required. The students are for the most part highly motivated by this challenge to do their own thinking. Either the reputation of the course or the events of the first week in class suffice to keep loafers away. Boredom does not seem to trouble the rest.

From 1937 to 1945, while B. F. Skinner was at Minnesota, at my urging a special arrangement was made to insure that superior students might come early under the influence of an especially stimulating and unconventional teacher. Each year I announced in the first lecture of the big introductory course that Skinner would take charge of a small segregated section of students whose previous scholastic standing had been especially high. He personally interviewed those who volunteered, told them how different their assignments would be, and invited the ones who impressed him to join his section, which they were free to do or not to do, as they wished. Partly through this device and in general through the appeal of his originality, Skinner quickly surrounded himself with a highly motivated group of students, many of whom were thus snared for advanced work. Alas, Indiana plucked him away to head psychology there. But an interest in behavior theory, and in experiments designed *ad hoc* to illuminate theoretical issues, still thrives among us, as the work of Meehl, MacCorquodale and Heron has demonstrated. More, and I predict much more, will be heard from them.

There can be no denying that the area from which the ubiquitously used stereotype "Minnesota psychology" has arisen is, to adopt that familiar but ridiculously anachronistic term, applied psychology. It all flowered from the appointment of Donald G. Paterson. I had served as a psychological examiner under "Pat" in the army, had followed in a general way his work in personnel psychology for the Scott Company and, when Dr. Mabel Fernald resigned the position in individual differences in 1921, knew at once whom we wanted if we could get him. We did get him, and he has been at Minnesota ever since, and served as adviser to 44 out of our 103 Ph.D. graduates and 131 of the 216 holders of a Minnesota Master's degree in psychology. Never was there a closer fit between the interests and abilities of a man and a job that was crying to be done. The closest partnership developed between Paterson and me at the department level, and between Paterson and Johnston in the formation of University policies and practices based on a recognition of individual differences among students. Minnesota's pacemaking role in this area is widely recognized.

When in 1924 the Committee on Human Migration of the National Research Council under Dr. Yerkes' chairmanship offered us a sizeable grant of funds with which to embark on a study of mechanical ability, it was chiefly Paterson's interests and energy (I was mostly the administrator again) which enabled us, after the necessary additional research staff was assembled, to push the project through to the completion recorded in *Minnesota Mechanical Ability Tests.*[9]

Paterson has been the chief representative of the department of psychology in two large research undertakings in the area where economics and psychology meet. In 1930, during the depth of the depression, an Employment Stabilization Research Institute was set up with the aid of substantial funds provided by three foundations. The Institute was composed of three projects. Paterson was chairman, and I was Associate Chairman of a committee

[9] D. G. Paterson, R. M. Elliott, L. D. Anderson, H. Toops, E. Heidbreder, 1931.

in charge of work in individual diagnosis and training. Our contribution is summarized in *Men, Women and Jobs,*[10] an informal report of research which did much toward laying down the pattern for the vocational guidance of adults in this country.

During Dean Johnston's long and progressive administration of the Arts College we worked earnestly and eagerly under him and with him. Since he, too, could do so much for us, an all-round symbiotic relationship developed. My personal role, however, was chiefly that of an adviser on whom ideas were tried out both in long personal conferences and in the sessions of the Arts College Advisory Committee. I helped develop the orientation course for freshmen on "Man in Nature and Society," first offered in 1923, and taught in it with enthusiasm. The content of the course and reading assignments ranged from astronomy through the gamut of the natural and social sciences to fine arts and the emerging Great Society. We instructors made it starkly clear to our students that we were neither omniscients nor authorities, but simply lay discussion leaders, presumably educated but out to learn a lot more ourselves. We did learn more, and so did the students, as was neatly demonstrated in Paterson's published appraisal of the course.

One other specialized area of Minnesota's activity which I shall touch upon is clinical psychology. My contribution to it, apart from the minor one of a course in Biographical Psychology, has been to assist in promoting the unusual teamwork between psychology and the Department of Psychiatry in the Medical School, and to serve as administrator of the Veterans' Administration program for training clinical psychologists. Three members of our department hold appointments also (two of them their chief appointments) in the Medical School. These include Professor Starke Hathaway, of "Multiphasic" fame, who has paved the way for the altogether exceptional recognition which our psychiatrists accord clinical psychology.

In 1924 at the invitation of Dana Ferrin of the Century Company (later merged into Appleton-Century-Crofts), who was acting on the recommendation of Boring, rare friend (and phenomenon) to so many psychologists, I undertook the editorship of a new series of texts in psychology to be known as the Century Psychology Series. The amount of space I shall allot it here falls far short of the place it occupied in my professional life. Nothing that I have ever put my hand to has been more satisfying. Boring himself gave the series a mighty initial boost with his *History of Experimental Psychology.* Garrett, Paterson, and Thorndike followed. To date 42 volumes in all have been published. The Series tells its own story, and anyone who knows my interests can surely see them in its composition. I have only to record my thanks to an unfailingly helpful publisher, who in the person of Dana Ferrin has become a prized friend, and to authors who trusted us, gave our suggestions a hearing, and often endured editorial tinkering.

[10] D. G. Paterson, J. G. Darley with the assistance of R. M. Elliott, 1936.

First plans for the Century Psychology Series had hardly been completed when I became eligible for that most delectable concession in academic life, a sabbatical year. I made mine a sheer spree. What more appropriate, I solemnly asked the authorities, than that a teacher in the Orientation course should visit the Orient? "Besides there is lots of 'psychology' there." So off I went to fulfill a long indulged daydream of getting myself in the course of eight months entirely by land from Beirut on the Mediterranean to Saigon on the South China Sea. My route led by automobile over the Syrian desert, Persia and Baluchistan to the western railhead of India. Thence through Kashmir and the northern provinces of India. Eventually out of Assam on foot from Manipur over the mountains to the Yu River in upper Burma. Thousands of G.I.s were later to prove that I did not have the copyright on that route that I then supposed I did. Travel in Burma and later in Siam, also entered by a week's journey on foot, was mostly in small native boats, tying up at night to sleep either on sand flats or in rest-houses. In both countries my lifelong interest in Buddhism was gratified by many illuminating contacts. Then by car from Bangkok to incomparable Angkor and so to the sea again. I was defeated by Chang-tso-lin's revolution in my plans to go up the Yangtze to the gorges, and to visit the tightly locked-up collections in Peking, and since I was rather satiated with travel anyway, I settled in Japan for just a month, and without any premeditation dashed off an amateurish travel book. By a narrow margin I made up my mind to send it to New York instead of leaving it in the wastebasket. Its very amateurishness helped anyway to make it an honest travel book. It also sufficed to tell my friends how a solitary unarmed psychologist meets a tiger in the jungle and how the world looks to him when he is not in his office on the banks of the Mississippi.[11]

Now to drop back to shop. I have saved to the last any reference to the over-all setting of psychology on our campus because I felt that I first had to make clear how the core department developed. The report of the Harvard Commission on "the place of psychology in an ideal university" puts great emphasis on integration, recommending that "the teaching in psychology would be conducted by a single comprehensive department of psychology" whose functions would include pre-professional training courses and training in research for both graduate students and for those who intend to become non-academic practitioners of applied psychology.[12]

We have achieved this integration in great measure, though not in some respects, and these I cannot bring myself to deplore. Once Education ceased to be an Arts College department as it did at Minnesota in 1915, it was inevitable that it should have a considerable number of educational psycholo-

[11] The Sunny Side of Asia, 1928.
[12] The Place of Psychology in an Ideal University   Report of the University Commission to Advise on the Future of Psychology at Harvard, 1947, cf p. 30.

gists on its staff. No one can imagine a college of Education without educational psychology in the role of a key subject, maybe even its heart.

The Institute of Child Welfare, since its founding in 1925 under the able direction of John E. Anderson, whom I first suggested for the position, also has its separate staff of psychologists, in part because it was first set up by an outside Foundation which wished to have it so.

But at the graduate level especially, the courses given by both these groups of psychologists are open to qualified students from other departments, and vice versa. We do not, however, enjoy the arrangement with respect to Education and Child Psychology which is advocated by the Harvard Commission when it recommends that "[all] the psychologists in the professional schools should hold joint appointments in their professional schools and in the department of psychology." I have wondered a good deal how much would be gained if this plan were adopted. That some overlapping in courses could be eliminated and expense saved is certain. On the other hand, I am positive that our psychology would be unwise to surrender its place on the Councils of both the natural and the social sciences in the organization of the Arts faculty and let itself be absorbed wholly into Education.

In other instances we do achieve integration through the use of joint appointments, and they work well. There are seven staff members, all with Ph.D.s in psychology, whose primary affiliation is with professional faculties or with the administrative personnel of the University rather than with Arts, but who are also part-time salaried members of our department. They give instruction in psychology and may direct the work of graduate students.

Reversing the relationship, there are six staff members salaried wholly by our department with part-time affiliations elsewhere in the University. These thirteen men, I think, support our conviction that Minnesota has long since broken what the Harvard report calls "the tradition of separatism and autonomy in the various faculties of a university" and achieved in good measure "interchange, collaboration, and mutual confidence between the faculties." More cooperation of this kind is sure to develop on our campus.

My own preference is for functional integration of psychology through collaboration of this kind — like the planting of shoots which take root wherever there is congenial soil — rather than through moves toward centralized administrative organization which in an extreme development would lead to one compact Institute of Psychology within the university. From that kind of proposal I shrink, as one likely to lead to a state of things in which organization and autonomy might easily be mistaken for ends in themselves, especially if this occurred at the cost of developing functions and services at all the various points where the need for them was first felt.

But in these matters, of course, especially in a vast country with many successful types of educational institutions, there is room for experimentation and variety. What will count most is that psychology is everywhere on the march.

⁰ ⁰ ⁰ ⁰ ⁰ ⁰

Looking back at what I have written I see little, and the reader will see less, of the inner dynamics, the personal give and take, of our Minnesota story. I plead but two among several reasons for my failure to add the coloring to this record. First, enmeshed as we were in the flux of a very large, lively, and self-conscious college within the university, much has been decided for us. Problems and pressures have arisen peremptorily and we have done what we could to meet them without even attempting to express our own preferences and personalities in bold original departures, or in strivings for over-all coherence and unity.

Second, it seems to me that I have really been little aware of even my own role at the majority of the junctures in our history. And though I would like to pleasure myself here with writing thumb-nail personality sketches of my chief colleagues, I would still be usually at a loss to tie these in significantly with the genetic history of the department. It must be that at least as an administrator I am much more the extravert than I once supposed, though I hope I have remained capable of empathy toward my associates. Or I may even be a living exemplar of dear (and peppery) old Holt's theory of the conscious cross-section. "The stream of consciousness," he wrote in neo-realistic vein, "is nothing but this selected procession of environmental aspects to which the body's ever-varying motor adjustments are directed."[13] So I seem to myself to have moved these thirty-two Minnesota years among the situations picked out by my "searchlight," just busy getting on with things, and finding a way around, adjusting to, or subduing the "procession" of difficulties.

Turning to the intraceptive vein, I am aware that in an autobiographical essay of this sort I have no mandate to write about much that is meaningful and precious to me: about friends, about music, art, science in general, astronomy and ornithology, about an appetite for reading which would be positively omnivorous had not almost all novels lost power to charm me. All these so delightful interests have brought joy to my leisure, while during many working hours, I never forget, it has been my privilege to be *paid* to examine the universe.

Then, apart and above, I come to my adored and, for me, matchless wife who by her laughter, her intelligence, her comradeship and her love, has utterly transformed my life. Not even this greatest of my blessings can find more than mention here.

Instead, in briefest epilogue, I wish to say that I am aware of a profound difference in a life viewed prospectively, as one peers ahead through unlifted

[13] From "Response and cognition" reprinted in *The Freudian Wish*, 1915, p. 189.

mists toward what may lie ahead, and that same life viewed retrospectively, once the so brief present has become the destined past, as, looking backward, I now feel it to be. In the obsessive feeling that it was destiny after all, lies the paradox. For in truth I stand with those who believe that some men — and I include myself — at some times and places, achieve freedom in the full and valid meaning of that splendid word.

Yet now I look upon my past as though it all had to be, granted my origins, my makeup and the forks in the road along which I have come. Despite the risks I run of suppression, distortion, and reconstruction in recall, it seems to me now that once I came under the influences I did at Dartmouth, Harvard psychology was thereafter the only possible next step. Surely, I now feel, I could not, being myself, remain at Yale even with a double promotion, once the Army had showed me something of a larger and to me more challenging America. Surely when I reached Minnesota through the always beneficent hand of Robert Yerkes, so much in evidence in this story, I with my assets and limitations was already cast in the role of administrative chairman of a good department of psychology in a propitious environment which expected some ground-breaking developments from us rather than a staid conservative psychology. Surely I had to love teaching, with my background, and especially to love teaching psychology, coming from an enlightened home, with my educational influences and debarred, as I felt I was, from a career in one of the more rigorous sciences.

Surely it is clear that I have been fortunate and that mine has been a good life to live.

AGOSTINO GEMELLI

THIS autobiography will tell only of my career as a psychologist, and, since that career began comparatively late, I shall omit mention of the years between my birth in Milan on January 18, 1878, and my last years as a university student.[1]

During those last years at the University of Pavia I devoted myself to histological research on the central and peripheral nervous systems, and, after earning a medical degree in 1902, I continued this work under the tutelage of Professor Camillo Golgi, who later received the Nobel Prize for his discoveries in the microstructure of the nervous system. I carried on research in this field until 1913, publishing my results in a number of papers.

I was eager, however, to come to grips with more general problems, for histological research did not satisfy my thirst for wider knowledge. This desire led me to inquire into the difficult problem of the relationship between reason and faith, and as a result I was converted from militant Socialism and positivistic materialism to Roman Catholicism and Scholastic thought. After I had completed the prescribed philosophical and theological courses, I became a Franciscan monk and a priest.

Later I received honorary degrees in Philosophy (Sacra Congregazione delle Università degli Studi), in Sacred Theology (University of Siena), in Law (Catholic University, Washington, D. C.), and in Science (Universities of Freiburg, Sofia, Coimbra, Budapest and Athens).

In 1909, following my conversion, I founded the *Rivista di filosofia neoscolastica,* and thus introduced in Italy a philosophic movement which, at first, paralleled Cardinal Mercier's school at Louvain. As time went on, however, our movement assumed a more distinctive character, becoming, thanks to a large number of collaborators and students, one of the most important schools of philosophy in Italy. Its line of thought, following the fundamental thesis of Scholasticism, emphasized the evaluation of scientific discoveries, and I undertook to exhibit the basic facts, particularly those

---

[1] This autobiography was submitted in English.

achieved by the biological sciences. Perhaps it was this work which led me
to take a special interest in the progress of experimental psychology, so that
from the first I urged my philosophical collaborators on the *Rivista* to attempt
to evaluate the results of experimental research in the field of psychology,
and to reconsider and assess such results from the point of view of philosophy
and in philosophical terms. At that time all I knew of experimental psychology was the teaching of Wilhelm Wundt, and I had been impressed by his
statement: "There is no psychic fact without a corresponding organic fact."
I had, however, no real training in the field, and I could not, therefore, form
a critical estimate of the discoveries, with which I was familiar only through
the descriptions in the famous German journals of the time.

In 1934, twenty-five years after the founding of the *Rivista di filosofia
neoscolastica,* I published a special issue in which I reviewed our contribution to the development of Neoscholastic thought. In that issue I wrote an
article[2] in which I defined my position as a philosopher in relation to experimental psychology. This position I shall illustrate later.

THE FORMATIVE PERIOD

The preceding paragraphs are prefatory to a description of my later development. Now I should like to show how, while inquiring into philosophical
problems and without neglecting my histological research, I became interested in psychology and came finally to live it and to devote to it all my
scientific effort. In those years, still spurred on by the desire to master general problems, I studied the most fundamental aspects of biology, and in
my book, *L'enigma della vita* (1910), which was translated and reprinted
several times, I reviewed the problems then under discussion by biologists
in an effort to reach an evolutional and at the same time finalistic theory of
the development of living beings and of their adaptation to their environment.

At Bonn I worked under Verworn in the physiological laboratory, and
under Nussbaum in the laboratory of general biology; I followed Edinger to
Frankfurt-am-Main in order to further my research on the nervous system;
from Hertwig I learned of the new discoveries in the mechanics of development. More important, I learned from Hans Driesch the means of interpreting vital processes. As an histologist I used the discoveries of all these
schools in order to perfect my work on the nervous system, but I had long
since understood that I must not confine myself to the study of the morphological side of the structures revealed to me through my histological
technique; rather I must widen my outlook and consider the general laws of

    [2] Il punto di vista della neoscolastica alla moderna psicologia ("The point of view of Neo-
scholasticism with reference to modern psychology"), *Riv. Fil. neo-scolast,* 1934, 26 (Suppl),
1–25.

life. This conclusion was a vitally important one for me as it effected my entrance into a new field of study and caused me to examine the living organism not only in order to understand its morphology, but also with a view to modifying experimentally its reactions and behavior — at least in the case of animals.

Thus I came to examine the role of the organism in the genesis of emotion. It was the day of the James-Lange peripheral theory and of Revault d'Allonnes' research. The James-Lange theory, as we know, caused a reaction in the opposite direction, it caused its opponents to look for the seat of the emotions in the central nervous system. All sectors of the nervous system were tested out, and, by successive elimination, the conclusion was finally reached that the centers of emotion were to be found in the thalamic nuclei.

My own work covered the studies of Sherrington, Pagano and others, with a view to testing their theories. It has been recently superseded by the discoveries of Hess and his followers, who have gone further in localizing these centers. We now know that the emotional reaction of the cat, that was injected with adrenalin by Cannon, is not the same as the animal's reaction to an adequate stimulus. The same can be said of the cat whose caudate nucleus is stimulated by my methods and the methods of Pagano and Hess. We now know that our research went for nothing, for autonomic diencephalic centers are closely connected with the subcortical centers which come into play in emotional reactions. Since there are anatomical and funtional relationships (some proved and others presumed to exist) between the autonomic and subcortical centers, we can say that the emotional response involves the cerebral cortex, the subcortical centers, and the autonomic centers — in a word, the whole central nervous system. The relation of emotion to the endocrine system, and the relation (admitted by Hess) between adaptive behavior and the autonomic system, lead us further to believe that the whole organism has a share in emotional life. Therefore, when we seek to localize a center of emotional life, we are misunderstanding the very nature of emotion, for the emotions involve the whole of personality in both its biological and psychological aspects. We must remember that the research on localization was all conducted on animals and aimed at causing an emotion, i.e., at causing a psychic event that, as we shall see, violently affects the whole organism.

At this stage of my work, however, I had no experience in psychological methodology, and this particular problem seemed to me not only obscure but, in fact, insoluble. At any rate, I repeat, I began my research with Sherrington's results, which I believed contradicted the James-Lange theory. In Sherrington's cases the emotions were aroused even without the connections between the central and peripheral nervous systems. I thought that the great English physiologist's experiments did not confirm the theory that the cardio-vascular changes serve to heighten and color the emotional reaction; certainly in the cases mentioned above nothing of the kind had been noticed.

Revault d'Allonnes had, however, his own explanation of Sherrington's experiments — he stated that, in apathetic dogs (dogs whose brains were intact but in whom the nervous links had been cut) there was a real lack of emotional response and that such seemingly emotional reactions were in fact simply automatic mimetic reactions, due to the fact that the mimetic centers were still intact. Now, were such an explanation true, we should have to conclude that Sherrington's experiments, instead of disproving the hypothesis of emotion's peripheral nature, do in fact prove its truth. Otherwise the animals would have been rendered unemotional by the inability of the peripheral stimulation to reach the centers.

In an effort to solve this problem I used dogs and cats, whose spinal cords I had cut between the sixth and seventh vertebrae. After the animals regained their reflex activity, although apathetic, they still experienced anger as intensely as before the operation and expressed it in the same way.

After keeping these animals under observation for some time, I again operated, removing the cerebral cortex according to Bechterev's technique. Following the operation the animals showed serious changes, and, by the time these changes had disappeared, the whole pyramidal tract, connecting the cerebral cortex to the medulla oblongata and transmitting impulses to the motor nerves, had become atrophied. I definitely confirmed this state of atrophy when, after the animal's death, I performed an autopsy and made an histological examination.

I found a most interesting condition in these animals whose receptive centers for peripheral sensations were removed while the mimetic centers were left intact. Mimicry was thus preserved but emotional experience was completely lost even while the animals responded to external stimuli in the usual way. Rough treatment caused them to gnash their teeth, bristle, etc.; they automatically showed anger and sorrow, but did not experience either. By fondling them I could produce signs of joy like purring or tail-waving, yet the animals remained absolutely unemotional. I therefore concluded that even if the thalamus is necessary for emotional reaction, it is not the center of emotion.

Was I justified, however, in accepting this conclusion? In order to be doubly sure I took these same animals which had already been decorticated and had their spinal cords cut, and by means of injections I stimulated the caudate nucleus in an effort to find out whether I could produce some characteristic emotion. After this treatment, my animals did indeed show a typical psychic excitement. When they heard a noise, they showed unmistakable fear and walked about with hanging heads, cringing bodies and drooping tails; they trembled and barked piteously. Or again, a dog would clearly show anger by snarling furiously and jumping at a stick which I shook at it. These experiments prove that in an animal whose brain has been cut off from its internal organs, an emotion can still be produced by stimulating the caudate nucleus. In other words, the sensations initiated by the internal organs are not necessary to the production of emotion, and the nerves linking these organs with the brain do not belong to the nervous circuit which is the physical substratum of emotions.

As I said before, the experiments I carried out in 1910 have lost much of their value since Hess' work, for it is understood today that the problem of the nature of emotional processes cannot be solved by looking for the hypothetical centers of emotional life. In my work, however, I reached a conclusion (in which I was perhaps influenced by the point of view of Scholastic philosophy) which in my opinion still preserves its value.

In emotional life, I concluded, there are two aspects: the psychic and the organic. Their union and integration gives to emotional reactions their typical characteristics. The physical reactions accompanying the various emotional conditions are not, however, typical of any specific emotion, being but two-dimensional, whereas the emotional conditions are multi-dimensional. Emotional conditions can be antagonistic; yet no antagonism can occur in their psychological counterparts. The same emotional condition, moreover, can produce different organic reactions in different subjects. For all these reasons and several others we must realize that it is useless to look for the explanation of the heterogeneity of emotional conditions in the heterogeneity of organic response. The somatic factor is not the differentiating factor of emotional conditions. Hence we must follow a different line. We must examine facts and processes of emotion as kinds of behavior and express them in terms of action without postulating any doctrinal principle. This concept led me to make other studies which I shall mention later.

This research on the emotions had an enormous influence on my life as a scientist since it brought me in contact with F. Kiesow, the professor of psychology at Turin University. He had brought to Italy the tradition of his own teacher, Wilhelm Wundt. For many years Kiesow strenuously defended the autonomy of psychology in a spiritually hostile world. On the one hand, physiologists claimed the right to absorb psychology into their own science; on the other hand, idealistic philosophers like Croce and Gentile maintained that experimental psychology is but a vestige of positivism, a theory they believed to have been exploded. Kiesow, almost alone — for Sergi was dead, and De Sanctis and Colucci were not yet in a position to make themselves heard — fought for experimental psychology, and it is owing to him that psychological research is active in Italy today. Had he done nothing else for his science (and indeed he did much), Kiesow would deserve our gratitude.

Kiesow came to see me and urged me to devote myself, with his help, to psychology, and I agreed with great enthusiasm. I still honor the man who opened my eyes to a new horizon in my scientific life. Later I went to Bonn to study with Kulpe, whom I followed to Munich. Thus I became a psychologist.

These pages I write to show how difficult were the beginnings of our science in Italy, where the new psychology developed through the indirect influence of Wilhelm Wundt.

LATER PROFESSIONAL LIFE

From 1911 to 1914, when I became a professor, I was deeply absorbed in the study of psychology, but from 1914 to 1921, owing to World War I, I had to abandon my work. In 1915, however, I undertook to test the flying aptitude of pilot candidates — the first time that such tests had been made in Italy. As a medical officer attached to Italian Supreme Headquarters, I tried to apply psychological methods to various military situations. Thus, for instance, I studied cases of amentia due to shell shock, and I stated before the Allied Commission that the theory that shell shock is attributable to injury of the nervous system is wrong, and that such patients were in fact neurotic subjects whose neuroses were revealed by the psychic traumata.

I also applied aptitude tests in various military situations. Psychology as applied to soldiers absorbed me to such an extent that I wrote a book, *L'anima del nostro soldato* (1917), which was translated into several languages. In a number of publications I pointed out the necessity for aptitude tests for all military personnel in order to obtain specialists for the many operations that modern war requires.

In 1920 Kiesow and I founded the *Archivio di psicologia, neurologia e psichiatria,* a journal which publishes the writings of the chief Italian psychologists and psychiatrists.

In 1921 I founded the Università del Sacro Cuore at Milan, which was soon officially recognized by the Government as a "free university," that is to say, it had the same rights and obligations as the State universities. In fact its degrees are conferred as by the authority of the State.

Along with the founding of the University I took upon myself the task of establishing a psychological laboratory, which was quickly completed and furnished with apparatus and books. In 1943 it was practically destroyed by bombs (two-thirds of the University buildings were destroyed), but we rebuilt it, and in 1946 it was as efficient as ever.

Because of the fine equipment many post-graduate students came to our laboratory to gain further knowledge; they came first from Italy, and later, among other places, from Bulgaria, Rumania, Jugoslavia, China, Japan,

Switzerland, Ireland, the United States and Sweden. The publications of our students were collected in the *Archivio di psicologia, neurologia e psichiatria* (eleven volumes to date), and in the *Contributi del Laboratorio di psicologia* (fourteen volumes to date, and the fifteenth in preparation). My activities and those of my students have been described by one of the latter, Professor A. Manoil, who now teaches psychology in Missouri. In 1938 he published *La psychologie expérimentale en Italie: l'école de Milan,* in which he comments on my work and the direction of my study.[3]

The Psychology of Comparison

Now I wish to describe some of my contributions to psychology. First of all I shall mention my study of the method of equivalents, which I investigated along the lines suggested by O. Kulpe at the beginning of my scientific activity in this field. My experiments were not aimed so much at establishing the equivalence of variously perceived distances as at exploring the process of comparison, a process which played an important role in Külpe's theory of the formation of thought. Its study consists in ascertaining the relations between different contents of consciousness.

In the course of my research I established two facts: (1) the variability of the observed equivalences is smallest for middle values and largest for the extreme values of the stimuli; (2) it increases with the relative difficulty of comparison, and so decreases with the ease of the comparison. I also worked with pressure and weight stimuli to ascertain the various factors involved in these comparisons. To me the most interesting fact is this: In the process of comparison of distances, weights, pressures, etc., the subject relegates to the periphery of attention the intensity, length, magnitude and other sensory characteristics of the stimulus, and exercises a kind of selective action which is fundamentally a process of elementary abstraction leading to the formulation of a judgment. That is to say, his comparison becomes an absolute judgment by means of a latent, potential knowledge (trace) regarding the standard stimulus which remains constant even when the stimulus ceases to be objectively present. The subject's judgment is not quantitative, as it might seem at first, but qualitative — at least the qualitative element is always present.

In the process of comparison, therefore, we have a unique activity. In the case of tactile distances, weights and pressures, the subject formulates a judgment based on the perception of a relation between the two stimuli. In

[3] A. Manoil also published a *Bibliografia riguardante la "Scuola di psicologia"* della Università Cattolica di Milano (2nd ed.), 1948. The reader who desires to learn more concerning my own conceptual position in psychology is referred to the following: *Introduzione alla psicologia* (2nd ed.), 1949; *La personalità del delinquente nei suoi fondamenti psicologici e biologici* (2nd ed.), 1949; *L'età evolutiva* (2nd ed.), 1949; *La psicologia del pilota da velivolo* (1948); *L'operaio nell' industria moderna* (2nd ed.), 1948, (with F. Bottazzi) *Il fattore umano del lavoro,* 1942.

the case of the comparison of two distances according to the method of equivalents, we have a series of comparisons arranged so as to arouse by means of a gradual variation of stimuli (distances between two points) various states of consciousness that represent the whole range of differences between the two distances compared, from the greatest difference on down to the judgment of subjective equality. Thus it is possible for us to analyze the constituent elements of the various states of consciousness corresponding to the various physical stimuli, and to observe the gradual development of the factors underlying the judgments of difference and of equality.

This process of comparison has various stages, in which the factors in question vary according to the difference in the magnitude of the distances compared. The stages in every process of comparison for every series leading to a judgment of equality are: (a) preparation of the subject, (b) apprehension of the standard stimulus, (c) pause, (d) apprehension of the comparison or variable stimulus, (e) formation of the judgment, and (f) verbalization of the judgment.

The apprehension of the standard stimulus consists in representing it with special regard to the process of comparison, so that the subject considers the one character to which the *Aufgabe* has called his attention, *viz.*, the comparison between two distances, or two weights, etc. That is to say, the differences are apprehended only with regard to the fact that they are to be compared later with other distances.

Two phenomena are due to the influence of the *Aufgabe:* (a) in apprehending the comparison stimulus, the subject possesses a *latent knowledge* of the standard stimulus, now absent; and (b) the subject apprehends the comparison stimulus in respect of its relation with the standard stimulus.

The experiences of "greater" and "shorter" distances, of "heavier" and "lighter" weights, etc., have a qualitative content. The increase or decrease of a weight or distance is a qualitative variation, and at the same time it is possible to place such variations in serial order.

I should like to emphasize the fact that the apprehension of this relationship is due to a different activity than is the apprehension of the content of two sensations. The process of comparison issues from a special psychic activity of comparing. With these results we come to the threshold of the formation of thought, which is by its very nature relational. Thus my research on the method of equivalents parallels the research by Külpe and his students on the thought processes.

The Psychology of Perception

I also devoted myself with special interest to the study of perception, to which the Gestalt school had brought some new and attractive ideas.

Unfortunately space does not permit me to review the results which were attained in this area, under my guidance, by my students Gatti, Galli, Cossetti, Zama and Fabro. Many of their findings are mentioned in recent general books on psychology. I shall speak only of my research on the origin of perception, as I believe this is an aspect of my work which is little known outside Europe.

As we know, the Gestalt school tried with great insistence to prove that, when one has, let us say, the perception of a geometrical design, prior experience is not sufficient to explain its origin. Certain followers of this school admit the influence of experience, but they claim that experience plays a role only after the original sensory organization has been formed, and that then all secondary sensory organizations are merged in the original organization by means of learning and the influence of intelligence.

My research and that of my collaborators was directed toward exploring this important point, and we noted that the Gestalt school denied the influence of experience. They mistakenly believed that perception consists only of this sensory organization or synthesis, whereas the synthesis is merely the primitive nucleus of perception which can be completed only by the inclusion of "meaning" or significance. It is in this way that past experience modifies sensory data. We shall never tire of repeating that the Gestalt school was obviously inspired by sensualism, and therefore opposed the introduction of an element that is not supplied by the senses. The Gestaltists thus had to deny the influence of previous experience and of the significance of the object perceived, else their whole theory of perception as a pure product of the senses would have fallen in ruins.

This line of thought takes us to the study of the genesis of perception. The multiplicity of sensory stimuli experienced at a given moment is paralleled in the psychic world by groupings, by the formation of large or small units that are more or less isolated from one another. Thus we have a formation of sensory organizations or units, which are derived from sensory elements. We recognize these sensory structures in a special way: We do not see, hear, or touch colored surfaces, shapes, rhythms, etc.; instead we deal with objects, *i.e.*, with sensory organizations so permeated with meaning that we can count them, name them and recognize them in the future.

These meaningful sensory units are parts of more complex units. The immediate world around them is also an "object," a "thing" perceived, recognized among other objects whose shapes, measurements and similarities we know. This "meaning" of the "thing" perceived is not something which is added at a later time; it is an essential constituent. In perception, for instance, we have the inclusion of an intellectual element, like numbers and measurements, which are ideas in themselves. It is what Michotte correctly called the *"prise de signification."* The existence of this intellectual element gives a precise character to intuitive organization, such that only by analysis can the object be separated from its meaning.

Perception does not always reach this complex and complete level. In psychic life we find perceptual units of various magnitude and comprehensiveness. From these elementary perceptions, in which we single out one physical quality from the others, we rise to the complex structure of large perceptions which still possess unity, like the perception of a whole day or of a whole range of activities. Many of our simple perceptions never pass beyond the first state. In everyday life such simple perceptions are frequent — for example, the perception of a color. On the other hand, many perceptions grow progressively richer, in consequence of the addition of new data, both images and intellectual elements. The object then becomes an organized system of sensory data, images and thoughts. At this stage perception reveals a clearer and clearer outline of organization. In its "whole" it integrates and organizes first the varied and manifold sensory data, then presently the images. (For instance, in listening to a piece of music what we hear first is a musical phrase, not the isolated sounds.) By the inclusion of images, which evoke past perceptions, in the texture of actual "data," known objects can be immediately recognized. Finally, we must not forget that intellectual elements also enter into such organizations. For instance, the sight of a watch is accompanied by the knowledge of the meaning of its dial and hands. Along this line of development perception becomes progressively more and more intellectual and at the same time less purely sensorial. Thus the perception of a name, read or heard, becomes at once equivalent to intellectual knowledge. I succeeded in proving experimentally, not only by what complex process perception is reached, but also the phases of this constructive synthesis.

To indicate the relative importance of the constituent elements of perception, let me briefly list these phases:

(1) The subject feels the "presence" of the object.

(2) The subject recognizes the object as a definite shape which he "knows." The transition from the first to the second phase can be effected in various ways. Sometimes it is so rapid that the two phases appear as one.

(3) The subject "understands" the meaning of the object; he understands what it is.

(4) The subject discovers the name of the object.

The last two phases can merge with one another and they in turn with the first two, so that the subject cannot distinguish between them and says he has known and named the object as soon as he has seen it. By various devices, however, we can separate these phases and so analyze the process.

The two main essentials of this process are, then, organization of sensory data and the attribution of significance. In some cases the subject cannot find the significance or meaning, or he reaches it only after a delay. Such a disparity shows that *significance* is something different from the *organization* of sensory data. Significance is not, however, something added from the outside; it is incorporated in the perception, so that the object becomes personal and occupies a definite position in reality. It also completes perception so that we can recognize objects and can know their measurements, number, equalities and differences. Significance is so intimately connected with sensory organization that perception is not complete or even useful without it. It is significance that allows us to name objects, to give them meaning and relationship with the world of other objects.

We must maintain, therefore, that the "organic configuration" or "sensory organization" of the followers of Gestalt psychology is not perception. Thomas Verner Moore took the same stand, even though he accepted the immediacy of a primary sensory synthesis that is independent of past experience. Moore, however, held also that, in order to have perception, a second operation is necessary, one in which the elements of past experiences are merged with the primary sensory organization. According to him this second operation consists of two stages: (1) the placing of the object in its proper perceptual category, and (2) the placing of it in the perceptual category of other objects to which it is related. Here I think Moore is including in perception certain processes which are purely intellectual. I myself think it is more correct to say that the final stage is the attainment of significance by the organized sensory data. At any rate what is important in Moore's thought is the role of previous experience in the development of the perception of an object. Past experience is a formative and directive element of sensory organization, but it comes into being through significance.

The Role of Movement in Space Perception

Because I am a pilot, I have been able to undertake a great deal of research on aviation, both as a doctor and as a physiologist. From such observations I have come to the conclusion that perception prepares and anticipates action. Its biological purpose is to regulate and direct the reactions of animals and men. Perception is not merely a means of knowledge, for it makes possible the adaptation of action to ambient conditions.

The organization of human and animal behavior requires man and animal to know how to behave, each in his world. We must know whether we can move objects, lift them, break them, bend or handle them, lean on them, go around them, throw them around, and so forth. We must, therefore, know whether they are large or small, heavy or light, hard or soft; and we must know how they are related to us — what happens if they fall on us or run against us, as well as how they are related to one another and how they behave in our world. In other words, "things" are related to us and to each other, and our activity must be adjusted to their characteristics, positions and relationships.

Until recently psychologists have not often inquired into these relationships. We have examined and discussed only theoretical problems concerning functional relations, and the most generally accepted opinion is that these relations are the product of a secondary elaboration of the sensory data, one which tends to give these relations a significance that is not inherent in the data. Gestalt psychology, which revolutionized the point of view of the psychologists who study perception, also stressed a new aspect of the problem of functional relations. Even so, this problem has been too much neglected.

In my plane flights I found that orientation in space is directly connected with the pilot's perception of the position of his own body. That is to say, the picture of the shape of his body determines his perceptive construction of the space in which he is flying. In this picture there is always an interesting factor. The plane is identified with the pilot's body; while objectively it is a part of outside space, subjectively it is perceived as belonging to what we call personal space, *i.e.*, the space occupied by the subject's body. It is as though the body were magnified to the length and breadth of wings, tail and cockpit. The pilot automatically uses this subjectively extended construction of the shape of his body in judging and correcting the position of the plane. This is an illustration of the fact that outside space and personal space are interrelated. Similar situations can be observed in ordinary life, as well as under certain experimental conditions.

If a person stumbles while climbing stairs, he immediately tries to snatch at a support. The hand that shoots out toward the railing is perceived as something going out from him, and is detached from his conception of his body. It is something that becomes detached as a "part" from the "background" of the body. It is still "his" hand, but at the same time it becomes something which acts by itself and which possesses a comparative autonomy.

Whether or not the hand reaches the railing, the action has been accomplished as far as the body is concerned. If the railing is not reached, the "part," the hand, re-enters the "background," *i.e.*, the picture of the body. Here we have even more clearly evidenced what we already observed in the case of the pilot: There is an outside phenomenal space, and there is also our own phenomenal space. Chiefly by means of kinesthetic and tactile sensory data do we construct this outside space in relation to our own space, *i.e.*, to the schematic pictures of our own bodies.

In order to explore the meaning of this process, we must begin with the previously explained theory of perception regarded as a construction, a structure erected from the fundamental "data" supplied by the sensations. These data, it will be recalled, are organized into a whole by means of several factors, especially by meaning.

In the aforementioned case the wrong movement, made in climbing the stairs, is followed by the movement of snatching at the railing. The picture of outside space has been corrected by the sensory data successively supplied by the movement towards the railing, and it was because of this movement that the person had the necessary data for measuring the distance between himself and the railing; he was able to effect a corrective movement. In this way kinesthetic and tactile sensations correct and complete perceptive constructions built on visual data.

"Outside space" and "personal space" are not wholly separated realities. They are mutually related, and their interrelation continually changes. The relation is effected by means of our motility, by which we come out of ourselves, so to speak, to enter the outside world, or the outside world "enters" into us. Motility gives us data for the perceptual construction of the outside world.

There is no space *in* or *on* which we *act*, which is different from the space we *perceive* and *picture* to ourselves. The two spaces are not the products each of a different function. Neither do we have a motility that is clearly separated from a "perceptual capacity." Indeed, these two stages and processes are so intimately connected that we have to say that motility is not purely conative but also cognitive.

In conducting a certain experiment one of my collaborators, A. Galli, made the following observation. The subject, shown a picture which he was to reproduce in a drawing, felt the need to trace the same picture in the air. There was no question of his learning a movement. A movement only fixes the perception of the picture in consciousness. I repeated this experiment on a larger scale and found that the experience occurs when the subject sees the picture for a short time only. Perception, it seems, is not complete without correction and supplementation by the motor response. It is apparent from the behavior of some subjects that they are not trying to find a way to reproduce the picture, but seeking only the better to fix the perception of the picture itself.

This phenomenon becomes even more evident in the study of the acquisition of manual skills. In teaching certain manipulations aimed at the achievement of a specific skill, I noticed that the movements are learned through a process of organization or structuration, such that they are better suited to reach their ends quickly and with precision. During this process each movement influences the successive one by acting as a stimulus, *i.e.*, by acquiring a cognitive value or function. Each link has the function of speeding up and improving the operation because of a better knowledge of the controlled by the previous element, and in turn controls the following element.

At this point I came into contact with the well-known work of Buytendijk and Palagyi. As I have explained, I was able to separate the intuitive organization of the sensory data from its meaning and to show that the growth and union of the two are effected in two distinct stages. The study of the manifold factors acting on "intuitive organization" is important, because, by changing the influence exercised by the various factors, it becomes possible to show the multitude of conditions that act on perception, both in the organization of sensory elements and in their connections with the intellectual element. It is also possible to show how the influence of these factors appears for the most part in the variations caused by the reciprocal influences of meaning and intuitive organization. In fact, the study of variations throws light on the mechanism of perception, and we can understand how the organization of sensory elements must appear to us who have opposed Gestalt theory.

I cannot accept the Gestalt theory that fundamental elements (sensory data) play no part between stimulus and inner experience (perception). On the contrary, perception appears to me to consist of the organization and construction of sensory data (intuitive organization) connected with meaning. Palagyi's "virtual movements" are part of the series of factors mentioned above, the factors to which we owe the construction of perception.

When we perceive a picture, we can fuse the various sensory data and build a perceptive whole, mostly because of virtual movements which allow us to connect and combine the sensory data into a configuration. From this point of view the data supplied by touch acquire greater importance and significance than has hitherto been realized. In this connection we might recall Katz's splendid work which showed the importance of the tactile factors in perception. Touch gives us information that we could not otherwise have (whether objects are smooth, hard, elastic, etc.). My collaborators have shown that the tactile factors influence our whole perceptive life. It is, in short, due to tactile data (combined, of course, with visual data) that movement becomes a fundamental factor in organizing perception.

My study of response also led me to investigate the organization of automatic movements, and the results I obtained have thrown new light on the problem of perception itself. I showed that, in order for us to have automatic movements, we require an adequate perception of a particular situation and also the reproduction of a suitable action. These conditions can be obtained only by means of this true configuration or organization of movements, which Palagyi studied theoretically and Buytendijk illustrated in animal activities. The facts become more obvious in the case of such complex automatic movements as we find in the manual skills.

In other studies I have found that manual ability is present only when its constituent movements are assembled in an organized and solidly structured whole. In order to achieve and preserve such structuration, we need "virtual movements," which guide the movement series towards its goal. The function of virtual movements becomes especially clear in those manual skills which approach artistic abilities in complexity.

When the guidance of the virtual movements is missing, the true movements become vague and uncertain, losing their sensory-motor organization. It is by means of these virtual movements that the various movements are organized into wholes, like a gesture or some other complex movement. In order to complete these complex movements without attending to them and controlling them, we must control the virtual movements, which continually inform us that the successive partial movements are all adapted to the final goal. I think I can infer from my study that perception and movement have always been regarded as two quite distinct activities. That is true in the sense that the two are based on two very different psychic processes. It would, nevertheless, be a serious mistake not to realize that they are in fact the expression of two opposite sides of our psychic activity, and it would be an equally serious error to believe that perception consists of a passive attitude toward events or to strip action of all its cognitive elements. In fact, perception must also be regarded as a form of activity, and a dynamic conception of its function becomes increasingly clear as we explore its laws.

In short, we build our world of perception out of the data supplied by the outside world. We build it each in our own way, according to our conscious life, past and present, but also according to the purpose of our action. Therefore we continually correct and adapt it to the new situations in which we find ourselves. All overt actions influence this perceptual construction of the world. It might be said that the stream of our perceptual consciousness is invaded by our motivating activity which thus profoundly modifies our perception of the outside world and our conception of it. In its turn, motor activity is continually guided by perception, which allows us to correct individual, partial movements and to adapt them to our needs.

Feeling, Emotion and Instinct

Now I should like to recall my contribution to the study of feeling. I began this research from a functional point of view and found that the organism never stops trying to reach an inner and outer equilibrium in its life — an equilibrium which must constantly be re-established, for it is destroyed just as soon as it is reached. The variation of external conditions must be accompanied by an inner adaptation, both passive and active. This adjustment the organism accomplishes by using the world for its purpose. In order to preserve life, the living being must at the same time both assimilate the outside world and defend itself from it. It must, in order to preserve its vital equilibrium, keep its organs alive by nutrition and coordinate their functions, *i.e.*, it must fit them for the preservation and the reproduction of life. This process encounters a number of objective necessities, to wit, the needs of the living being. These needs increase as life becomes richer and more complicated. They are subjectively translated in our consciousness where they become inclinations. These inclinations are only the psychological form of a need, and, as needs are objective necessities for the direction of activities along this or that line, we hold that the inclinations themselves can be defined as objective necessities, as natural directions of activity toward definite goals. Inclinations are fundamentally biological, and they are unconscious, as is life itself. They are forces, orientations of energy.

These terms are not facts, but only the principal and invisible causes of facts. Forces are known only through their effects and are thus perceived indirectly. This rule holds true for inclinations, which are not immediate psychological data although they dominate the whole of psychological life. Only conscious states are psychological facts, and inclinations are not conscious states; but certain conscious states do reveal inclinations, and these states are divided into two classes: (1) acts or movements and (2) emotional states or feelings.

In my interpretation of emotional states I have divided them into two classes. The first includes emotional feeling, the elementary feelings like pleasure and pain and the innumerable feelings due to coenaesthesis (hunger, thirst, well-being, discomfort, depression, fatigue, strength, etc.). These feelings cannot be defined analytically, for they are elementary primitive states of consciousness which we recognize directly by intuition. They are named according to the organs in which they are localized, or from the causes producing them, or by the inclinations and instincts that they express.

There is another class of feelings, however, which are preceded by a state of consciousness and which are sometimes called higher feelings. They cannot be defined except from the functional point of view. In introspection subjects describe some of their feelings as *subjective* and some as *objective*. This distinction between the two classes is based on the belief that the difference between the two is such that there can be no shifting from the one to the other; some authors, however, deny this view, and not without reason.

My experiments show that three fundamental elements are necessary for the higher feelings: (a) a cognitive state of consciousness, such that the subject faces a situation involving a stimulus; (b) some organic sensations which the subject notes as inner phenomena; (c) a movement of pleasure or disgust, repulsion or inclination, etc., which quickly follows the organic sensations and accompanies them, without, however, becoming confused with them. Then there is (d) a fourth element, instinct, so far neglected. I believe there is no emotional state where the movement of attraction or repulsion does not correspond to some instinct. Even in everyday life we use the same word for a specific feeling and the corresponding instinct. On the other hand, we have no instinct without a corresponding feeling of repulsion or attraction. In a word, no emotional state acts in us unless the corresponding instinct also acts.

Through the concept of instinct we can explain how a state of consciousness (idea, memory, perception) causes a specific emotional state. And, since every instinct is a biological factor, we may say that we have an emotional state only when a state of consciousness rouses a determined biological complex corresponding to that emotion. For example, the touch of a knife blade on my skin does not in itself arouse any biological factors; it is simply a perception. At most the coldness of the blade may cause some unpleasantness (objective feeling). If, however, I also know that the knife has a special meaning, that it is a menace to my life, then I feel repulsion and disgust, accompanied by the instinct for self-preservation (revulsion), which produces the emotion of fear.

The biological factors constituting instinct are therefore the real causes of the emotional state. Without them such a state would be incomprehensible. In my example there is no definite relation between the knife in itself and my feeling of fear. The knife, as such, can have many uses and should not excite fear. Nearly always there is such a discrepancy between the stimulus and the emotional state since the stimuli causing emotional states are apt to be inadequate. While the situation dangerous to life is an adequate stimulus to fear, and a piece of music is an adequate stimulus to pleasure, the same stimuli can be inadequate for the production of higher feelings if they are not connected with certain circumstances which arouse particular biological factors. If an inadequate stimulus causes a given feeling, it means that it has something in common with the biological factors constituting the instinct on which that emotional state is based. It is this common element that provides the link.

At the bottom of every emotional state, therefore, there is a biological element, instinctive in character, which reconciles the inadequacy of the psychic causes to the emotional state. Thus we can understand how an inadequate stimulus can produce pleasure, joy, sorrow, or any other feeling connected with the instincts leading to defense, anger, flight, etc. Beneath the level of our feelings we have the tide of our deeper and more complex tendencies. The play of emotional stimuli depends upon those tendencies which come to life under the particular circumstances surrounding the action of the stimulus.

The Psychological Analysis of Language

For the last few years I have given all my time to the study of the nature of language, and for that purpose I did considerable work in electroacoustical sound recording. It is an exciting experience to follow the vibration of the voice recorded by the microphone on the fluorescent screen of a cathode tube, but the best results are obtained by filming such vibrations. Then one can analyze them in order to discover the harmonies of sounds, their structure, tone and intensity. One can determine statistically the components of language and show with the greatest exactitude how phonemes vary when they are elements of a living language, *i.e.*, how words, phrases and sentences are constructed and transformed. Up to now phoneticists and linguists have depended upon auditory perception since graphic methods were inadequate for the task, but in auditory perception there are many sources of error which explain the previous discrepancies in results. It is, moreover, impossible to make a subject repeat a phrase in exactly the same way. Electroacoustical methods allow us: (1) to preserve words and phrases, and to hear them again and again in order to compare them objectively, (2) to determine the constituent elements of each phoneme and to discover their changes in words and in sentences spoken with a particular emphasis or tone (negatively or interrogatively, slowly or quickly, etc.); (3) to compare subjects of different races, age or sex, and also the dialects of a specific language in order to determine individual and social influences on language, (4) to compare the two aspects of language, genetic and perceptive, in order to establish the laws governing the perception of language; (5) to study the changes of language with relation to the organism and the anomalies of language, both individual (due to anatomical or functional alterations of the vocal organs, etc.), and collective (due to social causes); and (6) to ascertain the differences due to the psychic condition of a subject, and thus to establish the characteristics which make language an index of personality.

My research has revealed the profound differences shown by all elements of language. It would be vain, however, to look at single phonemes for the characteristics which make language a vivid manifestation of the activity of the human mind. A brief examination of the behavior of phonemes and syllables is convincing proof that their variations have a function which it is impossible to discern unless phrase-units or sentence-units are treated. It is through the variations of phonemes and syllables apart from their value as single elements that they acquire a particular meaning in a specific sentence and in a specific situation. Phonemes and syllables take on a particular look, or "acoustic weight," a pregnancy of meaning, a special function every time stress, intonation, pitch, and so on, make them the one element of the sentence which causes an especially significant psychic resonance in the listener. For a psychologist the phoneme is, therefore, the elementary unit of language, but he must look for the meaning of language in the stream of language.

We must also not forget that language is a function which requires at least two participants. The speaker does not merely produce sounds, nor does the listener merely receive them, for they both build a system of sounds possessing meaning or significance. Motive and acoustic function regulate and influence each other.

The various movements which give rise to language are organized into wholes and constitute "forms" of various degrees. Sensory data constituting words and sentences become meaningful wholes. Such motor and perceptual organization is regulated by the law of relative constancy, so that every unit or group resists being dissipated or weakened by such factors as rapidity in speaking and singing, emphasis, nearness of certain consonants to certain vowels, etc. There is also a "pregnancy" of form, which may be inferred from the position of a part of the word or sentence. The same laws, therefore, rule the motor and perceptual organization of speech as rule the learning and performing of complicated movement, the perception of colors and geometrical figures, and so on.

Language, let me say in conclusion, appears to be regulated by the speaker by means of the laws of form and is perceived by the listener as a unified organization. On a general level these studies of language had been previously treated, though with a different approach, by Heinz Werner and Eliel Lagercrantz, but their inadequate apparatus (Rousselot's ear) prevented them from discovering the mechanics of language which I have described.

My research has also revealed individual variations, *i.e.*, language peculiarities of the individual. When a subject with a "good ear" repeats a spoken or sung vowel under constant conditions, we obtain a series of comparatively uniform oscillograms. The same result occurs in the case of syllables. There are only qualitative differences, which appear chiefly at the beginning and at the end of phonemes.

In the case of even the most common *words* (father, mother), however, we find large differences which become even more evident in complete sentences. Oscillograph recordings, made simultaneously with victrola or wire recordings, have shown the number and importance of "individualisms" in speech. This finding is not surprising for language changes from time to time even in a single subject. Words record differences in age, sex, race, dialect habits, psychic states (chiefly emotional states), etc. A word or sentence, repeated many times, loses the distinctive characteristics of living language and becomes a response mechanism without any expression or meaning; thus it reaches greater uniformity. Only when the word is *living*, *i.e.*, possess a real meaning, is it rich in "individualism."

These individualisms, which I have been able to record and analyze, do not, however, violate the laws of language. They merely show the influence on language of various individual factors, both internal and external, without preventing understanding or making it unduly difficult.

Actually our ears operate as filters, so that we eliminate distortions and recognize words and their elements. When an expert observes the oscillograms of words or sentences spoken with intense meaning, he can recognize the various phonemes, see where they begin and end, and determine their mutual influences and the effects of stress, tune, etc. However, even with the greatest of variations (which show at one end the personal characteristics and individual freedom of the speaker, and at the other the mechanization of uniformity caused by habit, haste, etc.), language can still be understood, thanks to certain unconscious integrating mechanisms, provided only that the phonemes and words preserve a minimum of constant elements.

Electric filters are very useful in the experimental study of these integrating processes, for we can use the technique of electroacoustics to isolate some constituent elements of the complex sounds of speech and to establish the limits of distortion within which it is still possible to understand single phonemes, words or sentences. These partial breakdowns, although they do not achieve the perfection of those obtained by methods of interference, are nevertheless easier to effect. I have experimented with them myself and have discovered that if we suppress wide zones of frequency or subtract most harmonics from sounds, we can cause the disappearance of individual timbre; yet we can still recognize the words acoustically provided we retain certain characteristic elements of vowels and half-vowels.

The study of oscillograms also enables us to consider language as a series of numerous and varied auditory stimuli so grouped as to form organizations which possess meaning and which are perceived and understood as such by the listener.

Among many subjective variables we have the fact that the speaker's attention can be directed either to the individual parts of speech or to the whole. Such transforming factors (which are to be deemed subjective when the word is considered as a speech action, *i.e.*, as the production of sounds possessing meaning) become objective factors of transformation when the word itself is regarded as a perception of sounds possessing meaning. On the other hand, objective conditions of transformation in the speaker become subjective to the listener.

With automatic electroacoustical analytical methods it is possible to conduct a comparative examination of different subjects. As we have seen, we can study individual variations; as well as richness of harmonies of single phonemes, their length, variation in pitch and intensity, etc. All these elements combined give a recognizable individuality for every voice.

Emotional states also cause differences, which appear as structural modifications, but the chief cause of such variation is the meaning of what is spoken, as expressed by changes in intensity and pitch, by pauses, etc.

In the future the student of electroacoustics must try to determine the relationships between the variations of vocal characteristics, on the one hand (average pitch, individual pitch, deviations, number of words per time unit, number of pauses, modifications of syllable, word and sentence pitch, modifications of harmonics, and of their intensity and richness, displacement of resonance zones), and, on the other hand, he must determine meaning, as well as the speaker's subjective state, type, age, sex, etc. It is a fertile field of research, and so far it is largely untouched. It is impossible to emphasize too strongly the technical possibilities for research which electronics now offers.

Mental Disease

We might now describe my application of psychology in the selection of pilots, soldiers, telephone girls and bank clerks, my work in the field of industry, and on the scholastic and professional orientation of young people, and my studies on psychic abnormalities; yet I do not wish to unduly extend this scientific autobiography. Let me comment only on my latest studies on mental diseases.

I succeeded in establishing that psychoses are diseases[4] because they are brought about by organic morbid processes which can be studied by general pathology, and that psychoses are mental because they represent types of repression of psychic life. With this radical change of perspective, a discussion on the "psychic" or "organic" causes of a given mental disease becomes merely a discussion of the normal or morbid character of the variation of mental functions. This approach to the field shows clearly the weakness of the theory that claims that a psychogenetic mechanism is the sole cause of mental disease, or that such disease is always the result of an organic alteration. In other words, it is a serious mistake, in defining any kind of mental disease, to formulate such a definition exclusively on the evidence of its psychic manifestations and its psychogenesis. It is equally erroneous to define it merely in the light of the organic evidence, or of the disease's organic manifestations, or of its "localization," and to consider the modifications of psychic functions merely as minor phenomena. In either case the mistake is fundamental since man's organism cannot be separated from his psychic life. What we call "personality," to use a fashionable but ambiguous term, is the whole man considered in the light of his organic factors and activities.

Every mental disease has a negative aspect consisting of the absence or the alteration of psychic functions, and it has a positive aspect, consisting either of a new organization or of a regression of psychic life. It is quite

---

[4] For simplicity's sake I shall use the term "disease" to designate arrested development and disintegration of mental processes which appear after full development has been attained, as well as neuroses and psychoses which I consider in a different category.

easy to explain or understand certain diseases such as progressive paralysis (the result of the spread of syphilitic infection to the central nervous system) by the resultant great change in mental functions. We may, therefore, safely state that progressive paralysis is a disease of an organic nature which also presents general and typical manifestations of mental functions. The proof becomes somewhat more difficult in other mental diseases. It may be stated with confidence, however, that mental disease is a more or less marked loss of both reason and will power. It is a regression of the personality resulting from a process which renders automatic and determined those psychic functions that would naturally tend to bring about progressive increase of undetermined acts, an increase characteristic of that liberty which is the typical manifestation of psychic life. Furthermore, such a regression is also the result of a more or less marked alteration of the organism, especially of its central nervous system.

Such a conception of mental disease is the outcome of a correct consideration of the interrelationship existing between organic life and psychic life, and of what is incorrectly called the "physical" and the "moral." Cartesian dualism forced a separate consideration of organic and mental life, leading indirectly to the extreme consequences of a mechanistic theory, and, logically enough, to the reaction represented by the various psychogenetic theories. Enlarging our field of inquiry to the problem of the origin of man, on which the various anthropological theories depend, we should observe that Cartesian dualism is responsible for an absurd theory put forward by some authors in an attempt to reconcile opposite contentions, the theory that the body of man is derived from an animal source while his soul is the result of a creative act — as if it were possible so to separate the fundamental "dimension" of human personality. Organic functions, however, may be investigated separately, and the same rule applies to psychic functions; but these investigations may meet particular — and indeed fundamental — exigencies of method. Indeed it is sometimes necessary to conduct scientific inquiry according to different standards. This analytic procedure necessarily assumes that results under any given standard of inquiry should not be construed as an explanation of the whole living being, and this basic principle obviously also applies to the mentally affected person.

The picture we have attempted to outline shows man as a hierarchy of structures and functions that reciprocally act one on another, being organized in such a way that the higher structures and functions involve and integrate, to quote Sherrington, the lower structures and functions which are, as it were, overlapped by the former. No one of the lower functions can account for any one of the higher functions, even though the latter constitute a necessary condition for the former. Thus psychic structures and functions have a particular position of their own, and each lower structure and function stands out as a necessary condition of its immediately higher one. Yet the lower do not "explain" the higher, because the superior or higher functions integrate the inferior or lower ones.

It should be noted that certain psychic functions, since they are instrumental in adaptive behavior (functions of perception, of motion, of speech, etc.), are strictly bound to organic structures, which are either the receptors of a stimulus or the executors of movements. Certain other functions which are responsible for adapting life and behavior to needs, conditions and aims, are founded upon structures which direct energy upon definite objectives. The peak of the structural scale is occupied by the higher functions of volition and knowledge. These functions, using their own proper structures and the functions of the lower structures, direct life toward the attainment of its ends, which are an ever-increasing store of knowledge and the fullest enjoyment of freedom.

Mental disease is a disintegration or regression that may affect only a portion of these functional or structural strata. There is no such thing as a pure psychogenesis of mental disease. Such a tenet is one of the fundamental mistakes of psychoanalysis and is just as serious a mistake as is limiting the nature of psychosis and neurosis to organic processes. Neurosis and psychosis are regressions affecting any of the functional and structural strata of human personality. They especially involve organic alterations, regressions or modifications which are necessarily accompanied by psychopathological disintegrations.

To hold that every mental disease is a pathological alteration of personality affecting all the dimensions of personality implies that a pathological process or an organic alteration is the necessary condition of mental disease. This statement must not be construed as a confusion between neurology and psychiatry, each of which is distinct in its own field. Both are, it is true, cerebral pathologies, but as Ey rightly observes: "La Neurologie a pour objet propre les désintégrations fonctionnelles, partielles ou instrumentales, sans modifications, substantielles de la vie psychique, tandis que l'autre, la Psychiatrie, a pour objet les dissolutions globales des fonctions psychiques supérieures qui altèrent sinon aliènent la vie psychique."

No one will dispute that *tabes dorsalis* is a neurological disease, not only because it affects the neuro-axis, but also because it involves partial disintegration of the elementary inferior functions (sensations). Similarly it is agreed that progressive paralysis is a syphilitic meningoencephalitis, that is to say, an organic affection with typical mental characteristics. Nevertheless, while it is obvious that *tabes dorsalis* belongs to neurology and progressive paralysis to psychiatry, the differentiation between the varieties of a disease like schizophrenia is more difficult.

We are all aware of the numerous theories which have been advanced in an attempt satisfactorily to explain the psychic manifestations of these diseases, but not one can be considered satisfactory. The symptomatology of the various forms of schizophrenia clearly discloses a psychic regression, a dissolution and a disintegration. The followers of the various psychogenetic theories of schizophrenia attempted in vain to account for these facts. One may admit that its origin is referable to an organic cause. Possibly it may be traceable to a pathological process of the nervous system. But what is the nature of such a process? The fact that this question still remains unanswered merely shows that our methods of inquiry, for all their virtues, are nevertheless inadequate. It is indisputable, however, that organic processes are involved, since the regression, involution and psychic dissolution clearly show that personality itself has been fundamentally affected by these processes.

It may seem odd for a psychologist to draw such a conclusion. I must, however, insist upon it, for as a psychologist I am convinced that man must be made the object of psychological study of his entire person or, in other words, of his personality. The term "mental disease" might itself be a source of misunderstanding if it were employed to indicate the limited field of the psychogenesis of mental phenomena. In my opinion such an attempt is just as incorrect as is the search for the final causes of mental diseases in a limited region of the nervous system. A mental disease is a disease affecting the whole of man, and schizophrenia clearly belongs to this category.

The foregoing account of mental disease represents, I think, the very great asset that modern psychiatry can hand over to psychology. The theory I have described has the merit of enabling the psychologist to appreciate psychology as a biological science concerned with man in his entirety and of proving its value in the light of the progress made by modern psychiatry.

PERSPECTIVE

I close with a personal reflection. I began to study psychology in 1913 when experimental psychology in Italy was despised by the current schools of philosophy (idealism), and when physiologists denied its autonomy. As I now come to the close of my life, I can see that at last the autonomy of psychology, and its biological character, are fully acknowledged. Thanks to its application in industry, military life, aviation, education, etc., the value of psychology is now appreciated. It is indeed a triumph, and the credit for it goes to those pioneers who have preceded my generation: F. Kiesow, S. De Sanctis, G. C. Ferrari, and others less known outside Italy.

I am still working hard, directing my own laboratory, because we still must work to extend the application of psychology. With Professor M.

Ponzo of the University of Rome, who like me was·a pupil of Professor Kiesow and has brought along as many younger students, I can look with satisfaction at almost half a century spent in the service of psychology.

Today many younger men are teaching and planning to teach at the universities. They enter upon a very different situation than that encountered by Professor Ponzo and me at the beginning of our careers, for psychology has gone far since Kiesow, trained in Germany with Wundt, came to Italy more than fifty years ago.

ARNOLD GESELL

WILLIAM JAMES doubted that the science of psychology can ever become so refined that biographies will be written in advance of the life career. Even autobiographic retrospection, however objective, has its shortcomings. I shall simplify my task by limiting it to a simple account of my education and my professional activities. It may prove tempting along the way to indulge in a few comments and to hint as to causes and effects. But I would acknowledge at the outset, in matters biographical, the metaphysical force of Melville's matmaker scene:[1] — the shuttle, the warp and woof, and the strokes of Queequeg's impulsive sword, " . . . this easy, indifferent sword must be chance — aye, chance, free will, and necessity — no wise incompatible — all interweavingly working together."

I was born just seventy years ago in Alma, Wisconsin, a picturesque, two-street village on the bank of the upper Mississippi. The two parallel streets, one well above the other, notch the steep bluffs which slope sharply into the river. Here I grew up, the eldest of five children, in a closely united family. My father placed a high premium on education for all of us, as did my young mother who, in her middle teens, had already won a reputation by successfully teaching a difficult elementary school. The principal of the local high school, in our eyes, stood at the top of the cultural hierarchy. At any rate, I was very early oriented in the direction of a teaching career. In due course I attended a normal school.

But, as with all children, the truly basic part of my education was non-academic, pre-curricular, and extra-curricular. It consisted in the everyday life at home, in the varied household chores, in the regular observance of anniversaries and festival occasions, and in a direct identification with community happenings, made possible by the intimacy of a village environment. The very absence of radio, motion pictures, and comics made experiences more vivid, more configured, more eventful. Memorial Day, for example,

---

[1] Herman Melville, *Moby Dick or The Whale,* 1851, Chap. 47. "Queequeg and I were mildly weaving what is called a sword-mat, for an additional lashing to our boat . . ."

was meaningful; it had the sincerity of a folkway. Early in the morning, children climbed the bluffs to pick wild flowers; each child clutched his own memorial bouquet, fell into line on the mile-long upper street, and marched in procession behind blue clad survivors of The Grand Army of the Republic. Each child, individually, placed his flowers on a great table; a judge with flowing white beard spoke some words; guns spoke a mysterious salute.

Hills, valley, water and climate concurred to make the seasons distinct and intense in my home town. Each season had its own challenges and keen pleasures, accentuated by the everchanging, yet enduring river. It would take a special kind of depth psychology to determine in what manner the rhythms and impressions of Nature influence the early growth of the mind. I think that Walt Whitman has given us some real hints in his cataloguing poem, "A Child Went Forth."

But I do not wish to suggest that the boys in our river town spent most of their time contemplating the tranquil beauties of Nature. There was jubilation when the calm of the majestic valley was shattered by two long and three short blasts from the deep steaming throat of a packet boat. "She's going to land!" So we all rushed to the dock to look upon the crowded, hurried happenings, particularly the antics of the Negro roustabouts from the land of cotton. And on Saturday nights a brawny crew of river men from the near-by logging works would descend upon the town in their calked boots. There was more than one tavern in our town.

This leads me to comment on how very much of a child's psychology comes through his eyes. He is forever looking, scanning, watching. His vision is tireless, insatiable; and in the compact, candid life of a village of the eighties and nineties he could see a great deal.

During my boyhood I saw the dark as well as bright facets of our microcosm. I saw death, funerals, devastating sickness, ominous quarantines, accidents and drownings at close range. Acute and chronic alcoholism were common sights open to public view. Epileptic convulsions occurred on the street and sidewalk. A muttering "crazy man" walked endlessly back and forth in his garden. A condemned murderer stared at us through the bars of the county prison. A watchdog was poisoned and a burglary committed in the blackness of night. Strange and sobering things kept happening as though they were part of the normal course of existence. None of these experiences was overpowering; but cumulatively they left a deposit of impressions, which sensitized a background for my clinical studies in later life.

The scientific age was ushered in for us when incandescent Edison lights were installed to replace kerosene lamps. On graduation from high school (1896), I demonstrated, as my commencement exercise, the wonders of the new electrical era. By electrolysis I produced a tubeful of hydrogen, which on ignition flashed and popped for the audience. For further edification I tapped the electric current of the local dynamo. With the aid of the village blacksmith I had made a horseshoe magnet, powerful enough to grapple a flatiron, and to hold in mid-air the suspended weight of the juvenile demonstrator!

Chautauqua did not come to Alma, but teachers' institutes did. And for some obscure intellectual reason, I attended these institutes. The official state institute conductor, C. H. Sylvester, must have been amused at my presence and my young seriousness. In any event he befriended me; he gave me a pocket microscope, and took me on a nature study trip to the top of the bluffs. He was one of the original faculty of the Stevens Point Normal School (now Teachers College) which was being established among the frontier pine stumps of north central Wisconsin. Because of him, I elected to attend this far-away school, from which I graduated in 1899. It was a vital, progressive institution and I owe much to it. I had a stimulating course in psychology under Professor Edgar James Swift who had been trained at Clark University and who, in due course, directed me toward Clark and G. Stanley Hall.

Despite the excellent instruction and class work at the Stevens Point Normal, I recall most vividly my extra-curricular activities. I was captain of the second string football team, and editor-in-chief of the *Normal Pointer*. This journal carried my first printed article, an oration entitled, "John Brown: The Man," which placed second in the local oratorical contest. The following year I had better luck (interwoven with some free will and necessity) with an oration which placed first in the local, state, and interstate contests.

During my junior year, for summer reading, my mentor, Mr. Sylvester, had given me the distinguished two-volume treatise by W. E. H. Lecky, entitled *History of the Rise and Influence of the Spirit of Rationalism in Europe*. While I was much too immature to digest this scholarly work, it made a deep and lasting impression, by virtue of its exalted, eloquent diction and its noble aura of liberal humanitarianism. A by-product was the second aforementioned oration which was entitled, "The Development of the Spirit of Truth." The theme, espoused not without adolescent fervor, concerned intolerance, persecution, and freedom of thought. This was before the two world wars and the current Korean conflict. May I, nevertheless, quote two sentences of the prophetic (?) peroration of 1899: "But if the past has been dark with despair, the future is bright with hope. That 'Every great truth must be baptized in blood' will no longer be the law of progress. . . . "

Soon after graduation I was appointed teacher of the Stevens Point High School, a sort of omnibus post which I held for two years. The duties included teaching U. S. history, ancient history, German, accounting, commercial geography, and coaching and refereeing of football. I do not recall any significant intellectual achievements during this period.

The next two years were spent at the University of Wisconsin. I had a brief course in comparative psychology under Jastrow, but my interest for a time gravitated toward American history. I came under the dynamic and friendly influence of Frederick Jackson Turner, the acknowledged leader in the history of the Western Movement. He gave me an opportunity to do a minor bit of investigation in the early history of Mormonism, using the Schroeder Library which was carefully guarded because of its apocryphal items. This was my first definite experience in research, unless I except an earlier study, at Stevens Point, on the development of advertising in America. While at the University I also wrote a thesis on "A Comparative Study of Higher Education in Ohio and Wisconsin," and a commencement oration on "Shaftesbury and Child Labor." I was an active member of Athena, a unique debating society, which specialized in joint intramural debates in the days when forensic prowess excited more collegiate enthusiasm than athletic contests. In an intercollegiate debate with Michigan I argued unsuccessfully against the wisdom and constitutionality of a Federal Income Tax.

Influenced by the advantage of income as well as opportunity, I was pleased to accept the principalship of a large high school, after securing my Ph.B. I greatly enjoyed the many diversified experiences of my year with the body of lively students at Chippewa Falls, Wisconsin.

The next two years were spent at Clark University, with the help of a tuition scholarship. Here I received my doctorate in psychology in 1906, and an honorary Sc.D. in 1940.

As a Clark man, I would like to formulate, if space permitted, my specific indebtedness to each and all of the distinguished group of professors who still remained there after the hegira to the University of Chicago. Burnham had a carefully wrought and sympathetic historical approach to problems of child hygiene, Chamberlin, in anthropology, was notable for his warm and catholic protagonisms, Hodge for his informal, leisurely interpretations of ecology; Sanford in experimental psychology, was an exemplar of precise thinking, joined with an attractive personality. The venerable psychiatrist, Dr. Edward Cowles, conducted impressive demonstrations of psychotic patients.

G. Stanley Hall was the acknowledged genius of the group at Clark. Although the term genius is often overused, we can safely apply it to his intellect. True genius may be regarded as a creative developmental thrust of the human action system into the unknown. Hall embodied such thrusts, almost inveterately, in his thinking and in his teaching. He had, in addition, an empathic propensity to revive within himself the thought processes and the feelings of other thinkers. This same projective trait enabled him to penetrate into the mental life of children, of defectives, of primitive peoples, of animals, of extinct stages of evolution. What if he could not verify his prolific suggestive thrusts, what if he seemed unsystematic and self-contradictory, what if he exaggerated the doctrine of recapitulation — he nevertheless was a naturalist Darwin of the mind, whose outlook embraced the total phylum, and lifted psychology above the sterilities of excessive analysis and pedantry. In many ways, no doubt, he must now be considered outmoded. But as a teacher his so-called defects became virtues, and I still find in his writings a catalytic quality. Indeed if the young psychologist of today ever needs a little refreshment of spirit, perhaps he can read with profit some of the page-long sentences that issued from the ardent, exuberant mind of G. Stanley Hall.

There is a certain pathos in Hall's autobiographic confession in which he says, "The dominantly sad note of my life may be designated by one word, isolation." This note is implicit in the brooding quality of his eyes, which were the arresting feature of his Jovian countenance. But when at the Monday evening seminar or in the lecture room his interpretive mind began to coruscate there was no sense of isolation in the listening student.

I wrote three published papers while at Clark. The titles suggest a trend toward clinical psychology, but I had not yet concretely envisaged a professional goal. One paper dealt with "Accuracy in handwriting, as related to school intelligence and sex."[2] The second paper[3] brought me into quasi-clinical contact with a surpassingly strange individual whose senile delusion made him the inspired, nocturnal amanuensis of the Almighty. I analyzed the weird symbolic manuscript and drawings, which he esoterically penned in the deep hours of the night. The third paper,[4] my dissertation, dealt with the manifestations of jealousy, normal and abnormal, in animals and in man at ascending age periods beginning with infancy. When I was exploring thesis possibilities, Hall once suggested that I study the infants at the Foundling Hospital of New York; I was unable to carry out this plan at the time, but only a few weeks ago I examined a series of infants in this very hospital, in connection with a motion picture film which I shall mention later.

Following my doctorate I spent short periods as counsellor in a boys' camp, as elementary school teacher and settlement worker (East Side House) in New York, and as instructor in psychology at the State Normal School of Platteville, Wisconsin. With suddenness came a summons to join Lewis M. Terman as professor of psychology in the Los Angeles State Normal School. The double lure of California and my friendship for Terman sufficed. Soon he and I were in our respective citrus groves on opposite sides of Valley View Road, Casa Verdugo. It was a happy association. I had known Terman at Clark when he was engaged in his path-breaking study of Genius and Stupid-

[2] *Amer. J. Psychol.*, 1906, 17, 394–405.
[3] A case of symbolistic writing with senile delusions, *Amer J Psychol.*, 1905, 16, 519–536.
[4] Jealousy (Ph D dissertation, Clark Univ), *Amer J Psychol*, 1906, 17, 437–496

ity, a study which retains momentum in his hands to this day. At Los Angeles his interest in Binet and the measurement of intelligence was gathering strength, and came to notable fulfillment at Stanford University.

In the summer of 1909 I visited Witmer's psychological clinic at Philadelphia, and spent a few profitable weeks at the Vineland Training School, where Goddard was adapting Binet to a pioneering program of research. I was greatly impressed by the informality and sincerity of the work at Vineland, both in its scientific and humanitarian aspects. This marked the beginning of my lifelong interest in backward and defective children. In later years (1911–1915), Goddard and I worked together directing the New York University summer school for the training of special class teachers of backward and defective pupils.

Meanwhile I had built a bungalow in my chosen orange grove and I had married Beatrice Chandler. I had nothing to teach but psychology to groups of eager students. It seemed time to settle down. But at this very time I was overtaken by a strange, subdued kind of restlessness, a vague sense of unpreparedness for a task which was taking shape in my mind. I wished in some way to make a thoroughgoing study of the developmental stages of childhood. But with all my training I lacked a realistic familiarity with the physical basis and the physiological processes of life and growth. To make good this deficit I would have to study medicine. The decision was made, and it had the moral and insightful support of Mrs. Gesell. Five years later (1915) I received my medical degree from the School of Medicine at Yale University.

I had met Mrs. Gesell when she was on the faculty of the Los Angeles Normal School. As a recent graduate of the University of Chicago, where progressive education was in its heyday, she was creatively introducing liberal methods into the early grades of the model training school. These methods and her imaginative spirit are reflected in the better chapters of a book which we wrote in collaboration under the title of *The Normal Child and Primary Education.*[5]

In the fullness of time other collaborators of sorts appeared upon the scene, for I was destined to have a son and a daughter and a fine series of five grandchildren: two grandsons and three granddaughters. They all have taught me a great deal, and still keep teaching, but we have never permitted any scientific preoccupations to cast a baleful veil over us! On graduation from Vassar my daughter, Katherine (now Mrs. Joseph Walden), lent a willing hand in the compilation of a pictorial volume entitled, *How a Baby Grows* (1945). My son, Gerhard, has had to deal with corporate bodies of greater magnitude; he graduated from the Yale Law School and is an active attorney in Washington, D. C.

[5] Gesell & Beatrice Chandler Gesell, 1912.

The year 1910–1911 was transitional. I spent months in the medical laboratories of the University of Wisconsin. Most of my time was devoted to the study of human anatomy (under Bardeen) and histology (under Miller). It was for me an entrance into a new world, and I enjoyed the solid footing.

In 1911 I was appointed Assistant Professor of Education at Yale University. A new department was being formed under the aegis of Professor E. C. Moore, formerly superintendent of the Los Angeles Public Schools. Under the part-time arrangements of my appointment I was able to carry out a full program of medical study in combination with teaching courses in the graduate school at Yale. Yandell Henderson in physiology, Russell Chittenden in organic chemistry, and George Blumer in clinical medicine, were among my instructors. Dean Blumer was friendly to my plans. Without hesitation, he made available a room, a table and a chair in the New Haven Dispensary for the establishment of a psycho-clinic for children. This (in 1911) was the beginning of the Yale Clinic of Child Development. I probably designated myself as "director" even before I had a paid assistant in the person of Margaret Cobb Rogers. In due course I had an able staff and the title of Director was formalized by the fellows of the corporation in 1930, when I was assigned to the Board of Permanent Officers of the Yale School of Medicine.

On attainment of my medical degree I was promoted to a full professorship in the graduate school, but continued on a part time basis because I had also accepted a post as school psychologist for the State Board of Education of Connecticut. This position, the first of its kind I believe, under state auspices, involved interesting duties. I travelled from one rural school to another, often by horse and buggy, to identify handicapped pupils, and to set into operation, so far as possible, individualized programs in their behalf. By the organization of special classes for retarded pupils I also gave official assistance to city school systems and county homes for dependent children. Surveys and a manual entitled, "What Can the Teacher Do for the Deficient Child?" were published as public documents. In 1919 I was appointed by the governor to the Connecticut Commission on Child Welfare and wrote portions of a two-volume report dealing with the status of handicapped children and formulating administrative and legislative recommendations. The report led to the setting up of a Division for Educationally Exceptional Children under the State Board of Education. I was ineligible for war service, but in the fall of 1918 I undertook a mental survey of the elementary schools of the City of New Haven. The results were published by the Yale University Press.[6] New Haven developed an excellent system of special classes under the direction of Miss Norma Cutts. At about this time I set up an experiment to determine the capacities of subnormal girls in factory

[6] *Exceptional Children and Public School Policy,* 1921.

work. The cooperation of the employment division of the Candee rubber company indicated a growing recognition of the social aspects of the problem of feeblemindedness. A report of the experiment was published.

Although these social welfare activities consumed time they did not dull my interest in the clinical aspects of child psychology.[7] I was regularly examining children of various ages by appointment, and making special studies of selected conditions, such as cretinism, hemi-hypertrophy (a rare anomaly associated with amentia), cerebral palsies, a case of *pubertas praecox,* and the remarkable physical and mental correspondences of a pair of highly gifted twins. These cases yielded impressive evidence of profound mechanisms of development.

Concurrently I became increasingly interested in the normal developmental characteristics of the period of infancy and the pre-school years. From the standpoint of diagnosis, prevention and social control it seemed clear that there should be more concentration on the first years of life. I wrote a postwar book which undertook to define concrete possibilities in the field of early child care. I was pleased when Cubberly accepted the manuscript for publication in his famous Riverside series. The term "pre-school" was just coming into vogue and the book was entitled, *The Pre-School Child: From the Standpoint of Public Hygiene and Education* (1923). The pre-school period had been called the No Man's Land in the field of child welfare. The first World War pointed to the important medical and social problems involved.

Our clinical service gave special attention to the youngest age groups; and with the aid of graduate students we made a systematic survey of the developmental patterning of behavior at ten age levels in the first five years of life. One purpose was to define normative criteria which could be used in the diagnostic appraisal of normal, deviant and defective infants. I was not specifically interested in the psychometry of intelligence, *per se,* but rather in the diagnosis of the total developmental status as expressed in motor, adaptive, language, and personal-social behavior patterns. The approach was and remains essentially comparative.

To demonstrate the clinical significance of the comparative approach to medical students, I brought two pairs' of normal infants of disparate ages into the clinical amphitheatre. This was, I think, the first time that these students were definitely invited to observe normality as a clinical entity. The infants sat in their mothers' laps, side by side, confronting a table on which

---

[7] If I recall correctly I was a charter member of the ancient and long extinct American Association of Clinical Psychologists, which in 1918 met in Baltimore, where I presented a paper for a Symposium on "The Field of Clinical Psychology as an Applied Science." I still hold a $25 diploma duly signed (1922) by Executive Officer Wells and President Knight Dunlap, certifying membership in the section of consulting psychologists of the American Psychological Association "This instrument is valid only during membership "— I am quoting — and "neither the American Psychological Association nor any member thereof, other than the holder, is or shall be liable for the acts of the holder"

test objects were simultaneously placed. The infants reacted appropriately to the comparative occasion, simultaneously they displayed their developmental disparity.

Out of these studies and clinical applications came another inevitable book. I shall reproduce the title in full length, because it sums up the scope of our research program at that time: *The Mental Growth of the Pre-School Child: A Psychological Outline of Normal Development from Birth to the Sixth Year, Including a System of Developmental Diagnosis.* Illustrated with Two Hundred Action Photographs. This volume was included in the official list of 37 most notable books published in 1925, compiled by the American Library Association for the Committee on International Intellectual Cooperation of the League of Nations.

This recognition apparently reached the attention of the Laura Spelman Rockefeller Memorial, which foundation made a timely grant in support of our work. And this grant in turn was the first of a generous series of grants continuous throughout the subsequent 25 years into 1950, by The Rockefeller Foundation, the General Education Board, The Carnegie Corporation, and more recently, the American Optical Company. For the record I should like to state that all these grants created not only an opportunity; they created conditions of intellectual freedom for the research staff and director. In not a single instance was there the slightest interference, direct or indirect, in our research methods or objectives.

Here it is convenient to mention the special support which was given to our photographic program. I had come to the conclusion that cinematography should be used not only for purposes of documentation, but also as a research instrument for the analysis of the morphology of behavior patterns. Visible behavior is a form of motion, or, if you prefer, it is formed motion. Instantaneous photography freezes motion. Cinemanalysis is a method for systematic time-space study of frozen sections of motion, within a given episode, or in relation to a sector of the ontogenetic cycle.

From a monistic standpoint, the primary problems of a developmental psychology are morphological. The fundamental scientific riddle is always one of pattern or form. The cinema helps us to capture this form and to define its lawfulness in terms of (a) the behavior moment; (b) the behavior episode; and (c) a whole developmental epoch. Cinematography by itself bakes us no scientific bread, but as a tool for psychological research its potentialities are inexhaustible.

Our first contact with the cinema was in 1924 in our small laboratory at the Department of Education building at 28 Hillhouse Avenue. With the cooperation of Pathé Review[8] we made the first photographic survey of the

[8] In our later photographic program we made use of one of the original Pathé cameras which had been used in the historic filming of "The Birth of a Nation." Our film bore the title, "The Mental Growth of the Pre-School Child." The book bearing the same title was named after the film.

behavior development of the pre-school child, from early infancy to school entrance. The filming was done under the sputter of arc lights, and the infants made a surprisingly good adjustment to the novel situation. With the expansion of our research program, the clinic was moved in 1926 to the homelike environs of a spacious residence at 52 Hillhouse Avenue. Cinematography had an important place in this program. In collaboration with Professor Raymond Dodge, a member of the Institute of Psychology, and Professor Henry Halverson, Research Associate in Experimental Psychology on the clinic staff, we planned and installed a one-way vision observation dome for the systematic photographic recording of infant behavior at lunar month intervals. The sizzling arc lights were replaced with soft and cool Cooper-Hewitt illumination. The developmental examinations of infant behavior were made with careful regard for standard procedures by Helen Thompson, Ph.D., Research Associate in Biometry; by Catherine Strunk Amatruda, M.D., Research Pediatrician; and by myself. During this early period research and diagnostic examinations were also made by Elizabeth E. Lord, Ph.D., Ruth W. Washburn, Ph.D., and Marian Putnam, M.D., all of whom were especially interested in the clinical aspects of child development.

At first the cinema records were limited to the normative progressions of infant development, but from time to time instructive clinical deviations were similarly documented. In 1930 a supplementary Rockefeller grant made possible a parallel naturalistic survey supervised by Alice V. Keliher, Ph.D., which documented the infant's daily life under domestic conditions with the mother's immediate care. A homelike studio unit was constructed which permitted optimal 35 mm. cinema records of the baby's behavior day — his sleep, waking, feeding, bath, play, bodily activities and social behavior. The naturalistic survey was continued for two years in the Hillhouse unit. The two surveys, with the accompanying stenographic and other protocols, supplied the source data for *An Atlas of Infant Behavior* (1934). This work in two volumes (Yale University Press) was illustrated with 3200 action photographs derived from the original films. The normative volume delineates typical trends from age to age. The naturalistic volume depicts individual differences.

Scientifically controlled cinematography fortunately is a paradoxical form of embalming. It not only preserves the behavior in chemical balm, but it makes that behavior live again in its original integrity. The cinema registers the behavior events in such coherent, authentic and measurable detail that for purposes of psychological study and clinical research the reaction patterns of infant and child become almost as tangible as tissue.

Accordingly we have taken great pains to safeguard our films with a view of giving them archive permanence and research accessibility. Each film was catalogued by library methods and identified in specific footages and content. Over the years we have assembled some 200,000 feet of 35 mm. film, and over 100,000 feet of 16 mm. film to constitute a Photographic Research Library. The photographic collection has recently been taken over by the library of the Yale School of Medicine, where the Yale films of child development will be made available for students and investigators.

In 1929 an interesting movement within the university became articulate. The Human Welfare Group issued a booklet entitled, "Yale Proposes to Study Man." This group was a voluntary association of existing activities and at the time included the Yale School of Medicine, the Yale School of Nursing, the New Haven Hospital and Dispensary, and the Institute of Human Relations. "In the Institute of Human Relations, designed for co-operative research, are the child development study unit, the comparative psycho-biology unit, the graduate divisions of psychology and the social sciences, and a research and clinical group in mental hygiene and psychiatry." President James R. Angell, with his extensive background in psychology, the dynamic dean of the School of Medicine, Dr. Milton Winternitz, and the young and rising dean of the Law School, Robert M. Hutchins, were deeply concerned in this educational and scientific projection.

While the projection was in the blueprint stage, the staff of the Clinic of Child Development were given the rare opportunity to plan in detail for their needs and equipment in the Georgian building which was speedily erected as an integral part of the medical center. In 1930 we moved into our attractive and highly functional quarters which comprised a wing of the new building, with provisions on five floors as follows: 1. guidance nursery, clinical files, and photographic research library; 2. clinical examination suites and observation rooms; 3. photographic dome and laboratory rooms, 4. conference room, library and offices; 5. infant out-patient service and studio unit for clinical photography. The architectural arrangements were highly favorable for maintaining an integrated program of research, with a fair balance of collaboration and independent activity. The Clinic of Child Development occupied these quarters until my retirement in 1948.

My temporary association with the Human Relations Institute entailed no marked changes in the activities of the clinic. The close proximity with medical school and hospital and our basic objective led to an increasing emphasis of the pediatric and child guidance aspects of our program. The clinic had become a defined entity, operating on a separate budget, under the general administration of the School of Medicine. Yale thereby was the first institution to accord departmental status in a medical school to the new field of child development.

As a scientific movement "child development" is somewhat characteristic of America. Child psychology as a self-contained discipline and child study in its Victorian sense have come under the correlating influence of the life sciences. Child development may be regarded as a branch of biology or of anthropology which is concerned with early human growth in its physical, mental and cultural manifestations. The first conference on research in child development under the auspices of the committee on child development of the National Research Council at Bronxville, N. Y. (October 1925) marked a milestone in the diversification of the scientists whom it brought simultaneously within speaking distance. Even anatomists and physiologists proved to have important cross-fertilization contributions toward an understanding of the child mind. Scammon was a most stimulating participant in this rather unique conference.

Similarly, George E. Coghill was to demonstrate the significance of the neurophysiological approach for developmental psychology. His Cambridge lectures are gathered in a thin volume entitled *Anatomy and the Problem of Behavior* which bids fair to become classic. I was a great admirer of Coghill's work. We found common strands of interest in amblystoma and in the human infant.

The activities of the clinic were now varied enough to present their own problems of administrative coordination and scientific correlation. The clinic functioned both as a research unit and as a community service clinic for some fifty social agencies, with an increasing number of referrals from states throughout the country. A devoted, cooperative staff made it possible to maintain a reciprocal balance between basic and applied research. The research program took shape in terms of our cumulative experience, which was clarified from time to time by a series of collaborative publications. The normative investigation which began with infancy was gradually extended to include a charting of thirty-four progressive age levels embracing the first ten years of psychological growth. The concept of development proved to be a far-reaching integrating factor. It enabled us to study the defects and deviations of maldevelopment by the same methods used in the study of normal individual differences. In the course of years the clinic came into contact with an extraordinary variety of developmental manifestations – in the pre-school children attending the guidance nursery, in the developmental supervision and survey of the feeding behavior of well babies, in the study of the visual functions of infants and school children, in the pre-adoptive examination of foster children, and in the diagnostic service for atypical and handicapped infants and children. It was a rare privilege to come into intimate and recurrent contact with all these embodiments of growing humanity. Some of the children we were able to follow from infancy into adolescence and maturity.

This has been true of the infant twins T & C, for recently we attended their simultaneous weddings. As infants they showed such amazing identity in mental and physical development that they led us to devise the method of co-twin control to analyze the relationships between maturation and learning. Twin T was specifically trained, C was reserved as a control and as a criterion for later comparisons in a series of studies by graduate students. Research Associate Thompson, myself, and Louise B. Ames made an exhaustive, comparative analysis of the extensive cinema records. The results of this biogenetic study of the twins from early infancy into adolescence are summarized in a monograph by Gesell and Thompson.[9] I make special mention of this study because I regard the method of co-twin control, critically used, as a powerful method for psychological and clinical investigation.[10] It even has a kind of biometric merit because a highly identical co-twin criterion represents the summation of a statistically vast number of variables otherwise beyond experimental control.

The progress of the normative survey of normal development was reported in a series of volumes which appeared in natural sequence. In collaboration with Thompson the statistical trends in the first year of life were elaborately analyzed in two volumes.[11] The data on the first five years were codified in a joint publication by all the research members of the staff.[12] This volume is in a sense a cooperative sequel which covers in detail the territory staked out by the earlier work on *The Mental Growth of the Pre-School Child.*

The increasing volume of clinical examinations, the cumulative observations of the children attending the guidance nursery, the periodic contacts with the parents of these children, and similar contacts with children of elementary school age all led to better understanding of the problems of child care at ascending levels of development. Here again was an area of study which required close conjunctive effort and the coordination supplied by the integrative concept of development. Two organically related volumes comprising the first ten years of life resulted from this cooperative undertaking in which five members of the staff participated. Dr. Frances L. Ilg as a pediatrician in charge of the guidance service brought her rich clinical experience and insights to bear. Janet Learned, as principal of the guidance nursery, made intimate observations of the individual and interpersonal behavior of the young children; Glenna Bullis, assistant in research, conducted visual skills examinations which furnished many sidelights on maturity traits; Louise B. Ames, curator of the Yale Films of Child Development, through her many studies by the method of cinemanalysis helped significantly to define the developmental characteristics at all the age levels involved.

[9] Twins T and C from infancy to adolescence. a biogenetic study of individual differences by the method of co-twin control, *Genet Psychol. Monogr*, 1941, 24, 3–121.

[10] For a statement of the underlying principles, see Gesell, The method of co-twin control, *Science*, 1942, 95, 446–450.

[11] *Infant Behavior Its Genesis and Growth*, 1934, *The Psychology of Early Growth*, 1938

[12] *The First Five Years of Life*, 1940.

The characteristics were formulated in terms of growth gradients. Some 3000 concrete behavior items were available for codification in relation to ten major fields of child development for seventeen age levels from birth to ten years.

The two volumes just mentioned have recently been combined into a single volume to serve as a college textbook for courses in child psychology and child development.[13] Most of my teaching at Yale has been at the graduate and postdoctoral levels, although I have enjoyed occasional sessions with undergraduates. I participated in the annual proseminars formerly conducted by the department of psychology, and have given numerous brief courses to student nurses and to various lay and professional groups interested in child behavior and child welfare. My medical teaching has consisted chiefly in seminars, clinical demonstrations at the New Haven Hospital, and individual conferences arising out of the day-to-day work of the clinic. In my lectures I make free use of audio-visual aids, and have found it advantageous to bring the still lantern slide and the motion picture into close juxtaposition for cross reference. Occasionally I have been able to bring the living subject into direct comparison with a motion picture record of his earlier behavior to establish the significance of growth. I have televised one of our developmental films and am convinced that this medium holds great educational possibilities.

From time to time I have spoken on the radio in connection both with educational and social welfare programs. On invitation of the International Broadcasting Division of the U. S. Department of State we prepared scripts and a dramatic documentary on the work of the Yale Clinic of Child Development. These programs were transmitted in various foreign languages. The March of Time in its regular 1946 series, and in the later Educational Forum edition, made a documentary film delineating the activities of the clinic. This film has had wide showing both in this country and abroad. The clinic has also prepared educational exhibits for the International Congresses of Psychology (New Haven, 1929), of Mental Hygiene (New Haven, 1930), and of Pediatrics (New York, 1947). The University of Chicago, in its domestic and foreign broadcasts of the Human Adventure series, included a program on the work of the clinic. There have also been foreign language translations of several books from the clinic.

Teaching opportunities have not altogether vanished with retirement. The New School Associates of New York has invited me to participate in a pioneering experiment in adult education. I am scheduled also to conduct a continuous two-day seminar in clinical child development at the next annual meeting of the American Academy of Pediatrics of which I am a fellow.

[13] *Infant and Child in the Culture of Today*, 1943; *The Child from Five to Ten*, 1946, *Child Development: An Introduction to the Study of Human Growth*, 1949.

In 1949 I was honored by an appointment to a national lectureship of the Society of Sigma Xi. This brought me into very pleasant and stimulating contact with audiences at medical schools and universities throughout the East and Southeast. Although I enjoy the interpersonal experience of a lecture audience, writing has been my main channel of communication.

It remains to mention the publications which have a medical as well as a psychological orientation. The relationship between medicine and psychology raises moot questions, but all will agree that psychology is comparable to physiology as a fundamental of medical science. Indeed psychology is often semantically indistinguishable from physiology. Biologically considered the mind has structure and architecture as well as dynamic functions. The child comes by his mind as he comes by his body, through the organizing processes of growth. To paraphrase D'Arcy Thompson, the fabric of a behavioral organism is always a mechanical configuration. We may think of the unitary action system as a "fabric" which is exquisitely structured in its every detail. Because this organic "corpus" is governed by profound laws of growth, a potential clinical science of child development must be concerned with the principles and methods of developmental diagnosis. There is a corollary to this proposition: Development as well as disease falls within the scope of clinical medicine.

Pediatrics is, as Osler put it, "the specialty of general medicine." It has become the largest and most highly organized specialty in America. As such it is concerned with the supervision of health and development as well as with sickness. Over one half of the pediatrician's time and an equivalent proportion of the general practitioner's pediatric practice is devoted to well children. In 1935 the American Board of Pediatrics set up the field of Growth and Development as a basic requirement for specialty certification. This formal action marks an important step in the evolution of preventive medicine, a step which also has implications for the future of child psychology and child psychiatry.

In my own view the protection of mental health, beginning with infancy, should be primarily based on a science of normal human growth, and only secondarily on psychopathology, particularly a psychopathology conceptually derived from a study and theory of adult symptomatology. The relativities of the growth process are all pervasive. They influence even the morphology of emotions and the formation of Rorschach responses. They operate strongly in psycho-therapeutic situations, and in the innumerable problems of child care.

A good example of the ubiquitousness of growth factors was found in the field of infant feeding. A systematic analysis, by Dr. Ilg, of the naturalistic cinema records in conjunction with periodic observations at well baby conferences established developmental progressions in breast and bottle behavior, and in the mastery of cup and spoon. Intensive studies of feeding and sleep behavior through detailed daily records demonstrated noteworthy individual differences. These were the first systematic studies of the principle of self-regulation now widely applied in the management of infant feeding. The results of the studies and their pediatric implications were reported in a joint volume entitled, *Feeding Behavior of Infants: A Pediatric Approach to the Mental Hygiene of Early Life* (1937). In a later volume already mentioned (1943) we named and described the "rooming-in" arrangement for the care of newborn infants.

Pediatrics as the broadest specialty of general medicine is in a position to focus on the dynamics of growth with a minimum of ideology. It might in time bring into being a new type of child psychiatry and a genetic form of constitutional medicine. Cultural factors inflect but they do not generate the basic progressions and the ontogenetic patterning of behavior. There is a constitutional core of individuality which is manifested in growth characteristics.

These characteristics came to our attention not only in the periodic examinations of normal research subjects, but also in the stream of clinical cases which flowed through the diagnostic and advisory service. In 1928, in a volume entitled *Infancy and Human Growth*, I assembled a group of growth studies of normal and defective infants, covering a wide range of individual differences. Ten years later I reviewed these same cases to determine whether the earlier findings and prognoses still held good. These comparisons and other studies reported in the volume *Biographies of Child Development* (1939) indicated that developmental examinations of infant behavior with clinical appraisals have a significant degree of reliability.

There was no doubt about the demand for such appraisals on the part of social agencies, parents, and physicians. With the help of the late Dr. Catherine S. Amatruda, a pediatric clinician and teacher of rare skill, we had built up an infant out-patient service to which an extraordinary diversity of developmental conditions were referred — normal mentality, retardation, amentia, cerebral palsies (mild and devastating), convulsive and endocrine disorders, blindness, deafness, foundlings, dependents, and infants born out of wedlock, referred for possible adoption. All such cases called for diagnosis, prognosis and supervision, with an appraisal of their growth potentials based chiefly on an examination of the presenting patterns of behavior.

On the basis of our clinical experience, and the correlated normative studies, we issued in 1941 a medical manual on the principles, procedures and applications of *Developmental Diagnosis*. In an enlarged second edition (1948) this manual details case studies of eighty-seven forms of maldevelopment and deviation. Examination techniques, equipment, and developmental schedules for the first three years are described.

In another publication entitled *The Embryology of Behavior* (1945), the developmental approach was carried downward to the levels of fetal infancy and the neo-natal period. The neo-natal data were mainly based on a continuous study of a neonate who immediately after birth was transferred, with his mother, to the resident suite of the clinic. Continuous observation and photographic documentation were maintained night and day over a period of two weeks.

A fetal-infant by definition is a viable infant, prematurely born and still living in the fetal period. Under very favorable hospital conditions we were able to make systematic observations of the behavior characteristics of a group of fetal infants ranging from twenty-eight to forty weeks in fetal age.

Many years ago Perez asked a blunt question: Does the fetus belong to psychology? The subtitle of the Embryology volume was intended to suggest an affirmative reply; it reads "The Beginnings of the Human Mind." Although this volume deals with the humbler spheres of behavior — with the developmental patterning of muscular tonicity, electro-tonic integration, respiration, sleep, body posture, ocular and manual reactions — it is believed that these behavior phenomena have implications for a genetic psychology. Huxley was right when he insisted that the study of embryology subtends the entire life cycle. The higher as well as lower orders of behavior were built up by evolutionary processes, and they survive only through embryological (ontogenetic) processes however much they bear the final impress of acculturation. Learning is essentially growth; and even creative behavior is dependent upon the same kind of neuronic growth which fashions the capacities of the archaic motor system, *in utero* and *ex utero*. The performances of genius belong to a hierarchical continuum, because there is only one physiology of development. There is but one embryology of behavior.

It happens that as I write I am in the midst of recording a commentary for a motion picture bearing the title, "The Embryology of Human Behavior." For much of the past year I have been working on this project with a team of technical experts who are equally interested to produce a conceptual type of film suitable for medical and other advanced students. The project is under the joint auspices of the Office of Naval Research, and the Medical Film Institute of the Association of American Medical Colleges.

At the clinic we have long been interested in the utilization of films for teaching. Educational films are generally designed for congregate showings and group instructions. With this purpose in mind we have produced a series of sound films, and edited an additional series of silent films. But in the training of postgraduate physicians in the methods of developmental diagnosis we have placed our films on an individualized self-instruction basis.

The student threads the film, in an individual desk projector, and grinds it through to suit his interest and his needs. It may be a normative record which depicts the behavior patterns of eyes and hands, typical of a 16-weeks level of maturity. It may be a clinical record of a cerebral birth injury which depicts the behavior patterns distorted by a neurological lesion. In principle such film analysis is comparable to the student's use of his individual microscope in the study of histology. Cinemanalysis is a kind of laboratory self-instruction which visualizes the patterned conformations of behavior.

During recent years there has been a growing demand for postgraduate training in the methods of developmental diagnosis. To meet this demand the Yale Clinic set up medical externships of variable duration for physicians specializing in pediatrics or child psychiatry. The diversified out-patient intake of the clinic provided opportunities for observation and progressive participation in the diagnostic and advisory service. A systematic course of cinema self-study with conferences and full-time clinical participation over a period of two years was regarded as the standard requirement for specialization. A sizable number of externes both from this country and abroad were trained by these arrangements. It has been demonstrated that the field of developmental pediatrics offers professional opportunity for persons with clinical aptitude, and an adequate background of clinical experience in general and developmental work. Developmental Pediatrics may be defined as a form of clinical medicine which is systematically concerned with the diagnosis and supervision of child development, normal and abnormal. Under favorable arrangements postgraduate training in this field can be closely integrated with the educational provisions for internes and residents attached to the responsible department of pediatrics.

Since my chronological retirement in 1948 I have not experienced any loss of interest in the doctrine of development. There are too many fields of endeavor in education, in child care, and in child guidance, where a developmental philosophy and a developmental approach are badly needed both for child and adult. The concept of evolution strangely enough has had a much wider acceptance than the correlative idea of ontogenetic development. And in America there has been, in my opinion, an excessive emphasis on learning and conditioning at the expense of heredity and constitution. I ventured to elaborate this point of view concerning a biological psychology in an address on scientific approaches to a study of the human mind, delivered at the inauguration of the Psychological Museum, Garfield Park, Chicago.[14]

During the past four years (1948–1952), I have had the privilege of working as research associate in the Harvard Pediatric Study. The director, Dr. Francis McDonald, was interested in having the developmental point

[14] Scientific approaches to the study of the human mind, *Science*, 1938, 88, 225–230 Reprinted in *Studies in Child Development*, 1948.

of view and the methods of developmental pediatrics incorporated in the procedures of child health supervision instituted for the numerous groups of G.I. families at Harvard. A report is in preparation and will soon be in press.

At Yale University, thanks to a supplementary two year grant in aid by the American Optical Company, it became possible during the period from 1948 to 1950 to continue an investigation of the developmental aspects of child vision. This investigation had evolved as a natural culmination of many previous studies at the former clinic of child development. McGinnis, as a graduate student, had written a doctoral thesis on early eye movements and optic mystagmus. Bing Chung Ling, visiting fellow, had made a thorough experimental study of sustained visual fixation in the human infant from birth to six months. Halverson, Castner, and Ames published various papers on eye-hand behavior based on minute cinemanalysis. I had made a four-year study of the mental growth of a blind infant, a case of complete, bilateral anophthalmia. Dr. Frances Ilg and Glenna E. Bullis investigated individual and age differences in the normal patterning of visual behavior, as manifested in the developmental examinations, visual skill tests, and spontaneous adjustments to spatial situations in home, nursery and school. Two research optometrists, Dr. G. N. Getman and Dr. Vivienne Ilg, made objective determinations of visual functions by retinoscope, phoropter and other analytic procedures. The combined data clearly revealed significant trends in the ontogenesis of visual behavior. These trends were formulated for a score of maturity levels from birth to ten years, in terms of eye-hand coordination, postural orientation, fixation, projections, visual manipulation of space, and changes in the speed, direction and brightness of the retinal reflex. The findings were reported and interpreted in a volume entitled, *Vision: Its Development in Infant and Child* (1949). This outlines a concept of Developmental Optics.

It seems appropriate to make special mention of the subject of child vision because visual perception is one of the most fundamental problems for a science of psychology. Organic evolution and human culture both have placed a high priority on the capacity to perceive with eyes and brain. The development of vision in the child is complex because it took countless ages of evolution in the race to bring vision to its present advanced state. Moreover vision is so profoundly integrated with the total action system of the child, that it must become a major key for the clinical and systematic study of individual differences. The concept of development adds a useful dimension to all problems of visual care — diagnosis, supervision, prevention, training and re-education. The problems go beyond acuity and refraction. Developmental optics is concerned with the ontogenesis and organization of visual functions in their dynamic relation to the total action system.

An autobiography of necessity deals with what is past. But since developmental research constantly reckons with potentials, a concluding look toward the future is perhaps permissible. Developmental research, by its very nature leaves an impress on the researchers themselves. This has been the experience of our research staff. In their many years of reciprocal association they have become closely identified with numerous infants and children, whose careers they have been following through basic sectors of the life cycle. These children are now trending into the teens, and moved by a common impulse a small nuclear group of investigators have determined to utilize the amassed data and to project their studies into the period of early adolescence. As in the past one stage of investigation by a kind of inevitability has defined the next ensuing stage. In 1950 the Gesell Institute of Child Development was incorporated to continue a program of developmental research in close association with clinical and guidance services in New Haven, Connecticut.

With an achieved perspective on the first ten years of life, it is important to learn to what extent the mechanisms of early development continue into the years from ten to sixteen. What are the year by year transformations in maturity traits? And what are the developmental indices of individuality? Do such indices have a significance for constitutional medicine? These are primary questions on which we lack elementary knowledge to an amazing degree. They are important questions for child psychology and for a clinical science of child development. A clinical science of child development might eventually prove to be one cornerstone of a more comprehensive science of man. A science of man under the heightening pressures of the second half of this atomic century should help to define the mechanisms and principles which underlie child life and family life. This alone can enable man to act more consciously and more rationally as an agent in his own evolution.

CLARK L. HULL

MY first paternal ancestor of whom there is record in the United States was a semi-heretical Church of England clergyman who came to this country in 1635. The early generations of his descendants lived in Massachusetts and followed the sea, but later ones engaged in agriculture, first in Rhode Island, then in Connecticut, and later in New York. In religion the early generations were Quakers; one of my great-aunts was hanged on Boston Common because she practiced this faith. Later generations became Baptists; my grandfather was a very pious, austere deacon of that Church. My father, on the other hand, made no religious profession whatever.

I was born in a log house on a farm near Akron, New York, in 1884. My father was a tall, powerful man. He had a violent temper and when aroused became very profane. My mother, a Connecticut woman, was a quiet person, rather shy, and in her youth was given to extreme blushing which was very embarrassing to her. She was married at the age of fifteen. Father had little schooling because he was required to work when a boy, and my mother completed teaching him to read after their marriage.

My family migrated to Michigan when I was three or four years of age, and settled on a good but unimproved farm. My brother Wayne, who is sixteen months younger, and I accordingly grew up under pioneer conditions. We helped to clear the farm of trees, remove the stumps, plow the fields, and husk the corn, once we split a few hundred fence rails, and occasionally we cut wheat and oats with a cradle where the stumps were too close together for the reaper to operate.

I attended a one-room rural school in the tiny village of Sickels, then a place of twenty or thirty inhabitants. When farm work was heavy, in spring and autumn, our parents sometimes found it necessary to have my brother and me miss school, but we attended more of the nine months taught each year than most other boys did at that time and place. I found arithmetic easy, but grammar difficult. When I was sixteen an ambitious teacher named Della Kennett taught us algebra and physical geography. At seventeen I passed a teachers' examination and later taught in a one-room rural school for a year.

When I was eleven or twelve years of age, some traveling evangelists known as Christian Crusaders staged a violent revival at the local Methodist Church, the only denomination active there at the time, and I, among a dozen or so other boys and girls, was "converted" and joined the Church on probation. This experience aroused in me for the first time serious thought about religious matters, with the result that before the period of probation ended I had become very doubtful regarding the whole religious hypothesis. I finally announced my conclusions in open meeting and withdrew my affiliation.

The year of teaching, together with the religious crisis that preceded it, made me realize my profound ignorance and stimulated me powerfully to secure an education. The following year I attended high school at West Saginaw, in an adjoining county, where I lived in the home of the superintendent of schools, N. A. Richards, and did work around the place in exchange for my maintenance. Here I used a telephone for the first time, and learned something about urban life. Mr. Richards, a very religious man, lent me a number of books bearing on religion and gave me others, some of which I still have. Every morning the household knelt for family prayer, but I remained quietly sitting. When Mr. Richards spoke to me about the matter I formally refused to join in this ceremony, and gave my disbelief as the reason. For a time he seriously considered sending me home, an event which might have changed my entire life, but in the end his wife persuaded him to tolerate me. I left at the close of the school year but carried on a correspondence with him for some thirty years, until his death.

During the next two years I attended the academy of Alma College, graduating at the end of that time. I worked for my room and board in a small hotel. In high school I was older than the other students, but in the academy the students were of about my own age. I found languages extremely difficult, but mathematics of great interest. Indeed, the study of geometry proved to be the most important event of my intellectual life, it opened to me an entirely new world -- the fact that thought itself could generate and really prove new relationships from previously possessed elements. Later, in the writing of a prep school paper in English composition, I tried to use the geometrical method to deduce some negative propositions regarding theology. This ultimately led to the study of Spinoza's *Ethics*, while I admired his brilliance I could not accept some of his postulates and therefore I rejected nearly all of his theorems.

At the Alma Academy graduation I attended a special dinner where apparently some contaminated food gave about a score of us severe cases of typhoid fever. Several died, including "Old Buck" Ewing, my beloved geometry teacher. I myself was so ill I barely survived. The high fever gave me a permanent total amnesia which extended over the four-week period of highest temperature and left me in addition with a generalized bad memory for names which has continued to the present time.

I was too feeble to return to school that autumn but was able to teach a rural school the latter part of the year. The following year I returned to Alma College as a freshman, and this time worked for my board and room in a sanitarium. For two years I took a special course composed mostly of mathematics, physics, and chemistry, with emphasis on the last. This course was designed to lay the groundwork for the study of mining engineering at another institution. At the end of this preliminary training I secured the job of determining the manganese in iron ore, at the Oliver iron mines of Hibbing, Minnesota.

Two months after I went to Hibbing a small epidemic of poliomyelitis developed there and I, now an adult of twenty-four years, was a victim along with several children. This left me with one leg so badly paralyzed that I could not walk without crutches. Moreover, my general health was greatly enfeebled. A year was required to recover even partially from this shock, and this period was spent at my parents' home on the farm in Michigan.

This turn of events showed me that I must make new plans for a life occupation, and I employed the convalescent year and the two following ones in reaching a decision. One possibility was that I enter the ministry of the Unitarian Church, which at that time I considered essentially to be a form of free, godless religion. The preparation of ethical sermons of mainly philosophical content seemed attractive, but the contemplation of the probable necessity of attending an endless succession of ladies' teas and related functions led me to abandon the idea.

What I really wanted was an occupation in a field allied to philosophy in the sense of involving theory: one which was new enough to permit rapid growth so that a young man would not need to wait for his predecessors to die before his work could find recognition, and one which would provide an opportunity to design and work with automatic apparatus. Psychology seemed to satisfy this unique set of requirements. Accordingly I made a preliminary survey of the subject by studying the fourteen hundred pages of William James' *Principles of Psychology*. When I began this task my eyes were so weak that I could read very little, so my mother, who with her agricultural background had never before considered anything remotely like this, began reading to me. Later my eyes improved and I was able to read normally.

After a year of convalescence I had recovered enough to walk, first with only one crutch and later with a cane, by wearing a steel brace which I had designed and my brother had constructed at a local blacksmith's shop. I then secured the position of teaching the upper grades (seventh, eighth, ninth, and tenth) of my old home school, which had recently expanded into a two-room school. This work was deeply satisfying, and I believe that the teaching was the best I have ever done. I secured a second-hand compound microscope from Alma College, for about fifteen dollars, and set up a simple biological laboratory in the back of the schoolroom. During my two years there, my family drove me with a horse and buggy the one and one-half miles to and from this school nearly every school day; for this I have always felt very grateful.

At the end of this two-year period, though I had bad health, little money, and no prospects, Bertha Iutzi and I decided to marry. I had nearly all the money I had received from my teaching, and she had a little from her own teaching. We pooled our resources and entered the University of Michigan, I as a junior and she as a special student. I found the generally free atmosphere at Ann Arbor a gratifying contrast to the narrow provincialism of the small Presbyterian college I had previously attended. Indeed, it was like entering a new life.

The free election system operating there permitted me to concentrate largely on psychology during my two years of residence, much as would a graduate student. Looking forward to a future involving considerable scientific writing, I elected an excellent rhetoric course mainly concerned with exposition, and chose psychological subjects as my themes, much to the disgust of the young women theme readers who worshipped Robert Louis Stevenson. The outstanding course in psychology of that time, and of my life for that matter, was a year of experimental psychology with Professor W. B. Pillsbury giving the lectures and Professor J. F. Shepard in charge of the laboratory. They made a great combination, and each was incomparable in his own way. During my senior year I carried out a small experimental research project involving learning, under Shepard's direction.

Because of my interest in the psychology of reasoning I took a course in logic, under Sellers. In connection with this course I designed and constructed a logic machine mainly of concentric sheet-metal plates on which could be set up, one at a time, all the syllogism types and formal fallacies. When so set the machine would reveal to inspection and a little manipulation all the implications, both universal and particular, of each syllogism and fallacy.

At graduation my savings were gone so I sought a teaching position. The only opening available to me was a temporary position teaching a little psychology and various other things in a normal school at Richmond, Kentucky, at seventy-five dollars per month. This gave me a revealing view of the sturdy students from the mountains, the casual attitude of the students from the "blue grass" country, and the generally sterile nature of the faculty of that normal school. In spite of teaching twenty classes a week I found time to build a crude exposure apparatus, operated by hand, with which to do some preliminary experimental work on the evolution of concepts, those experimental results ultimately found a place in my doctoral dissertation.

During this year I tried to secure a graduate fellowship in psychology from Cornell and from Yale, but both institutions turned me down. Since in this connection I had asked Professor Pillsbury to write a recommendation for me, he knew of my desire to do graduate work. It happened that at about that time Professor Joseph Jastrow wrote to Pillsbury, asking him to recommend someone as a part-time teaching assistant in psychology at the University of Wisconsin. Although Pillsbury was severely ill at the time, he and his wife kindly attended to the matter, recommending me for the position. I received the appointment and grasped at the opportunity — this time at fifty dollars a month. This was one of the most fortunate events of my life, and I have always felt profoundly grateful to the Pillsburys for their extreme kindness in the matter.

I found Professor Jastrow a kindly person to serve under, but I learned little from the years of association with him. His mind could scintillate in a brilliant fashion but his approach to psychology was largely qualitative and literary. My teachers at Wisconsin who were of chief value were Professors Daniel Starch and V. A. C. Henmon.

Professor Jastrow had a remarkable linguistic fluency. He would sometimes lecture for five minutes at a time in perfectly good sentences, yet hardly say a thing. Naturally it was difficult to quiz on the basis of such lectures. When the students would complain about their inability to understand the lectures I used to reply with the true formula: "Professor Jastrow has genius of a kind but it is not of the pedagogical variety." Yet, curiously enough, he could give special lectures to popular audiences in various large cities which would sparkle with wit and completely hold his listeners, who would pay real money to hear him.

As an assistant my tasks were to take the roll in Jastrow's elementary psychology one semester each year, conduct oral quiz sections based largely on the lectures, and take charge of the laboratory instruction of an originally very small but gradually increasing class in experimental psychology. I also quizzed in much the same way during alternate semesters for a supposedly parallel course in elementary psychology given by a philosopher, Professor Frank Chapman Sharp. Paradoxically, this course by a philosopher had more content than Jastrow's course on the same subject. Sharp was meticulously specific and the quizzing task was much simpler. He was an excellent model for clarity of thought and statement.

Soon after I began my graduate work at the University of Wisconsin I started keeping a permanent notebook of original ideas concerning all sorts of psychological subjects as they came to me. This was begun mainly as a compensation against the bad memory which persisted from the typhoid fever. For example, when reading a new book I would enter in my notebook not what I had read, because that was permanently available, but the new ideas which the reading suggested to me, or occasionally the reasons why I did not agree with the author whose work I was reading. Sometimes on returning from a seminar I would write out my views on the subject discussed, in great detail and without inhibition. I also formed the habit of writing similar but briefer notes on the margins of all my books. Because of this habit I purchased the most of the books that I used appreciably, utilizing the university library relatively little. I now have twenty-seven volumes in this series of notebooks. They contain the growing plans for apparatus and empirical investigations of all sorts developed throughout my academic life, and the origin and evolution of my various theories.

Somewhat to my surprise I have found that these notebooks were not chiefly valuable as supports to my memory. While from time to time I have read over portions of their contents to recover things I have been uncertain about, their main value has been as stimuli to systematic thinking. I have frequently found that an idea would occur to me with apparent clarity and completeness, but that when I started to write it down in my notebook there was much more to it than I had at first realized, as often the new portion was more important than the original notion. Sometimes the new portion thus made explicit would indicate that the original "hunch" was quite absurd, or at least rather different logically from what it had at first appeared to be. I have frequently tried to induce promising graduate students in my seminars to keep systematic notebooks on original ideas, and to this end have sometimes purchased notebooks for presentation to them. Very little evidence has reached me that the practice was adopted by any of them.

The vacation before I began my regular work in the Wisconsin laboratory I spent at my old home in Michigan. Pursuing my plan to investigate the evolution of concepts by an adaptation of the Ebbinghaus methodology, I designed and constructed with the few hand tools there available an automatic memory machine which I used throughout most of my dissertation experiment. The drum was made from a tomato can fitted with wooden heads. The automatic stepwise movement of the drum was controlled by a long pendulum; the coarse-toothed escapement wheel controlled by the pendulum was filed from a discarded bucksaw blade. To substitute for a needed gear, a thread was reeled around a large, flanged wooden wheel and then around a spool pinned to the escapement shaft, and the shaft of the large wheel was turned by a heavy lead weight. At that time a person with a little initiative could construct a useful behavior laboratory in a wilderness, given a few simple tools and materials; this is true to a considerable extent even now for a wide range of important experiments. Men trained in laboratories where everything is provided, including a skillful mechanician, often are helpless when they go to serve a small college which usually has little laboratory equipment.

Professor Jastrow wished me to work on a three-dimensional perceptual project involving the matching of the postures of two identical white plaster casts of bullocks' heads to an exact measurable extent in all three dimensions when viewed from a distance of about ten feet. As Jastrow's assistant I designed and supervised the building of the rather complex and expensive apparatus by an expert mechanic. Considerable work was done on this project by various persons, but it never came to anything. At the same time, however, I continued to work on the research project concerning the evolution of concepts, the apparatus of which I had already constructed.

The general technique which I was to use developed fully during my first year. Professor Shepard had given me a small Chinese-English dictionary containing the common ideographs and radicals (common strokes running through families of characters) of that curious language. With practice I became fairly adept at drawing with a fountain pen the characters as they appear in print. In general the task of the subject was to learn by a prompting method the nonsense names given by me to twelve of these characters, each having a different radical. Then twelve new characters, each having the same radical as one of those previously memorized, would be put on the drum of the apparatus and learned, the response in each case being the same as to the previous character having that radical. As new sets of characters were learned the subjects gradually became able to respond to them at sight and, incidentally, to isolate the individual radicals so that if requested they could draw them with a pencil. Strictly speaking, the process involved should be termed "generalizing abstraction."

The technique employed was capable of many variations yielding a number of quantitative differences in economies of learning, which were my main objectives at the time. However, as I look back on it the chief finding of the study was of a different sort: the curve of the actual evolution of the concepts began to rise very slowly at first with positive acceleration, followed by a much longer period of negative acceleration.

The work on the dissertation extended through four full years. During the first two years of this period I was a half-time assistant, and during the second two years I was officially a full-time instructor even though I continued to do many of the assistant's tasks, such as taking roll in lectures, reading examination papers, and so on.

My next major experimental project was an investigation of the influence of tobacco smoking on mental and motor efficiency.[1] This investigation was

[1] The influence of tobacco smoking on mental and motor efficiency, *Psychol Monogr.*, 1924, 33, No. 150.

undertaken at the request of a local member of a committee composed mostly of academic men together with a wealthy breakfast-food manufacturer, all of whom were primarily interested in creating a public opinion opposed to tobacco smoking. It was assumed by them that smoking had a very bad effect. Their preliminary objective was to secure clear evidence of this so that their propaganda against tobacco would be convincing. Among their various efforts to this end they approached me concerning the possibility of making some precise experimental determinations of the effects of smoking on behavioral efficiencies.

Following the opinions and practice of Rivers and of Hollingworth, I concluded that this would depend primarily on whether I could devise a neutral control dose that the subjects would not spontaneously distinguish from the tobacco. I took my cue in this matter from tales which I had heard to the effect that people smoking in the dark ordinarily do not know when their tobacco has ceased to burn. Accordingly I purchased two identical pipes of conventional design but with rather large bowls. One pipe was used in actual tobacco smoking and remained normal in every way. The second pipe was used as a secret control device. After it had been smoked in enough for it to have a definite tobacco odor, there was installed in its bowl a special metal capsule containing an electrical heating element combined with an asbestos moisture-holding device. When supplied with a suitable amount of current this pipe gave a close sensory duplication of what was received in actual smoking, eighteen of the nineteen subjects did not detect the control device, though trial showed that people who had been told about it could detect the difference without difficulty. For this reason no slightest suggestion of the deception was given the subjects and elaborate care was taken to make all the experimental arrangements, such as blindfolding, seem perfectly natural so as not to arouse their suspicions.

At about this time Professor Starch was called to the Harvard School of Business Administration, which left his course in psychological tests and measurements open. This was offered to me and I accepted it gladly. I had taken the course as a pupil under Starch and found it of much interest, especially the mathematical manipulation of the test data. I changed the name of the course to "Aptitude Testing," and worked very hard trying to develop a scientific basis for vocational guidance. I looked forward hopefully to the day when aptitude tests would be much more efficient than they have come to be, expecting that the Thurstone factor approach would be more effective in improving tests than it has proved. At that time most works on tests were rather naive in the matter of validation and in their methodology of combining tests into batteries so as to yield a maximum of prediction in use. In an effort to improve this state of affairs, I gathered up the material I had assembled for the course and made it into a little book which I called *Apti-*

tude Testing (1928). The first company I submitted this to rejected it. It happened that Professor Lewis M. Terman previously had suggested its publication by the World Book Company, so I next submitted the manuscript to him and he accepted it at once. This was the beginning of a long and pleasant relationship with Professor Terman.

In the testing field at that time, if the work of assembling a battery was to be precisely checked for accuracy, the product-moments correlation computations needed to be performed very meticulously and laboriously, involving every individual score. It happens that I am very prone to make small errors in such computations, even when using an ordinary calculating machine. In order to reduce most of such computations to a quite mechanical system and thus avoid this type of error, I conceived the idea of building a machine which would do nearly all of the correlation work automatically. After I had constructed a partial working model with funds furnished by the university, it became clear that the final construction would be much more expensive than I had expected. I therefore appealed for substantial aid to the National Research Council through Robert M. Yerkes, then in charge of a major section of research, and received in all about five thousand dollars. With this money two complete machines were built — a preliminary model and a second, improved model, the latter is now on exhibit in my office at Yale.

This was possible only because I found a mechanician, named H. S. Kidder, who was a kind of genius. He could not read mechanical drawings, and I could not make them, so we got along very well by making marks free-hand on bits of paper at his workbench. I had an idea how the wheels should go around to do certain things, and so did he; we accordingly easily understood each other. Every day or two I would spend a few minutes in the shop to see how the new part was coming along, and would tell Kidder about the next small part to be made. The task as a whole took so long that some skeptical people apparently thought the machine would never work. They would smile a little when they inquired about its progress, as if it was a joke. This at length became a little nettling. However, in the course of time the machine was completed and it really worked exactly according to plan.

The survey leading to the publication of *Aptitude Testing* left me with a fairly pessimistic view as to the future of tests in this field, and I abandoned it permanently.

At about the time that I accepted Starch's course in tests and measurements, Professor Jastrow gave up an introductory course of lectures to premedical students. I had been conducting the laboratory part of this course for some time, so when invited I took over the lectures. Among the innovations I introduced into the course was the subject of suggestion, hypnotic and otherwise, which I believed to be active on a large scale in medical practice. I had never seen a person hypnotized, though I had entreated Professor Jastrow to demonstrate the technique to me. A medical student had given me a "hypnotic crystal" which he had secured by mail from England; but he could not hypnotize with it. Late one night a student suffering from a bad phobia came to my home pleading for hypnosis to "save his life." I brought out the "crystal" and tried it on him as the books described the hypnotic technique, and to my surprise the man went into a deep trance almost at once. This was the beginning of a long series of experiments in this field.

In its long history, hypnosis had been investigated mostly by persons without behavior experimental training. Moreover, until recently the subject has largely tended to attract experimenters with a peculiarly unscientific type of approach. As a means of correcting this state of affairs I instituted an experimental program which utilized fully the quantitative methodology customary in experimental psychology. In all, this work extended over a period of about ten years, along with other major projects such as aptitude testing, learning experiments, behavior theory, and so on. The earlier and better portion of the hypnosis program was carried out at the University of Wisconsin. There it was the custom to have the better undergraduates write a bachelor's thesis, and with those majoring in psychology this was automatically based on an experimental investigation. The hypnosis program offered many appropriate problems for such studies. I encouraged these bright young people to pursue their work seriously with a view to making a contribution to science. After they had been given a year of experimental psychology as preparation, it was an easy matter to teach them the hypnotic technique and many of them did very well. One factor which aided materially in securing the cooperation of the students was that I not only helped them considerably with the preparation of the manuscripts for publication, but in addition the thesis study was always published over the student's own name.

Twenty persons in all took part in this work, which yielded a total of thirty-two published papers. While the program was in progress I shifted my activities to Yale, where almost at once hypnosis investigations encountered opposition, mostly from the medical authorities, so that before long the experimental work had to be terminated. Indeed, in order to complete the experimental series which I had planned I found it necessary to seek assistance from some of my former pupils who were teaching in the Middle West where the superstitious fear of hypnosis was not nearly so great. Professor Everett F. Patten, of Miami University, gave notable help in completing these investigations. When the program had gotten well under way, while I was still at Wisconsin, Professor Richard M. Elliott, editor of the Century Psychology Series, approached me about writing a book on the subject. This book, *Hypnosis and Suggestibility*, was completed and published in 1933, four years after I had joined the Yale faculty. I was especially indebted to St. Clair A. Switzer, my research assistant at the time, for aid in its final preparation.

Despite its technical nature this book seems to have been read quite widely, not only by academic persons but by the general public as well. Occasionally throughout the years since its publication I have received letters about the subject from various parts of the world; these are often written in red or green or purple ink, and show other peculiar characteristics which almost always make it easy to identify them before they are opened. Usually they are concerned with neurotic symptoms suffered by the writer, who hopes to secure relief through hypnosis. Many such letters are very pathetic, but my commitments to pure, as contrasted with applied, science have prevented me from considering them.

Not very long after Professor Jastrow turned over to me the lectures in pre-medical psychology, he asked me to take the lectures in experimental psychology also, as he had lost interest in this field. As already stated, I had conducted the laboratory part of this course since the beginning of my graduate work. This was the one course above all others that I desired to give, because I felt then, and still feel, that it constitutes the foundation of a truly scientific psychology. For several years I had been gradually shifting the exercises in the laboratory from the almost purely sensory processes (in which I found them) toward the higher processes, such as free association, simple learning, retention, generalizing abstraction, and so on. As a means of facilitating the laboratory instructions, I had from the first prepared with care for each student's use mimeographed sheets telling how to conduct the experiment and how to work up the results statistically. This was followed by a series of questions designed to lead the student to think through his observations of the subjects' behavior in the light of his previous experimental observations and general knowledge.

Even at the time of my undergraduate work Professor John B. Watson's ideas about behavior were in the air. Professor Shepard, who as a graduate student had come into contact with Watson at the University of Chicago, mentioned him in a rather sympathetic way. Later Watson's two main books were published and they became a center around which the current psychological world tended to be oriented. Personally, while inclined to be sympathetic with Watson's views concerning the futility of introspection and the general virtues of objectivity, I felt very uncertain about many of his dogmatic claims. In this connection I recall the semi-fanatical ardor with which at that time some young people, including a few relatively ignorant undergraduates, would espouse the Watsonian cause with statements such as, "Behaviorism has made a greater contribution to science than has been produced by psychology in its entire previous history." This attitude on the part of some precipitated equally violent opposing claims.   The zeal of both sides took on a fanaticism more characteristic of religion than of science.

Not long after the behavioristic movement swept over the country, the equally zealous *Gestalt* movement came out of Germany.   I used to talk over these issues for hours with a bright young graduate student by the name of Joseph Gengerelli, who was working in the Wisconsin laboratory at the time.   I early made an attempt to secure a foreign fellowship to go to Germany and study with Kurt Koffka, but without success.   As an alternative I conceived the idea of bringing Koffka to the University of Wisconsin for a year.   This move, while very expensive, was successful. When Koffka finally arrived his personal charm captured everyone.   However, his expository approach was strikingly negative.   At least half of his time was spent in attacking Watson.   I listened to his lectures with great interest.   While I found myself in general agreement with his criticisms of behaviorism, I came to the conclusion not that the Gestalt view was sound but rather that Watson had not made out as clear a case for behaviorism as the facts warranted.   Instead of converting me to *Gestalttheorie*, the result was a belated conversion to a kind of neo-behaviorism — a behaviorism mainly concerned with the determination of the quantitative laws of behavior and their deductive systematization.

Perhaps in view of the stormy history of behaviorism and *Gestalttheorie* during the period now drawing to a close, I may here insert my personal conviction regarding the matter of attack and defense in science.   On some occasions these controversies have been so marked that they have approached a kind of warfare.   It has always seemed to me that the efforts involved were to a large extent wasted.   A view attributed to Edward L. Thorndike is to the effect that the time spent in replying to an attack could better be employed in doing a relevant experiment.   At least that is the policy which I have personally followed, especially where there were circumstances indicating considerable personal heat in the matter.   Moreover, I have generally been unwilling to divert the course of my investigations because of such attacks.   This has sometimes been falsely interpreted as evidence that no reply could be made.   I have an intense aversion to controversies, especially those involving personal elements.

An important factor involved in the development of my theoretical views was the fact that Watson had early seized on Pavlov's conditioned reflex work as furnishing valuable evidence for the new objective science.   In 1927–28 Anrep's translation of Pavlov's *Conditioned Reflexes* became available and I at once began an intensive study of it.   This work raised many more questions than it answered, and naturally it led to a great variety of experiments. Many of these were designed to determine whether the habitual behavior as revealed by ordinary trial-and-error experiments performed in this country was essentially the same as or different from what was revealed by the conditioned reflex. Preliminary examination showed that both sets of phenomena are probably produced by some of the same basic behavioral laws but that these laws are acting under different conditions. Later analysis has led to the conclusion that probably in simple trial-and-error learning there is a considerable complication created by extinction effects arising from the non-reinforcement of the erroneous portion of the responses, together with generalization effects of both positive habits and inhibition.

In 1929 I was called to the Institute of Psychology of Yale University as a research professor of psychology. The Institute shortly was incorporated in the Institute of Human Relations. I had no formal teaching duties, though I always did a certain amount of graduate instruction in order to keep in contact with the young. This usually consisted in the conduct of a two-hour seminar once each week. Sometimes the seminar was open to everyone and given without credit. On these occasions I tried to have no one in the class except those who really wished to secure what I had to give. Since under this arrangement I did not have the task of passing judgment on the work of the students, great freedom of discussion was secured. The subject matter taken up usually concerned some problem in systematic behavior theory which I was working on at the time.

As the result of the consideration of these behavioral problems over a number of years, probably influenced considerably by my early training in the physical sciences, I came to the definite conclusion around 1930 that psychology is a true natural science; that its primary laws are expressible quantitatively by means of a moderate number of ordinary equations; that all the complex behavior of single individuals will ultimately be derivable as secondary laws from (1) these primary laws together with (2) the conditions under which behavior occurs; and that all the behavior of groups as a whole, *i.e.*, strictly social behavior as such, may similarly be derived as quantitative laws from the same primary equations. With these and similar views as a background, the task of psychologists obviously is that of laying bare these laws as quickly and accurately as possible, particularly the primary laws. This belief was deepened by the influence of my seminar students, notably Kenneth W. Spence and Neal E. Miller. It has determined the most of my scientific activities ever since, and the longer I live the more convinced I am of its general soundness.

The Institute of Human Relations was a loose organization of behavioral scientists from various fields, mostly psychologists, sociologists, and cultural anthropologists, assembled at Yale by James R. Angell, Robert M. Hutchins, Milton C. Winternitz, and later by Mark A. May, for the purpose of making a unified, *i.e.*, integrated, contribution to the social (behavioral) sciences. One obvious method of attaining such an integration would be to have a scientific *Fuhrer* direct in detail to that end the work of all the individual scientists. But such a procedure conflicts with the democratic ideals prevalent in the United States of America. Moreover, such a dictatorial practice would not permit the institution to profit from the rich supply of original ideas possessed by the individual workers. The problem was resolved by the personnel becoming familiar with and convinced of the general soundness of the theoretical system which I was developing and teaching through the seminar.

The influence of these ideas was brought to bear on the Institute and related personnel quite definitely in 1936, when several of us, including Neal E. Miller, John Dollard, and O. H. Mowrer, ran an open seminar specifically concerned with the essential identities lying in conditioned reflexes and behavior laws generally on the one hand, and, on the other, in the phenomena considered by Freud and his psychoanalytic associates. I prepared the agenda and Mowrer prepared abstracts of the significant parts of the discussions. These were mimeographed and sent out widely after each meeting. Much interest was aroused, sometimes as many as seventy people attending. For the first time in the six-year history of the Institute of Human Relations its personnel were induced to assemble for a serious discussion of the integration of the social sciences. In addition, Miller spent vast amounts of time explaining the system to members individually.

As a result of these various activities the empirical research projects carried out by several members of the Institute came, in time, to stem in a general way from the system and to reflect its logical unity and integration.

An example of the growth of my theoretical approach may be seen in the origin and development of one aspect of it. This occurred during the summer of 1931 at Pennsylvania State College, where I taught a class in advanced learning theory. One day after class, William M. Lepley handed me a short memorandum scribbled on a scrap of paper. When I looked at it later I did not understand it. During the afternoon while driving I overtook Lepley and his wife out walking. I invited them to ride with me, and when up on the side of a mountain I took the occasion to inquire about the memorandum. It turned out to be the hypothesis that the remote excitatory tendencies of Ebbinghaus were essentially identical with the delayed or trace conditioned reflexes of Pavlov. While I had been working for some time with both these concepts, the identity had never before occurred to me and I was tremendously impressed. Later Lepley published a matured version of his idea.

At once I began to work out the complex logical implications of this hypothesis when applied to rote learning, especially in regard to the Pavlovian notion of the inhibition of delay. I read a preliminary version of my ideas on the subject in a symposium at the Pittsburgh meeting of the American Association for the Advancement of Science, in December of 1934. A revision of this, which presented a formal statement of definitions and postulates together with the formal deduction of eleven theorems by a method resembling that of geometry, was published in the *Psychological Review* in November of 1935.[2] Further work on the problem convinced me that the geometrical method was very clumsy for such deductions and I abandoned it (1938) for that of ordinary mathematics. This of course required the formulation of the postulates in such a way that they could be converted into equations.

Somewhat later, while attending a Paris Congress, I met Dr. J. H. Woodger of the Middlesex Hospital Medical School in London, and he convinced me of the value of using symbolic logic in the really difficult problem of precise definitions, a matter logically required in a theoretical system. The following winter he secured a subsidy, came to this country, and worked with me on the problem a good many weeks but was forced to return to London before anything publishable was written. Largely because of the delay of the mail in crossing the Atlantic at that time we were unable to complete what Woodger had begun, so that Dr. Frederick B. Fitch of the Philosophy Department at Yale finally wrote out the eighty-six definitions and formulated the eighteen postulates in symbolic logic.

I myself was able to deduce a few of the theorems mathematically but soon was forced to seek help from those having special training in this field. First, Robert T. Ross gave very valuable aid in formulating the postulates mathematically, then Marshall Hall, and later Donald T. Perkins, worked out the detailed mathematical proof of the many theorems and corollaries to which the system finally extended. Finally, Carl I. Hovland carried out a large number of behavior experiments to check the empirical validity of numerous theorems derived by the mathematicians and prepared an account of the relevant experimental literature.

The technical nature of the rote-learning monograph that developed from this work precluded any considerable number of the sales which normally pay for such publications. In order to reduce the costs which are very high in this particular type of publication, my secretary of many years past, Ruth Hays, typed up a special copy of 329 pages on a machine known as a Vari-typer, which possessed print-like letters as well as all the Greek and

---

[2] The conflicting psychologies of learning — a way out, 1935, 42, 491–516.

mathematical symbols. These pages were then photographed and reproduced by a photo-offset process, and this most complex monograph thus finally appeared in book form, signed by all six of us. At the very least it is believed to represent in a clear manner the form which the more scientific works on behavior theory of the future should take. The monograph was entitled, *Mathematico-Deductive Theory of Rote Learning* (1940).

During the years when the rote-learning monograph was in preparation, Eleanor Jack Gibson and Dr. Hovland were developing, quite independently, somewhat similar theories of rote learning which in my opinion had better sets of postulates than those used in our monograph. Mrs. Gibson has published her theory. While always favorably impressed by their work, I later became completely convinced of its general soundness by the striking similarity which I found between rote learning and the heterogeneous compound trial-and-error learning of rats.

The preparation and publication of the rote-learning monograph was a kind of dress rehearsal for the publication of the behavior system as a whole, which I had gradually been developing throughout my academic life. When I was still an instructor at Wisconsin, Professor Sharp had proposed that he and I collaborate in writing an introductory psychology, but I had declined because I felt that there were far too many basic questions upon which I had not yet made up my mind. However, by 1939 my views regarding many problems had sufficiently crystallized so that I was ready to put forward a draft of them. At first I had intended to write a fairly elementary work to be called a "primer" of behavior. As I look back now it seems unfortunate that I was not able to do this. However, as the system developed it became evident that when complete it would require at least three volumes: one volume stating the primary principles, with appropriate explanations and illustrations, a second volume stating the deduction from these principles of the more common forms of individual (nonsocial) behavior, and a third volume presenting a parallel set of deductions of the more elementary forms of social or group behavior.

In September of 1936 I had made a move in this direction in presenting a miniature statement of my maturing system, in my address as retiring president of the American Psychological Association at Hanover, New Hampshire. During that summer I had worked very hard preparing the copy for several hundred sets of mimeographed sheets in which I made an attempt to put the major elements of the system into a miniature logical structure *more geometrico*, complete with definitions, postulates, and thirteen theorems. These theorems included the formal derivation of simple trial-and-error learning (III, IV, and VI), of antedating (or anticipatory) reactions from stimulus traces, the presumptive behavioral basis of expectation (VII and VIII); and of the fractional anticipatory goal reaction (r_G) which as a stimulus (s_G) would tend to bring about purposive striving behavior, this in turn bringing about reinforced goals (X, XI, and XII). I was greatly aided in this extremely difficult task by Douglas G. Ellson, at that time my research assistant. This miniature logical statement was published in the *Psychological Review* of January, 1937.[3]

As the work progressed on the preparation of the manuscript of what became the *Principles of Behavior* (1943), many problems presented themselves about which I was uncertain. However, I realized that at best the book would be difficult reading. Accordingly where there were two views of about equal probability of proving ultimately to be true, I usually presented the simpler one without equivocation, and that only. All equations were relegated to terminal notes. For the same reason most controversial questions were ignored as such, and my own view was presented as simply and clearly as possible. Moreover, since the behaviorial implications of the postulates or principles, except for a few relatively simple illustrations, were to be presented at length in the two volumes which were to follow, most of these questions were also necessarily left until later. Some of the more important illustrations were: the probable multiplicative relation of habit strength (SH_R) and drive (D) to produce reaction potential ($_SE_R$), ($_SE_R = {_S}H_R \times D$); compound conditioned stimuli; the competition between responses with different delays in reinforcement; and the patterning of stimulus compounds. I felt that in the long run it was better for the advancement of science to state views clearly enough for any error to be easily detected and quickly removed than to seek defense in cloudy ambiguity which is difficult or impossible to disprove.

In this connection I must state that this volume really grew in my seminar and, in a larger sense, in the Institute of Human Relations. The names of Neal E. Miller and O. H. Mowrer are specifically attached in the book to certain principles contributed by them. Above all I am indebted to Kenneth W. Spence. As a student Spence was research assistant in the laboratory of Professor Yerkes, and worked with apes for some years. Even so, he was very close to me and we carried on an active technical correspondence after he left New Haven. He gave me detailed suggestions and criticisms regarding the text of *Principles of Behavior,* and after he became chairman of the psychology department at the University of Iowa he directed many able empirical studies which contributed materially to the later development of the system.

The volume which resulted was rather different from those commonly offered to psychologists. Naturally its readers displayed a certain amount of misunderstanding concerning the meaning of the system, especially when it was first published; some of this was rather bitter. On the other hand,

---

[3] Mind, mechanism, and adaptive behavior, 1937, 44, 1–16

there were a few fairly sympathetic reviews.   In general I have found the hostile examinations much more helpful in the continuing development of the system than the more friendly ones.   As time has passed, however, the comments have become more serious and understanding, and have been on a more objective and generally significant level.   Among the most heartening outcomes have been the letters I have received from graduate students not only in this country but in Britain, Norway, South Africa, and Japan, regarding research projects based on the system.   Two faculty men in Japan recently asked permission to translate the book.

As soon as the manuscript of *Principles of Behavior* was completed, I began writing the second volume of the series.   In a rather detailed way I had a fairly clear idea about how the more complicated phenomena of behavior were derived from the published postulates of the system; these phenomena included simple trial-and-error learning, various sorts of compound trial-and-error learning, the acquisition of skills, different types of discrimination learning, the reaction to objects in space, maze learning, the assembly of behavior segments, value and valuation, language or social pure-stimulus acts, reasoning, and so on.   In the course of four years or so I completed the preliminary draft of twelve chapters, or about six hundred manuscript pages. However, as time passed I became progressively more engrossed in the equational formulation of the several postulates and their quantitative implications in the fairly complicated forms of behavior as shown by experiment. This was in part caused by a new and radical development in the quantification of my symbolic constructs which occurred during the revision of the preliminary draft of these twelve chapters preparatory to publication.

Sometime previous to 1937, Professor E. C. Tolman had proposed the use of intervening variables in the field of behavior theory, and had devised a system of symbols to represent his proposed concepts.   In 1943, in my *Principles of Behavior*, I had followed the same practice but with a largely different set of concepts.   As a matter of fact, the use of precisely quantified intervening variables has so long been a matter of standardized practice in the physical sciences that it rarely causes comment.   By 1945 I had become much concerned about this type of quantification in behavior studies, especially the quantification of habit strength, of primary motivation or drive, and of reaction potential, together with a suitable unit in each case; and I became convinced of the necessity for making these quantifications before proceeding any further.   This turned out to be a very laborious process requiring several years of meticulous labor, the active cooperation of four other people besides myself, and ultimately extending to four technical articles in its publication.   In addition, Harry G. Yamaguchi in his Ph.D. thesis (1949) elaborated experimentally some of the details of the quantification of the hunger drive in rats, thus giving rise to three additional articles.

Basically the methodology of quantification used by us stemmed from a sagacious method of scaling devised by L. L. Thurstone around 1927, and applied by us to the reaction latencies of rats on a Skinner box lever. The unit employed was a kind of equalized dispersion (Thurstone's σ_k) of the reaction potentiality ($_S E_R$). Whether or not the method of quantification utilized and the units devised by us will prove to be generally useful remains to be seen. However, it seems almost certain that *some* quantification of important behavioral constructs must ultimately be necessary before the behavior sciences can develop very far.

A matter inherently connected with the intimate use of a set of primary principles in the quantitative deductive derivation of a theoretical scientific system is the realization of their inadequacies. One such lack which became apparent in 1948 was the presumptive fact of stimulus-intensity dynamism (V) — that the stimulus intensity involved in reaction evocation has an important bearing on the reaction potential of the resulting response. Because of a severe attack of coronary thrombosis which I suffered at about that time, with the consequent uncertainties of completing my projects, I did not take the time to set up an appropriate experiment to determine this law clearly and specifically as I should otherwise have done. Instead, I made the best approximation I was able by using some visual data published by James McKeen Cattell in 1886. This provisional arrangement yielded the value,

$$V = 1 - 10^{-.440 \log S},$$

where S is the intensity of the stimulus used by Cattell on his human subjects.

A second such inadequacy, closely related to stimulus-intensity dynamism, involves the quantitative law of the fall of the intensity of the stimulus trace following the onset and/or the termination of the stimulus, together with the generalization on this trace as a continuum in response evocation. Here again if time were available a special series of experiments should be set up in an effort to arrive at dependable quantitative equations in this field. As in the stimulus-intensity dynamism case above, I made the best immediate approximation I was able by using two latency studies from Spence's Iowa laboratory. Here a major goal was to secure primary empirical equations which imply that antedating reaction tendencies based on stimulus traces are definitely stronger than perseverating reaction tendencies, a matter well known empirically. Actually this trace-intensity problem had caused me great embarrassment in 1936, when I considered the matter of antedating reactions in my miniature system formulated at that time. It now looks as if it would have been impossible of solution then because of the lack of the principle of stimulus-intensity dynamism. The most we can do with these very complex phenomena at the present moment is to call attention to them by such provisional considerations as are available and trust the future to the on-coming youth.   It would be nice to know how these and similar scientific problems turn out.

Along with the additions to the postulates just described, a part of the postulate concerning behavioral oscillation ($_SO_R$) was dropped as being almost certainly erroneous.   In 1943 I had assumed that the oscillation of reaction potential had a normal or chance distribution and that the mean values throughout its range are always constant.   In the course of the attempt to quantify reaction potential, my collaborators and I found strong evidence that this distribution deviates perceptibly from the Gaussian form in being mildly leptokurtic, that its range is by no means constant, and that it probably has a range near zero at the absolute zero (Z) of reaction potential. The revised set of postulates was recently published without comment.[4]   I plan to present these principles, with a running explanation of their origin, as the introductory chapter of the second volume.

The protracted attempt to quantify some of the more important intervening variables involved in our behavior system, together with my frail health, has delayed the completion of the second volume of the system much beyond the time I had originally planned.   Had I known that this delay would occur I would not have left so many matters uncompleted in the *Principles*.   As a matter of fact, for many years I have felt that by far the most important portion of the system for civilization in general would be found in the third volume, which would concern the strictly social relationships among human subjects.   But as time passes I realize that I cannot possibly write this book, much as I desire to do so.

I believe that one of the greatest sources of international conflict and , human misery lies ultimately in our prevalent subjectivity.   It is bad enough to have religious considerations interfere with the evolution of science.   It is even more surprising and quite as unfortunate to have an international socio-economic system of politics do so.   Let us hope that with a sufficiently clear objectivity in our behavioral science these biases and their deplorable sequels will largely disappear.   Perhaps the most effective means to that great end will be the accurate and wholly convincing determination of the primary laws of human behavior, together with the scientifically true and unmistakable definitions of all critical terms involved.   These laws should take the form of quantitative equations readily yielding unambiguous deductions of major behavioral phenomena, both individual and social.   Present achievements are small, but the goal at least now seems fairly clear.

[4] *Psychol. Rev*, 1950, 57, 173–180.

WALTER S. HUNTER

I WAS born in Decatur, Illinois, on March 22, 1889, the second son of George Hunter and Ida Weakley Hunter. My father at that time was in the real estate business, but he (and my mother) had been reared on a farm in Shelby County, Illinois, and had only moved to Decatur some four years before I was born. My father had had a high school education, including a course in natural philosophy (physics) which gave him a lively interest in scientific problems for many years. Although he was a devout Presbyterian and maintained close connections with the church until his death in 1949, his attitude toward my own studies and even toward my boyhood reading on evolution was one of great tolerance. My more remote ancestors on both sides of the family seem to have been farmers, except that my paternal grandfather, Anderson Hunter, was connected with the carriage-making trade for a time in his youth in Ohio. My numerous uncles and aunts have all been farmers in the Middle West, but their children have frequently gone into the professions and trades with considerable success, one cousin, Hubert Hunter, having been editor of an El Paso newspaper. Originally, the Hunter stock came to the United States from Scotland via the north of Ireland, they arrived at an undetermined date in the eighteenth century and migrated from the east coast into the Ohio country about 1800.

Concerning the early years that I spent in Decatur there are but few things that I remember which may have been significant in my later intellectual life. I entered public school at the age of six, progressing at the usual rate from one grade to the next. By my tenth year I had become a great reader of stories of the Wild West, of natural history, and later of Stanley and Livingstone's adventures in Africa. It is interesting in retrospect that I attended the same elementary school with Lybrand Smith who was later to become a Captain in the Navy, Assistant Coordinator of Research and Development during the war, and a good friend of the Applied Psychology Panel, NDRC. Unfortunately I do not recall him as a boy although we had many friends in common.

163

In 1901, when I was in the sixth grade and just before I was 12 years old, life took an unexpected and sudden turn which landed me on a farm in Texas eight miles north of Fort Worth and four miles from a two-room school in Saginaw which was open some six months in the year. My mother had died after an extended illness, and my father, not wishing to rear two boys by himself in the city, moved to Texas whither his own father had gone some ten years earlier. From February of 1901 to April of 1905, I attended school in Saginaw during the term and worked in the fields in the summer. Indeed, until my graduation from the University of Texas in June, 1910, I did a man's job in harvest, threshing, and plowing in the summers. By 1904, at the age of 15, I was embarked on a highly stimulating series of activities. Darwin's *Origin of Species* and *Descent of Man* were purchased and read from cover to cover. In addition I had discovered a Chicago firm which sold paper-bound copies of the great classics of English and American literature. I seem to have bought at least fifteen of these which I read and partly memorized. During the year I also took a correspondence course in electrical engineering, organized an Athenian Literary Society in Saginaw with myself as president, and served as the local correspondent for the North Fort Worth paper. During the school year of 1904–5, I reached the end of what the Saginaw school could offer. My thought was to enroll as soon as possible in the Texas Agricultural and Mechanical College for the course in electrical engineering, but my teacher persuaded me that I should first obtain a liberal arts education. The suggestion was that I attend the preparatory school of Polytechnic College, Fort Worth, and then secure an Arts degree. Thanks to her recommendation, and to the quick reading of a required book on civics, I was able to qualify for admission to the senior class of the Preparatory Division. Although I did various odd jobs at the college from 1905 to 1908 in order to earn a part of my expenses, I can record, with a tolerant smile at the accuracy of grading, that my average at the end of the first year was 99.6, which secured me a scholarship in the college freshman class the following fall. I also joined one of the literary societies where I secured experience in parliamentary procedure, in oratory, in debating, and above all in getting along with people.

My interest in psychology was first aroused by my roommate, a former normal school student, who lent me a psychology text by Noah K. Davis, professor at the University of Virginia. From Davis I turned to William James' *Psychology, Briefer Course,* and then being seventeen and ready to be a college freshman the following year, I decided to become a psychologist. Dr. W. B. Rinker, professor of German and philosophy, advised me to lay a foundation for such a career by studying biology, chemistry, physics, mathematics, German, and French. It therefore came about that I spent the following two years in the study of some of these subjects, plus English and history, and then transferred to the University of Texas in order to begin a concentration in psychology. C. S. Yoakum, fresh from his doctoral work at Chicago (1908), was in charge of the subject which was at that time a division of philosophy. Due to the necessity of meeting new degree requirements within two years, it was impossible for me to enroll in chemistry or to increase my knowledge of physics. I did, however, study biology intensively, increase my mastery of German and French, and attend all of the psychology courses that were offered. In the 1909–10 academic session, I was an assistant to Dr. Yoakum at a salary of $15.00 per month. This sum was enough to cover my share ($5.00) of the rent of a large room shared with another student and to pay ($10.00) for simple but entirely adequate meals. My grades continued high, and at the close of my senior year, Angell offered me a scholarship for graduate work at Chicago.

Of my courses in Texas the most interesting one was on animal behavior using as a text Margaret Washburn's recent book *The Animal Mind* (1907). Yoakum had published a study of the behavior of squirrels based on work at Chicago under Watson, and he was in addition freshly informed and enthusiastic about the field. My own reading on the subject became fairly wide for an undergraduate student with the result that for the spring quarter laboratory work I asked for permission to repeat and extend J. E. Rouse's Harvard study of the maze behavior of pigeons (1906). Since there was no adequate space in the laboratory for such an experiment, I constructed an outdoor cage in the back yard at the rooming house and conducted the experiment each morning before breakfast. Fortunately the spring weather in Texas was favorable that year, and the work was completed without disturbance. Under H. A. Carr's guidance that fall, the results were put in final form and published.[1]

Immediately after graduation in June, 1910, I left Texas for Chicago in order to begin graduate work. W. B. Pillsbury of the University of Michigan offered the only course that summer that I now remember, the psychology of reasoning. My major concern was to get oriented and to determine in what subject I should minor. Had I followed my own inclination, the choice would have fallen on biology. However, it seemed necessary to take into account the fact that the only teaching positions for psychologists involved either a combination of psychology and philosophy or of psychology and education. I chose philosophy. In retrospect, and in view of the date at which the decision was made, it still seems to have been a wise one. I not only secured a broad understanding of a fundamental branch of human thinking and an insight into various theoretical problems in psychology, but in the early years of my teaching I derived great satisfaction from the conduct of courses in ethics, Kant, and the history of English philosophy.

[1] Some labyrinth habits of the domestic pigeon, *J. animal Behav.*, 1911, 1, 278–304.

Graduate work in psychology at Chicago in 1910–12 was on a very modest scale compared with its status in the years after 1920. The animal laboratory was housed in a small frame building which had been the department's headquarters when Watson was working on color vision in monkeys in the unfinished attic space. The departmental offices, library, and human experimental rooms were in a three-story brick apartment building. In spite of Dr. Angell's high position in the University administration, no adequate provision for psychology was ever made, although new buildings for other departments were provided. Perhaps this was due in part, as Vice-President J. H. Tufts told me in 1925, to the fact that the University could never decide whether psychology was a social or a biological science and hence could not determine where to place the building! Angell and Carr gave all of the graduate instruction in psychology in those years, work that was generously supplemented by offerings in other departments and by visiting professors in the summer term. No specific courses in learning, statistics, or in specialized experimental areas other than space perception were available. To Harvey Carr I believe I owe in large measure my high regard for careful experimental work and my low regard for loose thinking. To Angell I owe an equally important but more general debt, a broad interest in the field of psychology and an alertness to systematic issues. Both of these men were my good friends in post-doctorate years, aiding and giving me wise professional counsel on request.

In the fall of 1910 Carr suggested two problems to me as suitable for doctoral research: one the electrical changes in the retina, a subject on which recent experiments had been reported; and the other an analysis of the ability of animals to respond in the absence of a stimulus to which they had been trained. I chose the latter problem, later named the delayed reaction, because of my interest in the evolutionary development of such complex behavior as thinking, and probably because, with only an elementary knowledge of physics, I felt unsure of my ability to experiment on retinal potentials.

Two of Carr's students had already made exploratory studies of the delayed reaction using the rat, but the work had not been carried to a conclusion nor, so far as I learned, had any theoretical analysis been made by them. My own work began with the rat and indicated a lack of ability in this animal to respond correctly after a delay when gross bodily orientation was lost. Inasmuch as L. W. Cole had reported in 1907 that raccoons showed an ability which he interpreted as due to images, I decided to use raccoons in the delayed reaction. The result was a marked success in demonstrating a type of behavior not found in the rats. Later, dogs and young children were used as subjects. There were some rhesus monkeys left by Watson still in the laboratory; but they were wild and before I got around to working with them, there was no time left. This was, of course, unfortunate in the light of later experiments by others since the monkey is substantially superior to the raccoon in the delayed reaction. Research on this problem proceeded daily, without a missed day, from October 1910 until March 1912.

The monograph on the "Delayed reaction in animals and children"[2] received a very cordial reception from psychologists, as did the oral presentation of the findings to a meeting of Mid-West psychologists held in Chicago in the spring of 1912. Although the terminology used in the monograph would be considerably changed in writing today, the essential method is still current in experimental studies and the theoretical analysis of the problem has not been rejected by the various investigators who have published on the problem from 1913 to 1950. The 1937 revision of the Stanford-Binet uses a delayed reaction test for two-year-olds based on the method which I employed in 1917[3] with my daughter, Thayer, 13-16 months of age.

In addition to the delayed reaction research, I published a brief paper reporting evidence that rats could learn by being put through a response and I formulated, directed and prepared for publication a study by two graduate students which repeated and adequately controlled one of L. W. Cole's raccoon experiments which had been interpreted by him as demonstrating the existence of images in animals.[4] The results secured indicated that the assumption of images was entirely unwarranted in accounting for the behavior.

I accepted an instructorship at Texas in 1912. Although my salary began at $1,200 and never in four years exceeded $2,000, and although initially I had some debts, including the cost of my trip back to Texas, prices were low by 1920 or 1950 standards. I not only managed to survive, I married Katharine Pratt of Cleveland in January, 1913, bought furniture for a five-room apartment, attended the APA meeting in New Haven (1913), and became the father of a daughter in September 1914. My four years at Texas were happy and productive, marred only by the death of my wife in April of 1915.

My research got under way in January, 1913, immediately after my return from receiving the doctorate at Chicago, with studies on the after-effect of visual motion and on the auditory sensitivity of the rat. The work on visual motion seems to me to be among the best of my publications,[5] and I was gratified later to have it cited in Pillsbury's textbook (1916). I am still of the opinion that the account of the retinal factor of "streaming" in relation to visual after-movement stresses the essential retinal process involved and that fading after-images are not notably involved. The auditory studies utilized a T-shaped apparatus which became the prototype for the later

[2] *Behav. Monogr*, 1913, 2, No. 1.
[3] The delayed reaction in a child, *Psychol. Rev*, 1917, 24, 74–87.
[4] F. M. Gregg and C A McPheeters, Behavior of raccoons to a temporal series of stimuli, *J animal Behav*, 1913, 3, 241–259.
[5] The after-effect of visual motion, *Psychol. Rev.*, 1914, 21, 245–277, Retinal factors in visual after-movement, *Psychol. Rev.*, 1915, 22, 479–489.

widely used T-boxes and T-unit mazes. The results indicated that rats could discriminate readily between noise and tone, but that they showed no capacity for response to tones of the frequency used, below 4000 d.v. These results were again confirmed in a paper I published from Clark University in 1927. Although later investigators, working after 1930 and with improved methods of tone production, have demonstrated tonal sensitivity in the rat, they have found extremely poor sensitivity to the lower frequencies which I used.

In addition to my own studies, I planned and directed other work by my students. Alda Grace Barber completed a master's thesis on the localization of sound by the white rat[6] which was extensively quoted in the years to follow and which served as a stimulus for investigations in Germany. J. U. Yarbrough, now of Southern Methodist University, published a master's thesis on the delayed reaction in cats using the same type of apparatus that I had used at Chicago, but using both sound and light as stimuli. Binnie D. Pearce, J. U. Yarbrough, and I published two articles in the 1917 *Journal of Animal Behavior* on habit interference, using both visually and auditorily controlled habits. These were pioneer studies, using habits whose exciting stimuli were known, and giving quantitative data on habit strength and interference. When my infant daughter was between 13 and 16 months of age, I tested her on the delayed reaction by hiding a toy, or another small desired object, in one of three boxes placed directly in front of her. This experiment indicated that a child of this age could delay successfully for at least 15 seconds even though gross body orientation had been changed. Although this study was published in the *Psychological Review* for 1917, it was either overlooked or forgotten by psychologists who, writing from 10 to 12 years later, rediscovered the method and named it the direct method of studying the delayed reaction.[7] All in all, the four years at Texas resulted in the publication of ten experimental papers by myself and three students, plus four theoretical notes, and some miscellaneous reviews.

In 1914 as a result of a suggestion from Angell, R. M. Yerkes, Editor of the *Journal of Animal Behavior*, invited me to become a member of the editorial board of the Journal. I served in this capacity through 1917 when the Journal ceased publication to appear later (with *Psychobiology*) as the *Journal of Comparative Psychology*. In 1916 Howard C. Warren transmitted an invitation from S. I. Franz asking me to assume editorial responsibility for the annual comparative psychology number of the *Psychological Bulletin*. This appointment, which I accepted, was not honorary, but involved selecting the authors of the general and special reviews, approving the manuscripts,

[6] *J animal Behav*, 1915, 5, 292–311
[7] The delayed reaction tested by the direct method a correction, *Psychol Bull*, 1929, 26, 546–548.

and transmitting them to the editor. These two appointments, coming when I was from 25 to 27 years of age and bringing me into personal contact with great men in psychology, significantly stimulated my scientific and professional activities.

I resigned as adjunct professor of pyschology at Texas in the summer of 1916 in order to accept the professorship of psychology at the University of Kansas just vacated by R. M. Ogden. At 27 years of age, I was referred to as "the beardless professor" (I had a mustache), and Angell wrote that I might be getting promoted too fast for my age, although he himself had recommended me for the Kansas position. My salary was the beginning one for full professors, $2,500.

Kansas had an excellent laboratory in a new brick building which provided ample space for teaching and research. I promptly sequestered two rooms for animal work and began a series of experimental studies. F. C. Dockeray was a continuing staff member and D. G. Paterson, who had recently received his master's degree with Rudolph Pintner at Ohio, was the new instructor. One of the first questions that Paterson asked me was "What is the reliability of the maze?" This question, which I did not at first understand and which I could not answer, was the initial stimulus for work which Paterson began in 1917 and which Carr and Angell at Chicago accepted as a suitable problem for a doctor's thesis. Paterson was to carry out the experimental work at Kansas but was to be a candidate for the doctor's degree at Chicago. The entry of America into the War stopped the work after it had barely begun, and Paterson later went on to fame as a psychologist without ever receiving his doctorate. However, when I returned to Kansas after the War, Oakland Maupin (later Mrs. W. T. Heron), W. T. Heron, and I conducted a series of experiments on the reliability of the maze and the problem box, the results of which had extensive repercussions among psychologists. The first of these studies appeared in volume one of the *Comparative Psychology Monographs* for 1922 and the final study under my direction appeared from the Clark University laboratory in the *Journal of Comparative Psychology* for 1936, under the authorship of Sidney H. Newman. No one of the numerous students of reliability has succeeded in devising for rats a method of maze training or a maze pattern which gives results of a satisfactory reliability without using the Brown-Spearman formula for predicting reliability of a whole test. And this formula is not applicable to learning data as Newman clearly demonstrated. The wide scatter about the mean performance in learning experiments with rats poses a serious problem in the control of experimental conditions, a problem, however, which is still neglected in favor of an effort to secure some sort of data on the relationship between specified variables, the hope being that by pooling enough unreliable data something having statistical significance may emerge.

Paterson made another contribution, aided and abetted by me, which was not only significant in animal psychology, but which reveals the status of methodology in 1917. He published in the *Psychological Bulletin* of that year a critical review of the Johns Hopkins maze studies by Ullrich, Bassett, and Hubbert indicating that the authors had made no effort to determine the statistical reliability of the differences between the found averages and that, when such calculations were made, most of the differences were unreliable.

I spent nine years as a professor at the University of Kansas with sixteen months' leave for military service in connection with the Army testing program. These were pleasant and profitable years. In August of 1917 I married my former graduate student, Alda Grace Barber, whose paper on the localization of sound in the white rat has been referred to above, and in March of 1920 our daughter, Helen Barbara, was born. During the total period, I published eight experimental papers, six theoretical ones, an elementary textbook, directed the research represented in five experimental papers, edited the annual comparative psychology number of the *Psychological Bulletin*, finished for J. B. Watson the editing of the final volume of the *Behavior Monographs* (1922), and became the first editor of the *Comparative Psychology Monographs* (1922–27). Although my first published paper in 1911 had been on animal behavior, and although through the years since then most of my experimental work has been with animals, I was particularly interested in my years at Texas and Kansas in becoming recognized as a general experimental psychologist rather than as a specialist even in so broad a field as animal behavior.

Certain of my Kansas publications deserve special comment either because they represented stages in the development of my scholarly interests or because they had a greater or lesser influence on the research of others. My paper on the laws of association[8] in which I argued that the second term of an associative sequence need not be imaginal but could be sensory or perceptual was significant for me in two ways: (1) It brought me my first and only correspondence with E. B. Titchener, in which we argued the matter back and forth without reaching an agreement since he wished to exclude all "meaning" and I could not agree. And[1] (2) it was the last paper that I wrote which could be classified as subjective psychology. Although Warren discussed the paper in his *History of Association Psychology* (1921), it has had, I believe, no further influence, perhaps because of a loss of interest in the general problem.

Two papers that appeared in 1920 had a greater significance. One was on the temporal maze,[9] which I had first reported at the APA in 1918, follow-

---

[8] A reformulation of the law of association, *Psychol Rev*, 1917, 24, 188–196.

[9] The temporal maze and kinaesthetic sensory processes in the white rat, *Psychobiol*, 1920, 2, 1–17.

ing some preliminary observations that I had made as early as 1916 in Texas. The temporal maze problem, and its sub-form, the double alternation problem, raised for the first time the question of an animal's ability to react to a temporal sequence of cues where spatial cues were absent or controlled. The surprising result was obtained that rats had essentially no ability to learn a complicated temporal sequence[10] and hence could not depend on a merely temporal sequence of kinaesthetic stimuli in learning the ordinary maze. The theoretical analysis of double alternation behavior indicated that some internal supplement (perhaps a symbolic process) needed to be added to the cues which were in double alternation if success was to be attained. In later years at Clark my students and I carried out extensive experiments on double alternation with rats, raccoons, monkeys and children with the result that double alternation and the temporal maze became well established and recognized methods in the study of animal behavior. My last contribution on the problem was with Susan Carson Bartlett, using young children as subjects.[11] There are theoretical grounds for placing the double alternation problem in the same category as the delayed reaction as a method for demonstrating the presence of symbolic processes, although the logic is not quite so rigorous.

A second paper from 1920 which still seems significant dealt with the modification of instinct from the standpoint of social psychology.[12] In addition to the modifications which were generally recognized on the stimulus and response sides of such behavior, evidence was cited, particularly from Whitman's studies of pigeons, which indicated that habits formed prior to the appearance of unlearned behavior could modify the behavior when it did appear. Such a view is fundamental, of course, in the social control of late-appearing drives. The discussion further pointed out that an important and heretofore neglected phase of instinct modification lay in the changes which the individual and society made in the biological ends to be attained.

In 1920, also, I reported to the APA a study of the relation of degree of Indian blood to score on the Otis Intelligence Test.[13] I was led into the problem partly by my Army experience and partly by my acquaintance with George Ferguson whose doctoral thesis at Columbia had been on Negro intelligence and who had conducted similar studies on whites and Negroes at Camp Lee, where I was associated with him. The conclusions that I drew from the data were conservative, pointing out only that when the data were treated statistically in various ways there was a definite positive relationship between increasing amount of "white blood" and intelligence score.

[10] For some positive evidence, see W. S Hunter and J Nagge, *J genet Psychol*, 1931, 39, 303–319.
[11] *J exp Psychol*, 1948, 38, 558–567.
[12] *Psychol Rev*, 1920, 27, 247–269.
[13] The relation of degree of Indian blood to score on the Otis intelligence test, *Psychol Bull*, 1921, 19, 91–92; and *J. comp Psychol.*, 1922, 2, 257–277.

My *General Psychology* (1919) was begun in 1916. As published, it was at least 30 per cent smaller than the original manuscript. This reduction was directed by the publishers because the postwar increase in costs would have made it impossible to compete, so they said, with the books by Pillsbury and Angell which still sold for about $1.10. Even so, there was some question that the volume contained too much factual material for an elementary text. Although its financial returns were never as large as those of texts published after World War II, it went through six printings prior to 1923 and was translated into Chinese in 1926. The primary influence which led me to incorporate the various fields of psychology into the book was my successful use of Angell's *Chapters from Modern Psychology* as a supplementary text in beginning courses. Since 1919, few elementary texts have appeared which have not covered the entire field of psychology, although they may not begin as my volume did with separate chapters on the various fields.

By 1922 I had come to the belief that behaviorism represented essentially the only adequate scientific point of view in psychology and that some of Watson's pronouncements represented less the necessary details of behaviorism than his own prodigious effort to fill in the experimental gaps with hypotheses pending further work. Such a shift in my own point of view was signaled by a brief note[14] and then followed up in 1924 and 1925 by four articles on the nature of consciousness, the symbolic process, the subject's report, and general anthroponomy and its systematic problems, published in the *Psychological Review* and the *American Journal of Psychology*. Some amusement has been aroused by the term anthroponomy which I substituted for psychology both here and in my later (1928) *Human Behavior*. The term psychology is vastly misunderstood by the general public even today, and within the Services in both World Wars it has been expedient to use a variety of other terms to designate psychological facilities just to avoid prejudice and misunderstanding. Where, as in the case of the Applied Psychology Panel, NDRC, the term psychology has been used, constant vigilance and good humor have been necessary to safeguard the large quantity of sound work in progress. I was never under any delusion that the designation of the science would be changed to anthroponomy, but the path of our science would have been much smoother in its public relations had some nonpsychic term designated it. My general views on the nature of psychology are still well represented by three papers published in 1925, 1926, and 1932.[15]

In connection with my teaching, I organized a course on learning, making use of both human and animal behavior. At that time (1918) the only important books available were Thorndike's educational psychology (1913)

---

[14] An open letter to the anti-behaviorists, *J Phil*, 1922, 19, 307–308.
[15] General anthroponomy and its systematic problems, *Amer J Psychol*, 1925, 36, 286–302, Psychology and anthroponomy, *J genet Psychol*, 1926, 33, 322–346, The psychological study of behavior, *Psychol Rev*, 1932, 39, 1–24.

and J. W. Baird's translation of Meumann (1913), and there were few courses in the universities outside of schools of education. The field as I organized it found fair expression in the chapter on learning which was published in Murchison's *Foundations of Experimental Psychology* (1929) and which was not without influence, I think, in the subject's development. My shift to behaviorism led me to develop a senior seminar on the principles of psychology in which a thorough critical canvass was made of the source materials on structuralism, functionalism, and behaviorism. This course had a particularly enthusiastic reception at the University of Chicago in the summer of 1922, and I have reason to feel that, in the various universities where I have presented it and in my own department to the present time, the analyses presented have been helpful to the students by sharpening their critical wits as well as by giving them some historical perspective on points of view in psychology.

Before terminating my account of the years at Kansas, something should be said about my work in World War I and about the decisions that I had to make concerning the future of my career. Let us consider the war first. Although as an experimental psychologist I could not see my way clear in the spring of 1917 to promise to help in the preliminary phases of the Army intelligence testing program, August of that year found me under great pressure from W. V. Bingham to accept a commission as a first lieutenant because of the failure of one psychologist to pass his physical examinations. I first served under C. S. Yoakum at Camp Lee, and then became chief psychological examiner successively at Camps Lee, Sheridan, and Devens. My records show that I was involved in only two technical contributions to the testing program. The one of lesser importance was to secure at Devens, and to encourage the Washington office to order secured elsewhere, data on the national origins of the troops tested. On the basis of large amounts of such data gathered throughout the Army, there was shown to be a clear superiority in scores of the men from Northern Europe as opposed to those for men from Southern Europe. (No consideration was given to the selective factors which might be operating in immigration.) These Army findings were later used by C. C. Brigham in defense of Nordic superiority and other wild racial theories in his *Study of American Intelligence* (1922), and they are said to have affected the postwar United States selection policies on immigrants. The more important contribution from the Camps under my direction came from Camp Lee. It should be recalled that psychological examination was at first only authorized in four camps. If it failed there to win the support of military men, testing was to be discontinued. By late November examining in the four camps was completed, and psychologists awaited word from Washington on the future of the program. It was at this time that E. S. Jones, now of the University of Buffalo, came to me and proposed that our group prepare a set of charts depicting the test status of all organizations in the 80th Division. This he and the Staff did, using bar diagrams for the superior and inferior men in each unit, diagrams that are reproduced in practically all reports of testing in World War I. The material was sent to Washington and laid before the Surgeon General and the Training Committee of the General Staff in support of the recommendation for the continuance of the work. I am told that the charts of the Camp Lee report were largely influential in the favorable decision that was reached in December. The contribution by E. S. Jones came at a critical time for the future of military psychology in this country.

The decisions concerning my future career to which I referred above were as follows: In the fall of 1917, President Lowell of Harvard invited me to lecture the following year on animal psychology inasmuch as R. M. Yerkes had resigned. The decision was a difficult one, but I had already committed myself to the Army and therefore declined the invitation with some regret. In 1919 I received offers of professorships from the State University of Iowa and Ohio State University. After wrestling with the attractions of significant salary increases, I declined in favor of Kansas. The offer from G. F. Arps at Ohio, in the light of later history, was particularly amusing. Arps, whom I had known in the Army, wanted me to teach educational psychology, using as an argument that there was no future to the study of animal behavior now that the War had shown what applied psychology could do. The fact is, of course, that the most prolific period in animal behavior studies was just getting under way. In addition to the decisions required by these offers, the early postwar years required me to decide whether or not I would continue as a research man or become involved in university administration. I was urged to be dean of the summer session and then to be dean of the graduate school. Both pressures I resisted successfully, but again at a financial sacrifice.

In the spring of 1925 when I received an invitation to become the first G. Stanley Hall Professor of Genetic Psychology at Clark University, I was at first very loath to accept because of the recent extremely adverse report on Clark by an investigating committee of the American Association of University Professors. However, after friendly counsel from Angell, Warren, Boring, and Watson and after a visit to Clark, I accepted the appointment and held it for eleven years. I was particularly pleased with the prospect of teaching only graduate students and of having the balance of my time for research and scholarly work. The location in New England was an additional asset. My graduate students enabled me to extend my research through them to an array of problems in animal behavior and learning which on my own personal resources of time could not have been undertaken. They published a total of twenty-two experimental papers in the eleven years on such topics as: olfactory sensitivity in the rat, sensory control of the maze, form discrimination in the rat, similarity and emotion in retroactive inhibition, effects of inverted vision on spatial behavior, vision in raccoons and monkeys, double alternation in monkeys and children, reliability of animal and human mazes, conditioning and voluntary control of the pupillary reflex, stimulation deafness, and verbal *vs.* conditioned reflex methods of threshold determination. Special mention should be made of Luberta Harden, Norman Munn, Wayne Dennis, Robert Leeper, Clarence Hudgins, G. de Montpellier (now of Louvain), and E. H. Kemp. Two highly competent young men, P. H. Ewert (inverted vision) and John Liggett (olfactory sensitivity) died shortly after receiving their doctorates and before their early promise could be realized. Of other students who passed through the Clark department and on whose professional preparation I may have had some influence, mention should be made particularly of Frank Geldard, Clarence Graham, and Lorrin Riggs.

My own major publications during the Clark period included 21 experimental papers, five theoretical studies, four chapters for books of the Clark Press, and the textbook *Human Behavior.* The theoretical papers were largely concerned with the development of my general views on behaviorism and psychology in general, including a discussion of the basic phenomena in learning[16] which I still find adequate on the specific issue. Of the others, the one which attracted the most attention and which brought me numerous letters dealt with Lashley's theory of equipotentiality. Although I had followed Lashley's work from its beginning, I had never been converted to his interpretation of neural functioning. The immediate stimulus for writing the critical paper came from a talk which E. G. Boring gave to the Clark Colloquium in early 1930 and in which he assumed the soundness of Lashley's position. I immediately re-read everything that Lashley had written, and published my own interpretation of the problem.[17] Although the experimental evidence which has come in on the topic since that day has now favored and now opposed the view that the rat's brain is equipotential, the issue has never been clearly and definitely settled with reference to maze learning. I am inclined to think that it cannot be settled by experiments with the rat until someone can demonstrate some such restricted cortical localization for proprioception as exists for vision. The general conclusions to which I came and the total setting of the problem were given in my vice-presidential address to Sec. I, AAAS in 1933.[18]

Of my other experimental papers I attach most importance to those dealing

[16] Basic phenomena in learning, *J gen Psychol*, 1933, 8, 299–317.
[17] A consideration of Lashley's theory of equipotentiality of cerebral action, *J gen Psychol*, 1930, 3, 455–468.
[18] The stimulus-neural control of behavior during and after learning, *Science*, 1934, 79, 145–151.

with the sensory control of the maze habit, with double alternation responses (including the tri-dimensional maze), and with muscle potentials in learning. I tried to demonstrate that inactivity due to cold retarded forgetting in the cockroach; but possibly because the control animals rested in the dark in place of being active during the interpolated period, no positive effects were secured. The lead, however, was a good one and has since been followed up in various other laboratories. Using an adaptation of Warner's (1932) apparatus, I also initiated a series of conditioning studies. This work was primarily concerned with such problems as the relation of conditioning to extinction, and to maze learning, gradients and curves of conditioning, and a comparison of conditioning with regular reinforcement and conditioning where the animal could avoid the shock reinforcement. The latter condition was definitely the more favorable. Some of these studies published in England and Poland[19] have not always come to the attention of American psychologists even though abstracted in the *Psychological Abstracts*.

In the summer of 1925, H. C. Warren invited me to become editor of the *Psychological Index*. I was already involved, through my chairmanship of an APA committee, in the planning for the *Psychological Abstracts* whose editorship I had been asked to assume if the journal were established. Since my schedule at Clark was to be light, and since work on the *Index* promised to fit in well with work on the proposed *Abstracts*, I agreed to assume the editorship. Heretofore I had been only an associate editor of the *Psychological Bulletin* (1916–24) and as such not closely associated with the Board of the Psychological Review Publications. From now until my resignation from the *Abstracts* at the close of 1946, I was to profit greatly by friendly professional association with Warren (until his death in 1934) and the other editors. The Board meetings had an intimacy and a value which are no longer possible under the enlarged program of the APA publications. (No editor ever received a stipend, a fact which amazed my European colleagues. Indeed, during the ten years that I edited the *Index* my allowance for editorial expenses, including allowances for foreign editors, rarely exceeded $50 per year.) Beginning with 1927, I enlisted the cooperation of V. M. Bekterev of Leningrad, USSR, both on the *Index* and the *Abstracts*. Thus began the first formal effort in this country to secure access to the Russian psychological literature, an effort which to this day continues with inadequate success in spite of varied efforts to improve the situation. The *Psychological Index* was discontinued with volume 34 in 1936 because of the undesirability of maintaining two bibliographical journals. My preface to that last volume contains a brief historical summary of the journal's history.

[19] Conditioning and extinction in the rat, *Brit. J. Psychol.*, 1935, 26, 135–148, Gradients in the establishment of conditioned locomotor responses to serial stimulation in the rat, *Kwartalnik Psychol.*, 1936, 8, 5–12.

The *Psychological Abstracts* has been in existence longer than the professional lifetimes of most APA members and probably few know or remember how it was started. S. I. Franz, editor, and S. W. Fernberger, associate editor, began publishing abstracts in the *Psychological Bulletin* in 1921 and continued this practice through 1926. In December, 1921, the Psychological Review Company proposed to the APA that the Association aid the Company in starting an abstract journal. A period of five years then elapsed during which a committee of the Association and one from the National Research Council struggled with the problem. The two committees were able in 1926 to secure a ten-year subsidy of $75,000 from the Laura Spelman Rockefeller Memorial, in no small degree as a result of the interest taken in the proposal by Beardsley Ruml of the Memorial.

In the fall of 1926 I went to Europe to visit psychologists and to select foreign editors of the *Abstracts,* leaving the editorial office and the final arrangements for volume one, 1927, in charge of R. R. Willoughby, who had become assistant editor and who was to render valuable assistance to the journal through 1939. In Europe I visited the psychologists in Manchester, Cambridge, London, Paris, Louvain, Hamburg, Berlin, Leipzig, Geneva, and Bologna, seeking advice and gathering impressions of my foreign colleagues, some of whom were already cooperating on the *Index.* I was also able to renew my contacts in Berlin with Kohler, who had spent the previous year at Clark, and to become acquainted with Wertheimer and Lewin.

The foreign psychologists who joined the editorial board of the *Abstracts* gave freely of their time without remuneration and contributed greatly to the success of the journal. They also gave me a significant insight into psychology in their various countries as well as a deeply appreciated hospitality at the time of this visit and again in 1931 when I spent eight months in Europe on sabbatical leave. On this latter trip my friendship with Ranschburg and his wife in Budapest was particularly heartening, and my later sorrow at their tragic deaths during the 1945 siege of Budapest was correspondingly depressing. During the 1931 trip, I read a paper in French before the Société de Psychologie at the Sorbonne on geotropisms in the rat, and presented a discussion of the sensory-neural control of behavior at the Cambridge meeting of the British Psychological Association. C. S. Myers who presided at this latter meeting remarked that, while William James wrote like a novelist and his brother Henry like a psychologist, I spoke like a physiologist and it was the physiologist (R. S. Creed) on the program who spoke like a psychologist. During my stay in Paris, I wrote the paper on the "Psychological study of behavior" which was delivered that fall (1931) in Toronto as the presidential address before the APA. I have seen no reason to change my views on the nature of psychology as expressed in that account.

As has perhaps been clear from much that has preceded in this autobiography, my intellectual history has been much influenced by my colleagues here and abroad as well as by the intellectual give-and-take between myself and my graduate students.   With my foreign colleagues I have long maintained contact, particularly with Bartlett, Michotte and Piéron.   At Clark I was much influenced by J. P. Nafe, Hudson Hoagland, and Wolfgang Kohler, as well as by W. J. Crozier of Harvard.   I was a visiting lecturer at the latter university from 1927 to 1929, commuting from Worcester.   The course on animal behavior with its introduction to behaviorism was apparently a novel experience for the Harvard students and one not without influence on their thinking and research.   It is interesting to look back at the old class roll and find the following names among others. D. W. Chapman, W. A. Hunt, F. S. Keller, B. F. Skinner, and R. W. White, all now prominent psychologists.

As may be gathered, I was happy at Clark University.   My research was proceeding at a satisfactory rate, and my professional contacts were most stimulating.   I resigned as editor of the *Comparative Psychology Monographs* in 1927 after the conclusion of volume four because the start of the *Genetic Psychology Monographs* by the Clark Press made it seem unwise to me to have two such series edited from the same university.   I delivered an address by invitation at the 10th International Congress of Psychology (Copenhagen, 1932) on a behavioristic view of voluntary action, utilizing C. V. Hudgins' experiment on the voluntary control of the pupillary response.[20] I was offered the chairmanship of the psychology departments at Northwestern (1927) and Illinois (1928), and Carr had tried to interest me in coming to Chicago (1926).   I was elected to the American Academy of Arts and Sciences in 1933 and to the National Academy of Sciences in 1935.

In 1936 I accepted the professorship of psychology at Brown University, taking with me Clarence Graham as assistant professor and R. R. Willoughby as assistant editor of the *Abstracts*. One of my students at Clark, E. H. Kemp, had already been made an instructor at Brown, and I secured J. McVicker Hunt, recently at the Worcester State Hospital, as an additional staff member.   Together with Harold Schlosberg and Herbert Jasper (Donald Lindsley succeeded him in 1938) the Brown department had a staff which was not only a congenial one, but one whose professional productivity was to be of a high order.

With the move to Brown in 1936, at the age of 47, my professional life was changed significantly in various ways.   Heretofore, most of my energy had gone into my own research and that of my students, with my social services limited essentially to the editing of the *Abstracts* and the *Index*. At Brown I was in charge of a growing department with teaching and admin-

---

[20] Voluntary activity from the standpoint of behaviorism, *J genet Psychol*, 1934, 10, 198–204.

istrative duties at both undergraduate and graduate levels. I continued to edit the *Abstracts* (until 1947) with the help first of Willoughby, and then later of H. L. Ansbacher and my wife, Alda Barber Hunter, without whose efficient and continued help I could not have carried out my responsibilities during the war. My research time was inevitably greatly reduced; but in the fourteen years that have passed, I have published eight experimental papers, seven of a theoretical and general character, and directed six additional major experimental studies. My election to the American Philosophical Society in 1941 was particularly appreciated.

In 1936 I was appointed chairman of the Division of Anthropology and Psychology of the National Research Council. I had already served as a member of the Division in 1926–29 and 1933–36 and as vice-chairman in 1934–35, but these duties had not carried much responsibility. From 1936 until the war and then through it, first one obligation and then another had now to be met, not because I desired the task but because I could not avoid the responsibility.

I think that my chief accomplishment during the two years (1936–38) as chairman of the Division lay in the promotion of the interests of research in psychopathology. A conference on experimental neuroses and allied problems, held under my direction in 1937, was participated in by experimental and clinical psychologists, psychiatrists, and analysts. A Committee on Problems of Neurotic Behavior (1936–44) was established with W. R. Miles as chairman. Although it never succeeded in raising research funds, two accomplishments can be put to its credit: (1) the establishment of the *Journal of Psychosomatic Medicine* with the financial assistance of the Josiah Macy, Jr. Foundation and (2) the preparation of a report by William Malamud and myself (1941) on the importance of cooperation between psychiatrists and psychologists in the interests of national defense. Detailed joint statements were secured from selected pairs of psychologists and psychiatrists who were working together on clinical problems. These statements, which stressed the value of such cooperation, were transmitted to the Surgeon General in the interests of a more satisfactory development of clinical psychology and psychiatry in the Army medical service. Although there were no immediate consequences of the report, it served to educate the medical group concerned and it may have aided in the later development of military clinical psychology. During this period as chairman, I was also serving as a member of Council committees on aging and on work in industry. This latter committee brought me into contact with such stimulating men as L. J. Henderson (Harvard Fatigue Laboratory), Chester Barnard (recently of the Rockefeller Foundation), and Elton Mayo (Harvard Business School). I profited greatly by this widening of my horizons. Some of the results of the Committee's study are reported in a volume, *Fatigue of Workers* (1941).

In 1938, Dr. Carl Guthe, an anthropologist, succeeded me as chairman of the Division, but I was asked to continue as a member-at-large. The minutes of the 1939 annual meeting of the Division record a marked concern with the growing threat of war. A Committee on Public Service was authorized with the thought that such a title would camouflage the military defense interests of the group. I was asked to be chairman of the proposed committee, but I declined as I had previously declined the chairmanship of the Committee on the Selection and Training of Civilian Pilots, feeling that such committees should be in charge of men more professionally competent in the areas concerned than I was. (The Committee on Public Service was never actually established, partly because the Council disapproved of its title.) I did, however, serve as chairman of a conference on military tests and measurements which was in a very real sense the forerunner first of a Committee on Selection and Training (J. G. Jenkins, chairman) and second of the Advisory Committee to the Adjutant General's Office on the Classification of Military Personnel, established following the 1940 meeting of the Division with W. V. Bingham as chairman.

In order to complete the picture of these beginning days of military psychology in World War II, it is necessary to revert to April, 1939. Dr. Guthe and I, after the Divisional meeting above described, held a conference with the Adjutant General's Office in order to learn of the Army's plans in the area of classification tests and in order to offer the Army the expert advice of the Council. We were cordially received and told that the Army planned to use the 1918 tests and procedures. Our assurances that these were quite outmoded and that the National Research Council was established to offer scientific advice to the Government were well received but with no indication that the Army realized the magnitude of the problem that confronted it. That fall, however, the Committee on Selection and Training was in contact with the Adjutant General's Office, and by April of 1940 an official request was received and approved for the establishment of the above Advisory Committee. I think the evidence is clear that the psychologists were among the first of the scientific groups to prepare for war.

In August, 1940, an Emergency Committee in Psychology was set up under the Division with K. M. Dallenbach as chairman and with members recommended by the six national psychological groups.[21] As a member of this committee, I was asked (December, 1942) to investigate the supply of psychologists in terms of the known military demand for them. The results of the inquiry led to the introduction of psychology in the Army Specialized Training Program where a curriculum, in whose specifications I had a part, of broad psychological coverage with an emphasis on laboratory and work-

[21] For the history of this important committee, see K. M. Dallenbach, The Emergency Committee in Psychology, National Research Council, *J. Amer. Psychol.*, 1946, 59, 496–582.

shop methods was put into effect. The ASTP psychologists suffered severely in morale after finishing the course due to the failure of the Army properly to assign them to duty; but they had taken perhaps the most intensive psychological training ever given a group, a training designed to give them a functional mastery of the subject with a primary slant toward selection problems. It was my thought in planning the preliminary version of the curriculum that it might well have significant postwar results in undergraduate teaching in the form of an increased use of laboratory and workshop methods.

Those of us who by force of circumstances were responsible for some of the planning for military psychology were neither ignorant of nor indifferent to the large range of non-experimental interests. I have spoken above of my concern in furthering the activities of the clinical psychologists. A conference on the psychological factors in morale was organized by the Division in November, 1940, and Gordon Allport was invited to serve as chairman. The conference proposed that the Division establish a Committee on Morale. The proposal was not favored in that form by the officers of the Council who felt that the problem extended far into the field of the social sciences and of education. Conferences on the problem were held in the spring of 1941 by the chairmen of the American Council on Education, the American Council of Learned Societies, the National Research Council, and the Social Science Research Council. It was the recommendation of the four Councils that a Joint Committee for Scientific Research in Morale be established, composed of six members chosen from psychology, public affairs, sociology, physiology and history with myself as chairman. This appointment I refused, but I did agree to study immediately the feasibility of the general proposal and make a report. Inasmuch as the Councils were interested in research and not in action programs, the net result of my study was a recommendation that a joint committee be not established at that time. This recommendation was accepted by the Councils, some of whose chairmen thanked me later for not encouraging them to enter the morale field.

June 1940 saw the creation of the National Defense Research Committee, referred to as NDRC, under the chairmanship of Vannevar Bush. (No psychologist was included in the long list of names associated with NDRC as published in *Science* for November 22, 1940.) In a letter dated November 15, Warren Weaver of the Rockefeller Foundation wrote me asking for recommendations of a psychologist to work with Section D-2 on sensory problems, particularly stereo-vision. My nominee was S. W. Fernberger, who two weeks earlier had been made chairman of a sub-committee of the Emergency Committee to deal with sensory problems. Fernberger later accepted an appointment with NDRC and did valuable work on fire-control problems throughout the war. I should like to quote here from a letter dated December 5, 1940, which I addressed to Weaver, copy to

F. B. Jewett, President of the National Academy of Sciences, as follows: "In looking over the description of the NDRC as published in *Science* for November 22, I am greatly concerned over the fact that Psychology is not represented either on Dr. Jewett's Division or on Dr. Carl Compton's. We have heard so often that this is a war of machines that we are apt to come to the conclusion that physics, chemistry and engineering will offer all of the contributions necessary for success, forgetting that men must operate machines and that their efficiency and morale are after all the fundamental factors." So far as I know this was the earliest statement of the man-machine problem which was to become the dominant problem of the later Applied Psychology Panel and which was to bulk so large in postwar military psychology. The statement, however, produced no immediate results.

I did not come directly into the NDRC picture until September, 1943, when Dr. Conant asked me to be chairman of the Applied Psychology Panel with which NDRC had decided to replace the Committee on Service Personnel, Selection and Training which had been operating on contract with NDRC since June, 1942, under the National Research Council. This Committee, created through the leadership of Leonard Carmichael, had done excellent work in opening up research problems in various areas of military psychology and in enlisting military interest in their solution. I accepted the chairmanship with its civil service status on the assurance that I could maintain an office in Providence in addition to the one in Washington. This was necessary since I needed to be able at night and on the week ends to supervise the *Abstracts* which could not be turned over to a new editor on the spur of the moment and during the war.

The history of the Applied Psychology Panel is well presented by C. W. Bray,[22] and I need here comment only on a few aspects of its activities. I received excellent support from the members of the Panel, from Dr. Conant's top NDRC group, from key military personnel, and particularly from my Technical Aides: C. W. Bray, John Kennedy, and Dael Wolfle. In return, I exerted caution in expanding the Panel's program beyond the capacities of the limited available research personnel. Even so, it was several times necessary to curtail or abandon one project in order to undertake a more pressing one. This was notably true when the Panel undertook the analysis of field artillery errors in gunfire and the problem of improving the accuracy of fire with the B-29 gunnery system. I think that my only specific contribution to the detailed work of the research teams was to suggest the development, by Lorrin Riggs of Brown, of an odometer-type scale for the field artillery panoramic sight (1944–45). This type of scale which minimizes reading errors was well received, and it has been

22 *Psychology and Military Efficiency,* 1948.

used in postwar military research as well as incorporated in a variety of military equipment.

On November 17, 1944, President Roosevelt addressed a letter to Vannevar Bush requesting his advice on what measures should be adopted in order to insure the continuation in peacetime of the high level of scientific advance then current for military purposes. Bush's report is contained in the famous volume *Science the Endless Frontier* (1945). One phase of the report concerns the discovery and development of scientific talent prepared by a sub-committee of which I was a member and of which Henry Allen Moe (John Simon Guggenheim Memorial Foundation) was chairman. At the first meeting of the Moe Committee, I urged that we approach the problem of scientific talent in a broad way to include not merely the natural sciences but the social sciences and the humanities as well.[23] Not to do so would be to formulate a national program on too narrow a conception of the value of research and would be an effort, through governmental subsidy, to draw the finest talent into the natural sciences and away from all other disciplines. I fought a hard battle for this point of view, with Moe's support but against opposition from some of the most distinguished members of the committee. A partial victory was won in the sub-committee, and Bush incorporated references to the social sciences in the main body of his report. It was not, however, until President Truman requested the Congress to include more than the natural sciences in the proposed National Science Foundation that the chances were improved for such inclusion. Indeed, up to that time even the Social Science Research Council greatly doubted whether or not the social sciences should be included. I was a member of that Council in the period 1943–45. My question to the Council in 1944 on its attitude toward postwar research on governmental funds led to the establishment of a committee which brought in later a report on how social scientists could *aid the Government* in its research. When this report was seen to be beside the point, the committee restudied the question and was ready to recommend that social science not participate in the use of Federal funds for large-scale research. President Truman's request, mentioned above, came just in time to enable the Committee to reverse itself before submitting its report to the Council. Had this story been generally known at the time, some of the criticism of the natural scientists for attempting to exclude the social sciences would not have been made. (Public Law 507 — 81st Congress provides authority for a division of social science, if one is desired by the Foundation.)

Concurrently with the above activities in connection with the proposed

[23] It was not known at this time that another sub-committee would propose a National Science Foundation.

National Science Foundation recommended in the Bush report, the Secretaries of War and Navy requested the National Academy of Science to establish a Research Board for National Security which would function as an operating research agency during the liquidation of OSRD. Of the twenty civilian members of RBNS, four represented biology and medicine and I represented psychology. There is little to chronicle about the life of the Board. It was discontinued in March, 1946, due primarily to uncertainty in high governmental circles over postwar science plans. During its one year of existence, various rulings on budget matters prevented any allotment of funds to the Board. I can, however, record that psychology was cordially welcomed in the group and that plans were drawn up for its effective functioning. The only organizational problem that might be mentioned involved a choice between human engineering and psychology as the designation of the field and the relation of the work to medicine. The result of the deliberations was a psychology unit separate from medicine.[24]

I resigned as Chief of the Applied Psychology Panel in September, 1945, and returned to Brown to resume my academic duties. It seemed to me that my contribution to national defense and to the advancement of military psychology was complete, and that younger men should now take over with reference to postwar planning and the more distant future. I therefore sought to withdraw in their favor wherever possible. The unexpected climax to my war service came in June, 1948, when, with a group of engineers and scientists, I was awarded the President's Medal for Merit at ceremonies in Boston. The citation accompanying the award read, in part, as follows: "Dr. Hunter . . . recognized that research on the psychological and physiological capacities of man in relation to the new instruments of warfare could contribute materially to the more effective utilization of both military personnel and instruments." Commendation was given also "for applying the psychologist's knowledge of the nature of man to the designing of the weapon to fit the man and to the selection and training of the man to utilize the particular weapon." Thus, in a way, the citation was a validation of the principle embodied in my letter of 1940 to Warren Weaver. Although the medal was given to one psychologist, it was obviously a recognition of the effective work which all psychologists connected with the Applied Psychology Panel's program had done toward the increase in military efficiency.

Since September, 1945, I have not been able to devote myself entirely

[24] When the first National Science Foundations bills were introduced in the Congress, biology was included under the medical sciences. The undesirable implications of this were called to the attention both of Dr. Bush and of Dr. R. F. Griggs, the chairman of the Biology Division of the NRC. The bill was later changed to give the biological sciences divisional status and Dr. Griggs wrote me, "It is true that, thanks very largely to you, we have won the fight to have biology included by name and as a special Division of Biology."

to academic duties. I served as a member of the Scientific Advisory Group, Air Force Headquarters, in 1946–47. Since 1946 and 1947, respectively, ∟ I have been a member of the Undersea Warfare Committee, NRC, and a deputy member of the Research and Development Board's Committee on Human Resources. The failure of nations to establish peace and the consequent continuance of a cold war have given an importance and an urgency to the work of these groups which could not be ignored. One of the fruits of these labors is the publication of a volume, *Human Factors in Undersea Warfare* (1949), prepared by the Panel on Psychology and Physiology of the Undersea Warfare Committee under the editorship of D. B. Lindsley, my former colleague at Brown University.

In 1945, President Conant of Harvard University established an *ad hoc* commission of twelve under the chairmanship of Alan Gregg of the Rockefeller Foundation to advise on the future of psychology at Harvard, with particular reference to organizational problems and the place of psychology in general education. The Commission's report was published in 1947[25] too late to influence the changes which were made in the organization of psychology at Harvard. My own point of view, where it differed from that of others, can be detected in the dissenting footnotes which members of the Commission were encouraged to offer. My central thesis was that the future of psychology as a science and as a profession depended, from the educational point of view, primarily upon the maintenance of a solid groundwork in experimental fields and upon a closing of the widening gap between fundamental psychology and such areas as social and clinical psychology by requiring of all psychologists a common core of knowledge of experimental work supported by training in related sciences.

In May, 1946, The Carnegie Corporation and the Carnegie Foundation, concerned as they had been for many years with the problems of educational testing, established a Committee on Testing with President Conant as chairman to consider ways and means by which the programs of four nonprofit national testing agencies (The Graduate Record Office, The College Entrance Board, the Cooperative Test Service, and the Educational Records Bureau) might be made more effective, better integrated, and hence more serviceable. The Corporation asked me to serve as an adviser to the Committee, and this I did during the summer of 1946. After a detailed study of the problem, I recommended to the Committee that a single national testing agency be established by the merger of the four groups above listed. Such an agency should be independent, have its own governing board, be nonprofit making, and should be so organized that fundamental research on human abilities could be undertaken in addition to general service functions. If all four groups were unwilling to

[25] *The Place of Psychology in an Ideal University,* 1947.

merge, I recommended that the new agency be composed of those that were willing. The Committee acted in accordance with the recommendation except that it proposed to tie the new agency, administratively, to the American Council on Education, a plan which seemed to me unwise.[26] However, as discussions proceeded between the interested parties on the complicated details of the proposed merger, it became clear that only an independent agency could accomplish the end in view. The result was the establishment in 1947 of the Educational Testing Service by a merger of the testing groups above listed, with the exception of the Educational Records Bureau which chose to remain independent. ETS with the increased financial resources at its command can engage in fundamental research, and it has already established a fellowship program. The accomplishment of a basic research program in addition to the more or less routine development and revision of standard tests has long been a serious weakness of the testing agencies, a weakness which can now be corrected.

Of the publications which I have made from Brown University, I attach most importance to the following in the order listed: (1) the study with Marion Sigler (Wessell) on the span of visual discrimination as a function of time and intensity of stimulation[27] where it was shown that the Bunsen-Roscoe law, $I.t = C$, holds within limits, a study greatly aided by my colleague Clarence Graham; (2) the continued studies of double alternation; and (3) my presidential address to the Eastern Psychological Association "On the professional training of psychologists."[28] In addition, I took great pleasure in summarizing the heredity-environment symposium held by the Society of Experimental Psychologists,[29] since it carried me back to my 1920 paper on the modification of instincts and reassured me that the denial of instincts by psychologists in the twenties had been too hasty.

I am happy to be counted among the many workers who have brought about the change from a psychology of experience to a psychology of behavior. The fundamental issue in behaviorism is not, and never was, the particular speculations of any one behaviorist — of Watson for example. Behaviorism is the point of view in psychology which holds that an adequate account can be given of psychological problems without reference to the terms consciousness and introspection. So thoroughly has psychology been permeated by this point of view that the term behaviorism is currently seldom used, although the term behavior is constantly employed and although only a negligible number of studies even purport to deal with consciousness.[30]

---

[26] For the Committee's preliminary report, see *School and Society*, Oct. 19, 1946, 63, 247–276.

[27] *J exp Psychol.*, 1940, 26, 160–179.

[28] *Psychol. Rev*, 1941, 48, 498–523.

[29] *Psychol Rev*, 1947, 54, 348–352.

[30] Some observations on the status of psychology, In *Miscellanea Psychologica Albert Michotte*, Louvain, 1947.

Since my first paper in 1911, two-thirds of my publications and those of my students have been in the central area of psychology, the field of learning. Nevertheless, I have not thought of myself as a psychologist with a specific program to be worked out in detail. Rather, I have looked for problems where, as it seemed to me, the expenditure of experimental and theoretical effort might push forward the boundaries of knowledge significantly and on a varied front. Such a point of view results in a less integrated body of experimental findings than that which follows from the adherence to a program; and yet were it possible to relive the period, my choice would again be for the varied rather than for the programmatic approach to experimentation.

DAVID KATZ

IT seems unlikely that even a professional astrologer could have predicted from my horoscope that psychology would become my lot; in any event for those who are interested I might state that I was born on the first of October, 1884, in Kassel, in the Prussian province of Hessen-Nassau, the seventh child in a family consisting of five sons and three daughters.[1]

Kassel, a medium-sized city, is situated in extraordinarily lovely country, with a history rich in artistic traditions, and its fine schools offered excellent educational opportunities for the young. Among the most cherished memories of my childhood and youth are the excursions around our town with my family and friends. Short visits to relatives in the country led to an early acquaintance with nature based more on feeling and observation than on studies. These first contacts of the child, however, developed into the deep interest of the schoolboy in zoology, and an even more intense interest in botany. The magic world of plants must have taken strong possession of me at that time; otherwise I cannot understand why, as a child, the profession of gardener appealed as an ideal to me. But there were also later reactions to this early state of mind: my deep interest in research dealing with the "sensory" life of plants which was furthered by the development of time-lapse movies, and by investigations on the validity of Weber's law in botany, as carried out, for example, by W. Pfeffer.

In its cultural aspects my native city offered unusual opportunities in the fine arts and in the theater. The picture gallery of Kassel had one of the finest collections of Dutch art; I often spent hours there, standing in reverent admiration before Rembrandt's masterpieces. A modern philosopher has well defined history as *Sinngebung des Sinnlosen* ("giving sense to the meaningless"). Therefore we should be careful in attempting to relate meaningfully the events and experience of childhood to our later development. I believe, however, that it is not a post-factum rationalization to connect my discovery of the secrets of light and shade, as revealed by Rembrandt's paint-

[1] Submitted in German and translated by Peter Welti of Clark University.

189

ings, to my later lively interest in psychological problems of color and illumination. My numerous visits to exhibitions of pictures and art museums were not inspired by the mere transitory enthusiasm of an adolescent. The real reason was a profound interest, based on my own natural predisposition for artistic creation — an interest which has lasted all my life, causing me to deal with problems of the fine arts, and in 1914 leading to the publication of an essay on the Spanish painter, El Greco.

Few German cities had a better theater than Kassel. The admission price for schoolboys was so low that even our very modest allowances permitted us to attend dramatic performances frequently. There is hardly a classical opera, or a play by Shakespeare, Goethe or Schiller, to which we were not introduced in those days. Way up, in the last row which usually passed sentence on the fate of a play or an actor, we experienced Aristotelian catharsis. There, intoxicated by overpowering aesthetic experiences, burning ideals and noble plans were born — and indeed some of the plans became reality. I doubt whether the movies of today could be called a primary educational factor as compared with the stage of my youth. To attend the theater and concerts became a need which outlasted our student days.

Attendance at school normally began at the age of six. However, at the insistent request of my mother, who was unable to control my very active disposition, I was admitted at the age of five. This had the advantage of enabling me to leave school at the age of 17, and to begin university studies. In secondary school I was especially interested in biology as well as in physics, chemistry and mathematics. Strangely enough, I did very well in Latin, too, I often had to take over when no one else in class could go on, and thereby attained honorary title of the teacher's *refugium ultimum*. I cannot say that I took an ardent interest in the classical authors whom we read at that time; rather I was much more attracted by the neatness, the precision of expression, and the logical sequence of this ancient language toward whose mastery I was lured as if motivated by a sort of intellectual game. Later on, as fate had it, I was obliged to teach in two foreign tongues, and would have been very thankful then for a better background in English and French. Unfortunately I never rose above the average in those two modern languages taught in school. Despite my four years' stay in England and the now 14 years' residence in Sweden, I never learned to express myself in the language of these adopted countries with the same ease and fluency as in my mother tongue. Personal experience of the greater fatigue engendered by expressing oneself in a foreign tongue was the starting point for research which I published under the title *Blendungsphaenomene und konnektive Hemmungen bei Denkprozessen* ("Phenomena of blinding and connective inhibitions in thought processes"), and briefly referred to in my *Gestalt Psychology* (1950).

Discipline at school was very strict. How often we were referred to Kant's "categorical imperative"! Militaristic ideas, however, which pervaded history as well as other subjects, can hardly be said to be in line with the humane principles of Kant's philosophy. It was not until years later, during my stay in England, that I became familiar with a society whose attitude is completely opposed to militaristic thinking. There I came to a clear understanding of how dangerous the principles of German education could become under certain political constellations; at that time, of course, we had no inkling of this. As a result of my thoughts on the differences between German and English education, I published in Sweden *Deutsche Erziehung (German Education)* in 1940, and in 1948 I published an essay *"Der Spielgedanke in der englischen Erziehung"* ("Play in English education"), which appeared in the *Neue Schweizer Rundschau.*

While speaking of my schooldays, I might mention that I began early to give private lessons, specializing more and more in mathematics. My experience in this field convinced me that genuine lack of talent in mathematics at the secondary school level was not as frequent as was then generally assumed, and indeed is still assumed today. This lack of talent proved in many cases to be only superficial. The student's difficulty was often caused by some unfortunate occurrence, such as temporary absence from school which resulted in a gap in knowledge fatal to normal progress. For that reason I used to start my lessons from the very beginning, without regard as to whether the pupil made any visible progress in school during that period of recapitulation. My method was very successful, even in cases which seemed hopeless, and I acquired quite a reputation. Especially in the period before Easter, when promotion to a higher class was under consideration, I was overwhelmed with offers for private tutoring. When I started graduate work, the money I thus earned became quite important — even if it was a very modest sum. Of lasting value was the pedagogical insight which I gained by this experience.

I entered the University in 1902, and specialized in mathematics and natural science. One of my reasons for choosing Göttingen, the small but famous university town, was its short distance from Kassel which made it less expensive to carry on my studies. The academic freedom of the University and the attitude of the students, less burdened by practical considerations than today, enabled us to study in a different way than is now possible. We did not restrict ourselves to major and minors, but attended lectures delivered outside of our own departments in the hope of broadening our general education. Not only in Göttingen but also during my studies in Berlin and Munich, I therefore attended courses in fine arts, music and economics. In Berlin I occasionally heard the lectures of Georg Simmel, who was one of the first to include sociology in the academic curriculum.

Since the curriculum in mathematics and the sciences (usually preparatory for secondary school teaching) included courses in general education with philosophy as a central core, I attended many philosophy lectures. Among the courses in philosophy I was very much attracted by the public lectures on the immortality of the soul given by the philosopher, Julius Baumann. I cannot remember how, or even whether, Baumann solved this problem. The profound discussions of this cultured and erudite old gentleman on the relations between body and soul aroused my desire to inquire even more exhaustively into these problems. I believe that these lectures made me think of psychology for the first time. Yet something else contributed to this idea. In my first semester I met one of G. E. Muller's students who was engaged in an experimental research problem. He persuaded me to take part as a subject. Although these experiments dealt with lifted weights and were rather dull, my scientific imagination was stirred. It dawned on me that it was feasible to study empirically the relation between body and soul. (It might be added at this point that Fechner's original weights were at the Gottingen Institute, a present from Fechner to Muller.) The first encounter of the young student with technical laboratory apparatus, including such an exact measuring instrument as the Hipp chronoscope, must have strengthened his belief that here, finally, an examination of the relation between body and soul seemed possible in the pattern of scientific measurement. After thus entering the hallway of psychology, the decision to attend the lectures of Muller himself quickly followed. I was deeply fascinated, and soon decided to make psychology my major study; philosophy and physics became my minors.

The final oral examinations in psychology were based entirely on lectures and did not require independent reading of psychological literature. Muller used to lecture very systematically. Most important was his course in the field of general psychology, he also taught courses on the Psychology of Colors, on Psychophysics and on Imagery and Memory. Muller's lectures always were prepared with admirable care. Psychology students were also required to attend a full year's course in physiology, which was given for medical students. These lectures, filled with numerous demonstrations and delivered by the outstanding physiologist, Max Verworn, greatly influenced my scientific development and soon directed my interest to the border province between psychology and physiology. Courses in psychiatry, next to physiology the most important connection between psychology and medicine, were not required for students of psychology. I attended them only cursorily, a fact I have regretted ever since.

As a rule Muller used to propose the subject of a dissertation to his students, having in mind that every single dissertation should be a real contribution to psychology; hence the choice of a problem and the methods of solution presupposed a clear understanding of the present situation of research – an understanding which was impossible for the beginner. Thus it quite often happened that the topic of the thesis proposed to the student was far beyond his grasp, and he therefore had to be closely supervised by Muller himself. At the time that I asked for his advice Muller was interested in the problem of the formation of comparative judgments in connection with his theory about absolute judgment, and proposed for me a study on the psychology of comparison in the field of time experience. I plunged into the general problem of time consciousness and was fascinated by its philosophical aspects, which had been treated by St. Augustine and Kant. Of the two general forms of experience, time appears to be of greater importance than space. Not all psychological events have spatial qualities, but none lacks temporality. Despite this fact it is astonishing how little even now the psychology of time has captured the imaginations of experimental psychologists.

The main purpose of my dissertation, however, was less a thorough analysis of the experience of time itself than a study of the question of how the comparison takes place in the judgment of the relation of two intervals of time. It became clear that frequently correct judgment of this relation, based on the absolute impression of the second time-interval, was possible if a special "set" (*Einstellung*) had been formed toward the range of time-intervals presented in the experiment. Thus the importance of the phenomena of *Einstellung* in psychology, in the specific forms of sensory, motor and connective sets became clear to me. My research led me to reject the current opinion that a comparison between two sensory impressions, separated by a steadily growing interval, could be considered a parallel to forgetting in memory experiments. My work, moreover, contributed to the current discussion concerning the possibility of immediate recognition or discrimination without the intervention of reproduction of past experience. This possibility, defended by Harald Hoffding against Alfred Lehmann, I was able to verify.

My dissertation, published in 1907, was of less significance in my scientific development than a short study on children's drawings, published in 1906. It did not deal with free, *i.e.*, imaginary, drawings by children, as had been the case in earlier publications, but rather with the copying of objects. This procedure was very fruitful and made possible a direct analysis of child perception. The drawings clearly showed the tendency toward *Pragnanz*, with the well-known tendency toward orthoscopic representation as a special case. In this study I already touched upon the problem of color constancy – a starting point for further experiments which occupied me for many years to come.

At the time I began my studies there was not a single chair of psychology in Germany. Psychologists like Muller, for instance, occupied chairs of philosophy, and had to deal, at least in their classes, with some philosophical problems outside the realm of psychology.   Even a *Privatdozent*² in psychology had to be concerned with philosophy to a certain extent.   Thus I regularly gave an Introduction to Philosophy, and occasionally lectured on Aesthetics and English Empiricism.   The governments of the German states did not meet the growing needs of our aspiring science by creating special chairs of psychology, as would have been appropriate; instead they followed the policy of appointing psychologists to existing chairs of philosophy.   For that very reason the representative of our field occupying a chair of philosophy often appeared a usurper, opposed by his own faculty and even by the public.   Consequently objections were raised against psychology, which on the surface appeared to be factual, but which in reality were due to human, all-too-human prejudices; indeed quite a few philosophers became prejudiced against this new branch of science which was trying to gain a firm and independent footing.   There were, of course, comforting exceptions, among them Ernst Cassirer, who was himself very well informed in psychology and tried to make psychological knowledge useful for philosophical analyses.   The union between psychology and philosophy at that time, however, had by no means merely a negative value; a positive consequence consisted in the fact that a psychologist with a solid and broad philosophical background was less threatened by the dangers of over-specialization.

To me phenomenology, as advocated at that time by Edmund Husserl, seemed to be the most important connection between philosophy and psychology.   None of my academic teachers with the exception of G. E. Muller has more deeply influenced my method of work and my attitude in psychological matters than Husserl by his phenomenological method.   This method coincided partly with the descriptive method in an attempt to understand directly given facts without presupposition and prejudice, as had been done previously with eminent skill by the physiologist, Ewald Hering, in the field of vision.   I became friendly with Max Scheler, another philosopher who showed a sympathetic attitude toward psychology; he was a genius in his own way, but not free of eccentricities.   His life, it was said jestingly, oscillated between cloister and saloon.   Associated at times with Husserl and his Gottingen circle, Scheler was a fascinating teacher who exerted a deep influence on many a young scholar.   Both Husserl and Scheler took an ardent interest in analyses of the kind I have published in my two books on color and touch sensation.   Husserl's philosophy was characterized among other things by its opposition to the so-called psychologism, *i.e.*, he was against the opinion that philosophy must be based on psychology.

Thus Husserl's attacks were directed against empiricists like Hume. Hume, in his opinion, had confused the question of the history of the development

² A *Privatdozent* was a lecturer admitted to teaching after special examination which included a scientific thesis beyond the doctoral dissertation.

of thinking — which is, as a matter of fact, psychologically explainable — with the question of the validity of thought. One can be a psychologist heart and soul without being a "psychologizer," and I myself believe that the limits of psychological cognition are correctly drawn by Husserl. This attitude has, however, no great consequences in the work of advancing the frontier of psychological research. An entirely different situation arises if one takes into consideration certain consequences for the psychologist arising in a phenomenological study regarding the difference between relations of facts and relations of insight *(Wesenseinsichten).*

The findings of classic memory psychology are without exception characterized as facts connected with each other empirically, as, *e.g.,* the decrease of associations in time. All laws of psychological connections are of that character. The order of colors, however, which might be thought of as geometrically represented in one pattern or another, is based on an insight into its nature *(Wesenseinsicht).* Unlike psychological or psychophysical connections of facts, it does not require statistical treatment. Here might be the place to point to the danger of misinterpretation of the relation between psychology and statistics. This danger existed in the older experimental psychology and appears again today, although on a higher level. Statistics is an absolute necessity for psychology, but it always will be an auxiliary science. It should never be an end in itself, as it seems to become here and there among the younger generation. Psychological insight cannot be replaced by statistics, however specialized.

As I have previously stated, I spent one of my semesters in Berlin, but my studies there had no great influence on my development as a psychologist. I did not attend the lectures of Carl Stumpf, but I fail to recall why not. Schumann's lectures on freedom of will did not impress me particularly, but I got quite a bit out of Max Dessoir's lectures and seminars on aesthetics, which really came up to my expectations. Dessoir's book, *Vom Jenseits der Seele* ("Of the Soul Beyond This World"), awoke my interest in occult phenomena. Later in Rostock I frequently devoted lectures to the subject "Science and Occultism." Whatever may be the truth concerning the genuineness of occult phenomena, the psychological insights I gained from these lectures proved to be very interesting.

After obtaining my doctor's degree in 1906, I considered it more useful for the accomplishment of my scientific plans first to do my military service. Unexpectedly I was released after a few months and decided to go for one semester to Munich; there Theodor Lipps had gathered around him a rather large group of younger scholars, among them Aloys Fischer, Max Pfander and Moritz Geiger. I attended Lipps' lectures and seminars, but his method, directed more towards speculation than towards empirical research, was not to my taste. Though my visit at Munich was not scientifically very profitable,

I was greatly stimulated by the cultural life of this South German city.   On my way back from Munich to Northern Germany I stayed for some months at Kulpe's Institute at Würzburg.   Here I did some limited experimental research on individual differences in the apprehension of figures as a casuistic contribution to individual psychology.   Kulpe received me in a very friendly manner and at his Institute I met quite a few younger psychologists, who were much devoted to him.

After my return to Kassel during the spring of 1907, I received a letter from Muller asking whether I would like to fill a vacancy at the Institute of Göttingen caused by the transfer of his former assistant to Berlin.   I immediately accepted the offer.   This decision was the one which did most in shaping my further scientific career.   For a long time it had been the tradition of Carl Stumpf in Berlin to import his assistants from Gottingen.   First he had appointed Fr. Schumann; when Schumann was called to Zurich, N. Ach succeeded him; Ach left for Konigsberg and was followed by Rupp.   But now the usual traffic got blocked: Rupp, for want of proficiency, was not called away from Berlin, thus obstructing my advance which should have led me to Berlin and from there possibly even farther.   However, Gottingen meant for me exciting and happy times in research and study.

Even now I am not sure whether my contract as an assistant stipulated any well-defined duties; I only know that I spent my entire day from early morning to late afternoon and frequently part of the night in the laboratory, occupied partly with administrative matters concerning the Institute, partly with my own research.   Regularly every morning Muller appeared in the Institute to make his rounds, like the head physician at a hospital.   Every student working on his dissertation was requested to remain in his room in order to report on the state of his research and to plan the continuation of his experiments.   There was no dissertation published at the Institute of Gottingen for which Müller himself was not a subject.   This personal supervision of their work by the master stimulated the students and increased their feeling of responsibility.

Muller jokingly called the Institute of Gottingen the last stronghold of old Prussian parsimony.   The laboratory indeed looked more like a poorhouse than a place for research.   The budget was absolutely insufficient.   Occasionally Muller paid the bill for the water-supply, amounting to about one dollar, out of his own pocket, which had an unexpected result: The office of the Prussian *Oberrechnungskammer* in Berlin, which controlled the finances of the universities, sometimes inquired about the sources from which the bill for the water-supply of the third quarter, for instance, had been paid.

There is a story about an astronomer who conducted a tour on the occasion of the installation of a gigantic telescope at an American observatory. He asked which part of the instrument the audience considered the most important; there were many answers, all of which he rejected. "The most important part of the apparatus," he said, smiling, "is the investigator, sitting in front of the lens." This story contains a moral for experimental psychology, too. There were times during the development of our young science when one was inclined to judge the importance of the scientific work by its technical apparatus, and to see in the precision of measurement made physically possible by the apparatus, a guarantee for precision in the psychological sense. Of course the value of a psychological study lies in its inner significance, and the apparatus has to be judged in terms of its adequacy for the solution of the problem at hand. The classical observations of Hering in the fields of color- and space-theory, or the fundamental experiments of Ebbinghaus on the psychology of memory, were carried out by very simple techniques. It is true that many sensory-psychological experiments now require a rather complicated arrangement A psychologist interested in the electroencephalogram is badly handicapped without technical equipment of top quality. Cooperation with physiologists and technicians will become more and more important for the psychologist. But this does not imply that a psychologist with original ideas cannot be successful even though he has to work with moderate means. Neither in Gottingen nor afterward did I ever have the chance to work in a well-equipped laboratory. Thus, forced to make a virtue out of necessity, I tried to carry on my experiments with quite simple machinery. Nevertheless I always have appreciated useful and elegant technical equipment; in fact I have been interested in technical inventions all my life. As a schoolboy I invented an automatic fire-alarm, and while I was in active service during the first World War, I constructed a gadget for candles which prolonged the period of burning by 100–200 per cent. At that time I also proposed to the military authorities a transparent bullet-proof optic shield, based on the episcotister-principle. A rotating disc, with a few narrow slots extending over only a few degrees, appears transparent; this device obstructs vision very little, and under high illumination it even improves it. If the episcotister is made of steel, the observing eye behind it is protected against splinters of average penetration. My interest in constructing various apparatus led to two patented inventions in the psychological field. I own a German patent for a percussion instrument which I constructed while doing research on the sense of vibration. On top of an open box containing a pillow, a thick sheet of cardboard is placed, at the bottom of which leaden figures are fastened. The forms of these figures have to be determined by percussion. This apparatus has been used at several medical schools in Germany for demonstration of and training in percussion. My "scriptochronograph," which permits measurement of temporal relations in writing with a high degree of precision, was patented in Sweden.

In spite of its poor financial condition, the Institute at Gottingen strongly attracted young scholars from Germany and from foreign countries. Among the students who were trained there or who spent some time in research, I might mention N. Ach, Raymond Dodge, Paula Ephrussi, V. Henri, E. R. Jaensch, O. Kulpe, Lillien Jane Martin, William McDougall, G. Révész, E. Rubin, Fr. Schumann, Charles Spearman, and Laura Steffens; during my assistantship I met most of these psychologists personally. In that golden age of the Institute there were more than a dozen predoctoral research studies carried out at the same time. With the outbreak of World War I in 1914, when all its members were called to active duty or volunteered, the Institute became deserted.

The training in methods provided by the Göttingen Institute was exemplary, and was ideally suited for the psychological problems that had to be solved. In the course of such experimental training the student became familiar with the scientific techniques whose applicability in psychology was well-nigh limitless. There was only one question: Were all the problems we dealt with of such importance that they justified the great amount of time and work we spent on them? If at times an immense amount of statistical technique was introduced just to study the time and space errors of the positive or negative type in lifting of weights, a critical student might well ask himself whether all this was not making psychological mountains out of mathematical molehills. As a matter of fact, psychology as carried out in Göttingen as well as in other universities needed psychologizing, paradoxical as it might seem. With respect to perception, this meant liberation from interests in purely sensory functions; as to memory, it meant supplementation by investigations directed toward the analysis of biologically important forms of learning; as to the theory of motivation, it meant the replacement of a static view, working with association and reproduction, by a dynamic theory based on drives, instincts and needs.

One of the courses required by Müller dealt with the psychophysics of visual sensation. This topic was treated almost exclusively from a physiological point of view, and was supplemented by speculative ideas based on those of Johannes Müller concerning the nature of intraorganismic optical psychophysics. Psychological questions were touched upon only slightly. This lack of psychology in the treatment of a field so rich in fascinating phenomena, and, moreover, the lack of psychological data in the literature dealing with that field, troubled me very much and was one of the reasons why I started the research on color. Underlying this work — published in 1911 in a book entitled *Die Erscheinungsweisen der Farben und ihre Beeinflussung durch die individuelle Erfahrung* ("Modes of Appearance of Colors and Their Modification through Individual Experience") — was this question: Why not study the psychological phenomena of color directly instead of restricting oneself to problems which can be handled just as well or even better by a sensory physiologist? The phenomenological method in the field of colors proved to be very productive. It appeared that up to then psychology had been concerned with rather remote and isolated color experiences. The spectral colors occupied the main interest; they are best defined in terms of physics, and have little bearing on the color experiences of everyday life. I occasionally explained this situation by saying that most people die without ever having looked through a spectroscope. It appeared to me a psychological nuisance to talk of colors *in abstracto* instead of starting with actual appearance of the colors. In so doing one first has to take into account the spatial modes of appearance, such as "film colors" and "surface colors." Furthermore, one must recognize the significance of illumination versus local colors, and the necessity of facing the manifold problems of color constancy. The explanations of Hering, based on the workings of certain physiological equipment (*viz.*, pupil, interaction of elements of the visual field, etc.) plus the psychological factor of "memory color," soon proved to be insufficient. They were replaced by a holistic theory, according to which the valence of local colors is determined by the structure of the total visual field. This theory was anything but empirical; thus the title of my book, which summarized the most important results of the investigation, was actually a misnomer. But since it had been formulated at a time when I still was influenced by the Hering theory, and perhaps out of some kind of laziness, I did not change it. The problems of color constancy and of other phenomena of constancy, as one knows, remained major topics of perception for quite some time to come.

The volume on color led in 1911 to my formal admission as *Privatdozent*, for financial reasons, however, I kept my assistantship until the beginning of the first World War. When I entered military service – my experience during the war will be mentioned later – I was given a leave of absence as an assistant. Müller, who wanted to save money for the Prussian government, stopped the payment of my small salary (100 marks per month) so that during the next four years I was left with the small pay of a member of the medical corps, and later of an ordinary soldier. I suppose I was the only assistant in a university in all Germany who fell a victim to the rigorous attitude of his master, and who thus contributed an extra sum for war expenses.

The book on color was well received. I was especially proud of the comment of Ewald Hering, whom I visited during an educational trip, in his laboratory in Leipzig. Carl Stumpf, who always showed much personal interest in me, let me know through Müller that he would formulate the topic of the prize essay of the Prussian Academy of Sciences in a way which would come close to my interests. I still own the copy of this text, with Stumpf's handwritten greetings on it. It read: "Investigate systematically and state the role that experience plays in human perception. The question is not to collect the many facts in physiological and psychological literature, but to determine the forms of sensory experience as clearly as possible both as to their nature and as to the limits of their efficacy, and to show the factors and the laws common to the various sensory fields." The prize was 5000 marks, an enormous sum for that time, and especially to me in view of my own financial position. The public announcement of the topic was set for July 9, 1914. Unfortunately I was unable to compete. Some weeks later the war broke out, and I served almost continuously, first with the Red Cross, later, until March, 1918, at the front. From the formulation of the prize topic it may be seen how strongly impressed Stumpf was (and, for that matter, scholars in general) at that time by the all-important role which individual experience plays in perception.

Immediately preceding the war I completed some other studies, primarily in the field of animal psychology. I worked with Géza Révész, with whom my friendship dates back 50 years. These studies, dealing with chickens, in part concerned the sense of vision and form, and in part their memory. Our experiments received a good deal of notice, they furnished a necessary supplement to the memory experiments on humans, and were contemporaneous with similar animal experiments which had been begun by American investigators. As a result of this research we received an invitation from the famous neurologist, L. Edinger of the University of Frankfurt, to work as guests in his laboratory; Edinger had carried out fundamental research concerning the localization of psychological functions in the older and newer parts of the brain. The experiments with chickens started a long sequence of research in animal psychology, which I carried on with my students at the small laboratory in Rostock and concluded in the Zoological Garden of London. With animals it is always a drive, mostly hunger, which makes them perform in the laboratory situation. Thus through work with animals we became more familiar with genuine biological forces; we came closer to a dynamic way of psychological thinking which later on prevailed more and more in human psychology.

At the outbreak of the war I enlisted as a volunteer in the army. At first I was rejected for front-line service and worked with the Red Cross. After a short course in the care of the wounded, I was assigned to an ambulance train which transported wounded from the front lines back to Germany. The journeys home were always very fatiguing, but the trip back to the front was stimulating because of intensive discussions with the numerous professional men who made up the corps. We had plenty of opportunities to contact all kinds of people, and by and by became real experts on the intricate workings of the railroad. At times tragicomic incidents occurred. Once I was taking a walk through the streets of Hamburg; I was wearing the Red Cross uniform. Suddenly several persons came up to me and asked for help for a man who was lying in the street. My practical knowledge of medicine was hardly good enough for first aid, and I was therefore quite relieved when the victim's alcoholic breath convinced me that he did not require my help.

Owing to a serious cold which resulted from the train trips, I had to quit service with the medical corps toward the end of 1914. I returned for a short time to Gottingen. Early in 1915 I was called to active duty, and the next year, in the spring of 1916, I volunteered for the front. The work in a so-called Schall-Messtrupp (sound-ranging crew) was not without psychological interest. The task was to plot the positions of enemy artillery and to direct the fire of our own batteries. The time of these spottings was measured by stop watches which provided an opportunity to study the factor of the personal equation. At times we used the *Richtungshòrer* (direction-finder), apparatus constructed by von Hornbostel and Wertheimer. These experiences in auditory localization inspired later studies on auditory localization in animals.

I fought in Russia and in North France, became vice-sergeant, later sub-altern, and received the Iron Cross. In the spring of 1918 I was ordered to the Engineering School in Hanover, a research institute for the study of artificial limbs, where I worked with a military physician of high rank and a professor of engineering of the school. This was a new field of applied psychology, the psychology of prothesis. To fit the amputated person with an efficient artificial limb was a very important step in the rehabilitation of the disabled.

Specifically my work consisted in the study of the sensory-motor function of the stumps, especially of persons operated on according to the Sauerbruch method. Sauerbruch's method is as follows: Channels are pierced through the muscles remaining in the stumps — for instance, in the case of the arm above the elbow, through biceps and triceps. The inner side of these channels is lined with a piece of skin taken from the chest. If these channels are pro-vided with a pin which is connected by a thin chain with the mobile part of the artificial limb, a motion of the voluntarily innervated muscles can be transferred to the artificial limb. In using biceps and triceps and the stump as a whole, combinations of motions can be achieved which cause the arti-ficial limb to operate almost like a natural one. In the summer of 1950 I met a group of technicians and physicians in Berkeley who were also engaged in studies on Sauerbruch-amputees.

These amputees present interesting subjects for experiments which can be conducted in a manner analogous to the classical experiments of Weber and Fechner, but which are not feasible under normal circumstances. Normally in every activity of the muscles the motion of the innervated muscle calls for an action of its antagonist. In the stumps, however, one finds muscles where antagonistic action — *e.g.*, such as that between biceps and triceps — is lacking. It is therefore possible to carry on experiments on lifted weights with one of these muscles, without the participation of the antagonist. The validity of the Weber-Fechner law has been proved even in these cases. Looking at the problem as a whole, it seems strange that this law could have been derived in the first place from such a complicated process as the lifting of weights. This classical field of research in experimental psychology also shows typical constancy phenomena. They manifest themselves in cases of lifting weights by different body parts (arm, leg, head, teeth) — which I investigated in collaboration with my students. These phenomena also appear when the lifting arm is immersed in water, thus eliminating its own weight almost entirely, and finally when the back of the lifting hand is burdened by an additional weight. Through these variations the classical weight-experiment has become a specifically psychological problem.

Theoretically the study of the "phantom limb," an illusion occurring after amputations, is of particular interest. Since the time of Ambroise Paré, the great war surgeon of the 16th century who dealt with this illusion, it has been noticed again and again, especially by the neurologists who were interested in the formation of the so-called body-image.

In 1919 my activity as a *Privatdozent* and Assistant of the University of Göttingen came to an end. I was called to Rostock where, on the occasion of the fifth centennial of the State University of Mecklenburg, a new chair of psychology and education was established. Consequently from that time on I had to deal with the whole field of pedagogy as well. I was always deeply interested in educational questions; in fact, after the first World War, it would have been difficult under any circumstances to disregard the wave of pedagogical enthusiasm flooding over Germany and carrying with it chiliastic hopes; after all, my professorship itself was a product of this very movement.

My interest in pedagogical research was restricted to its psychological aspects. In 1919 I was married, and in close cooperation with my wife, Rosa, née Heine, a pupil of Muller, I published a whole series of studies on pedagogical psychology. The most important one was the book entitled *Gespräche mit Kindern* (1927). This contribution to child psychology differed from other publications in the same field because of its special psychological method. The choice of dialogues as the raw material for our analyses, instead of the use of single words or sentences as in most examinations of child language at that time, gave the book its holistic character. Conversation was here recognized as the most important and most consequential cooperative action between two participants. There is no aspect of child psychology which cannot benefit from analyses of conversations.

Several years before my wife and I wrote this book, I published studies on abstraction in children.[3] I tried to answer the question whether children,

[3] *Studien zur Kinderpsychologie*, 1913.

under the same experimental conditions, are more impressed by colors or forms of figures. It seemed that younger children were more strongly influenced by color, older ones by form. In connection with experimental investigations on Kretschmerian types, the color-form problem was carried subsequently into personality research. Here it became apparent that the cyclothymic type is primarily inclined toward color, the schizothymic type primarily toward form.

Among other works in pedagogical psychology I published a book entitled *Psychologie und mathematischer Unterricht* (1912) in a series edited by the International Committee on Education in Mathematics. The book owes its origin to Felix Klein, the outstanding mathematician at Gottingen, with whom I often profitably discussed the relationship between psychology and mathematics. It dealt with such questions as working methods of mathematicians, sex differences in arithmetical abilities and the development of space and number ideas in normal children and in the feebleminded. The book was well received, especially among teachers of mathematics, and was soon out of print. I was asked to publish a second edition, but I declined since I was more interested in new problems than in an activity which consisted in collecting and revising existing material.

In 1925 I published my book, *Der Aufbau der Tastwelt* ("The World of Touch"), a work in which holistic views were systematically developed in opposition to the prevalent atomistic views. In order to do justice to the great number of natural touch phenomena, it was necessary to critically examine and reject the atomism of that time. A large part of the book, which has now been out of print for quite some time, deals with observations concerning the vibratory sense. Though the organs of this sense possibly are identical with those of the pressure sense, its function seems closer to the auditory sense than to that of pressure. Evolutionally the vibratory sense represents the bridge between pressure sense and auditory sense. In deaf people it functions vicariously for the absent auditory sense, and may even render music accessible to them. I was able to prove this in a study published in collaboration with Révész, *Musikgenuss bei Gerhorlosen* (1926). Many performances of animals, such as spiders, can only be explained by the existence of a vibratory sense.

If one holds in each hand a vibrator oscillating synchronously at a not-too-slow speed and with the intensity of vibration decreasing on one side and increasing on the other, one gets the impression of something moving through the air from one hand to the other. This is an interesting case of external projection which cannot be due to previous experience. Obviously our nervous system is capable of types of achievements which ordinarily remain unknown.

The psychology of hunger and appetite was a subject to which I devoted considerable efforts during my stay in Rostock.   I dealt with the problem in a short monograph, *Hunger und Appetet,* published in 1932 and now out of print.   The hunger drive, whose physiological aspects are sufficiently well known, offered the best chance to clarify the general laws of drives.   A two-component theory of hunger was advanced, according to which the satisfaction of hunger is not based solely on physiological factors but also, to a surprising extent, on field conditions.   In my theory of avidity I formulated for a specific case the principle of self-regulation of metabolism, which brought me into close contact with Gestalt psychology.

By means of my theory of the psychology of hunger I laid the foundation for a general psychology of needs.   Starting with the concept of need, one can divide the general psychology of need into three parts: a survey of existing needs, objects to satisfy them, and the technique of acquiring them. From the techniques as a whole, which I believe also include language and thinking, one can further separate the psychophysical apparatus as the instruments, as it were, on which the technique acts.   If based on the concept of need, many psychophysical investigations take on quite new aspects.

Despite its limited facilities, in time the Rostock laboratory attracted quite a number of students, most of them candidates for the doctor's degree. About thirty dissertations in various fields were published, most of them in the *Zeitschrift für Psychologie* which was the oldest psychological journal in Germany.   Schumann and I co-edited this journal from 1930 to 1933.   I also took part in editing the fourth volume of the *Psychological Register.*   For several years I represented psychology in the *Notgemeinschaft der deutschen Wissenschaft* (Society in Aid of German Science).   This organization supported scientific work and publications with rather large sums.   Among other projects it financed a small research laboratory of animal psychology in Rostock, probably the only animal laboratory of this kind in Germany.

In 1929 I accepted an invitation from the University of Maine in Orono to teach there as a visiting professor.   On this occasion I came into personal contact with American psychology for the first time, a contact which for me was extremely valuable and stimulating.   Robert H. MacLeod assisted me most graciously in the planning of that trip.   During the following year I received an invitation from the Ohio State University at Columbus, which I regretfully declined since I did not like the idea of leaving my numerous students again for a long period of time.

Rostock was not far away from Hamburg, Copenhagen and Berlin.   My friend, William Stern, worked in Hamburg, Rubin, one of my oldest friends, taught in Copenhagen.   I always maintained cordial relations with the representatives of the Berlin Gestalt School.   Everything at Rostock seemed to promise scientific success and happiness; then Hitler ascended to power and I was soon to share the fate of all non-Aryans.   At first it seemed that my military activity during the first World War would protect me against the loss of my position and all the misery which threatened my family and me. The government of Mecklenburg, however, easily found the means to trick me out of my job. The chair I occupied was declared to be unnecessary, and was suspended in spite of the fact that psychology had become the largest department of the University. My scientific career appeared to have come to an end; suffering and indigence seemed imminent.

In this desperate situation I received a call to the University of Manchester in the fall of 1933. At this university the distinguished historian, L. B. Namier, had organized a foundation which would enable a number of German scientists, victims of the Nazis, to carry on their research, and I was fortunate enough to be one of those invited. At first the Nazis denied me a passport — they really meant destruction. I owe it to my courageous colleague, the historian W. Schussler, that I finally obtained my visa. (It had been denied only some months before, when the British Association for the Advancement of Science had invited me to participate at its congress.) In the autumn of 1933 I left for Manchester, but with a heavy heart; my family had to remain in Rostock as long as my financial position in England was uncertain. Two years later, when the Academic Assistance Council took over my financial support and when the Leys Schools in Cambridge generously offered free tuition to my two sons, my family was reunited. Through these unhappy years my wife was a comrade whose courage did much to help me carry on.

Soon after my arrival in England I met Aveling, and to my surprise he asked, "Do you know that you have been in *Punch?*" This was news to me, and Aveling told me the facts. Since I had been unable to take part in the Congress of the British Association, as I mentioned above, my absence had been noted on the bulletin board at the meetings in the following way: "Professor E. C. Tolman speaks about the learning of rats. . . . Professor D. Katz withdraws." *Punch* quoted this statement and added: "A very tactful retirement."

As an Honorary Research Fellow I spent the following two years (1933–35) at the University of Manchester, where I enjoyed the hospitality of Professor T. H. Pear's laboratory. There I carried on research which led to the publication of my paper on "The tongue as a primitive sense-organ."[4] The experiments attempted to prove the hypothesis that the sensations conveyed by the tongue are archaic in character. Life originated in water where it passed through its first stages of development; when our animal progenitors left the water, the body surface dried up and an extensive change took place in the organization of the senses. As I have shown, dryness and wetness in

---

[4] *Mem Manchr lit. phil. Soc*, 1934, 78, 56–72.

a specific sense are experienced exclusively in the mouth. Thus this study is an experimental contribution to the genetics of sensory psychology.

In 1935 I moved to London, where I was invited to work in the laboratory of Professor Cyril Burt. London attracted me strongly because it seemed possible to continue the investigations on animal psychology which I had begun in Rostock. Julian Huxley, the director of the Zoological Gardens, planned to modernize zoological research which at that time was based entirely on morphology and systematics. For that reason he welcomed my proposal to complement the current methodology by psychological experimentation with animals. For two years my wife and I walked daily to Regent's Park. In the animal clinic we were given a small place to carry out our experiments. Two publications resulted from this work: "Some problems concerning the feeding behaviour of monkeys" and[5] "Behaviour of monkeys under light of poor visibility."[6] The first study was based on the earlier work in Rostock concerning the hunger instinct, and led to new insights into the regulation of the hunger instinct as a function of field conditions. The latter study, however, dealt with a new problem, namely, the change in animal behavior through elimination of a sense which normally predominates. In the case of monkeys, which as a rule depend mainly upon sight, that experimental condition was accomplished by drastically reducing illumination. When our own eyes had become sufficiently adapted as a result of a longer stay in the almost-dark room, we were able to watch the animals, who at the same time and because of their slow adaptation, were almost blind. There are, of course, countless experiments on the behavior of animals in which sight has been destroyed by operation; in contrast to these studies the conditions of our experiments, however, made it possible to return to the normal situation at any time. Experiments of this kind offer new possibilities for the study of the problem of vicarious perception in animals.

When I gave two lectures on animal psychology for the children of the Royal Society of Arts, I learned how much interested the English public was in these problems. The response to these lectures was so great that even *The Times* and the *Manchester Guardian* published editorials about them. At that time I was already working on a book which was published under the title *Animals and Men – Studies in Comparative Psychology* (1937). It summarized the research I had carried out in cooperation with my students on animal psychology, and included pertinent contributions of other scientists. For quite a time it had been a principle of mine to study, if possible, unsolved problems of human psychology by means of animal experimentation. In doing so one is often able to decide between two hypotheses which, in terms of human psychology, would be equally probable. If one has to choose,

[5] *Proc. Zool. Soc.* (London), 1936, Part 2.
[6] *Proc. Zool. Soc.* (London), 1937, Series A.

for instance, between the physiological color-contrast theory of Hering and the one by Helmholtz, based on unconscious inferences, the fact that color-contrast exists in the lower animals (even in bees) decides the matter in favor of the physiological theory. How profitable the comparative psychological method can be has been shown by the experiments of one of my pupils, the Norwegian animal psychologist, Th. Schjelderup-Ebbe, concerning the laws of social rank-order in animals, which in some ways are analogous to the social hierarchy of human beings.

Comparative psychology is of decisive importance in the problem of the nature of man and his place in the universe. This problem obviously is the central question of modern philosophical anthropology. How can it ever be answered if not by comparison of man with his fellow-creatures? Thus my animal book attempts to contribute to anthropology, which in my opinion is basic to a satisfactory understanding of human psychology.

In England I was psychological adviser to the British Research Association of Flour Millers for two years. This association wanted a psychologist's assistance on two quite different problems. In bakeries the gluten content of flour is very important. The higher this content is, the easier the dough can be handled. Complaints of the bakers concerning too-low gluten content, which they based on a subjective touch sensation, could certainly be decided objectively; but these complaints, with time, became so annoying that the Research Association asked the psychologist to find out whether the bakers' subjective touch sensation was at all trustworthy. I was able to prove that doughs of various origin could be, to a certain extent, differentiated by tactual methods. Dough of very high gluten content seems "alive"; dough of very low gluten content seems "dead." The reliability, however, of this judgment at medium gluten content was by no means sufficient to uphold the bakers' complaints, which were based entirely on subjective touch sensations. The impression of greater liveliness is connected with the fact that more elastic dough enables the fingers to rebound easily — Sherrington's proprioceptive reflex. These experiences later caused me to examine the proprioceptive reflex more closely; they showed that in voluntary motions we continually take the recoil into consideration either by using it, avoiding it, inhibiting it, or letting it pass without interfering.

The second question which the Research Association had asked me to answer was of greater practical importance. In England a steady decline in bread consumption took on such proportions that it began to threaten the flour market. Even during periods of heavy unemployment the bread consumption of the most seriously affected families was not higher than that of the well-to-do, although no other article of food with the exception of potatoes produces as many calories for the same price. What was the reason for this decline, and what could be done about it? I came to the conclusion that this decline in bread consumption was partly due to a desire for the slim figure demanded by sports and the Hollywood ideal of beauty, and partly to the competition of new and more appetizing food.   To stop the decline of bread consumption I proposed to make the English bread tastier.   At the same time I recommended changing to new flour products and inducing agriculture to shift its emphasis from grain production to other foods.   The reason for the decline of bread as a main food staple lies in a change of appetite which can hardly be expected to reverse itself except through the emergence of unusual counteracting factors.   All this shows the importance of applied psychology for very significant problems of national economics.

An invitation of the Chartered Society of Massage and Medical Gymnastics turned my interest toward psychological questions of massage.   During my work with the hand as a sensory and motor organ, I had earlier come across two medical methods: palpation and percussion.   The effects of massage on healthy and sick bodies always involves psychological factors; there are certainly connections, for instance, between the age-old psycho-therapeutic effect of "the laying on of hands," and medical massage.   In this borderline field cooperation between medicine and psychology should produce many valuable results.   My lecture on "Touch in Massage and in General Medical Technique," which later was published, had a strange result: I was asked by the author of a textbook on massage to write a preface, a request with which I complied.

I shall always remember with deep gratitude the pleasant four years I spent in England, where I experienced so many evidences of noble humane feeling, while my home-country had fallen to a barbarism beyond human comprehension.   I would gladly have stayed in that country whose ways of thought and methods of work so greatly appealed to me.   It was, however, hard to foresee if and when it would be possible for me to enter academic life there in a full-time capacity.   From a disinterested source I received the suggestion that I apply for a vacant chair at the University of Stockholm, a suggestion that I followed up.   Since the will of the founder of this professorship, dating back to 1881, was quite ambiguous, the nature of the chair became the subject of much discussion.   Finally the opinion prevailed that a chair of pedagogy was closest to the founder's intention.   I might mention that at that time no chair of psychology existed in Sweden, and that it was part of the duty of the professor of pedagogy also to take care of psychology.

Three years elapsed between the time of my application and my appointment.   I finally received a telegram from the President of the University, Sven Tunberg, which read: "Royal confirmation — welcome in Stockholm."   Thus the decision finally turned out in my favor; the intrigues of German Nazism, which had permeated even into Sweden, were thwarted by the fearless and noble attitude of the Swedish authorities.   At last I had regained firm roots, had become a member of a university, and was able to carry out research in my own laboratory. As in Rostock I had to start from the very beginning, the only difference being that the organization in Sweden was more difficult because methods of instruction, curriculum, and kind of examination differed widely from continental forms. Though some adverse circumstances, particularly the outbreak of the second World War two years after my emigration to Sweden, hindered the full realization of all my plans, very soon a lively program of research began to take shape in the youngest laboratory in Sweden.

A part of our research work dealt with entirely new fields in which the point of view of Gestalt psychology was more strongly emphasized than before; this led to the publication of a small book on Gestalt psychology in which I tried to show the fruitfulness of the Gestalt approach; at the same time, however, I pointed out the definite limits of the holistic method. My familiarity with Gestalt psychology has been of long standing; when Koffka reviewed my book on color, he expressed his confidence that its investigations would have influence on psychological research in general. I am quite sure that Koffka had in mind particularly my holistic theory of color perception. In the book on touch I completely broke away from the prevailing atomistic view. Certainly our book on conversations with children was written in a holistic vein; and, finally, the theory of avidity had utilized the principle of dynamic self-regulation of the organism. Now some new problems were added to our work which offered new possibilities for a Gestalt-psychological application: the problem of mental work, which Kraepelin had subjected to a one-sided atomistic method; that of the transposition of action-configurations, the problem of the formation of the body-image; and, finally, that of characteristics of the thought process, including those I had called blinding phenomena.

The possibilities for applications of Gestalt principles in psychology have not been exhausted, but one has to be on guard against thinking of the Gestalt-psychological view as the only method in psychology. Many psychological facts cannot be interpreted in terms of the atomistic-holistic dichotomy; this is, for instance, the case with respect to qualities of sensation. The symbol concept is of high importance in the field of psychology of thinking, but offers little for considerations of theoretical concepts of Gestalt psychology. As things stand now, I cannot see how isomorphic views could be applied to a psychophysics of thought processes of a logical-conclusive character. Again, differential psychology can hardly be based on Gestalt-psychological views. Even if one acknowledges the revolutionary significance of Gestalt psychology in the development of our science, one should not forget the merits of earlier periods of psychology, neither should one fail to apply other methods of modern psychology to questions which are relatively unrelated to problems of configuration.

Occasional observations in widely different fields of animal as well as of human psychology led me to a problem in which I recently became very much interested — the problem of performances of the organism which are achieved under quite exceptional conditions, or, in other words, the problem of the activity range of the organism. It is rather difficult to fit these achievements into one of the existing theories of evolution; it is hard to see how they could have been developed in accordance with such hypotheses. It seems that the organism is richer in possibilities than is usually realized. There are, for instance, those well-known examples which show how the response mechanism of animals is capable of adapting itself at once to the new circumstances, as in the case of experimental amputation. There are, furthermore, cases of excellent distance orientation in artificially disorientated birds and dogs. These instances are so strange that nowadays some psychologists include them — somewhat hastily — under "extrasensory perception."

Concerning conditions that induce unusual forms of human reaction, I might refer to some of those made possible through modern techniques in the field of perception. If one throws on a screen a number of different movements, using several projectors at the same time, one sees clearly as many as three interpenetrating movements. Such experience does not exist in natural motion perception. It is easy to produce a film in which persons seem to glide through each other like ghosts, and where the law of impenetrability seems suspended. I might also refer here to the above-mentioned phenomenon of vibratory displacement, which does not occur under normal conditions. Then, too, with the help of two vibrators, it is possible to enforce displacement phenomena from one sensory field to the other; this occurs, *e.g.*, if one puts one vibrator close to the ear and holds the second one in the hand. These new achievements, occurring under exceptional conditions, are not restricted to perception. Under mescal intoxication the attributes of reality change radically; the limits between the ego and the surrounding world become blurred. It is a fascinating task to examine such phenomena which, without being occult, normally remain hidden.

Another pertinent problem relates to the formation of composite photographs. Photography enables us to produce composite pictures, such as those shown first by Francis Galton. In recent years I have studied such pictures extensively, and found the composite photograph valuable as a novel method of studying "collectivity," in terms of a concrete representation of statistical facts. One of the unexpected results was that a relatively small number of individual pictures, gathered at random, always show the same composite picture. Just as unexpected was the discovery of the beauty which these composite photographs always possess, a result which might provide food for thought even to a psychologist who is not usually prone to metaphysical speculation.

With the destruction of German psychology, America has assumed leadership in all fields of our science, and my desire to renew contact with American psychology was fulfilled in 1950 when I was invited to give the Hitchcock Lectures at the University of California at Berkeley. I must leave to fate whether I shall be able to take advantage of the great incentive I received from this renewed acquaintance with an extremely lively and productive science.

ALBERT MICHOTTE van den Berck

W HEN publication of my autobiography was proposed to me, my first
reaction was to decline this honor.[1] My life, academic and scientific as
well as private, has proceeded so simply, so regularly, and indeed so logically, that it seemed to promise little of interest to anyone outside my
immediate environment.

Upon reflection, however, it occurred to me that a collection of autobiographies might well gain by including the most varied samples of the
styles de vie of contemporary psychologists, and I yielded to the amiable
insistence of a few of my colleagues.

"Styles of life" may mean many things. It goes without saying that it
is only of scientific life that I am thinking. The aim of this book is to
provide a contribution to the history of psychology, including the details
which the French so aptly call *la petite histoire*. Thus, what is paramount
here, it seems to me, is that each of us should give an account of his
opinion concerning his personal contribution to our knowledge of psychology, as well as trace the individual evolution of his ideas and the
reasons which have provoked it.

Such is the spirit in which these pages have been conceived.[2]

I was born in 1881 at Brussels, the second and last child of a well-to-do
intellectual family, interested traditionally in both the fine arts and science.
Thus my youth was spent in a cultivated environment.[3] All my known
ancestors were Catholic and sincerely religious, as I too have been all my
life.

I entered the University of Louvain as a student in 1897 and studied
philosophy and science until 1905. There I had the good fortune to find
two great masters.

[1] Submitted in French and translated by Professor J G. Beebe-Center of Harvard University.
[2] I take the liberty of mentioning that a short biography, together with complete bibliography
and a list of all research undertaken in my laboratory, have been published in *Miscellanea Psychologica Albert Michotte*, pp I–XL, edited in 1947, on the occasion of my professorial jubilee,
by Editions de l'Institut Supérieur de Philosophie, Louvain.
[3] My brother Paul was also professor at the University of Louvain, where he taught Geography
and founded the Institute of Geography which bears his name.

The first was the incomparable man who later was to become the illustrious Cardinal Mercier. At the time, he was professor and President of the Institut Supérieur de Philosophie. From the very outset he was kind enough to show for me a solicitude and an affection which were truly paternal. His influence was determinative in my intellectual and "human" development. Even today I continue to feel its beneficent effects.

The second was the great neurologist, Arthur van Gehuchten, who introduced me to scientific work. It was under him that I carried out my first investigations.[4]

Mercier was greatly interested in psychology. When he founded the Institut de Philosophie, he wished it to include the teaching of psychophysiology. To this end he had procured the collaboration of Professor Armand Thiéry, who had worked with Wundt at Leipzig, and who organized a small laboratory in the Institut as early as 1894. It is there that I learned the first rudiments of our science. Thiéry, however, preoccupied with philosophical and theoretical questions, was not a laboratory man. In consequence, when my philosophical and scientific training had progressed sufficiently, Mercier strongly encouraged my plan to become a specialist in psychology. As a step in this direction I undertook under Thiéry a series of investigations on the distribution of tactile sensitivity.[5]

My next step was to go to Leipzig, where I spent two semesters, in 1905 and 1906. It was there that I really began to become familiar with psychology, for the Louvain laboratory was still in an embryonic state, and its library even more so. I steeped myself at that time in Wundt's *Grundzüge der physiologischen Psychologie*, and I familiarized myself with the techniques of experimentation. I had a great admiration for the system developed by Wundt, but I felt nevertheless that it was inadequate. I had already read a few works of Binet, and I had been struck by the accent he placed on the study of "higher processes" and by his extensive use of introspection.

In 1906 I had the opportunity of attending the Kongress für experimentelle Psychologie at Würzburg and of meeting Külpe. At once I was aware that I would find in him precisely what I felt to be missing at Leipzig. That is why I decided to go to his laboratory, and there I spent a few months in 1907 and 1908. I was perfectly happy in Würzburg, experiencing a true revelation. Indeed it is to Külpe that I owe my real maturation as a psychologist, not only because of my personal contacts with him and my participation in his seminar and his investigations, but

---

[4] A. Michotte, Contribution à l'étude de l'histologie fine de la cellule nerveuse, *Bulletin de l'Académie royale de Médecine de Belgique*, 1904, 515–556
[5] Michotte, *Les signes régionaux*, Louvain, Institut Supérieur de Philosophie, 1905.

also because it was through him that I discovered the works of Brentano, Mach, Meinong, Husserl, Stumpf, von Ehrenfels and others.

In 1909 I married Lucie Mulle. Our home which six children came to brighten has never ceased to be a perfectly happy one. I owe, indeed, great gratitude to my wife, for, although she is not an academic person herself, she has always understood admirably the duties required of me by my professorial responsibility and my scientific activity, and has always endeavored to relieve me of other cares.

Another event should also be mentioned here, one which had great influence on my career because it gave me the opportunity to concentrate all my efforts on the fairly specialized field which interested me most. After the war of 1914, the academic authorities, and especially Cardinal Mercier, who had become Chancellor of the University, decided to develop at Louvain the teaching of pedagogy according to modern ideas, and they were kind enough to call on me for collaboration. I took advantage of this opportunity to establish in 1923 with one of my former students, Professor Fauville, an "Ecole de Pédagogie et de Psychologie appliquée à l'Education." This change made it possible to develop and to diversify the teaching of scientific psychology. From then on the University provided lectures on individual psychology, mental tests, child psychology, adolescent psychology, etc., given by specialized teachers. Little by little new professorial appointments provided the opportunity to broaden the curriculum even further, and in 1944 our "School" was transformed into an Institut de Psychologie appliquée et de Pédagogie, which offered a thorough theoretical and practical education in all branches of psychology and was empowered to award academic degrees up to the Doctorate in Psychological Sciences.

This leads me quite naturally to say a few words concerning the factors which have determined the orientation of my scientific lifework throughout the course of its development, that is to say, my personal tendencies and the conditions under which I have worked.

There is a key idea which I have allowed always to guide me (a little too exclusively, perhaps). This idea is that each one of us, to give maximal effectiveness to his activity, must first of all try to become aware of his personal capacities, and, above all, of their *limitations*. He must manage, if possible, to bring all of his efforts to bear on the kind of work in which he considers it likely that he will attain maximal output.

Now tastes and aptitudes both had directed me from childhood towards experimentation. Furthermore, I felt especially attracted towards the exact sciences, and that is why my preferred field of activity has always been experimental psychology proper. Other branches, such as the social psychology of those days, the application of mental tests then still in their infancy, and, especially, psychoanalysis did not measure up to the standards set by my concern for precision. Consequently I have dealt with these subjects only to the extent demanded by my teaching. And yet I have always been convinced, and have stressed the conviction in my courses, that *social psychology* is of basic importance in the study of behavior, for it is quite clear that behavior is determined above all else by the *human environment* in which the individual lives. This essential complement of psychology, however, had to wait upon the future and upon the discovery of adequate methods of research.

For the rest, it seems a rather vain undertaking to try to establish a hierarchy of values in purely scientific matters. Any real problem — that is to say, any problem the solution of which will genuinely enrich our knowledge in any field and from any point of view — deserves the effort required for its study.

It seemed to me, I may add, that the stage of development reached by psychology at that time (and, indeed, perhaps its present stage) made it premature to venture on the construction of theories. There were too many theories for my liking in the works of most of the psychologists, theories that seemed to me to be singularly precarious. I felt convinced that the first thing to do was to know as exactly as possible the facts and the empirical laws controlling them.[6]

As I have just pointed out, at the beginning of my career my teaching was addressed only to the students of the Institut de Philosophie, for whom this field was of secondary importance and of little more than propaedeutic value. Some of these students, however, did show special interest in it and wanted to undertake research, but unfortunately they were not technically prepared to use experimental methods. The result was a kind of collaboration which has maintained itself, presumably by force of habit, throughout my whole career, even after the establishment of the Ecole de Pédagogie, which gave certain students the opportunity to enjoy a far better training.

As a matter of fact, I have always taken charge of the technical and instrumental sides and of the planning of experiments and have taken part in them personally, sometimes as observer, sometimes as experimenter. Indeed I have never had an assistant in the real sense of the word,[7] partly because the necessity of extending our teaching to new fields absorbed all the better young talent, partly because of budgetary limitations. I make no complaint

---

[6] Cf. p. 234.

[7] I must mention, however, that for the last thirty years I have had a technical collaborator of highest value, Mr. L. Roland, whom many psychologists know, and who, thanks to his admirable talent as a mechanic, has not only enriched the laboratory by a considerable collection of instruments, but has provided me with inestimable aid in carrying out my research.

in this matter. Our way of working gave me inestimable experience and made of my laboratory a sort of workshop like those of artisans of yore, or of painters, where the training of the "apprentices" depended ultimately on the experience which they acquired in the course of a period of active cooperation with their "master." This arrangement had very great charm, and it brought about between my students and myself relations of friendship which have been one of the joys of my life.

There is, however, a shadow over the picture. All of this work took an enormous amount of time. No sooner was one set of projects completed and their results analyzed, than I would find myself obliged to begin the study of other problems with new students. The result has been that even though I have done a great deal of experimentation during my life and thus learned much that I put to use in my teaching, and in my lectures abroad, a relatively important part of our work has never been published.

I must also confess that, dominated as I was by a passion for research, my joy in having brought a project to its conclusion, and in having found an answer to the question which had aroused my curiosity, was followed, naturally enough, by a dampening of my enthusiasm. Indeed, the idea of devoting myself afterwards to a painstaking task of composition, a task which, it seemed to me (though I have since learned better), would teach me nothing new, had for me no attraction whatsoever.

Maybe it will be possible for me, when I retire not too long from now, to publish what seems to me of some interest in this accumulated material.

What precedes is enough, I think, to make clear the character of my scientific work and to show that I have been, above all else, a laboratory investigator. It has been during my research work and in immediate connection with it that my ideas have been born and that my convictions have developed in regard to the major problems with which I have been concerned. Hence the best way to describe the evolution of my psychological thinking is to follow the development of the research tasks which I have undertaken with my students during the last forty years. Obviously I shall confine myself to the principal ones, but I shall also try to bring out, in connection with each, the conclusions which, in my opinion, seem to be of more general interest.

EXPERIMENTAL INVESTIGATIONS

My investigations fall naturally into three groups, corresponding to periods during which they assumed fairly different characteristics: the period extending up to the first World War, the one extending from 1920 to 1939, and, finally, the one from 1939 to the present.[8]

---

[8] A few of our laboratory investigations, particularly the ones which were of sufficient scope to provide material for a volume, have been published in a series which I called *Etudes de Psychologie*. Six volumes of this series have been published to date. The publisher is Editions de l'Institut Supérieur de Philosophie de Louvain.

Years 1905–1920

As early as 1905 I had been entrusted with the direction of the investigations of the laboratory of Louvain, with the status of assistant (then with that of lecturer in 1906, and of professor, beginning in 1908). After some early gropings, our investigations turned in the direction followed by the Wurzburg School and by Binet, becoming focused in the main on the study of the higher processes: logical memory, recollection, cognition and establishment of logical connections, genesis of meaning, voluntary choice, conscious motivation, etc.

We made extensive use of systematic introspection. We always tried, however, to complement introspection with a certain amount of objective control, seeking to discover the correlations that might exist between the data supplied by the *observers and certain objective symptoms*, like reaction-times or frequency of occurrence of certain sequences of these events under determinate conditions. As it turned out, we found correlations of this sort in many cases, and this put us on the track of interesting findings, notably in our studies of logical memory and of voluntary choice.

Thus, for instance, differences in reaction-times led us to recognize the role of the integrating function of thought in memory, an integration by which the items to be memorized become embedded in a complex relational unit (a Gestalt!) such that the reactivation of one of its aspects could bring about the reproduction of the others or make possible the intentional search for these others, and thus eventuate in a reinstatement of configurational unity.[9]

The result of all this was to provide a basis of personal experience for my convictions regarding the autonomy of thought processes and the shortcomings of traditional associationism and of the elementaristic conception of mental life. Our experiments on thought and on the meaning of words confirmed me in this way of thinking and brought out especially well the importance of the mental processes leading to the creation of symbols.

From this moment I was convinced that observational data justified, aside from any metaphysical considerations, the distinction of two levels of psychic activity: on the one hand, the level of sensory experience and of everything related to it (formation of units, associations, emotions, etc.), and, on the other, a higher level, that of thought. The latter was not to be conceived, in my opinion, as characterized by the intervention of new elements of mental life, but rather by a fertilization of sensory experience through the participation of special *functions* that allow the use of symbols and the formation of more comprehensive syntheses and permit relational thinking and reasoning.

[9] Michotte and C. Ransy, Contributions à l'étude de la mémoire logique, *Etudes de Psychol* , Louvain, Editions de l'Institut Supérieur de Philosophie, 1912, 1, 1–96; Michotte and T. Portych, Deuxieme étude sur la mémoire logique, *Etudes de Psychol.*, 1914, 1, 237–346.

The most important work of that period, however, was the one bearing on voluntary choice, in 1910.[10] We described there the various forms that choice, whether voluntary or not, could take between two possible actions; and we sought to determine the motivational conditions under which these forms occurred. To this end we carried out an analysis, both descriptive and statistical (very rudimentary), of the motivation involved, and examined the evolution which it showed with repetition of the situation in which the subject was placed.

This investigation led us to the conclusion that man has an immediate experience of his own activity (what we called "awareness of action"), a conclusion which agreed with the observations of Ach, but one which had been reached by us independently.

Furthermore, the study of what was then called determination (determining tendency) brought me to a dynamical conception of psychology which has dominated my whole work and led me to recognize the capital importance of permanent unconscious tendencies in the make-up of personality.

This contribution was in general well received by the critics, and Külpe wrote me a long and extremely flattering letter about it. I treasure the letter to this day, for it helped a great deal in the development of my self-confidence and was an inestimable stimulus to my later activity.

Then came the war of 1914, the burning of Louvain, and, to my profound grief, the death of my venerated father under tragic circumstances. I moved with my family to Utrecht, where my friend, Professor Zwaardemaker, lived; and, having been entrusted by the Belgian Government with the task of teaching the young university students who were in the part of our army that had been interned in Holland, I remained there until 1918. I occupied myself with various scientific projects, principally with the measurement of acoustic energy, in Zwaardemaker's laboratory.[11]

Years 1920–1939

My ideas had matured during the war, and I had done a good deal of thinking, particularly about the problem of introspection. The many discussions that had come up, both in Germany and in America, concerning the work of Külpe's school, and in particular Titchener's criticisms, together with the contentions of the behaviorist movement then coming into existence — all these had shaken my confidence in the scientific value of introspection as used at Würzburg and as I had used it myself up to that time.

[10] Michotte and E Prum, Etude expérimentale sur le choix volontaire et ses antécédents immédiats, Louvain, Editions de l'Institut Supérieur de Philosophie, 1910, also in Arch de Psychol , 1910, 10, 113–320, Michotte, Note à propos de contributions récentes à la psychologie de la volonté, Etudes de Psychol , 1912, 1, 193–233.

[11] Michotte, Note sur la mesure de l'énergie acoustique au moyen du miroir de Rayleigh, Arch. Néerlandaises de Physiologie, 1922, 7, 579–587.

Theoretical objections, as well as the *fact* that experiments of this type yielded *contradictory* results when performed under apparently identical conditions, by persons of marked competence but with different training, especially when the investigators belonged to different psychological schools — these were such as to warrant the greatest scepticism.   Besides, it was obvious that, in spite of the objections of the opposing side, everyone always remained convinced of the *correctness* of his own observations.

Since there was no court of last resort empowered to decide who was right and who was wrong, it followed that such experiments had only the individual value of a personal belief, and that, incapable of general verification, they could not be considered scientific.

Such being the case, I became convinced that it was a vain task to try to describe internal events and analyze them into elements, and that the only value of introspection must be an *informative* one.   In this connection, the verbal responses of observers come to be considered as differential reactions, allowing only for the discovery in the subject of the presence, the absence or variation of an event x, the nature of which necessarily escapes the experimenter and remains for him unknowable.

On the other hand, general information of this sort about the state of mind of the observer, about the way in which he understands the situation in which he finds himself, and about his own reactions to this situation seemed to me indispensable in all psychological experiments, even in those intended to bear solely on the external, objective behavior of the subject.

Such information is especially useful in one particular field, that of perception.   There it is possible to establish a parallelism between the relatively simple and limited responses of observers and the stimulus or the complex system of stimulation acting upon them.   Applying then the principle of concomitant variations, it is possible to establish the conditions for the phenomenon x, whatever its nature "in itself."   This is what has always been done in the experiments of psychophysics, and the procedure is obviously similarly applicable to the study of the perception of complex configuration.[12]

It is, indeed, in this field that a great many of our investigations between the two wars were concentrated.   Among other things, these researches were directed upon constancy phenomena in the tactile-kinesthetic field, upon sensory syntheses in that field, upon the relations between visual and tactile-motor localization, upon the relations between the reproductions of irregular figures when presentation is visual and when it is tactile-motor, upon the influence of the entire form of an object on the localization of its parts in the third dimension, upon induced movement, upon the genesis of visual forms whose parts appear successively, and so on.   In addition there were tachisto-

[12] Michotte, Psychologie et philosophie, *Revue néoscolastique de Philosophie*, Louvain, Editions de l'Institut Supérieur de Philosophie, 1936, *39*, 208–228.

scopic experiments and extensive investigations on the stroboscopic phenomenon. It would be tiresome to list them all. These instances will suffice to show with what they dealt.

Even in our first experiments in this field we obtained results and reached conclusions quite analogous to the fundamental principles of Gestalt psychology, a movement which was then still unknown to me, for I was cut off from scientific publications by the destruction of our University library during the war.

It was at the Oxford International Congress in 1923, where I met Koffka and Köhler, that I first acquired a close-up knowledge of Gestalt psychology, and so was enabled to note the similarity of our points of view. There remained, however, a certain number of divergences between us, particularly concerning the importance which I ascribed both to past experience and to needs and attitudes as factors determining the structural organization of perception. As my ideas evolved later, especially in the course of my most recent experiments, I was obliged to recognize that the influence of past experience is much less in principle than I had earlier imagined. It assumes its full importance only, it would seem, in the ambiguous cases (numerous, withal) where several types of structuration have more or less equal chances of establishing themselves because the objective factors of organization (proximity, similarity, symmetry, etc.) do not have the necessary strength to impose a particular form.

This question of the role of past experience, and likewise of needs, is connected with a thesis that has always been dear to me, namely that it is futile to try to study perception "in itself." Rather, perception should be considered as a "phase of action," in the framework of the activity of the individual, both motor and intellectual.

When seen from this point of view, the role of perception evidently does not reside in the mere presentation of objects of this or that form, of this or that color, for a completely isolated object remains devoid of meaning and thus of interest. It influences behavior only in so far as it has a signification[13] that is given to it by the relations that unite it to other objects, the relations in space and time, the relations of causality and of finality, etc. The problem of meaning thus takes precedence, in the long run, over the problem of form, and one might consider that it is, in theory, separate from that of perception because all meaning is, as was long thought, an extrinsic complement of the perceptive datum. Such is not the case, however, and this question arises all over again when one finds that it is possible to *perceive* also certain functional relations (as was shown much later by my experiments on the awareness of causality) and that certain complex experiences consequently possess an *intrinsic meaning*.

[13] Michotte, Rapport sur la perception des formes. Symposium "Gestaltwahrnehmung," *Proc. VIIIth International Congress of Psychology*, Groningen, 1926, 89–97.

Be that as it may, it is to a large extent these ideas concerning the importance of the meanings that certain objects or actions may have for a man or an animal witnessing them — it is these ideas that have prevented me from subscribing to a radical behaviorism. I had, indeed, become convinced that psychology was not a science of mental life but rather a science of behavior and actions. Nonetheless it seemed entirely evident to me that to make an exhaustive study of behavior it is essential to take into account the way in which men or animals understand the situation in which they are placed, the actions of other men or of other animals, as well as the actions that they themselves perform.

On the other hand, it is certainly the development of behaviorism that led me to concern myself more especially with motor reactions, beginning in 1924 and continuing for a number of years thereafter. These years witnessed the undertaking of a whole series of investigations closely linked one to another.

The starting point of the first of them was a strange observation which I had made on the speed with which it is possible to execute a chain of movements involving the successive striking of a series of targets, arranged irregularly in a plane with fairly large distances between them.[14] What I had observed was that the speed was practically the same when the subject had practiced the activity a large number of times as when he was performing the activity for the first time, provided that he had been allowed in advance the time necessary for examining thoroughly the positions of the points to be touched. In view of this finding, it was natural for me to wonder exactly what can be the role of motor training as such.

In order to settle this question, I adopted a technique, patterned after the old procedure of Marey, which made it possible to record on a photographic plate the trajectory described by the hand (the finger) of the observer. This record was combined with measures of time, etc. The kinesigrams thus obtained constituted the objective documents on the basis of which it was possible to study systematically the modifications that might take place in the form of the trajectories.

It immediately became apparent that training was accompanied by profound alterations in this regard. The trajectories took on a characteristic appearance quite different from that which they displayed before training. The orientation, the length, the form of each segment were obviously adapted to those of the following segments, and vice versa. All the parts were integrated into a continuous whole and changed as a function of the whole. It was the objective demonstration of the long-recognized fact that with practice motor reactions become unitary and global, and that they are set off all at once. Furthermore, they were no longer "conducted" by a visual schema,

[14] J. van der Veldt, L'apprentissage du mouvement et l'automatisme, *Etudes de Psychol.*, Editions de l'Institut Supérieur de Philosophie, Louvain, 1928, vol. 3, also Vrin, Paris, 1928

and the indication of the targets to be hit now only played a part like that of an order to salute or to take up an object lying on a table.

In addition, certain other experiments showed that the forms of the trajectories became stereotyped, recurring with marked self-identity in the course of successive repetitions. They also showed that the forms could maintain themselves even when the subject was made to respond in another plane or on another scale (transposition).

Moreover, since the forms shown by the kinesigrams were the mechanical resultant of the movements executed by the observers, it is evident that the characteristics of the kinesigrams must have been representing certain properties of the movements themselves. Thus, it became possible to assert that motor exercise results in the creation of global, autonomous *motor forms*, possessing properties similar to the properties of *sensory forms*. Here was an experimental demonstration of the applicability of Gestalt principles to the motor field, a new contribution to Gestalt psychology which, at that time, had pretty much limited itself to the study of the sensory domain.

This first experiment, however, had dealt with many other problems, and the use of kinesigrams had been, on the whole, more or less incidental. Then this emphasis changed. Our later experiments dealt more specifically with the motor forms themselves. The study of their spatial and temporal structures I called the "morphology of movement."[15]

In 1931 we began to study, by means of improved techniques, the problem of the deformations shown by trajectories recorded when the complex movements had to be executed at greater and greater speeds.[16] Deviations of trajectories relative to the "model" can, as everyone knows (in the case of writing, for example), be marked, and our task was to discover the factors which determine their form.

In this connection, however, a first point deserves to be noted. The model shown visually to the subject can eventually be structured in different ways by different people, each of whom can give an introspective description of the fashion in which he "sees" it. Now, the experiments showed that the form of the trajectory copied literally, without awareness by the subject, the sensory structure described by him. Thus there was here a veritable objective recording of the subjective organization, and, besides, a demonstration of the importance of the latter as a factor determining the reaction.

Nevertheless there are also other factors more purely motor in origin. Thus I noted that many of the trajectories executed at very high speeds and strongly deformed presented striking analogies with Lissajous' figures. This finding led me to suppose that the movements of the limbs controlling the

[15] Michotte, L'étude morphologique des réactions motrices, *Proc XIth International Congress of Psychology*, Paris, 1938, 29–41.
[16] G de Montpellier, Les altérations morphologiques des mouvements rapides, *Etudes de Psychol*, 1935, vol. 4.

form of the trajectory must in all likelihood be pendular movements, an hypothesis that was subsequently verified in 1938 in the course of new experiments, undertaken with other collaborators. These experiments involved analysis, by means of motion pictures, of the movements performed by the various segments of limbs, movements that resulted in the production of the trajectories under consideration. The results showed quite clearly the occurrence of continuous segmental movements of a pendular form.

As everyone knows, this type of movement corresponds to well-known physiological mechanisms which allow them to take place under optimal and singularly economical conditions. We concluded from this that combinations of movements of such a type should be considered as favored forms — "pregnant" ones — which establish themselves spontaneously, as soon as the situation permits it. Another analogy between motor forms and sensory forms!

We had, furthermore, observed that subjects have a tendency to introduce rhythm into their movements, and that the movements take on not only a spatial structure, but also a determinate temporal structure, which is elicited by the form of the model.

A related experiment was undertaken in 1938.[17] In it the subjects were to touch targets, adhering to a rhythm imposed upon them by audition. We found that this rhythmization of movements also produced modifications in the trajectory which were specific for the rhythm. These alterations were so characteristic that they recurred, for each rhythmic structure, after an interval of three months, maintaining an obvious degree of self-similarity without any noticeable effect from learning!

Whatever their origin, the deformations of the trajectories raised another problem. It seemed evident that they must result in a decrease of accuracy in the touching of the targets. We were led by this expectation to make a special study of this aspect of the matter in 1933. We used new methods, notably the so-called method of typtograms, which allows the recording of the dispersion of taps, combined with the taking of kinesigrams.[18] The results showed that, in general, our hypothesis was correct, that accuracy depends not only on speed, but also on the rhythm involved in the reaction. They also showed, however, that the forms of the trajectories followed by different subjects with the same degree of accuracy could differ markedly from one another.

A further series of experiments, in 1936 and the years following, dealt with training in accuracy in the case of rapid movements, the morphological characteristics of the automatic motor reactions of everyday life, the acceleration of movement, the transfer of motor training, and similar topics.

[17] Montpellier, Note sur le rythme dans les mouvements volontaires de la main, *J de Psychol*, 1946, 39, 467–473.
[18] H. MacNeill, Motor adaptation and accuracy, *Etudes de Psychol*, 1934, vol. 5.

Our experiments on motor reactions had constantly confronted us with the problem of rhythm, a situation that led us to undertake in 1935 a systematic study of rhythmic structure as such.[19] This study confirmed our view that rhythm must be considered a *temporal form,* analogous to spatial form and occurring in the various sensory modalities as well as in the motor sphere.

Furthermore, a thorough examination of spontaneous rhythmization disclosed to us the existence of an internal organization of the rhythmic measure which is truly astonishing for its structural complexity as well as for its extraordinary precision and for its stability.

I shall not go into detail, for it might lead us far afield, but it is important at least to point out that in spontaneous rhythmization the divisions constituting the complex measures were of two sorts: simple *successions* and *durations* which combined together in various ways. These divisions are functionally interdependent, for change in one is accompanied by changes in the others, in such a way as to maintain the over-all structure. Thus certain types of organization are favored, and when an experimenter seeks to impose upon his subjects the production of a different rhythmic form, their reactions tend to alter in the direction of the pregnant structure, at the price of systematic deviations from the proposed model.

Finally, it may be said, the favored temporal structure establishes itself spontaneously, always the same, when the total duration of the measure is varied over a considerable range and also when the reactions are performed by different bodily parts, like the hand, the foot, or the head. Thus there is transposition.

This work constituted a new contribution to the psychology of form and was, as far as I know, the first extensive experimental research bearing on these particular aspects of temporal forms.

Our experiments on motor reactions had allowed us to make numerous observations relative to learning, and this interest switched my research in two new directions — toward the law of effect, a topic to which I shall return in a moment, and toward the old problem of association.

As regards the latter, our first experiment in 1924 had clearly confirmed the views of Lewin concerning the eventual dynamic role of "associations by contiguity" by showing that connections established in this way are not sufficient in and of themselves to bring about the arousal of the induced term following the mere occurrence of the inducing term. Reproduction seemed rather to depend on the action of distinct dynamic factors, such as the influence of the task accepted by the subject. Furthermore, we had also observed that errors of reproduction, consisting in the

[19] P. Fraisse, Contribution à l'étude du rythme en tant que forme temporelle, *J. de Psychol.,* 1946, **39**, 280–304.

execution of reactions *learned* but different from the ones which the subject was asked to execute, occurred when there was similarity or fairly extensive partial identity between the form of the reaction demanded and the form of the reaction previously learned.

This discovery brought us back to our old experiment on logical memory, for in both cases there was the development of an over-all unitary configuration at the time of learning, and reinstatement of the entirety of the pattern at the time of reproduction, provided that a sufficiently characteristic part of the configuration should be present.

In all this there was an obvious analogy to the notion of the Gestalt school according to which the laws of association become confounded, in the last analysis, with the laws which control the formation of over-all structures.

In order to render more precise my ideas about this matter, I planned a new set of experiments in 1937, the purpose of which was to compare the chances of the arousal of one term by another (known objects or meaningless geometrical figures) when they had been simply presented simultaneously, juxtaposed in space, at the time of learning, and when, on the other hand, they had been integrated into an over-all unit. This over-all unit was sometimes purely spatial in nature, formed, for example, by partial superposition. At other times it was of an "internal" nature, like a picture representing certain functional relations between the two objects, as, for instance, a hatchet-cutting-wood. The general result was what one might easily have foreseen: The chances of arousal were found to be the greater, the more powerful had been the factors of unity at the time of learning. Temporal relations apparently enjoyed no special privilege in this matter.

These experiments further brought out clearly the need of applying a correction to the general principle. For arousal to take place, it is obviously necessary that the part to be reproduced should not have been absorbed by the over-all unit at the time of its formation, and that the part should thus have retained a phenomenal existence of its own. Such being the case, it seems that the general principle ought to be formulated as follows: Optimum conditions of arousal correspond to *the formation of the strongest unities compatible with the maintenance of adequate autonomy of the parts in the over-all units which they constitute.* This rule, let it be said in passing, seems to go far toward explaining the superiority of so-called logical memory.

With regard to the law of effect, we had found that, during motor practice of rapid reactions, the form of the trajectories changed successively at the critical points in such a way as to make performance of the trajectories *easier.* This change was wholly unconscious. The possibility of applying the law of effect to this phenomenon was obvious.

At this point I asked myself to what extent the *recollection* of rewards or punishments might influence *intentional* practice. With this in mind, we sought to determine whether the law of effect could not be interpreted, in part at least, in terms of the intervention of such conscious recollections. The experiments, analogous to those of Thorndike in their performance, dealt with the respective frequencies with which subjects remembered the rewards and punishments that had been applied to certain "connections" at the time they were being established. Our results showed that there was, indeed, a higher frequency of recollection of rewards, but — and this point is important — this superiority came in the main from the occurrence of *false* recollections, that is to say, of cases in which the observers thought that a connection had been rewarded, whereas, in fact, it had been punished. Therefore, in the end, the conclusion was negative; plainly it could not be the recollection of an actual reward which made the subjects fixate intentionally the connections that had really been rewarded in the course of the successive presentation of the series during the period of training.

Other experiments on the law of effect later had as their object the clearing up of the contradiction which seemed to me to exist between the general principle of the favorable effects of satisfaction, in Thorndike's sense on the one hand, and, on the other, the fact, noted by Lewin, that activities are better fixed in memory when they are interrupted in the course of execution, a procedure which seemed to me to constitute a sort of penalization. This contradiction led to an interpretation of the law of effect that was very different from Thorndike's. According to this new view the role of the reward would not be to reinforce a connection, but rather to maintain the state of tension aroused by the instructions given concerning the training. I shall not dwell upon this conception, which was developed at considerable length by Professor Nuttin and which provided the starting point for a whole series of his investigations.[20]

1939 and Years Following

The year 1939 was a turning point in my career and marks the beginning of a period during which I attacked, still using the experimental method, certain fundamental problems of phenomenology, the problems of causality, of permanence and of apparent reality in outer experience.

Causality

Having been asked to write an article for the *Tijdschrift voor Philosophie*,[21] I decided to treat in it the problem of the perception of action

---

[20] See on this subject J. Nuttin, De Finaliteit in het menselijk handelen en het Connectionisme. Een Studie over de wet van het Effect, *Tijdschrift voor Philosophie*, 1942, 4, 235–268
[21] Michotte, La causalité physique est-elle une donnée phénoménale? *Tijdschrift voor Philosophie*, 1941, 3, 290–328, La perception de la causalité, *Etudes de Psychol.*, 1946, vol. 6.

which had already been the subject of a paper presented before the International Congress of Psychology at Yale in 1929, and then of lectures given at the Collège de France in Paris in 1937.

Long since I had acquired the conviction, on the basis of personal observations, that "action" performed by objects or human beings on each other are perceived, just as simple movements are perceived. Wishing to confirm the correctness of this finding and to study it more critically, however, I sought for a means of verifying it experimentally.

It was then that I had the good luck to think of the possibility of producing systematically combinations of movements of several objects by making use of the well-known illusion of movement which occurs when a line is moved behind a screen having a slit forming an angle with the line. By this technique I was able to perform at once an experiment intended to represent the case of the impact of two billiard balls (actually, two spots of color) and the result was quite obvious. All the observers agreed in asserting that they "were seeing one of the objects hit the other and drive it away."

This finding, however, was only a first step, for its yield did not much exceed that of casual observation. The next task was to vary the conditions of the experiment so as to discover those which were determinative of this kind of response on the part of the subjects (genetic analysis).[22]

These conditions have turned out to be extraordinarily precise and definite, not only from the spatial aspect (length and direction of the trajectories) but also from the temporal aspect (duration of the contact of the two objects) and the aspect of movement (absolute velocities and relative velocities of the two objects). It was possible to conclude, by applying the principle of concomitant variations, that there existed a relation of direct dependence between a given system of excitations and the presence in the observer of an impression x, which he characterized by using expressions designating a causal relation. This argument, and others also based on the experimental data, amply demonstrated that this impression x must in any case be a specific Gestalt, different from a simple combination of movements to which had become attached an extrinsic meaning, like that which becomes attached to the visual form of the words of a language.

I then tried to find out whether it might not be possible to go beyond this conclusion and the point of view which I had adopted concerning introspection (cf. p. 00) and to shed some light on the *nature* of the impression itself.

Reflecting on all the data supplied by my work, I succeeded, thereupon, in formulating the theory of "ampliation" of movement[23] which shows, I think,

[22] Perception de la causalité, *op cit.*, 16 ff.

[23] The word *ampliation* must be considered a new technical name for a specific kind of phenomenon the nature of which is made clear, I believe, in Perception de la causalité, *op cit*, 122 ff, 208 ff.

that the *impression* received must be that of a genuine *production* of the displacement of the mobile item by the blow given it and must consequently possess an intrinsic meaning.

Naturally it was in order for me to extend what I had found in the visual sphere to the tactile-kinesthetic domain and consequently to the impressions of the causal influence that occur when we exert the pressure by our limbs on external objects. This investigation thus continued and completed my earlier work on "awareness of action" in inner experience (voluntary choice) by stressing this time a new aspect of the question: the perception of the action of one's own body.

All of these results were in obvious contradiction to the classical thesis of Hume, according to which it would not be possible to perceive the *production* of one event by another; and, insofar as the issue is one of fact, it seems that this point is now cleared up. It goes without saying, however, that my experiments, taking only the phenomenological point of view, imply no definite position concerning the epistemological problem of the value of the notion of causality. I am insisting on this point because already there have been a number of misunderstandings about this matter.

Study of the perception of causality led me to take up next two questions related to the perception of the activity of human beings.

The first was concerned with the specific aspects of the movement of living beings. Do such movements display certain special characteristics that lead us to consider them as produced by the animal itself (immanence)? The answer came out clearly when we found that it was easy to produce combinations of movements of inert objects (spots of color) which gave an impression quite analogous to that of the creeping of an animal — of a worm, for instance. Appropriate variations of these kinetic combinations showed that the impression was bound to certain of them and that consequently here was still another case of a specific perceptual configuration. It was later that we found it possible to formulate a fairly satisfactory theory of this perceptual configuration.[24]

The second question concerned another point, theoretically far more important. As certain authors believe it possible to "perceive" the intentional character of human or animal actions, one could well ask oneself whether this too might not be a case of a rather primitive specific impression, bound to the presentation of specific constellations of movements. Supposing these to be combined so as to give the observer the impression of a chain of activities involving several objects (inert objects, in this case), it was conceivable that, under determinate conditions, certain stages might appear to occur "in order to bring about the following ones," or might at least appear "pre-

[24] L Knops, Contribution à l'étude de la "naissance" et de la "permanence" phénoménales dans le champ visuel, *Miscellanea Psychologica A. Michotte*, 1947, 602.

paratory for these," etc. The results of our previous experiments and many observations on successive Gestalts show that such an hypothesis is by no means absurd, and that it was worthwhile to try the experiment.

Consequently we undertook trials in which human or animal actions, like pursuits, flights, detours, etc., were represented in schematic fashion by fairly complex combinations of movements of colored spots. Some forty different combinations were used, as varied as I could make them, but the result remained *negative* so long as I worked with observers not informed of the purpose of the experiments; the perceived chain of events seemed to them purely mechanical.

The slightest suggestion to the observers, however, leading them to suppose that representations of human actions were being shown, was enough to provoke the appearance of finalistic interpretations, and these interpretations naturally showed themselves to be largely independent of the systematic variations of the stimulus. The reports of the observers thus had a very different significance from those in the experiments on causality. Here we had obviously to do with cases of "extrinsic meanings."

This conclusion naturally remains valid only within the universe of our experiments, but these suffice at all events to show, it seems to me, that if there exists really a *phenomenal characteristic of intentionality* inherent in the perception of certain activities, it must occur under conditions markedly different from those giving rise to the impression of causality. We see, furthermore, how prudent one must be in these matters, and the care that must be taken to differentiate by adequate criteria a phenomenal characteristic, properly so-called, from an extrinsic meaning. This differentiation may, moreover, be all the more difficult in the present case, for the reason that a meaning of intentionality may be due — and probably is due in many cases — to a process of *projection* which is difficult to identify.

Phenomenal Permanence

While studying, during my experiments on the impression of causality, the various characteristics which it may display, I had examined the question as to whether it would be possible to elicit by my method the impression of the active compression of one object by another. The experiments were carried out as follows. A mobile object *A* (elongated rectangle) was made to move over and join an object *B* of the same shape. After joining *B*, *A* continued to move in the same direction, while *B* decreased in length as *A* advanced.

To my great surprise not one observer perceived this shortening of the object *B*. All agreed, on the contrary, in asserting that it was simply covered by *A*, which *slipped ahead of it* and gradually hid it. This fact was extremely interesting, because the hidden object seemed to remain present and self-identical, although some of it had become invisible (or, indeed, all of it).

I decided at once to proceed with a systematic investigation of this remarkable case of phenomenal permanence.

A great variety of experiments were performed. They showed that we were dealing here with a special phenomenon, and not, as one might have thought *a priori,* with an "interpretation," nor with an "assimilation" resulting from acquired knowledge or from a direct influence of past experience. The "theory" of this phenomenon, easily formed and confirmed by many facts, connects it also to the laws of structural organization and especially to those laws which control the attachment of the boundaries separating two objects to one or the other of the objects.[25]

Later we extended our investigations to other cases of apparent permanence and also to cases of non-permanence in which one has either the impression of a "creation" or that of an "annihilation" (air bubbles at the surface of a liquid, for instance). I then became aware that the whole problem must be envisaged from the point of view of the psychology of time. "Creation" and "annihilation" imply the existence of *temporal boundaries specific* to the object or process, whereas permanence is found when such specific time-boundaries do not exist.[26]

The problem of the belongingness of boundaries thus arises in the domain of time as well as in that of space, and the more my research develops, the more do I become aware that this problem is of truly capital importance for the understanding of the structure of the phenomenal world. What follows is one more example of its significance.

The problem of permanence is also bound to the problem of the perception of change (change of form, size, color, for instance), for there can be *change* only in so far as the "thing" that changes remains in certain respects what it was before; otherwise, there occurs but simple substitution of one object for another. For this reason we planned a further set of experiments for the study of this phenomenon.

Our attention was particularly drawn to the case in which an object or a group of objects becomes larger through the addition of new parts. This is an important case, for it seems actually to constitute the intuitive basis of the arithmetical notion of addition, and becomes consequently a starting point for all mathematics. Here again permanence is essential, for there can be real addition only in so far as the "parts" continue to exist in the "whole."

The findings led to the conclusion that the "adjunction" under considera-

[25] A. C. Sampaio, *La translation des objets comme facteur de leur permanence phénoménale,* Louvain, Editions de l'Institut Supérieur de Philosophie, 1943, Knops, *op cit,* 562–610.
[26] Michotte, A propos de la permanence phénoménale. Faits et théories, *Acta Psychologica,* 1950, 7, 298–322.

tion results in setting off a process of structural reorganization, one that involves, among other things, an apparent shift of the external boundaries of the object which seems to grow in size. Such growth leaves intact (for the time being, at least) the object's own existence, and consequently its permanence. I have called this occurrence the phenomenon of incorporation. Its role in the conceptual understanding of mathematical addition may well be important, but obviously that remains to be determined by investigations of another kind.

Apparent Reality

My work on the impression of causality steered me in a third direction. I had been struck by the fact that the subjects, who naturally were aware of the technique being used and consequently knew that it was only a matter of optical illusion, nevertheless had the impression of a real impact (in the physical sense of the word) between the objects, not that of the mere *representation* of an impact. This finding aroused my curiosity and I sought a way to approach experimentally the problem of the apparent reality of perceptual data. It seemed to me that a good procedure would be to compare systematically the cases in which apparent reality obtains with those cases in which there is none, and that the most obvious example is that of the volume represented in perspective drawings as compared to that aspect of the corresponding actual solids.[77]

The main point demonstrated by these experiments may be summarized as follows. The same combination of lines, objectively localized in a plane and constituting the perspective representation of a volume, may give rise, according to circumstances, either to the impression of an unreal volume (drawing), or to that of a volume which is entirely on a par, in respect of its apparent reality, with the volume of a physical object that serves as a basis of comparison.

The first eventuality occurs when the structural organization of the perception is such that the lines appear as drawn on a surface and as belonging to the surface. When, on the other hand, one succeeds — thanks to an adequate technique of presentation — in apparently detaching the lines from any plane support and in apparently making them free in space, there arises the impression of the reality of the volume.

This finding obviously made it possible to vary the conditions of the experiment in such a way as to obtain at will one or the other result, to pass gradually from one to the other, and thus to show that the characteristic of reality, in the case studied, is capable of occurring in various degrees.

[77] Michotte, L'énigme psychologique de la perspective dans le dessin linéaire, *Bulletin de la Classe des Lettres de l'Académie royale de Belgique*, 5th series, 1948, 34, 268–288, Le caractère de "réalité" des projections cinématographiques, *Revue Internationale de Filmologie*, 1948, 1, 249–261.

The conclusion can be drawn, it seems to me, that this characteristic must be considered a special *variable* of perceptual experience, which corresponds, as do the others, to a definite type of structural organization.

Résumé

Little by little there were thus accumulated many data, and I am trying still to add to them.[28] At present it is possible to foresee a general conception for which the lines begin to form with a fair degree of clearness.

It seems certain at present that sensory experience (and by this I mean all of the impressions that correspond directly to more or less complex systems of stimulation) has an infinitely richer content than one could have supposed.

It seems also that this richness is not the result of learning alone. On the contrary, all the facts observed indicate — at least in my opinion — that the fundamental structure of the phenomenal world is provided for from the outset by the operation of laws which determine the organization of the perceptual field when a certain degree of maturation has been reached. The role — important, indeed, without a doubt — of acquired experience would appear to consist in the main of completing, supplementing, confirming or correcting the edifice thus formed.

Our experiments suggest that this primitive structure presents itself in the guise of a world of "things" that are separated from each other — inert bodies or animate ones endowed eventually with specific vital movements.

These things normally possess a character of *reality* which differentiates them from the unreal, the imaginary.

Furthermore, most of them are *permanent* in the sense that their apparent existence is not uniquely determined by the *actual* action of the corresponding sensory stimulations, for they may phenomenally exist for a short time before or after the stimulation.

Finally, these things and the processes which they involve are bound to each other, not only by their spatial and temporal relations, but also by all sorts of functional relations — such as the many forms in which mechanical causality appears, the screen effect, pursuit, flight, etc. Thanks to these functional relations, moreover, both things and events have an intrinsic meaning antecedent to the extrinsic meaning which they may acquire later under the influence of the accumulation of data of experience.

In a word, there seems to exist in the phenomenal world, in the world of appearances, a sort of "prefiguration" of such abstract notions as the "categories" of the mind (substance, reality, causality), appearances which under-

---

[28] It is for this reason that only a part of the results obtained to date have been published.

lie the conception that man develops spontaneously concerning the physical universe which surrounds him.[29]

Perhaps this interpretation throws some light on the origin of these notions; yet it is necessary for us to emphasize the biological bearing of this spontaneous organization of the phenomenal world. It is spontaneous organization which must make it possible for the individual (man or animal) to adapt his reactions to the world before his personal experience has had a chance to structure it.

It should be clear, moreover, that this prefiguration justifies the profound analogies which exist between the behavior of animals and the behavior of men, despite the probable lack in the animals of those "superior" functions which give to men the capacity to understand intellectually the world in which they live.

Perspective

And now, having gone over again in my mind the whole course of my scientific life, which is nearing its close, I think that I may justly conclude that I have remained faithful to the conception of it which I developed in my youth and which was sketched in the first pages of this paper. I thought at first that I had special aptitudes for experimentation, and I have remained an experimenter during my whole career. I have constantly sought to accumulate data which were as solid as possible, capable of providing a base for the general syntheses which should, I felt, be reserved for the future, and also, perhaps, for minds more definitely oriented in that direction than was mine.

Nevertheless my life's work does not at all appear to me as a mere hunt for facts, as a pure accumulation of observations, which would have given it a rather sterile character.

The experiments that I carried out and the efforts expended to draw conclusions from them have always been dominated by my concern to provide a contribution to the understanding of one of the major problems which has never ceased to preoccupy me. And, if my work has borne fruit, it is precisely, I think, for this reason. Because I have *thought again and again* about the questions which interested me passionately, these questions have gradually ripened in my mind; the solutions, seen sketchily at first, have gradually become transformed and completed; and, finally, old problems have suddenly appeared to me, often after many long years, in an entirely new light. One can indeed say without exaggeration — of this I am pro-

[29] Michotte, La préfiguration dans les données sensorielles, de notre conception spontanée du monde physique, *Proc. XIIth International Congress of Psychol*, Edinburgh, 1948, Evening discourse II, pp. 20–22.

foundly convinced — that my work of the last ten years on phenomenology constitutes *the result of a whole life* of research and meditation.

TEACHING AND OTHER ACTIVITIES

My field of teaching was of necessity much wider than my field of research, although the former always drew much of its substance from the latter. After what I have already said, it is easy to understand that the ideas presented to my listeners were fairly eclectic and that they evolved considerably in the course of my career. Nevertheless were I to pick out their main feature and supply a label for them, I should be tempted to say that "my" psychology has been dynamic, both functionalistic and structuralistic. The reason is that all my problems were seen from the point of view of action, and that I accented the directive and energetic role of needs and tendencies and of the attitudes characterizing the acting personality. Furthermore, as might be expected, I stressed particularly the principles of the structural organization (Gestalt) of action itself, a veritable "cell" of behavior, and of the events which action encompasses, like perceptions, emotions, thoughts and motor responses.

My teaching was not restricted to the University of Louvain. A large part of my professorial career was devoted to lectures and courses which, presumably because of my knowledge of various languages, I had the honor to be invited to give at other universities in Holland, England, Germany, France, Switzerland, Italy, Spain and the United States of America. I should like to mention especially, in this connection, Stanford University, where I was called to teach psychology as a visiting professor during the summer session of 1929. Furthermore, I have many times presented my ideas on the results of our experiments to the International Congresses of Psychology, in which I have regularly participated since 1905, and also to certain meetings of foreign psychological societies.

Finally, we have recently inaugurated interlaboratory relations consisting of collective visits lasting several days by the members of one institute of psychology to another. This arrangement has already operated between Amsterdam and Louvain, and between Cambridge (England) and Louvain. Such an exchange has shown itself to be so useful and stimulating for all that it seems highly desirable to extend it in the future as fully as may prove practicable.

It is in this same spirit of collaboration that I founded, in 1947, with the generous support of my colleagues, a Société Belge de Psychologie, the existence of which seems to me justified by the growth of psychological research in this country.

In closing, I wish to stress most particularly the immense profit I have gained from my numerous personal contacts with foreign colleagues because of the opportunities of discussing with them problems of mutual interest, and of getting a close view of their work, and also of straightening out my own ideas in connection with the lectures which I was to give. All of this cross-stimulation has been a very great asset in the development of my scientific activity, quite aside from the many priceless bonds of friendship which have become established in the course of these many contacts.

JEAN PIAGET

A N autobiography has scientific interest only if it succeeds in furnishing the elements of an explanation of the author's work.[1] In order to achieve that goal, I shall therefore limit myself essentially to the scientific aspects of my life.

Many persons doubtless are convinced that such a retrospective interpretation presents no objective value, and that it is to be suspected of partiality even more than an introspective report. I myself had originally subscribed to this view. But, on re-reading some old documents dating from my years of adolescence, I was struck by two apparently contradictory facts which, when put together, offer some guaranty of objectivity. The first is that I had completely forgotten the contents of these rather crude, juvenile productions, the second is that, in spite of their immaturity they anticipated in a striking manner what I have been trying to do for about thirty years.

There is therefore probably some truth in the statement by Bergson that a philosophic mind is generally dominated by a single personal idea which he strives to express in many ways in the course of his life, without ever succeeding fully. Even if this autobiography should not convey to the readers a perfectly clear notion of what that single idea is, it will at least have helped the author to understand it better himself.

I.   1896–1914

I was born on August 9, 1896 at Neuchâtel, in Switzerland. My father who is still active, has devoted his writings mostly to medieval literature, and to a lesser extent, to the history of Neuchâtel. He is a man of a painstaking and critical mind, who dislikes hastily improvised generalizations, and is not afraid of starting a fight when he finds historic truth twisted to fit respectable traditions. Among many other things he taught me the value of systematic work, even in small matters. My mother was very intelligent,

[1] Submitted in French and translated by Donald MacQueen of Clark University.

energetic, and fundamentally a very kind person; her rather neurotic temperament, however, made our family life somewhat troublesome. One of the direct consequences of this situation was that I started to forego playing for serious work very early; this I obviously did as much to imitate my father as to take refuge in both a private and a non-fictitious world. Indeed, I have always detested any departure from reality, an attitude which I relate to the second important influential factor of my early life, *viz.*, my mother's poor mental health; it was this disturbing factor which at the beginning of my studies in psychology made me intensely interested in questions of psychoanalysis and pathological psychology. Though this interest helped me to achieve independence and to widen my cultural background, I have never since felt any desire to involve myself deeper in that particular direction, always much preferring the study of normalcy and of the workings of the intellect to that of the tricks of the unconscious.

From seven to ten years of age I became successively interested in mechanics, in birds, in fossils of secondary and tertiary layers and in sea shells. Since I was not yet allowed to write with ink, I composed (in pencil) a little pamphlet to share with the world a great discovery. the "autovap," an automobile provided with a steam engine. But I quickly forgot this unusual combination of a wagon and a locomotive for the writing (this time in ink) of a book on "Our Birds," which, after my father's ironic remarks, I had to recognize, regretfully, as a mere compilation.

At the age of ten, as soon as I had entered "Latin School," I decided to be more serious. Having seen a partly albino sparrow in a public park, I sent a one-page article to a natural history journal of Neuchâtel. It published my lines and I was "launched"! I wrote then to the director of the Musée d'histoire naturelle and asked his permission to study his collections of birds, fossils and shells after hours. This director, Paul Godet, a very nice man, happened to be a great specialist on mollusks. He immediately invited me to assist him twice a week — as he said, like the "famulus" to Faust — helping him stick labels on his collections of land- and soft-water shells. For four years I worked for this conscientious and learned naturalist, in exchange for which he would give me at the end of each session a certain number of rare species for my own collection and, in particular, provide me , with an exact classification of the samples that I had collected. These weekly meetings in the director's private office stimulated me so much that I spent all my free time collecting mollusks (there are one hundred and thirty species and hundreds of varieties in the environs of Neuchâtel); every Saturday afternoon I used to wait for my teacher a half hour ahead of time!

This early initiation to malacology had a great influence on me. When, in 1911, Mr. Godet died, I knew enough about this field to begin publishing without help (specialists in this branch are rare) a series of articles on the mollusks of Switzerland, of Savoy, of Brittany and even of Colombia. This afforded me some amusing experiences. Certain foreign "colleagues" wanted to meet me, but since I was only a schoolboy, I didn't dare to show myself and had to decline these flattering invitations. The director of the Muséum d'histoire naturelle of Geneva, Mr. Bedot, who was publishing several of my articles in the *Revue suisse de Zoologie* offered me a position as curator of his mollusk collection. (The Lamarck collection, among others, is in Geneva.) I had to reply that I had two more years to study for my baccalaureate degree, not yet being a college student. After another magazine editor had refused an article of mine because he had discovered the embarrassing truth about my age, I sent it to Mr. Bedot who with kindness and good humor responded: "It is the first time that I have even heard of a magazine director who judges the value of articles by the age of their authors. Can it be that he has no other criteria at his disposal?" Naturally, these various articles which I published at such a young age were far from being accomplished feats. It was only much later, in 1929, that I was able to achieve something more significant in this field.

These studies, premature as they were, were nevertheless of great value for my scientific development; moreover, they functioned if I may say so, as instruments of protection against the demon of philosophy. Thanks to them, I had the rare privilege of getting a glimpse of science and what it stands for, before undergoing the philosophical crises of adolescence. To have had early experience with these two kinds of problematic approaches constituted, I am certain, the hidden strength of my later psychological activity.

However, instead of quietly pursuing the career of a naturalist which seemed so normal and so easy for me after these fortunate circumstances, between the ages of fifteen and twenty I experienced a series of crises due both to family conditions and to the intellectual curiosity characteristic of that productive age. But, I repeat, all those crises I was able to overcome, thanks to the mental habits which I had acquired through early contact with the zoological science.

There was the problem of religion. When I was about fifteen, my mother, being a devout Protestant, insisted on my taking what is called at Neuchâtel "religious instruction," that is, a six weeks' course on the fundamentals of Christian doctrine. My father, on the other hand, did not attend church, and I quickly sensed that for him the current faith and an honest historical criticism were incompatible. Accordingly I followed my "religious instruction" with lively interest but, at the same time, in the spirit of free thinking. Two things struck me at that time: on the one hand, the difficulty of reconciling a number of dogmas with biology, and on the other, the fragility of the "five" proofs of the existence of God. We were taught five, and I even passed my examination in them! Though I would not even have dreamed of denying the existence of God, the fact that anyone should reason by such weak arguments (I recall only the proof by the finality of nature and the ontological proof) seemed to me all the more extraordinary since my pastor was an intelligent man, who himself dabbled in the natural sciences!

At that time I had the good luck to find in my father's library *La philosophie de la religion fondée sur la psychologie et l'histoire* by Auguste Sabatier. I devoured that book with immense delight. Dogmas reduced to the function of "symbols" necessarily inadequate, and above all the notion of an "evolution of dogmas" — there was a language which was much more understandable and satisfactory to my mind. And now a new passion took possession of me: philosophy.

From this a second crisis ensued. My godfather, Samuel Cornut, a Romansh man of letters invited me about that same period to spend a vacation with him at Lake Annecy. I still have a delightful memory of that visit: We walked and fished, I looked for mollusks and wrote a "malacology of Lake Annecy," which I published shortly afterward in the *Revue savoisienne*. But my godfather had a purpose. He found me too specialized and wanted to teach me philosophy. Between the gatherings of mollusks he would teach me the "creative evolution" of Bergson. (It was only afterwards that he sent me that work as a souvenir.) It was the first time that I heard philosophy discussed by anyone not a theologian; the shock was terrific, I must admit.

First of all, it was an emotional shock. I recall one evening of profound revelation. The identification of God with life itself was an idea that stirred me almost to ecstasy because it now enabled me to see in biology the explanation of all things and of the mind itself.

In the second place, it was an intellectual shock. The problem of knowing (properly called the epistemological problem) suddenly appeared to me in an entirely new perspective and as an absorbing topic of study. It made me decide to consecrate my life to the biological explanation of knowledge.

The reading of Bergson himself which I did only several months later (I have always preferred to reflect on a problem before reading on it) strengthened me in my decision but also disappointed me somewhat. Instead of finding science's last word therein, as my good godfather had led me to hope, I got the impression of an ingenious construction without an experimental basis: Between biology and the analysis of knowledge I needed something other than a philosophy. I believe it was at that moment that I discovered a need that could be satisfied only by psychology.

II. 1914–1918

It was during this period that the curious phenomenon to which I alluded in my introduction began to happen. Not being satisfied with reading a lot (this in addition to the study on mollusks and preparation for the baccalaureate degree which I received in 1915 at the age of eighteen), I began to write down my own ideas in numerous notebooks. Soon these efforts affected my health; I had to spend more than a year in the mountains filling my forced leisure time with writing a sort of philosophic novel which I was imprudent enough to publish in 1917. Now, in reading over these various writings which mark the crisis and the end of my adolescence – documents which I had completely forgotten till I reopened them for this autobiography – surprisingly I find in them one or two ideas which are still dear to me, and which have never ceased to guide me in my variegated endeavors. That is why, however unworthy such attempt may seem at first, I shall try to retrace these early notions.

I began by reading everything which came to my hands after my unfortunate contact with the philosophy of Bergson: some Kant, Spencer, Auguste Comte, Fouillée and Guyau, Lachelier, Boutroux, Lalande, Durkheim, Tarde, Le Dantec; and, in psychology, W. James, Th. Ribot and Janet. Also, during the last two years before the baccalaureate, we had lessons in psychology, in logic and in scientific methodology given by the logician, A. Reymond. But for lack of a laboratory and guidance (there was no experimental psychologist at Neuchâtel, even at the university) the only thing I could do was to theorize and write. I wrote even if it was only for myself, for I could not think without writing – but it had to be in a systematic fashion as if it were to be an article for publication.

I started with a rather crudely conceived essay pretentiously entitled "Sketch of a neo-pragmatism"; here I presented an idea which has since remained central for me, namely, that action in itself admits of logic (this contrary to the anti-intellectualism of James and of Bergson) and that, therefore, logic stems from a sort of spontaneous organization of acts. But the link with biology was missing. A lesson by A. Reymond on realism and nominalism within the problem area of "universals" (with some reference to the role of concepts in present-day science) gave me a sudden insight. I had thought deeply on the problem of "species" in zoology and had adopted an entirely nominalistic point of view in this repect. The "species" has no reality in itself and is distinguished from the simple "varieties" merely by a greater stability. But this theoretical view, inspired by Lamarckism, bothered me somewhat in my empirical work (*viz.*, classification of mollusks). The dispute of Durkheim and Tarde on reality or non-reality of society as an organized whole plunged me into a similar state of uncertainty without making me see, at first, its pertinence to the problem of the species. Aside from this the general problem of realism and of nominalism provided me with an over-all view: I suddenly understood that at all levels (*viz.*, that of the living cell, organism, species, society, etc., but also with reference to states of conscience, to concepts, to logical principles, etc.) one finds the same problem of relationship between the parts and the whole; hence I was convinced that I had found the solution. There at last was the close union that I had dreamed of between biology and philosophy, there was an access to an epistemology which to me then seemed really scientific!

Thus I began to write down my system (people will wonder where I got the time, but I took it wherever I could, especially during boring lessons!). My solution was very simple: In all fields of life (organic, mental, social) there exist "totalities" qualitatively distinct from their parts and imposing on them an organization. Therefore there exist no isolated "elements"; elementary reality is necessarily dependent on a whole which pervades it. But the relationships between the whole and the part vary from one structure to another, for it is necessary to distinguish four actions which are always present: the action of the whole on itself (preservation), the action of all the parts (alteration or preservation), the actions of the parts on themselves (preservation) and the action of the parts on the whole (alteration or preservation). These four actions balance one another in a total structure, but there are then three possible forms of equilibrium: (1) predominance of the whole with alteration of the parts; (2) predominance of the parts with alteration of the whole, and (3) reciprocal preservation of the parts and of the whole. To this a final fundamental law is added: Only the last form of equilibrium (3) is "stable" or "good," while the other two, (1) and (2), are less stable; though tending toward stability, it will depend on the obstacles to be overcome how closely (1) and (2) may approach a stable status.

If I had known at that time (1913–1915) the work of Wertheimer and of Kohler, I would have become a Gestaltist, but having been acquainted only with French writings and not yet able to design experiments for the verification of these hypotheses, I was bound to limit myself to the construction of a system. I find the re-reading of these old papers extremely interesting, inasmuch as they represent an anticipatory outline of my later research: It was already clear to me that the stable equilibrium of the whole and of the parts (third form) corresponded to states of conscience of a normative nature: logical necessity or moral obligation, as opposed to inferior forms of equilibrium which characterize the non-normative states of conscience, such as perception, etc., or organismic happenings.

After my baccalaureate, I took to the mountains for a rest. During that time I was formally registered in the Division of Science at the University of Neuchâtel, so that, soon after my return, I was able to graduate in the natural sciences and then to take my doctor's degree with a thesis on the mollusks of Valais (1918). Though I was all the while greatly interested in courses in zoölogy (Fuhrmann), embryology (Béraneck), geology (Argand), physical chemistry (Berthoud) and mathematics (group theory was particularly important for me with respect to the problem of the whole and the parts), I was very eager to move to a larger university with a psychology laboratory where I could hope to carry out experiments to verify my "system."

It was in this area of research where the mental habits acquired from contact with zoology were to serve me well. I never believed in a system without precise experimental control. What I wrote for myself during my years at the lycée I deemed unworthy of publication, because it remained mere theory; its real value seemed to me to be an incentive for later experiments, whose nature at that time, however, I could not surmise.

Nevertheless, during the year I spent in the mountains I was haunted by the desire to create, and I yielded to the temptation. Not to compromise myself on scientific grounds, however, I avoided the difficulty by writing — for the general public, and not for specialists — a kind of philosophic novel the last part of which contained my ideas (1917). My strategy proved to be correct: No one spoke of it except one or two indignant philosophers.[2]

III. 1918–1921

After having received the doctorate in the sciences, I left for Zurich (1918), with the aim of working in a psychology laboratory. I attended two laboratories, that of G. E. Lipps and that of Wreschner, and also Bleuler's psychiatric clinic. I felt at once that there lay my path and that, in utilizing for psychological experimentation the mental habits I had acquired in zoology, I would perhaps succeed in solving problems of structures-of-the-whole to which I had been led by my philosophical thinking. But to tell the truth, I felt somewhat lost at first. The experiments of Lipps and Wreschner seemed to me to have little bearing on fundamental problems.

[2] Here are some quotations from that work entitled *Recherche* (1917). It was a question of elaborating a "positive theory of quality taking into account only relationships of equilibrium and disequilibrium among our qualities" (p 150). "Now there can be no awareness of these qualities, hence these qualities can not exist, if there are no relationships among them, if they are not, consequently, blended into a total quality which contains them while keeping them distinct. For example, I would not be aware either of the whiteness of this paper or of the blackness of this ink if the two qualities were not combined in my consciousness into a certain unit, and if, in spite of this unity, they did not remain respectively one white and the other black. . . . In this originates the equilibrium between the qualities there is equilibrium not only among the separate parts in that way (and that occurs only in material equilibriums) but among the parts on the one hand, and the whole on the other, as distinct from the whole resulting from these partial qualities. . . . (It is therefore necessary to proceed from the whole to the parts and not from the part to the whole as does a physicist's mind)" (pp 151–153). "One can then distinguish a first type of equilibrium where the whole and the part mutually sustain each other" (p. 156), and other types such that there be coordinated interaction between the whole and the parts (p. 157) Now "all equilibriums tend toward an equilibrium of the first type" (p. 157), but without being able to reach it on the organic level "Therefore we call an ideal equilibrium the equilibrium of the first type and real equilibrium that of the other types, although every real equilibrium, whatever it be, presupposes an ideal equilibrium (p. 158). In contrast, the first type is realized on the level of thought It is "the origin of the principle of identity, from which the principle of contradiction is deduced," etc (p 163).

On the other hand, the discovery of psychoanalysis (I read Freud and the journal *Imago*, and listened occasionally to Pfister's and Jung's lectures) and the teachings of Bleuler made me sense the danger of solitary meditation; I decided then to forget my system lest I should fall a victim to "autism."

In the spring of 1919 I became restless and left for le Valais; there I applied Lipps' statistical method to a biometric study of the variability of land mollusks as a function of altitude! I needed to get back to concrete problems to avoid grave errors.

In the autumn of 1919 I took the train for Paris where I spent two years at the Sorbonne. I attended Dumas' course in pathological psychology (where I learned to interview mental patients at Sainte-Anne), and the courses of Piéron and Delacroix; I also studied logic and philosophy of science with Lalande and Brunschvicg. The latter exerted a great influence on me because of his historical-critical method and his references to psychology. But I still did not know what problem area of experimentation to choose. Then I had an extraordinary piece of luck. I was recommended to Dr. Simon who was then living in Rouen, but who had at his disposal Binet's laboratory at the grade school of the rue de la Grangeaux-Belles in Paris. This laboratory was not being used because Simon had no classes in Paris at this time. Dr. Simon received me in a very friendly manner and suggested that I should standardize Burt's reasoning tests on the Parisian children. I started the work without much enthusiasm, just to try anything. But soon my mood changed; there I was, my own master, with a whole school at my disposition — unhoped-for working conditions.

Now from the very first questionings I noticed that though Burt's tests certainly had their diagnostic merits, based on the number of successes and failures, it was much more interesting to try to find the reasons for the failures. Thus I engaged my subjects in conversations patterned after psychiatric questioning, with the aim of discovering something about the reasoning process underlying their right, but especially their wrong answers. I noticed with amazement that the simplest reasoning task involving the inclusion of a part in the whole or the coordination of relations or the "multiplication" of classes (finding the part common to two wholes), presented for normal children up to the age of eleven or twelve difficulties unsuspected by the adult.

Without Dr. Simon being quite aware of what I was doing, I continued for about two years to analyze the verbal reasoning of normal children by presenting them with various questions and exposing them to tasks involving simple concrete relations of cause and effect. Furthermore, I obtained permission to work with the abnormal children of the Salpêtrière; here I undertook research on numbers, using the methods of direct manipulation as well as that of conversation. I have since resumed this work in cooperation with A. Szeminska.

At last I had found my field of research. First of all it became clear to me that the theory of the relations between the whole and the part can be studied experimentally through analysis of the psychological processes underlying logical operations. This marked the end of my "theoretical" period and the start of an inductive and experimental era in the psychological domain which I always had wanted to enter, but for which until then I had not found the suitable problems. Thus my observations that logic is not inborn, but develops little by little, appeared to be consistent with my ideas on the formation of the equilibrium toward which the evolution of mental structures tends; moreover, the possibility of directly studying the problem of logic was in accord with all my former philosophical interests. Finally my aim of discovering a sort of embryology of intelligence fit in with my biological training; from the start of my theoretical thinking I was certain that the problem of the relation between the organism and environment extended also into the realm of knowledge, appearing here as the problem of the relation between the acting or thinking subject and the objects of his experience. Now I had the chance of studying this problem in terms of psychogenetic development.

Once my first results had been achieved, I wrote three articles, taking great care not to become biassed by theory. I analyzed the data, psychologically as well as logically, applying the principle of logical-psychological parallelism to my method of analysis: Psychology explains the facts in terms of causality, while logics when concerned with true reasoning describes the corresponding forms in terms of an ideal equilibrium[3] (I have since expressed this relation by saying that logic is the axiomatic whose corresponding experimental science is the psychology of thought).[4]

I sent my first article[5] to the *Journal de Psychologie* and had the pleasure not only of seeing it accepted, but also of noting that I. Meyerson who became my friend at this time had interests very similar to mine. He had me read Lévy-Bruhl and spurred me on by his encouragement and advice. He also accepted my second article.[6]

As for the third, I sent it to Ed. Claparède, whom I had met but once, and who published it in the *Archives de Psychologie*.[7] But in addition to accepting my article, he made a proposal which changed the course of my life. He offered me the job of "director of studies" at the Institut J. J. Rousseau of Geneva. Since he barely knew me, he asked me to come to Geneva

[3] *Cf.* Une forme verbale de la comparaison chez l'enfant, *Arch de Psychol*, 1921, 18, 143–172.
[4] *Psychologie de l'intelligence* (1947), Chap. 1.
[5] Essai sur quelques aspects du développement de la notion de partie chez l'enfant, *J de Psychol*, 1921, 38, 449–480.
[6] Essai sur la multiplication logique et les débuts de la pensées formelles chez l'enfant, *J de Psychol*, 1922, 38, 222–261.
[7] La pensée symbolique et la pensée chez l'enfant, *Arch. de Psychol.*, 1923, 38, 273–304.

for a month's trial. This prospect enchanted me, as much because of Claparède's fame as for the wonderful research facilities which this position would afford; on the other hand, as yet I did not know how to start out on any research! I accepted in principle, and left Paris for Geneva. I noted immediately that Claparède and Bovet were ideal *patrons* who would let me work according to my desires. My work consisted simply of guiding the students and of associating them with the research that I was asked to undertake on my own, provided it was in child psychology. This was in 1921.

IV. 1921–1925

Being of a systematic turn of mind (with all the hazards that this implies) I made plans which I then considered final: I would devote two or three years more to the study of child thought, then return to the origins of mental life, that is, study the emergence of intelligence during the first two years. After having thus gained objectively and inductively a knowledge about the elementary structures of intelligence, I would be in the position to attack the problem of thought in general and to construct a psychological and biological epistemology. Above all, then, I would have to stay away from any non-psychological preoccupation and study empirically the development of thought for itself, wherever this might lead me.

According to this plan I organized my research at the Maison des Petits of the Institut J. J. Rousseau, starting with the more peripheral factors (social environment, language), but keeping in mind my goal of getting at the psychological mechanism of logical operations and of causal reasoning. In this connection I also resumed, working with the primary school pupils of Geneva, the type of investigation I had done in Paris.

The results of the research is contained in my first five books on child psychology.[8] I published them without taking sufficient precautions concerning the presentation of my conclusions, thinking they would be little read and would serve me mainly as documentation for a later synthesis to be addressed to a wider audience. (The studies were the product of a continuous collaborative effort in which all students of the Institute participated, among them Valentine Châtenay who became my wife and constant co-worker.) Contrary to my expectation, the books were read and discussed as if they were my last word on the subject, some adopting my point of view of a genesis of logic, others strongly opposing it (especially in circles influenced by empirical epistemology or Thomism). I was invited to many countries (France, Belgium, the Netherlands, England, Scotland, the United States, Spain, Poland, etc.) to present my ideas and discuss them before university

---

[8] *The language and thought of the child* (1924), *Judgment and reasoning in the child* (1924), *The child's conception of the world* (1926), *The child's conception of causality* (1927), *The moral judgment of the child* (1932).

faculties and other teachers. (However, I had no interest in pedagogy at that time as I had no children.) This unexpected acclaim left me somewhat uneasy, since I realized quite clearly that as yet I had not organized my ideas and had barely entered the preliminaries. But one cannot say to the critics, "Wait — you have not seen what is coming" — especially when one does not know it himself. Besides, when one is young he does not suspect that, for a long time, he will be judged by his first works, and that only very conscientious people will read the later ones.

Two essential shortcomings existed in these first studies. One I was not aware of before studying infant behavior, the other, however, I knew perfectly well.

The first of these shortcomings consisted in limiting my research to language and expressed thought. I well knew that thought proceeds from action, but I believed then that language directly reflects acts and that to understand the logic of the child one had only to look for it in the domain of conversations or verbal interactions. It was only later, by studying the patterns of intelligent behavior of the first two years, that I learned that for a complete understanding of the genesis of intellectual operations, manipulation and experience with objects had first to be considered. Therefore, prior to study based on verbal conversations, an examination of the patterns of conduct had to be carried out. True enough, since one finds in the action of younger children all the characteristics he observes in the verbal behavior of older children, my first studies on verbal thought were not in vain; but my point of view would have been much more easily understood if I had found out then what I discovered only later: that, between the preoperative stage from two to seven years and the establishment of a formal logic occurring at the ages of eleven and twelve, there functions (between seven and eleven years of age) an organizational level of "concrete operations" which is essentially logical, though not yet formal-logical (for instance, the child of eight will be able to conclude $A < C$ if he has seen three objects under the form $B > A$ and $B < C$, but he will fail to perform the same operation on the purely verbal plane).

The second shortcoming stems from the first, but I did not quite understand the reasons then: I tried in vain to find characteristic structures-of-the-whole relative to logical operations themselves (again my theory of the part and the whole!); I did not succeed because I did not seek their source in concrete operations. So I satisfied my need for an explanation in terms of structures-of-the-whole by studying the social aspect of thought (which is a necessary aspect, I still believe, of the formation of logical operations as such). The ideal equilibrium (the reciprocal preservation of the whole and of the parts) pertains here to the cooperation between individuals who become autonomous by this very cooperation. Imperfect equilibrium characterized by the alteration of the parts in relation to the whole appears here as social constraint (or constraint of the younger by the older). Imperfect equilibrium characterized by the change of the whole as a function of the parts (and the lack of coordination of the parts) appears as unconscious egocentricity of the individual, that is, as the mental attitude of young children who do not yet know how to collaborate nor to coordinate their points of view. (Unfortunately, because of the vague definition of the term "egocentricity" — undoubtedly an ill-chosen term! — and because of the misunderstandings of the concept of mental attitude, this term has usually not been given its only clear and simple meaning.)

Though I failed at first to find the characteristic structures of logical operations which ought to correspond to the structures of social intercourse (at least I sensed at once the importance of the reversibility of thought),[9] I noticed that a certain degree of irreversibility of operations corresponded to the young child's difficulties in grasping intellectual and social reciprocity. But to put this hypothesis on solid ground I had first to study concrete operations.

During these years, I had discovered the existence of Gestalt psychology, so close to my notions concerning structures-of-the-whole. The contact with the work of Kohler and Wertheimer made a twofold impression on me. Firstly, I had the pleasure of concluding that my previous research was not sheer folly, since one could design on such a central hypothesis of the subordination of the parts to the organizing whole not only a consistent theory, but also a splendid series of experiments. In the second place, I felt that, though the Gestalt notion suited perfectly the inferior forms of equilibrium (those in which the part is altered by the whole or those in which, according to the very terms of the theory, there is no "additive composition"), it did not explain the kind of structure peculiar to logical or rational operations. For example, the sequence of whole numbers 1, 2, 3 . . . etc. is a remarkable operative structure-of-the-whole, since numbers do not exist alone but are engendered by the very law of formation itself $(1 + 1 = 2, 2 + 1 = 3,$ etc.). And yet this law of formation constitutes essentially an "additive composition." What I consider a superior form of equilibrium (the mutual preservation of the parts by the whole and of the whole by the parts) therefore escaped the Gestaltist explanation. From this I concluded that it was necessary to differentiate successive steps of equilibria and to integrate the search for types of structures with a more genetic approach.

V.   1925–1929

In 1925 my former teacher, A. Reymond, vacated his chair of philosophy at the University of Neuchâtel, and a part of its incumbency was given to

---

[9] *Judgment and reasoning in the child* (1928), p. 169.

me, though I was merely a doctor of sciences. (Since 1921, as *privat-dozent* in the Faculté des Sciences at Geneva, I also taught child psychology.) My duties at this time were very heavy: They included (in the Faculté des Lettres) the teaching of psychology, of philosophy of science, of a philosophy seminar, and also, of two hours of sociology at the Institut des Sciences Sociales. In addition I continued to teach child psychology at the Institut J. J. Rousseau. Since one learns by teaching, I expected that this heavy schedule would at least bring me closer to epistemology. In fact, for four years I devoted the course on philosophy of science to the study of the development of ideas as it can be observed in the history of science as well as in child psychology. The opening lecture on this subject[10] has since been published.

During these years many other problems occupied me. In 1925 my first daughter was born and my second in 1927 (a boy followed them in 1931). With the help of my wife I spent considerable time in observing their reactions, and also subjected them to various experiments. The results of this new research has been published in three volumes that deal mainly with the genesis of intelligent conduct, ideas of objective constancy and causality, and with the beginnings of symbolic behavior (imitation and play).[11] It is not feasible to summarize these books; the first two have not been published in English, but the third (written much later) is now in the process of being translated.

The main benefit which I derived from these studies was that I learned in the most direct way how intellectual operations are prepared by sensory-motor action, even before the appearance of language. I concluded that in order to progress in my research on child logic I had to change my method, or rather to modify it by directing the conversations toward objects which the child himself could manipulate.

In the course of experiments (undertaken in collaboration with my students at Neuchâtel and at Geneva), I had just discovered that children up to 12 years did not believe in the constancy of material quantity, *e.g.*, of the weight and the volume of a lump of modeling clay that changed its shape by stretching or flattening. I had observed in my own children that between the sixth and tenth month they did not possess the notion of the permanence of an object disappearing from view (a watch hidden beneath a handkerchief, etc.). Between the beginnings of a notion of constancy or permanence of concrete objects and the final mastery of the concept of constancy of physical properties (weight, mass, etc.), there had to be successive stages in the development of ideas of constancy which could be studied in concrete

---

[10] Psychologie et critique de la connaissance, *Arch de Psychol*, 1925, 19, 193–210
[11] *La naissance de l'intelligence chez l'enfant* (1937), *La construction du réel chez l'enfant* (1937), *La formation du symbole chez l'enfant* (1945)

situations rather than solely through language. Experiments on this problem I resumed again much later, after my return to Geneva, in collaboration with A. Szeminska and B. Inhelder.

Before leaving Neuchâtel, I concluded the research on mollusks by clearing up a question which had preoccupied me for many years, and which touched on the fundamental problem of the relation between hereditary structure and environment. Indeed, this last problem had always seemed to me to be central, not only for the genetic classification of organic forms (morphogeny), but also for psychological learning theory (maturation versus learning) and epistemology. Therefore it seemed worthwhile to me to utilize my zoölogical findings for studying, in however limited a way, that significant problem of morphogenesis. I have been aware of a variety of *Limnaea stagnalis* particularly abundant in the lake of Neuchâtel and remarkable for its adaptation to its environment. Its globular shape comes from the action of the waves which constantly force the animal to clamp itself to the stones, and thus cause an enlargement of the opening and shortening of the whorl during the period of growth. The problem was to determine whether these traits were hereditary. Observations on 80,000 individuals living in their natural environment and on many thousands grown in an aquarium led me to draw the following conclusions: (1) this variety exists only in large lakes and in those sections of the lakes where the water is roughest; (2) its traits are hereditary and survive in an aquarium after five or six generations; a pure species can be segregated which reproduces according to the Mendelian laws of cross-breeding. The variety is able to live outside the lakes; I deposited some of them in a pond where they are still thriving after twenty years. The hypothesis of chance mutation, independent of environmental stimulation, seems unlikely in this particular case, since nothing prevents this globular variety from living in any body of fresh water.[12] That experience has taught me not to explain the whole of mental life by maturation alone!

VI.   1929–1939

In 1929 I returned to the University of Geneva as Professor of History of Scientific Thought (in the Division of Science) and Assistant Director of the Institut J. J. Rousseau; in 1932 I became co-director, with Claparède and Bovet. Since 1936 I have also taught experimental psychology at the University of Lausanne one day a week. In addition, in 1929 I imprudently accepted the duties of director of the Bureau International Office de l'Edu-

[12] See Les races lacustres de la *Limnaea stagnalis*, L. Recherches sur les rapports de l'adaptation héréditaire avec le milieu, *Bull biol de la France et de la Belgique*, 1929, 18, 424–455; and L'adaptation de la *Limnaea stagnalis* aux milieux lacustres de la Suisse romande, *Rev. suisse de Zool.*, 1929, 36, Plates 3–6, 263–531.

cation on the insistence of my friend Pedro Rossello, who had become its assistant director. For two reasons this international office, which now is working in close collaboration with UNESCO, interested me. In the first place it was able, through its intergovernmental organization, to contribute toward the improvement of pedagogical methods and toward the official adoption of techniques better adapted to the mentality of the child. Secondly, there was, so to speak, an element of sport in that venture. Rossello and I had succeeded in having accepted a new organization essentially on an intergovernmental basis. But on the day the statute was signed there were only three governments participating: the canton of Geneva (the Swiss government itself was represented but undecided), Poland and Ecuador. Moreover we were the subject of poorly repressed opposition (I am speaking to psychologists!) by the Institut de Coopération Intellectuelle. We had to act quickly and with diplomacy. A few years later between thirty-five and forty-five governments were represented at the annual conferences called by the Swiss government (today this organization is sponsored jointly by UNESCO and the International Office of Education). This job has certainly cost me a good deal of time I might possibly have spent more advantageously on research in child psychology, but at least I have learned from it quite a bit about adult psychology!

Added to these non-scientific labors were other administrative duties; I had in particular the task of reorganizing the Institut J. J. Rousseau which ceased to be private and became partially affiliated with the University.

The years from 1929 to 1939 cover a period filled with scientific endeavors. Three principal events stand out in retrospect.

First, the course in the History of Scientific Thought which I gave in the Faculté des Sciences at Geneva enabled me to promote more vigorously the project of a scientific epistemology founded on mental development, both autogenetic and phylogenetic. For ten successive years I studied intensely the emergence and history of the principal concepts of mathematics, physics and biology.

Secondly, I again resumed, on a larger scale than before, the research in child psychology at the Institut J. J. Rousseau. This work I carried out in collaboration with most able assistants, particularly A. Szeminska, and B. Inhelder, who now occupies the chair of child psychology. Thanks to them, a series of new experiments could be performed that dealt systematically with problems of action (manipulation of objects), whereby the conversation that was carried on with the subject exclusively involved the child's own manipulatory conduct. By this method I studied the development of numbers with A. Szeminska, that of the ideas of physical quantity with B. Inhelder; I also started studies of spatial, temporal and other relationships with E. Meyer. The most advanced of these studies were published around

1940,[13] at a time when psychologists no longer had the opportunity of exchanging their ideas across frontiers, or often, even of doing research. Thus these books were little read outside of French-speaking areas, though they were the first to develop fully a number of problems on which my first books hardly had touched.

In the third place, the study of concrete operations finally enabled me to discover the operative structures-of-the-whole that I had been seeking so long. I analyzed in children four to seven or eight years of age the relationship of part and whole (by asking them to add pearls to a group of predetermined magnitude), the sequences of asymmetrical relationships (by letting them construct series of prescribed order), and the correspondences, item by item (by making them build two or more corresponding rows), etc. These studies led me to understand why logical and mathematical operations cannot be formed independently: The child can grasp a certain operation only if he is capable, at the same time, of correlating operations by modifying them in different, well-determined ways — for instance, by inverting them. These operations presuppose, as does any primary intelligent conduct, the possibility of making detours (which corresponds to what logicians call "associativity") and returns ("reversibility"). Thus the operations always represent reversible structures which depend on a total system that, in itself, may be entirely additive. Certain of these more complex structures-of-the-whole have been studied in mathematics under the name of "groups" and "lattices"; operative systems of this sort are indeed of importance for the development of equilibria of thought. I sought for the most elementary operative structures-of-the-whole, and I finally found them in the mental processes underlying the formation of the idea of preservation or constancy. Simpler than the "groups" and the "lattices," such structures represent the most primitive parts of a part-whole organization: I have called them "groupings." For example, a classification (whereby the classes of the same rank order are always discrete and separate) is a grouping.

I presented my first paper on this subject, although I had not yet thoroughly mastered it, at the International Congress of Psychology at Paris in 1937. At that same time I was trying to determine the logical structure of groupings of classes and relationships of which I was able to isolate eight interdependent forms. I wrote an article in 1939 on this topic which P. Guillaume and I. Meyerson published in their "Collection Psychologique and Philosophique."[14]

---

[13] Piaget and A. Szeminska, *La genèse du nombre chez l'enfant* (1941), Piaget and B. Inhelder, *Le développement des quantités chez l'enfant* (1941). *La genèse du nombre* will soon be translated into English.

[14] *Classes, relations et nombres   Essai sur la réversibilité de la pensée* (1942).

VII. 1939–1950

The war spared Switzerland without our really knowing exactly why. However great his concern, an intellectual of my age (43 years), no longer subject to military service (I had been definitely released in 1916), could only cross his arms or go on with his work.

When the professor of sociology at the University of Geneva gave up his position in 1939, I was, without my knowledge, nominated to that post; I accepted the call. A few months later Claparède fell ill of a disease which was to be fatal; I took over his duties, and, in 1940 was given the chair of Experimental Psychology and named Director of the Psychology Laboratory (there I found an outstanding co-worker in Lambercier). I continued editing the *Archives de Psychologie*, first with Rey, and later with Rey and Lambercier. A Swiss Society of Psychology was founded shortly thereafter and I assumed the presidency of it for the first three years, collaborating with Morgenthaler in editing a new *Revue Suisse de Psychologie*. There was much work to be done.

From 1939 to 1945 I carried on two kinds of research. Firstly, on assuming the responsibility of the laboratory made famous by the names of Th. Flournoy and Ed. Claparède, I undertook, with the collaboration of Lambercier and various assistants, a long-range study on the development of perceptions in the child (until the age of adulthood). The aim of this study was to better understand the relationship of perception and intelligence, as well as to test the claims of the Gestalt theory (which had not convinced me with respect to the problem of intelligence). The first results of this research, which we are still continuing, have already appeared in the *Archives de Psychologie*,[15] they seem to us rather instructive for a theory of structure. Whereas logical structures deal only with one of the various aspects of the objects (class, number, size, weight, etc.), but, as far as that aspect is concerned, are complete, the perceptual structures are for the most part incomplete because they are statistical or merely probable. It is because of this character of probability that the perceptual structures are not additive, but follow the Gestalt laws. These structures do not remain the same at all ages:They have a less active character in the child than in the adult, and are closer to the products of intelligence in the latter. These facts are of consequence in such matters as the degree of geometric-optical illusions as a function of age, the magnitude of perceptual constancy, etc.

Secondly, by utilizing a concrete experimental technique and analytical method of procedure, and with the assistance of many collaborators, I began

---

[15] Recherches sur le développement des perceptions (Recherches I à XII), *Arch de Psychol*, 1942–1950.

research on the development of ideas of time, of movement, of velocity, as well as on behavior involving these concepts.[16]

In 1942 Piéron was kind enough to invite me to give a series of lectures at the Collège de France; that occasion enabled me to bring to our French colleagues – it was during the German occupation – testimony of the unshakable affection of their friends from outside. The main content of these lectures appeared shortly after the war in a small volume which is now available in English[17] as well as in German, Swedish, etc.

As soon as the war was over, social exchanges were resumed with renewed effort. The International Office of Education had never completely ceased to function during the years 1939 to 1945; it had served particularly as a clearing house for the sending of educational books to prisoners of war. When UNESCO was being organized, the Office of Education participated in the preparatory conferences and, later, in the annual general conferences which decided on general policies and the work to be carried out by the two institutions. After Switzerland joined UNESCO, I was named by my government President of the Swiss Commission of UNESCO and headed the Swiss delegation to the conferences at Bayreuth, Paris and Florence. UNESCO sent me as a representative to the meetings at Sèvre and Rio de Janeiro, and entrusted me with the editing of the pamphlet "The Right to Education"; I also held for several months the interim post of Assistant Director General in charge of the Department of Education. When M. Torrès-Bodet offered me this post for a longer period, he put me in a somewhat embarrassing position; actually, it did not take me long to decide between the international tasks and the appeal of my uncompleted research: I accepted the offered responsibility, but for only a short time. I recently accepted, however, membership on the Executive Council of UNESCO, having been elected to it by the general conference at Florence.

While on the subject of international relations, I might mention that in 1946 I had the pleasure of receiving an honorary degree from the Sorbonne; I had been given the same honor by Harvard in 1936 during the unforgettable ceremonies celebrating the tricentenary of that great university. In 1949 I received the honorary doctorate of the University of Brussels and, that same year, the title of Professor, *honoris causa*, of the University of Brazil at Rio de Janeiro. Nor, while writing in this vein, do I wish to fail to mention the pleasure I felt on becoming a member of the New York Academy of Sciences.

But postwar social activities did not cause me to neglect my work. On the contrary, I have gone on a little faster for fear I might not finish in time

[16] *Le développement de la notion de temps chez l'enfant. Les notions de mouvement et de vitesse chez l'enfant* (1946).
[17] Piaget, *The psychology of intelligence* (1950).

if the world situation should again become troubled. That explains my many publications. This increase in output, however, does not imply hasty improvisation; I have been working on every one of these publications for a long time.[18]

First of all, with the help of B. Inhelder, I was able to carry out about thirty experiments on the development of spatial relations between the ages of 2 and 3, and 11 and 12,[19] a problem all the more complex because of the constant mutual interference of factors of perception and action. On the other hand, study of intellectual operations as the only reversible mental mechanisms (as opposed to perception, motor performance, etc., which are one-directional) led us to the investigation of the reactions of young children to an irreversible physical phenomena, such as that of mixture or chance.[20] I also finished a study on the genesis of probability with B. Inhelder, which was extended to include the wider problem of induction.

Secondly, I was at last in a position to realize my old plan of writing a genetic epistemology.[21] At the death of Claparède I had given up the course in history of scientific thought to take over experimental psychology. Since I had enough experimental data on the psychological processes underlying logico-mathematical and physical operations, it seemed the right time to write the synthesis I had been dreaming about from the beginning of my studies. Instead of devoting five years to child psychology, as I had anticipated in 1921, I had spent about thirty on it; it was exciting work and I do not in the least regret it. But now was the time to conclude it, and that is what I attempted in this general study. It is basically an analysis of the mechanism of learning, not statically, but from the point of view of growth and development.

Lastly, the Colin publishers asked me to write a *Traité de logique*[22] with

[18] I have often been asked where I found the time for so much writing in addition to my university work and international duties. I owe it first to the unusual quality of the men and, especially, of the women who have collaborated with me, and who have helped me much more than I can demonstrate here. After years spent in questioning children all by myself, with only small groups of students, latterly I have been helped by teams of assistants and colleagues who did not confine themselves to collecting facts, but took an increasingly active part in conducting this research. And then, too, I owe it to a particular bent of my character. Fundamentally I am a worrier whom only work can relieve. It is true I am sociable and like to teach or to take part in meetings of all kinds, but I feel a compelling need for solitude and contact with nature. After mornings spent with others, I begin each afternoon with a walk during which I quietly collect my thoughts and coordinate them, after which I return to the desk at my home in the country. As soon as vacation time comes, I withdraw to the mountains in the wild regions of the Valais and write for weeks on end on improvised tables and after pleasant walks. It is this dissociation between myself as a social being and as a "man of nature" (in whom Dionysian excitement ends in intellectual activity) which has enabled me to surmount a permanent fund of anxiety and transform it into a need for working

[19] Piaget and Inhelder, *La représentation de l'espace chez l'enfant* (1948), Piaget, Szeminska and Inhelder, *La géométrie spontanée chez l'enfant* (1948).

[20] *La genèse de l'idée de hasard chez l'enfant* (1951).

[21] *Introduction à l'epitémologie génétique.* I *La pensée mathématique*, II. *La pensée physique*, III. *La pensée biologique, la pensée psychologique et la pensée sociologique* (1949–50).

[22] *Traité de logique, esquisse d'une logistique operatoire* (1949).

the twofold aim of presenting concisely the operative methods of logistics (or modern algebraic logic) and of developing my own ideas on this subject. I hesitated at first since I am not a logician by profession. But then I was tempted by the desire to construct a schematic outline of logistics which would correspond, on the one hand, to the steps in the formation of operations (concrete operations of class and relationship — formal operation, or the logic of propositions), and, on the other hand, to the kinds of structures the fundamental psychological importance of which I had previously discovered. Since then I have written a shorter work, not yet published, which deals with structures-of-the-whole (groups, "lattices" and groupings) which can be defined by means of three propositions (the logic of the 256 ternary operations).

CONCLUSION

My one idea, developed under various aspects in (alas!) twenty-two volumes, has been that intellectual operations proceed in terms of structures-of-the-whole. These structures denote the kinds of equilibrium toward which evolution in its entirety is striving; at once organic, psychological and social, their roots reach down as far as biological morphogenesis itself.

This idea is doubtless more widespread than is generally assumed; however, it had never been satisfactorily demonstrated. After more than thirty years' work on the higher aspects of that evolution, I should like one day to go back to the more primitive mechanisms; this is one reason why I am interested in infantile perceptions. The reversibility characteristic of the operations of logical intelligence is not acquired *en bloc*, but is prepared in the course of a series of successive stages: elementary rhythms, more and more complex regulations (semi-reversible structures) and, ultimately, reversible operative structures. Now this law of evolution, which dominates all mental development, corresponds no doubt to certain laws of structuration of the nervous system which it would be interesting to try to formulate in regard to qualitative mathematical structures (groups, lattices, etc.).[23] As to Gestalt-structures, they constitute only one particular type among possible structures, and these belong to regulations rather than to (reversible) operations. I hope to be able some day to demonstrate relationships between mental structures and stages of nervous development, and thus to arrive at that general theory of structures to which my earlier studies constitute merely an introduction.

[23] Piaget, Le problème neurologique de l'intériorisation des actions en opérations réversibles, *Arch de Psychol*, 1946, 32, 241–258.

HENRI PIÉRON

ANCESTRY

ON my father's side I am descended from a male line of Lorraine glass-makers, the Piérons, of Clermont-en-Argonne.[1]   My great-grandfather and my grandfather died young, as was the rule with glass-blowers; to them had been given the name "gentlemen glass-makers" as compensation for the risks of an exhausting trade.   In fact my grandfather, who had married very early, died six months before the birth — in January, 1847 — of my father, Nicolas Dominique Piéron.   On the other hand, my grandmother, Julie Athanaïse Benoit, whom I knew well, died August 14, 1904, at the age of 79.   After the death of her husband, she came to live with her father, Jean François Benoit, a landowner of Folembray (Aisne) who had been a widower since the death of his first wife, Marie Collard, in 1832, but who later remarried.   My grandmother, in turn, was married again to J. A. Trousselle, a director of a sugar refinery in the neighboring village of Trosly.   Trousselle, whom I never knew, raised my father, with the help of his father-in-law, Benoit, who died in 1872, and of Benoit's mother.   "Maman Nini," as Benoit's mother was called, was an intelligent and autocratic woman, though quite indulgent toward her great-grandson.   She died in 1870 at the age of 96.

On the maternal side I come from two well-to-do farming families of Alsace.   My mother, Madeleine Wendling (February 9, 1853 — February 4, 1932) was born at Kaltenhausen near Haguenau; her father was Jacques Wendling (born in 1816) and her mother was Barbe Klipfel (born 1824).   Because of the German annexation of Alsace in 1871 I knew my grandparents only slightly, having gone to see them only once at Haguenau when I was three; their death occurred while I was still very young.

My father, though he liked to wander about the countryside instead of

[1] Submitted in French and translated by Donald MacQueen of Clark University.

257

attending the village school of Coucy-le-Chateau — three kilometers from Folembray — showed such superior ability that it attracted the attention of the authorities; he was given a scholarship which enabled him to continue his studies, first in a boarding-school in the small town of Chauny, and later, 1862, at the Lycée Charlemagne of Paris where he entered the third grade as a science student and studied at the Institut Favart at the same time. He was always at the head of his class and won all the prizes. In 1868 he ranked first in science at the École Normale Supérieure. The director of that school, on the recommendation of the head of the science department, expressed his opinion about him in these words: "He is an outstanding student who gives promise of becoming a first class professor. I will add that M. Piéron is an excellent young man, considerate and devoted to his schoolmates." After passing his professorial examination with top rank he went to the Lycée de Besancon as professor of higher mathematics. He was a substitute teacher at the Lycée of Caen in 1871, and was appointed to the Lycée Charlemagne at Paris in 1874. In the following year he was married at Kaltenhausen. In 1877 he was appointed to the chair of higher mathematics at the Lycée Saint-Louis; this position he held for fifteen years, teaching classes of over one hundred students. His reputation as a professor was such that it was necessary to turn away many more pupils desirous of taking his course than could be admitted. The number of his former students who had graduated from the École Polytechnique and École Normale Supérieure and subsequently occupied administrative positions in France was really considerable; he took great pride in the affectionate gratitude they always showed towards him. He was appointed Inspector of the Academy of Paris in 1892, and in 1894 was made Inspector-in-chief of Public Education. By special appointment, during the two years 1895–1896, he assumed the directorship of the Lycée Saint-Louis where he set up a scientific institute preparing students for the schools of higher learning. He died suddenly before reaching his sixtieth year, on Christmas day 1906, while on his way to visit the grave of his eldest son, Paul. My brother Paul had died at the age of seventeen on December 25, 1893, of pulmonary tuberculosis. A bust of my father, done by the sculptor Verlet, has been placed in the Lycée Saint-Louis by his former pupils.

My father was a very sensitive and tender-hearted man, but rather reserved and somewhat ashamed of showing his feelings. We never came into close emotional contact. Though he never tried to influence me intellectually or direct my thinking, he nevertheless watched steadily over me, without my being much aware of it. I was much like him in temperament, and on my part did nothing to establish closer personal or intellectual relations with him, after his death I have often regretted this neglect.

INFANCY AND ADOLESCENCE

I was born July 18, 1881, right in the middle of the Latin Quarter, at 65 Boulevard Saint-Michel between rue Soufflot and rue Gay-Lussac where the Luxembourg Garden opens its main gate on a large square, called then Place Médicis.

My first memories are closely linked with the balcony of the fifth floor apartment, where I stood so often watching the traffic in the street and viewing the Luxembourg Garden, the place where I used to walk and play, first under the supervision of a nurse, and later, of a young aunt, my mother's sister. At the age of four I watched from there the funeral procession accompanying Victor Hugo's body to the Panthéon; shortly afterward I watched with despair a carriage carrying off my aunt and a man whom I then considered a robber. It was my excellent uncle Théodore Bon, cousin of Pierre Loti, whom my aunt had just married.

It seems that I must have been a difficult child, strong-willed, very independent and often rebellious. Indeed, in my childhood I had violent conflicts with my mother, who was herself a very peremptory, yet very kind person.

When I was six, having learned to read almost without help, I entered a small private class where several pupils were taught in a family environment by a charming young lady. To my great delight I visited the Exposition universelle in the summer of 1889. It was with much regret that in October of that year I had to transfer into the eighth grade of the Lycée Saint-Louis — located in a rather grim neighborhood. The change was not really very great, however, for there were only three of us students under one very kind professor. The Lycée Saint-Louis was about to be transformed into a purely scientific school, and the lower classes were to be discontinued. The following year, because of this change, I had to leave the school where my father had taught, and was transferred to the Lycée Henri IV, near my home in the Place du Panthéon. With no great effort I gained top rank among three pupils, so I naturally won all the prizes. On graduation day I received them, amid the enthusiastic applause of the audience, and I was quite embarrassed about this apparently magnificent success since I sensed how ridiculously little I had done to deserve it.

During the following three years I kept my scholastic standing relatively high without much difficulty, although I did not show any particular brilliance. Before the beginning of the school year of 1893 my brother became very ill, and my mother took him to Arcachon, where he died on the 25th of December; these circumstances led my father to enter me as a boarding student at the Lycée Hoche at Versailles where M. Gazeau, one of my father's dear friends, was headmaster. In that school I became acquainted

with a rougher kind of existence, physically speaking; on rising in an un-
heated dormitory, I was obliged to break the ice in the washbasin before
washing. The dissatisfaction with this collective and continuously supervised
life often provoked me to acts of rebellion. However, the complete lack of
distractions made me work harder, so that at the year's end I won numerous
prizes which I felt this time were not unjustified. The following year I was
glad to return to Paris as a day student to attend, until 1899, the upper
classes of the Lycée Louis-le-Grand located opposite the Sorbonne. I found
once more a freedom of action which I fully enjoyed. Just as my father as a
youth had so often strayed away from his village school to go hunting birds'
nests, so I did not hesitate now and then to cut a boring class in order to
explore unknown sections of the great metropolis. My taste for solitude
generally steered me clear of the beer gardens of the Latin Quarter.

During the two years my father directed the Lycée Saint-Louis, we lived
in the school which was located on the Boulevard Saint-Michel; in the
autumn of 1896 we moved to the rue d'Assas, on the other side of the
Luxembourg Garden.

I was now entering my thirteenth school year, at the end of which time
I passed the first part toward my baccalaureate certificate (July 1897). That
year was very fruitful for my intellectual development, thanks to a keen-
minded and artistic though unassuming teacher, M. Morand, with whom
I got along very well. On the other hand a second professor, Casanova by
name, lacked common sense; we made life so impossible for him that he
eventually gave up trying to control our rebellious class and asked for leave
of absence. I remember particularly a New Year prank we played on him:
First, there was a speech in French, full of hidden meanings; while he was
applauding the first, a second speech in Latin was presented in which the
words "casa nova" recurred in various guises, then came a Greek speech
where the most obscene allusions were made through terrible plays on words,
while on the surface the whole thing looked like an official text of apparent
dignity.

In my final year I struck up a close friendship with Professor Victor
Delbos; he left during the school year to take the place of Henri Bergson at
the Lycée Henri IV. Delbos was succeeded by Marcel Bernès, a dull teacher
by contrast. Bernès was attacked in Le Temps by the great critic, Francisque
Sarcey, who accused him of teaching a Bergsonian philosophy far too obscure
and difficult to grasp. I wrote an article defending Bernès, and thus started
a controversy with Sarcey which went on for some time in the columns of
the newspaper; he calmed down after I had called him "mon oncle," a title
which pleased him very much.

It was during the year in which I passed the baccalauréat de philosophie
that current events in France stirred up violent arguments among us students;

the general excitement centered around the Dreyfus affair. I was violently pro-Dreyfus while my father, without taking part officially, had aligned himself with the opposite camp. We therefore avoided that subject in our conversations.

During that year, after an honest attempt, I definitely gave up the study of mathematics; I was influenced in this move by my father, who had always been careful not to play up the professor and sway my decisions. Purely abstract thinking without concrete content had no attraction for me, and, while recognizing the usefulness of mathematics as a tool, I could see in it only an accessory, not a goal in itself.

Philosophy had won me over by all that it implied of independence of thought and of universal criticism. Therefore I decided, as a beginning of my higher studies, to prepare for the *licence de philosophie.* My father, since he was closely attached to the École Normale Supérieure, was very anxious to see me enter the great school of the rue d'Ulm, as he once had himself. I was reluctant to give up, even to a slight degree, my newly-won freedom; but in order not to disappoint my father I agreed, while preparing for the *licence* as a student at the Sorbonne, to attend some of the courses of *Rhétorique supérieure* at the Lycée Louis-le-Grand, where preparation was given for the entrance examination of the École Normale.

I was then seventeen, and already sporting a beard; along with my secondary education I was nearing the end of the adolescent period.

I had enjoyed particularly favorable living conditions in a well-to-do family environment. Our social life was restricted almost exclusively to my father's university connections; thus we lived in a lively atmosphere where the occasional narrow-mindedness of the faculty wives was well counterbalanced by the great breadth of mind on the part of most of the men. Their modest but secure social position freed them from material preoccupations and enabled them almost always to carry on their intellectual pursuits with remarkable unselfishness.

The vacations, which we spent mainly at the seashore each year, were especially happy periods of a carefree life, full of opportunities to establish pleasant relations with friendly people of different professional interests, particularly merchants and newspapermen. Physical activities, restricted to fencing and dancing during the school year at Paris, were broadened to include walking and swimming, tennis, canoeing and sailing.

ADVANCED STUDIES

The first year of my higher studies decided my career; of all the branches of philosophy only psychology attracted me. Among the excellent teachers whose courses I attended, I found myself agreeing only with those whose teachings were based on positive and scientific methods; these were above all, Th. Ribot at the Collège de France; Pierre Janet at the Sorbonne, whose courses on experimental psychology, though outside of the preparation for the *licence,* I attended regularly; Lucien Lévy-Bruhl, who held the chair of philosophy in *Rhétorique supérieure* when I began my studies but was transferred to the Sorbonne in the middle of the year — a great teacher who exerted a strong influence on the students, making them truly his disciples; Victor Brochard, a splendid teacher who taught Greek philosophy. Brochard, who had become blind, was quite up-to-date on experimental psychology because of his close contact with his reader, George Dumas, a young professor of philosophy at the Collège Chaptal. I was thus fortunate that Brochard, a former schoolmate of my father, should favor me with his friendship. Other teachers I had were the sociologist, Henry Michel, with whom I was on friendly and familiar terms, and Ferdinand Buisson, whose extracurricular pro-Dreyfus activity provoked violent clashes among his students, even in class. The Sorbonne was then the scene of rather violent fights, particularly incited by anti-semitic groups in the Latin Quarter against whom Péguy, the poet, sometimes led the battle; I often joined in and twice suffered skull wounds which fortunately left no trace. One day I was almost knifed for having cried "Long live the Republic" near the office of the anti-semitic newspaper *La Libre Parole;* it was on the same day that President Loubet was struck with a cane at the races at Auteuil.

In our Republican group there were two students, sisters, one of whom was to become my wife, and the other the wife of my schoolmate and faithful friend, Eugène Frossard.

At that time the whole of France was really divided into two clans, typified by the Ligue des Droits de l'Homme for the defense of Dreyfus and the Ligue de la Patrie française for the defense of military authority which had condemned this innocent Jew. This division separated me from my childhood sweetheart, the daughter of one of my father's friends, to whom I was secretly engaged.

Despite the political unrest of the times, I passed the examinations for the *licence ès lettres-philosophie,* dispensing in a Latin dissertation the remembered treasures of Ciceronian redundancies. There was no longer any question of attending Normal School and, after two months of rest at the beach at Royan where we went each year, I came back to Paris planning to study for the *agrégation* in philosophy; this would assure a teaching position and especially allow me to continue my studies, particularly those concerned with the biological and psychological nature of man and its pathological deviations.

From the beginning I attended the neurological clinic at the Salpêtrière where Raymond had succeeded Charcot and where Pierre Janet gave consultations at which I served as his secretary. For training in experimental research I went to the psychology laboratory at the Sorbonne which was open on Thursdays and where I found, after a rather unencouraging welcome from Binet, such men as Jean Philippe, Victor Henri, the Swiss Larguier des Bancels and the Norwegian Aars. I went to the Faculté des Sciences where Félix le Dantec, a former pupil of my father, and a most precocious mathematician side-tracked to biology, drew me to the Laboratory of Alfred Giard, another of my father's schoolmates who had a strong influence on me.

There then began a ten-year period of research and study, continually interrupted by examinations and competitions. These studies were both of a philosophical and of a scientific and medical nature, with an orientation toward neuropsychiatry. It was during these years that I started my scientific career as a psychologist.

In the course of these years, after embittered conflicts, the "Affaire Dreyfus" finally calmed down, but new quarrels within the Latin Quarter again involved me in fights. With the Socialist students I took part in the demonstrations aimed at omitting a course in social philosophy which was to be given by Izoulet at the Collège de France. These demonstrations ceased only when the firemen, mobilized to protect the professor, had thoroughly soaked the demonstrators.

At the School of Medicine, with its clique of scientists headed by Eugène Gley, *agrégé* of physiology, I also took part against the clinical group, both interns and *agrégés*, in the defense of two professors from Nancy, who had been called to teach in Paris. These men, the histologist Prenant and the anatomist Nicolas, had not graduated in Paris and had not entered private practice, but had devoted all their time to their Laboratory; so the surgeons who had obtained their degrees in Paris wanted these chairs for themselves, especially the chair of anatomy to which Poirier had just been named.

I passed my *agrégation* only after two failures at the oral examination. One member of the jury, the inspector-general Darlu, a narrow-minded moralist and violently opposed to the scientific method in psychology, did not hesitate to announce that I would never pass. This incident induced Lévy-Bruhl to accept membership on the jury for one year, a membership which he had previously declined, and it was only because of him that I passed at the top of the group (there were 100 candidates for the seven vacancies); for the practice lesson I gave at the end of the test, the mark he proposed to the jury was 18 out of a possible 20; Darlu's proposal, not approved by the other members, Messrs. Lachelier, Hamelin and Rauh, was only two. Moreover, in my examination in Greek philosophy, I had the luck to get a quotation from Plotinus; this philosopher had been the subject of brilliant lectures by Bergson whose own thoughts bear close kinship to mysticism of Plotinus.

My studies for a degree in natural sciences — a certificate of advanced studies in physiology — were under the direction of Dastre, another schoolmate of my father, a clever, cultured and liberal mind. At that time I was fortunate to be initiated into rigorous experimental techniques, working under L. Lapicque, who was engaged in research on nervous excitability, and under P. Portier and Victor Henri; the latter had changed from experimental psychology to physical chemistry before going into theoretical physics; I had met him at Binet's.

At the Physiology Laboratory of the Sorbonne a poor opinion of clinical work and of medical physiology prevailed. My contacts with that outstanding man, Charles Richet, professor of physiology at the Medical School, left me somewhat perplexed: I very much admired his imagination and his bold ideas which led him to undertake some research with me on the treatment of the insane by carbonic acid narcosis (research which was interrupted by technical difficulties) at a time when no one had yet dreamed of the therapeutic effects of narcotics in mental medicine; but I also was struck by his lack of critical judgment which was painfully conspicuous, particularly in his thoughts on metapsychical experiences.

At the Dastre Laboratory I started my studies on the physiology of sleep which concluded in 1912 with my doctoral thesis in the natural sciences; the thesis concerned my discovery, undertaken with the help of a histological biologist, my friend, René Legendre, of the formation of hypnotoxins during experimental insomnia.

While helping Edouard Toulouse at the Asylum of Villejuif where a psychology laboratory had been started, I became initiated into psychiatry. I was at the same time engaged in research in normal and pathological psychology which I had begun with Nicolas Vaschide whom I had met at Pierre Janet's. Thanks to the facilities at Villejuif I was able to install a physiological laboratory, and thus to continue my research on experimental insomnia in the dog. The work called for close supervision of the dogs both day and night for about ten days by walking them and tending to them in order to prevent them from going to sleep. These experiments started a press campaign led by the journalist Gustave Téry, which involved me in a newspaper controversy and brought the antivivisectionists into the discussion. As far as I am concerned, I have always loved animals and only with great reluctance have I performed vivisections. But, even though I avoided as much as possible inflicting pain on the animals, for the good of science I have always defended the right to use them in physiological research.

Another study concerning the nycthemeral rhythm of temperature was made possible through the employment of night nurses in the Villejuif asylum. In collaboration with E. Toulouse, I established the inversion of the nycthemeral rhythm of temperature gradually induced by a reversal in living conditions, and the gradual return to the normal rhythm when normal conditions were reintroduced.

My first scientific publication appeared at the Fourth International Congress of Psychology in 1900, in Paris, where the *Exposition universelle* was also being held. Pierre Janet, who was the secretary general of the Congress, invited me to present a paper. Th. Ribot, director of *la Revue Philosophique*, who was very much interested in my work, also asked for my collaboration. I started to write for the *Revue* in 1901 and contributed to it during the many years when Lévy-Bruhl, after the death of Ribot, edited the journal in the same spirit of positive science.

During this period of advanced studies, I was completely dominated by a deep and far-reaching curiosity and an insatiable desire to acquire knowledge that drove me to read extensively, to observe, to experiment.

The summer vacations were essentially dedicated to research in biology and animal psychology in the marine laboratories at Wimereux where I fell under the spell of Alfred Giard. I also worked in the laboratories of the Ile de Tatihou near Saint-Vaast-la-Hougue, nominally headed by Edmond Perrier, director of the Muséum d'Histoire Naturelle, but in fact run by Raoul Anthony. At Arcachon I worked with the physiologist Jolyet. Jolyet was a deeply original scientist, who — accompanied always by his little dog, silent as he — spent his life between the two laboratories at Bordeaux and at Arcachon (where he later died) and his boat in the bay; I remember well those Sundays when all the workers would gather in his boat, conversing freely among themselves while the *patron* silently held the rudder.

In 1913 I was elected a member of the Société de Biologie. The many reports I wrote for this society allowed me to make public the wealth of data I had accumulated in my biological and physiological research. My research in experimental and zoological psychology stimulated many papers and discussions in study groups at the Institut Général Psychologique, which was founded in 1900, and at the Société de Psychologie, which separated from the Institut in 1905; this same year I had become a member of the Société which later, in 1909, elected me its president. As to my neuropsychiatric work, I took part in the meetings of the Société neurologique, the Société médico-Psychologique which in 1903 made me corresponding member and in 1910 a full member, and of the Société clinique de médecine mentale which I helped to form in 1908.

I may say that my whole life has been devoted to study and research, and toward this aim I found myself in complete accord with my wife whom I married in October, 1902. She has lent me her full spiritual support, and renounced all the pleasures of a social life, even accompanying me to the marine laboratories in spite of their complete lack of comfort.

CAREER

Edouard Toulouse, in his capacity of director of a department of the Asile d'aliénés at Villejuif — today the Hôpital neuropsychiatrique — founded a laboratory of experimental psychology. When this laboratory was attached to the École Pratique des Hautes Études on January 1, 1901, I was named assistant, while N. Vaschide became its *chef des travaux;* no salary went with that position, however. Therefore, after my marriage, in 1903, I accepted the chair of philosophy at the Collège de St. Germain-en-Laye, but continued to live in Paris and pursue my studies and research at Villejuif. When in 1904 Edouard Toulouse assumed the directorship of the *Revue Scientifique,* I was appointed general secretary of that important journal, which made it financially possible to remain in Paris without teaching in a provincial school. My wife and I left the family home in rue d'Assas, and moved into an apartment nearby at 96 rue de Rennes; there we lived until 1913, when we settled for good in the western suburb of Vésinet.

In 1907 I was deeply shocked by the death of my father. In that year I became the *chef des travaux* of the Villejuif Laboratory, succeeding Vaschide who had moved on as assistant director to August Marie's Laboratoire de Psychologie pathologique; J. M. Lahy replaced me as assistant. Several months later, having been appointed *maître de conférences* at the École pratique des Hautes Études, and after having resigned as general secretary of the *Revue Scientifique,* I organized a course in scientific psychology which, for the first time in France, was connected with a laboratory. At that time I was editorial secretary of the *Revue de Psychiatrie* and assumed also the secretaryship of a scientific encyclopedia published by O. Doin under the editorship of Edouard Toulouse. The war of 1914 was to stop its publication almost completely. In addition to these activities, I gave two series of lectures at the École d'Anthropologie.

In 1911 Alfred Binet died prematurely, and the people concerned with higher education were for a long time disturbed over the question of his successor as director of the laboratory of physiological psychology of the Sorbonne, affiliated with the École pratique des Hautes Études. Indeed, the candidates were numerous. There were Jean Philippe, assistant director of the laboratory; Th. Simon, medical chief of the Insane Asylum of La Seine Inférieure and Binet's collaborator; the collaborator of Georges Dumas at Ste. Anne, Revault d'Allonnes; Edouard Toulouse requested that his laboratory be joined with Binet's; Pierre Janet who had to leave his small laboratory at the Salpêtrière because of difficulties with Déjerine, Raymond's successor at the Charcot clinic, also competed. Ferdinand Buisson and the Minister Steeg supported Simon's candidacy, and Th. Ribot felt obliged to support that of Jean Philippe. But Louis Liard, the rector, who had founded the Sorbonne laboratory, and Bayet, the director of the *enseignement supérieur*, both thought that I was particularly equipped to assume this post. The physiologist, Eugène Gley, and Victor Brochard, the philosopher, also urged me to announce my candidacy, which I had not dared to consider even in my private thoughts. When Steeg, the Minister of Public Education, resigned because of political vicissitudes and the downfall of the government, in May, 1912, I was appointed director of the Laboratory with all of the responsibilities that it entailed. At the same time the Masson publishing house appointed me director of the *Année Psychologique*, and soon afterward ceded to me all its property rights.

The Laboratory had been grossly neglected by Binet for several years; there was hardly more to be found than the equipment and books that had been brought there in 1889 by its first director, the physiologist Henry Beaunis. There were practically no funds and no personnel except Jean Philippe, who became my assistant director; I myself had, at first, to perform the work of a laboratory attendant. I had to struggle hard in order to obtain, if not larger quarters, at least an assistant, funds for upkeep, and subsidies for new equipment. Little by little I was able to provide working facilities for a few students, whereas Binet, as far as I could see, had rather discouraged those who wanted to work under him. I thought of persuading the Faculté des Sciences to establish a course in psychophysiology, a hope not to be realized until 1949. In the month of August, 1914, the war came, and my efforts were interrupted for several years. I had been previously rejected for military service, but I was called up again, and was accepted. I rather quickly passed the officer's examination and expected to be sent shortly to the front as an officer. But, unknown to me, at the headquarters of the Health Department of Montpellier, to which my corps belonged, decisions were made by which I was assigned to the dean of the Faculté de Médecine, Professor A. Mairet, as Medical Assistant in the military section of neuropsychiatry. I remained in that auxiliary service for about four years before being discharged at the time of the Armistice. In that important .department of the General Hospital to which the insane asylum of Font d'Aurelle was attached, I, as the only assistant, with an intern as my sole help, had to assume heavy responsibilities, both in general medicine and in neuropsychiatry. But with the wealth of material furnished by the terrible hazards of war on mental disturbances and head wounds, I could not fail to carry on extensive research in physiopathology and mental pathology. Throughout the years I have been receiving many souvenirs from some of the old patients I cared for at Montpellier; and I remained in close friendship with one of them, Jean Milon, professor at the Lycée de Nîmes, until his death in 1938.

As soon as I was discharged I resumed my duties at the laboratory of the

Sorbonne, eager to contribute as much as I could to the reconstruction and progress of my country. With the *Compagnons de l'Université nouvelle* I became interested in pedagogical reforms and the problems concerned with the organization of instruction. Thanks to the efforts of Louis Liard, a law was passed which created the Instituts d'Université and which made it possible to break through the water-tight compartments of the Facultés. With the concurrence and support of Delacroix and Georges Dumas of the Faculté des Lettres, and of Étienne Rabaud of the Faculté des Sciences, I was able to get the University of Paris to organize an Institute of Psychology. Founded by a decree of 1920, this was the first of the French University Institutes. In this Institute, a training program in psychophysiology, and, a little later, in *psychotechnique* was established. By using, on the one hand, the laboratory of the Sorbonne, and on the other, a laboratory of applied psychology created at the École Pratique des Hautes Études and installed at the Sainte-Anne Asylum under the direction of J. M. Lahy, practical laboratory research was made obligatory for the diplomas of general psychology and of applied psychology. Soon I succeeded in establishing the higher diploma of "expert psychotechnician" of the University of Paris.

The great independent scientific schools such as the École Pratique des Hautes Études and the Collège de France (with Pierre Janet) were closely connected with this University Institute. Therefore I didn't have to leave the Institut when in 1923 I entered the Collège de France to occupy the chair of physiology of sensation which had been created for me.[2] The establishment of such a chair had been suggested by Eugène Gley and Pierre Janet in November, 1922, after the death of Pierre Boutroux who had been teaching the history of the sciences; but, by a small majority, the Assembly of the Collège had decided to establish instead a chair of Egyptology for A. Moret. In April, 1923, Gley-Janet's proposal was once more taken up, supported by Nageotte; the chair was created replacing a chair of Semitic Archeology which had become vacant at the death of Clermont-Ganneau. In July, 1923, I was appointed by unanimous vote of the Assembly of the Collège and of the Académie des Sciences. This was for me the crowning achievement of the career which I had entered. I was to offer a course limited to twenty lectures annually, which, in accordance with the great tradition of the school, had to be different each year. Though this entailed a considerable amount of preparation, it enabled me to develop successively

---

[2] Thanks to the establishment of the University Institutes, collaboration was assured between the University of Paris and the great independent scientific schools, such as the Collège de France which had been, at first, a rival of the University. The latter, which had a monopoly over education, had been founded on Latin scholasticism, and at first did not permit any other method of teaching. But in 1520 François I created a college of "Royal Readers," dependent only on him, to which he appointed men to teach Greek, Hebrew and mathematics That was the beginning of the Collège de France.

the various problems of sensory psychophysiology.[3] For the development of research in these technical fields, I had to organize a laboratory, obtain personnel, funds and quarters. Little by little I succeeded in these tasks. In 1926 the Laboratory of Sensory Physiology, attached to the École des Hautes Études, was put at my disposal; that laboratory was founded by the now retiring Charles Henry at the Sorbonne after he had separated from Binet. Successively I was given the help of an assistant, a laboratory attendant, a mechanic, and a sub-director. A temporary laboratory was installed above the lecture halls of the new Collège de France, and on a small plot of land still available I was able to erect a steel-prefabricated house for electroencephalography. At the same time my collaborator, Alfred Fessard, thanks to a subsidy from the Singer-Polignac Foundation, had been able to install a laboratory of cathodic oscillography in a small room of a temporary building. By 1937 this new research set-up, while not perfect had become satisfactory, and I was able to offer working facilities sufficient for a large number of researchers. In the meanwhile I was drawing up the plans for a large permanent laboratory which was to be installed in a Biology Building, the foundations of which, with three subcellars, were started in 1939. The work was stopped by the war, and only recently has it been possible to resume construction and complete the large excavation.

During this period of transition and development, facilities for research, thanks to the École des Hautes Études, were always available. This school, created by Duruy in 1868 for research purposes and training in research, comprised three scientific sections, a fourth section on historical studies, and a fifth on studies in religion. The last two sections had been well organized and with explicit regulations; but the scientific divisions were left to the good-will of the administrative offices, and no guarantees had been given concerning the status of the personnel, its selection, advancement, the allocation of funds, etc. With my colleague, André Mayer, I went to the director of Higher Education, M. Coville, to obtain the necessary regulations. Thanks to him, and in spite of administrative resistance, a ministerial decree of regu-

[3] The subjects of my successive courses (occasionally two subjects were treated in the same year) are given in the following chronological order· The laws of the Temporal Aspects of Sensations — Theories of Vision — Mechanisms of Achromatic and Chromatic Vision — Psychophysiological Problems of Perception — Cutaneous Sensitivity — Affective Sensory Reactions. Pain — Auditory Function — Theories of Hearing — Sensory Basis of Motor Activity — Visual Space — Qualitative and Quantitative Aspects of Sensation — Time of Reaction and Sensorial Latencies — Chemical Senses — Luminous Excitation and General Problems of Visual Sensation — Temporal Evolution of Visual Sensations — Sensory Functions of Animals — Higher Stages of Sensory Evolution of Invertebrates — Sensory Functions of Vertebrates — Color Vision — Mechanism of Chromatic Vision — Notions on the Developmental Stages of Sensation — Reflexogenic Sensitivity and Perceptual Reactions — Cerebral Substratum of Perceptual Reactions — Internal Sensitivity — Knowledge of Space — Present-Day Notions of Sensory Dynamics — Judgment of Intensity of Sensation. The last subject I am to treat before reaching the age of retirement (which has been instituted at the Collège of France since my entry into this school) relates to scientific concepts contributed by the pathology of senses.

lations was signed in November, 1925, by M. Yvon Delbos, whose divisional director was my friend and colleague, Henri Laugier. I was elected a member of a four-man steering committee in the department of natural sciences, which was the supervisory agency of seventy-five laboratories, among them the psychological institute. From 1926 on I was entrusted with the management of that department and, in 1937, became its president.[4]

It was not long before new administrative duties were added to the numerous ones which had already been assigned to me. I was very much concerned over the development in France of vocational guidance that people had been trying to organize since the end of the World War. Counselling services had been set up, and M. Julien Fontègne had been designated inspector of these services. But appeals were being made for the voluntary collaboration of retired educators who were guided by their own common sense, but who had no preparation of any kind for counselling and for the handling of techniques of screening.

In my laboratory at the Sorbonne my wife had devoted herself for years to the task of assembling and validating tests adequate for psychological examinations. I succeeded in convincing M. Labbé, the general director of the Services of Technical Instruction who had taken the initiative in the field of vocational guidance, of the necessity of creating a center for the training of vocational counsellors, and for a study of the techniques to be used and their evaluation. The University of Paris agreed to take this establishment under its wing. But the Service of Technical Instruction was loath to accept this proposal. It was decided to subsidize a private agency with an administrative council over which Director Labbé would preside, and a steering committee made up of M. Fontègne, of the physiologist, Henri Laugier, who taught at the Conservatoire des Arts et Métiers, and of myself. As delegate of this committee I had charge of the direction of the Institut national d'Orientation professionnelle which had been founded in 1928 and was housed in a few rooms of the old Musée Pédagogique at 41 rue Gay-Lussac. But this building was falling into ruins; the Musée Pédagogique was moved elsewhere and, since the land was to revert to the Department of Higher Education, we ran the risk of not having any quarters just a few weeks before the opening of the Institut. I then secured from the Director of Higher Education, M. Cavalier, the provisional cession of the land and the building; soon afterward the Minister of National Education, M. de Monzie, officially assigned that estate to the Conservatoire National des Arts et Métiers,

[4] The laboratories of the École des Hautes Études receive help in personnel and in funds for equipment, but, except in special cases, this assistance depends on their having quarters at their disposal, either in establishments of the university or in private institutions. The research laboratories may accept students regularly appointed by ministerial decree who are eligible to obtain a diploma without university prerequisites. These laboratories are designed above all for the development of new branches of science.

with the condition that our Institut be allowed to use it. Thanks to the interest that Léon Labbé's successor, M. Luc, had in our Institut, a broad program of construction was drawn up which provided for the building of an Institut d'Étude du Travail et d'Orientation Professionnelle on the site of the Musée Pédagogique Museum. The plan called for the setting up of several laboratories: Applied Psychology, Psychobiology of the Child, Organization of Work (from the École des Hautes Études) and Physiology of Work (from the Conservatoire). After three years of temporary housing in the Conservatoire, in 1938, the Institut was installed in its new buildings. Thanks to M. Luc, who had remained Director of Technical Instruction, the Institut, threatened by the Vichy Government, was taken over by the state in 1941 as the Institut du Conservatoire National des Arts et Métiers, under the direction of M. Ragey. Since 1928 my wife has been directing the publication (interrupted only during the war years) of a Bulletin of this Institut.

In 1937 Jean Perrin, a close friend of mine since the days of the affair of the N-rays, built the Palais de la Découverte at the Exposition Universelle, there I set up a psychological display on the physiology of sensations. That year a small celebration was held to commemorate my twenty-fifth anniversary as director of the Sorbonne laboratory; it came at the very time when the installation of an elevator finally facilitated access to the quarters located on the sixth floor, up under the roof.

In 1939 at the Collège de France and at the Sorbonne we celebrated the centenary of the birth of Th. Ribot, which coincided with the 50th anniversary of the founding of the Laboratory of Physiological Psychology and of Pierre Janet's defense of his famous thesis on *l'Automatisme Psychologique.*

At that time I had the satisfaction of being able to promote work in the field of my own research. Under the National Research Center, which had been created in 1933 by Jean Perrin, groups of research workers had been organized, and as I had been elected to the Conseil supérieur I was able to act in favor of those whose research I was directing in the fields of my specialization.

And now for the second time war came and interrupted again the normal course of my activities.

As a member of a Committee on Air Biology of the Air Force Ministry I had agreed, in case of war, to assume command of a military service on psychophysiology and on selection of personnel under the *Inspection medico-physiologique* of the Air Force. In September, 1939, I went to Mérignac near Bordeaux to start my service at the airport with my collaborators Fessard and Durup, who had been sent there with their old military rank. A few months of intensive work followed, during which I learned to fly a plane so that I might better understand the abilities required of a pilot. But soon the military collapse of France came, and with it the interruption of our work. I had moved to Mérignac a large part of the laboratory equipment of the Collège de France and of the École des Hautes Études. The Rector of the University of Bordeaux succeeded in keeping it from the Germans and moving it, though with considerable losses, back to Paris.

During the German occupation, I was faced with the question of whether to leave Paris or stay. Though I was rather seriously threatened, I decided to stay in order to save and protect as much as possible those institutions and agencies for which I was responsible. Though I could not, therefore, join the armed resistance I still was able to protect, hide and help Jews and threatened members of the resistance forces. I also succeeded in helping to maintain a very active resistance center in the Institut in rue Gay-Lussac in spite of its being surrounded by Gestapo-held buildings.

I took temporary charge of the laboratory of Biométrie humaine du Centre national de la Recherche Scientifique, whose director, Henri Laugier, had left France, and whose assistant director, D. Weinberg, was forced to go into hiding. At the wish of my great teacher and friend, Louis Lapicque, I also took over his responsibilities as director of the Institut Marey — at least nominally; my collaborator, A. Fessard, carried on the actual work there.

After the trying period of the Occupation and the Liberation, and despite the many difficulties and the inevitable decline of my strength, I was able to return slowly to my normal prewar activity.[5]

All during my career a good deal of my time was taken up in innumerable committee meetings and commissions and by the work of many societies over which I had to preside at lengthy sessions (such as business sessions of the Sociétés de Psychologie, de Biologie, de Biotypologie, de Sexologie, de Zoologie, d'Education nouvelle, Féderation des Sociétés des Sciences naturelles).

In 1910 I was one of the founders of the Institut français d'Anthropologie; it had split from the Société d'Anthropologie of which I was then associate general secretary (with Verneau, Paul Rivet, Lapicque, Rabaud, Dussaud, and Lévy-Bruhl).

In 1940 I became president of the Association française pour l'Avancement des Sciences, which remained dormant during the Occupation; in this capacity I had the great satisfaction of directing the work for the great Congrés de la Victoire in 1945.

Scientific meetings played a rather important part in my life. I participated in the International Congresses of Psychology in Paris in 1900, in Rome in 1905, in Geneva in 1909, in Oxford in 1923, in New Haven in 1929, in Copenhagen in 1932. As president, and with Meyerson as secretary-

[5] In the *Bulletin de l'Institut national d'Étude du Travail et d'Orientation professionnelle* I published a few reminiscences of this period ("Souvenirs des années maudites," 1945, no. 1, 1–9).

general, I organized the 1937 Congress in Paris; also I participated in the Congress at Edinburgh in 1948, and the Congress at Stockholm in 1951. In addition to attending various national Congresses (Alienists and Neurologists, French Association for the Advancement of Sciences, in which through my efforts a section of Psychology had been created in 1914; New Education, etc.) I frequently took part in other International Congresses, such as those of Physiology, of Psychotechnique, etc.; I presided over the Ninth International Conference on Psychotechnique held at Berne in 1949.

These Congresses furnished opportunity for travel abroad and for personal contact with numerous scholars. On invitation I visited many countries, giving lectures or university courses (London, 1924 and 1950; Rio de Janeiro, 1923, 1926 and 1947; São Paulo, 1926; Barcelona, 1926; Liège, 1928; Madrid, 1929, Moscow, 1932; Bogota, 1933; Louvain, 1935; Santander, 1935). In 1933 I also had the honor of being invited by the World's Fair Committee of Chicago to give a lecture at the meeting of the American Association for the Advancement of Science.

SCIENTIFIC WORK

From the beginning of my scientific life my research was concerned with four main interconnected fields: general experimental psychology which I first started with Binet; psychopathology, where my orientation, through Pierre Janet, was toward neurology, and, through Edouard Toulouse, toward psychiatry; psychophysiology, to which I was introduced by Dastre's physiology and Lapicque's neurophysiology; and animal psychology, for which my interest was aroused by Alfred Giard, the keen observer in biology.

Work in animal psychology occupied me completely during the summer months till the beginning of the first World War. I was particularly interested in ant life; here I took my lead from experiments by Bethe in determining recognition factors between species and between colonies, and in analyzing homing mechanisms which are very different from one species to another. I was able to establish a factor of kinesthetic memory in the *Messor* ants by means of the often repeated and decisive experiment of displacing a worker returning to its nest: the insect, after having covered a distance equal to that which would have brought it home always starts looking for its nest. (V. Cornetz thought this experiment significant enough to link it to my name.) Fruitful research on autotomy and on homophany were completed by an experimental study on the memory of gastropods. These experiments involved the acquisition and extinction of the conditioned inhibition of skioptic reaction; the results brought out quantitative laws more or less identical with those which I had obtained in a study with humans on the memory of numbers. Animal psychology played a large role in my adopting a rigorously objective attitude. At the same time I also carried on research on sleep and on reflexes, and studies on mental pathology.

With Edouard Toulouse I developed laboratory techniques which were to play an important part in applied work. *La Technique de Psychologie experimentale* (1904 and 1909) was concerned with principles and methods of the application of instrument-tests and paper-and-pencil-tests; it was intended as a handbook for workers in the area of *psychotechnique*.

As a side line, N. Vaschide, who had a penchant for the metapsychics of Ch. Richet, interested me in experiments concerning evidence of telepathic communication; the results were negative. I participated in certain strictly controlled experiments; one, in particular, with G. Dumas, L. Lapicque and Henri Laugier, was a study of the nature of the "ectoplasm" that the famous medium Eva caused to materialize. These experiments established the materializations as fraud: We could show that the fraud was accomplished by regurgitation, although we were not able to get hold of the matter previously ingested.

It was also with G. Dumas and L. Lapicque that we studied in my laboratory at the Sorbonne a subject, discovered by Jules Romains-Farigoule, who pretended to be gifted with "paroptic vision." We found that this vision is really very easily explained by the existence of the slit caused by the nasal protuberance at the bottom of the blindfold. By serving as a subject himself, under the same conditions as the young lady brought by Jules Romains, George Dumas revealed the answer when he uttered his famous "I see!"

The psychophysiological research which I carried on was concerned particularly with sensory processes; and here I studied systematically the latencies of sensory responses. During the war years, my studies of the effects of neurological injuries, aside from the investigations on aphasia and disturbances of the reflexes, were concerned principally with the analysis of "psychosensory" disturbances (hemianopsias and cortical sensory syndromes).

After the war of 1914–18, my research became specialized almost exclusively in the field of physiology of sensations, without my losing sight, however, of problems of applied psychology, which I continued to pursue in collaboration with my wife. My principal work for more than thirty years has been in that field; my teachings revolved around it, my laboratory at the Collège de France was dedicated to it.

Besides engaging in research I always had a strong desire to be professionally well informed; this led me to read a great deal, to keep myself abreast as far as possible of all that was being done not only in scientific psychology but also in neighboring fields of physics, biology and pathology. The *Année Psychologique*, in which I published innumerable analyses during thirty-five years, has taken a great deal of my time and energy. I now leave the greater part of this work to my collaborators, A. Fessard and P. Fraisse.

If, in the course of my life, I have had the general satisfaction of finding the results of my studies confirmed by other scientists, very often even by those who did not know my work, I also had to disagree with them sometimes and to participate in rather lively controversies. One such controversy was in connection with the matter of the "N-rays." At the time of the discovery of radio-activity, Blondlot, the physicist in Nancy, described a new radiation indicated by an increase in luminescence of calcium sulphate; and his colleague, Charpentier, who was professor of biological physics of the School of Medicine of Nancy, contended that he had found an emission of these N-rays (N for Nancy) related to biological, and particularly nervous, activity. Such phenomena were, however, not found by other laboratories. I began studying the question, and became convinced that the observed increase of luminescence was due to suggestion. Having at my disposal the *Revue Scientifique* of which I was secretary general, I started an inquiry, and published a series of unsigned articles. Subsequently evidence was introduced to show the findings of the Nancy physicists to be erroneous; however, they never admitted their error.[6] The courage with which I had dared to attack reputed scientists (who were supported at that time by the Academy of Sciences, especially in the person of its permanent secretary, Mascart), brought me the friendship of the secretary-general of the Société de Biologie, E. Gley, a friendship which lasted until his death.

With Georges Bohn I had numerous controversies that extended over many years. He was a convinced supporter of Jacques Loeb's theory of tropisms, and of his explanation of the phenomena of life by elementary physicochemical mechanisms. We took opposite stands in many discussions, such as that before the Société de Biologie and at the Congrès de Psychologie at Geneva where Jacques Loeb and Bohn gave their reports on tropisms. With the entrance into our discussions of Anna Drzewina, his co-worker — and later his wife — our controversy became particularly vehement on the subject of the psychic autotomy, of emotional origin, which I had clearly demonstrated and whose existence was admitted even by Léon Frédéricq who had affirmed the exclusively reflex-like nature of this reaction in various *Arthropods*. Another subject of discussion between us was the mechanism underlying the protective anticipatory reaction in the *Coelenterata* which I discovered in 1906 and which appeared to be of the nature of Pavlov's cortically conditioned reflex.

With Selig Hecht I had only one polite controversy on the subject of the law concerning the variation, with time of exposure, of the retraction re-

---

[6] At the request of Alfred Binet, I published an article on this question of N-rays Grandeur et décadence des rayons N, *Année Psychologique*, 1907, 13, 143–169

sponse in the clam *Mya,* a law which he thought to be based on constant
relationship (Bunsen-Roscoe). I could show, however, that the variation
is hyperbolic — as has been often verified since.

During the 1914–18 war, I was involved in a controversy with the
biologist and physicist, Strohl, on the subject of the interpretation of the
patellar reflex in relation to observed pathological alterations. Like the
neurologists, Guillain and Barré, he attributed the initial jags of the registered curves to an ideo-muscular response. I was able to show that this
response, initially clonic, was in reality of medullary origin and was followed
by a tonic response equally reflex in nature which could be present alone
and be independently extinguished. On this point, too, I was later proved
to be correct.

Finally, without any direct controversy, I was able to prove that Wertheimer's isomorphic conception, which attempted to explain apparent motion
by a cortical short-circuit, could not be correct since an apparent movement
could be induced between visual impressions, one issuing from the left field
of the left eye, and the other from the right field of the right eye.[1]

FRIENDS AND PUPILS

The only serious and lengthy animosity which I encountered during my
career was that of Georges Bohn; clearly manifest in his earlier books, it
mellowed with the years. To many of my teachers, colleagues and collaborators I was bound in close friendship. Among former teachers I should
mention Pierre Janet, Alfred Giard and Lucien Lévy-Bruhl; with Edouard
Toulouse I maintained a continuous friendship based on mutual high regard
and complete trust.

Common problems often brought together specialists from diverse fields;
thus a small circle of friends was formed to study anthropology. To this
group belonged L. Lapicque, the physiologist; Et. Rabaud, the biologist;
and P. Rivet, the ethnologist; our discussions were enlivened by the witty
and charming Georges Dumas, who was loved by all.

I have already touched on my friendship with the philosopher and physiologist, Eugène Gley, a man of high intellect and genuine kindness. I should
also mention the admiration and love I felt toward the great physicist, Paul
Langevin; it was Langevin who asked me in 1944 to serve as vice-president
of a committee on the reform of teaching in France.

To a few of my closer colleagues such as Henri Wallon, Paul Guillaume,
André Mayer and the late Georges Blondel I was always affectionately devoted; I was still closer to Henri Laugier and René Legendre. My intimate

[1] Remarques sur la perception du mouvement apparent, *Année Psychologique,* 1934, 34,
244–248.

friendship with L. Marchand and Cl. Vurpas dates from my days at Toulouse where they served as internes, and from our common work on the wards of the Asylum of Villejuif.

I count many foreign colleagues among my dear friends; they include particularly many from the United States and Brazil. Many have passed away: Edouard Claparède, O. Decroly, G. Ferrari, C. S. Myers, C. E. Spearman, Adolf Meyer and K. Koffka; I also shall never forget the friendliness with which J. McKeen Cattell treated me, nor the sympathetic understanding of J. P. Pavlov both toward me personally and toward my work.

I am affectionately indebted to those who have worked — or still are working — in my laboratory: I. Meyerson, the late Marcel François, G. Durup, and P. Fraisse. I suffered a great loss by the premature death of some of my students, among them Dagmar Weinberg and Jeanne Monnin, and Chweitzer and Goldmann who were killed by the Germans.

I should like, too, to mention here Alfred Fessard, who became my collaborator in 1923 and whom I had the great pleasure of welcoming to the Collège de France in 1949 when he was appointed professor of general neurophysiology, a position that was especially created for him.

Among the foreign scientists who often visited my laboratory, I remember with pleasure Z. Bujas of Zagreb; Velinsky of Prague, who fled to Canada; Geblewicz of Warsaw; Kucharski who came from Poland and stayed at Paris where philosophy became his main interest; and those from the United States who became leaders in their fields: N. Kleitman, O. Klineberg, F. L. Ruch, G. Stoddard, D. Wechsler, and many others.

ONE PERSON, ONE WORK

After having written this autobiographical essay, the request for which I had accepted somewhat reluctantly, and after having turned my thoughts back to the past, it seems appropriate to close with a few general impressions.

I take some pride in stating that people in general have placed their trust in me — in my critical, though often severe, judgments as well as in my handling of human affairs; in all these matters my actions have always been governed by a concern for objectivity and impartiality, by a genuine attitude of kindness and indulgence, by the desire to help others, and by a profound respect for independence of thought. On the other hand, because of my lack of emotional demonstrativeness which made me appear cold, and my reluctance to influence other people's decisions, I never had enthusiastic disciples or faithful followers. Indeed, I tried to retain independence of thought, freedom of judgment and of criticism, just as I never wanted to impose my opinions on my pupils; I respected the independent thinking of my students, and was secretly inclined rather in favor of those who opposed me. I never belonged to any political or religious group. My father, always well-disposed toward the Church without being a real believer, had raised me in the Catholic faith; but soon after my first communion I drew away from religion to the point of finding it extraordinary that anyone could have religious faith and accept dogmas. I have, however, always respected the beliefs of others even where I did not understand.

Only conscious lies and dishonesty could arouse me, sometimes even to the extent of brief but violent bursts of anger. The need for truth and sincerity even when set against self-interest absolutely dominated me; along with a strong trend for order and clarity, it almost had the character of an instinct.

As for my work, it seems to me that I was successful in the establishment of a certain number of laws and well-founded facts without making any very widely acclaimed discoveries. The latter require both imagination — which I lacked, and without which there can be no genius — and perseverance, which my too-broad interests prevented me from exercising to the fullest degree — as was necessary, for instance, in the case of the discoverer of hypnotoxin. I deliberately have refrained from constructing any of those all-inclusive general theories to which one likes to attach a name. They belong to philosophy and not to positive science; I have always kept close to the field of positive science, never losing sight of empirical facts in my conceptual constructs and hypotheses.

The branch of the strictly objective psychology in which I worked is limited to the biological aspects of behavior; I have been not unaware, however, of the social aspects of human behavior, including man's spiritual life. My efforts have been directed toward the development of a scientific psychology in France that involves all its aspects; for many years I strove toward this goal almost single-handed. This development was made possible only through the establishment of necessary facilities for empirical study and the creation of agencies concerned with teaching and research. To a rather large extent my efforts have been successful, and after a period of decline, French psychology is now regaining an honorable place in the international field. Its growth, however, has been slow, and too short of the goal I hoped for to be fully satisfactory.

A summary of all that I have said above might probably be best compressed into this brief statement:

Son of a professor, reared in an academic environment, a professor myself, living with my wife in a communion of ideas and tastes, without family responsibilities, I dedicated myself wholly to a life of scientific research. My many findings have been of unequal value. My sustained efforts have been directed toward the development of an objective psychology in France, closely related to the biological and physiological sciences, though not neglectful of the social point of view and the social applications of *psychotechnique.* In these efforts I have been at least partially successful.

GODFREY THOMSON

I WAS born in 1881 at Carlisle, England, close to the Scottish Border, but
from the age of a few months up to my 44th year my home was on Tyne-
side, at Felling on Tyne and, after I married, in Newcastle upon Tyne.
Since 1925 my home has been in Edinburgh.

In Felling I went to the local Board School and was likely to have finished
my schooling at 13 had I not won a scholarship which gave me free tuition and
books at Rutherford College in Newcastle which I attended (travelling daily
by train) from 1894 to 1897. There I passed London University Matricula-
tion and various other examinations. In 1897 I returned to High Felling
Board School as a pupil-teacher and stayed there till 1900, at a salary of
£15 for the first year, and a little more in the succeeding years.

We pupil-teachers (there were five of us) went to school at 8:20 a.m. and
were taught by the headmaster till 9 a.m. Then we had private study till
9:30 when the opening exercises and the scripture lesson ended. For the
rest of the day we were teachers, of parts of classes or of whole classes,
sometimes of over 60 boys and girls, except for the twice weekly singing
lessons during which we again had private study.

On three evenings a week I went to Newcastle to science classes at Rutherford College, which had an evening department, returning by the 10:15 p.m.
train and getting home not much before 11. I do not remember thinking
this was a hardship, but I have since sometimes wondered how I stood it.
In 1899 I went up to London to sit for the London University Intermediate
B.Sc. examinations and passed.

One of my fellow pupil-teachers was of German parentage, and from him
and his family I began to learn German by contact, as it were; and I went
to Germany with him for a long summer holiday with his relatives in and
around Crailsheim, and became fluent although illiterate.

At Christmas, 1899, I sat for the Queen's Scholarship examination, success
in which gave to pupil-teachers free tuition at college and a small sum, £20
per annum, if I remember rightly, towards maintenance. I expected to do

well in the examination, but was frankly surprised when I was placed third in order of merit in all England, a high position which gave me free choice of college. I chose, however, to go again to Newcastle, to the Durham College of Science, part of the University of Durham. (It has since twice changed its name, quite early to Armstrong College and recently to King's College.) College did not begin till October, and in the intervening nine months I served as an uncertificated teacher, at what I thought the princely salary of £60 per annum. Also I looked round for some way of adding to my income while at college, and sat for and won the open entrance exhibition in mathematics and physics. My success in mathematics was rather a discovery to me, for in my London Intermediate B.Sc. I had taken chemistry, physics, and biology.

My course at Armstrong College (as it was soon called) was in mathematics, physics, chemistry and geology in the first year, and in mathematics, and physics in the remaining two years. In 1903 I graduated B.Sc. with distinction in each of those two subjects. Meanwhile I had in 1901 won the Junior Pemberton Scholarship, and in 1902 the Charles Mather Scholarship, to help with my maintenance. All through these three years I was simultaneously being trained as a teacher, and obtained the government certificate in 1902.

After graduating I obtained a post as physics master at St. Cuthbert's Grammar School, Newcastle, a Roman Catholic School. I was the only Protestant on the staff, and the boys addressed me as "Father," as they did the others, who were all priests. In the autumn, however, I was appointed Pemberton Fellow of the University of Durham, with an income of £120 per annum which enabled me to go to Germany to take a doctorate in physics and mathematics. I chose Strasburg (which was then German) because Ferdinand Braun was professor of physics there. He was the great wireless telegraphy expert of Germany and was awarded a Nobel prize in the same year as Marconi.

My professors at Strasburg, in addition to Braun, were Heinrich Weber, Theodore Reye, and Emil Cohn. My chief was of course Braun, in whose Institute I carried out the experiments on which my thesis was based. But perhaps I was influenced most by hearing Reye, for my mind was, and is, geometrical rather than algebraic in its approach to mathematical problems, and I felt his to be the same. Yet Cohn's lectures on the electromagnetic field, using vector methods, also fascinated me; and from him I heard, as early as 1905, lectures on Einstein's first relativity theory. I began experimental work at first on selenium cells, a problem I had brought with me from England, but soon changed to another research. My thesis was *"Über den Durchgang Hertzscher Wellen durch Gitter"* and I obtained my doctorate in 1906 with the mark *summa cum laude,* the examination success of which

I am most proud. Among my friends were two young Russians, assistants at the Physical Institute, Mandelstam and Papalexi, who later became professors of physics at Moscow and Leningrad, respectively. I made many student friends, especially among my *Vereinsbrüder* in the M.N.St.V.

Then in 1906 I had to return to some form of teaching which would satisfy the obligation I had undertaken when I accepted a Queen's Scholarship in 1900, namely to teach, for nine years out of the first twelve after qualification, in "an elementary school, the army, the navy, or the workhouse"! I came back to Armstrong College as assistant lecturer in education to train school teachers, in which capacity I had to deliver lectures on educational psychology, on which I had had very elementary lectures between 1900 and 1902 while training. But I now had to study the subject more intensely, and felt the change pleasant from studying only dead matter in the province of physics, much as I had enjoyed that. I began some amateurish experimenting in psychology. This acquired interest in psychology led me, in 1911, to go up to Cambridge for the long vacation, where my Newcastle friend and colleague, Professor T. H. Havelock, introduced me to Dr. Charles Myers. In that summer I worked through the experiments in Myers' textbook, in the tiny house in Mill Lane which was the predecessor of the present psychological laboratory at Cambridge, the foundation stone of which I saw laid that year. Myers and I were alone in the laboratory, he working upstairs on gramophone records of native music from the Torres Straits expedition, while I experimented on hired boys and on college servants downstairs. He was very interested in my mathematical training and one day brought me William Brown's little book, *The Essentials of Mental Measurement,* to the enlarged later editions of which, in our joint names, I was destined to contribute a great deal, for Brown went largely over to medical and psychoanalytical work. It naturally interested me very much to find a branch of psychology where my mathematical training might enable me to make a worthwhile contribution. At first it was the psychophysical methods which I attacked. When I sent my first paper to Myers, as editor of the *British Journal of Psychology,* it was returned with a referee's remark "The writer does not seem to know of F. M. Urban's work." Indeed I had never heard of him, but Myers lent me the necessary journals, and I was able to supplement, and in at least one respect to correct, Urban's work, placing what we called the Constant Process or $\phi(\gamma)$ Process of Fechner and Müller on a basis which made it a precursor of the modern Probit Method, as has lately been recognized, although its calculations were clumsier. Shortly before the first World War Urban, who was a professor at Philadelphia, offered a prize for the best set of calculations on his lifted weight data, and I and my wife spent several months carrying these out, and sent in our effort soon after the outbreak of war. I heard nothing about the result until after the end of the war when Professor Titchener, one of the judges, informed me that our entry was adjudged the best.

Urban was of Austrian nationality, which he had not changed in spite of his residence in the U.S.A., and since he was on holiday in his home town, Brünn, in August, 1914, he never got back to America. He had in his possession then another MS. of mine which I had sent to him in his capacity as editor of an American psychological journal, and in 1919 I received a letter from him enclosing a German translation. He had made this translation and preserved it, but destroyed my English original. In May, 1938, my wife and I visited him in Brünn, at a time when there was once more much talk of war.

At the same time in 1914 as I was preparing the Urban competition MS. I was writing the first of my articles on factor analysis. Spearman and Hart had published their article making sweeping claims for the theory that all correlations between psychological tests were due to only one factor, g, unless the resemblance between the two tests was so great that they shared a specific factor. I found it possible to make a set of artificial test scores (using dice) without any general factor, which nevertheless gave correlations which satisfied Spearman's mathematical criteria for the Two-factor hypothesis. I was going to read this paper at a meeting of the British Psychological Society, and it was announced. But when I learned that Spearman could not be present because he was engaged on military duties, I asked the secretary to preserve my paper till the war should be over. Meanwhile, in early spring of 1915, I myself undertook military work. I had served from 1899 till my marriage in 1912 in a volunteer battalion of the Northumberland Fusiliers, in the college company, which had become the university Officers Training Corps, and I now returned as its adjutant and served in that capacity to the end of the war, and thereafter until 1923 as its commanding officer.

My intention to let my MS. lie in cold storage until the end of the war was however shaken by the continued appearance of articles by adherents of Spearman's hypothesis, and so I caused it to be published in 1916 in the British Journal of Psychology under the title of "A hierarchy without a general factor." That "hierarchy" I had made intentionally, distributing the numerous small links so as to imitate the correlations required by the Two-factor theory. But while planning further artificial examples I stumbled on the fact that design and intention were unnecessary, for random arrangements of numerous small links gave a close approach to the correlations of a Two-factor hierarchy, an approach which could be made as close as desired by increasing the number of small random links. I published this in 1919 in the Proceedings of the Royal Society of London, together with an explanation based on the fact that sampling errors in correlation coefficients are themselves correlated, strongly if two correlation coefficients have a variable in common, less strongly if that is not the case. That article adumbrated (in the language of 1919) what I consider to be a very important mathematical fact which has received insufficient consideration, namely (in more modern language) that the random interplay of a large number of small independent influences produces a matrix of correlation coefficients which can be reduced to a low rank, or even to rank unity, by substituting certain fractions for the unities in the diagonal cells of the matrix. The correlations can then be explained, and could have been produced, by a small number of common factors (or even only one) together with a specific factor peculiar to each variable. *Can* be so explained, and *could* have been so produced — but really they were produced by the random interplay of a large number of small independent factors. This fact seems to me to have a bearing on the remarkable phenomenon so familiar in our lives — so familiar indeed that we do not think it remarkable — that quantitative changes can and do, when they reach certain thresholds, produce qualitatively new values or entities; and some bearing on E. L. Thorndike's Quantity hypothesis.

When I came to Edinburgh in 1925 I encouraged Dr. John Mackie to put my discovery into rigorous mathematical form which he successfully did. His papers were published in the *Proceedings of the Royal Society of Edinburgh* and elsewhere. In 1935 I summed up my ideas on this work in a paper "On complete families of correlation coefficients and their tendency to zero tetrad-differences, including a statement of the Sampling Theory of Abilities," in the *British Journal of Psychology* for July.

The psychological meaning of all this is that if, when we attack some task, some test, our ability to solve it depends upon a large number of things — genes we have inherited, pieces of information we have acquired, skills we have practiced, little habits of thought we have formed, all and sundry influences from past and present — then the correlation coefficients between performances in tests will show exactly the same relationships with one another as they would have done had our ability depended on our possession of a small number of common "factors" (plus specifics). This does not prove that we have no such "factors." But it does show that perhaps we haven't, that perhaps they are fictions — possibly very useful fictions, but still fictions.

Shortly after I was demobilized in 1919 I received a completely unexpected letter from Karl Pearson. "I am writing to you," he said, "on the assumption that you may be a young man and not definitely fixed at Newcastle. Beside your papers I do not know anything of you personally. But they show me that you are interested in one side of our subject and are not afraid of computing. I have been wondering whether there would be the least chance of your considering the question of a post in the Galton Laboratory." I can still recapture the thrill that letter gave me. But I was hoping to succeed in 1920 to the chair of education at Newcastle (as, in the event,

I did) and Karl Pearson agreed with me that for financial reasons I ought to stay at Newcastle in the hope of that promotion, to which he helped me very materially by writing to the electors. I was head of the department at Newcastle for five years, but for one of them, 1923–24, I was on leave in America. That arose out of a letter — again an unexpected letter from one I had never met — from E. L. Thorndike, supported by a more official one from Dean James Russell, inviting me to Teachers College, Columbia University, for a year. My predecessor came back to re-occupy the Newcastle chair for a year, and we sailed for New York, my wife and I and our small son, aged six. That was the beginning of many friendships, with the Hollingworths, the Poffenbergers, the Gates', Rudolph Pintner, McCall, but especially with Edward Thorndike who became one of my dearest friends, and for whose ability and greateartedness I have infinite admiration. It was a tremendous stimulus to work in that environment, and in addition I felt, without actual contact, the influence of T. H. Morgan who with his squadron of "terrible men" was raiding, not like his grandfather the lines of communication of Federal armies, but the uncharted land of genetics. I was very interested in genetics, as anyone concerned with intelligence testing is bound to be, and read a lot in the library of Morgan's department. But chiefly I was concerned with running a big psychology class in parallel with one of Pintner's, and although I do not read my lectures I did in that year write them out, and published them under the title "Instinct, Intelligence and Character."

I returned to my post in Newcastle in 1924, as I had promised to do, and expected to remain there permanently despite an invitation from Dean Russell to cross the Atlantic for good. But in 1925 I accepted an invitation to allow my name to be considered for appointment to the chair of education at Edinburgh University and the directorship of the teacher training college, Moray House, and began my work there that October.

I must, however, go back to 1920 when, as the newly appointed professor of education at Newcastle, I gave two Saturday evening public lectures on intelligence tests, in which I had become very interested. These led to an invitation from the education authority of the county of Northumberland to confer with them on a problem in which Dr. Andrew Messer, chairman of one of their committees, thought intelligence tests might help. This problem was how with most justice to select 11-year-old children in the primary schools for the privilege of free secondary school education. It was a problem which had a personal interest for me for, as I said earlier, I would myself have had no education beyond the primary school had I not won a free place in a secondary school in a competitive examination.

Northumberland had for some years held such competitive examinations at age eleven or a little younger, in the ordinary primary school subjects. They had found, however, that a large number, indeed a large majority, of the primary schools of the county never put forward any candidates, and that nearly all the free secondary school places were won by pupils from a few schools near Newcastle. Primary schools in the mining villages and in the remote valleys of the Cheviots did not supply candidates and this, it was feared, was because these schools could not compete with the better staffed and more lavishly equipped suburban schools in preparing pupils for such an examination. But intelligence tests, it was hoped, might discover in those schools some children of potential secondary school ability even if their environment and their poorer primary schooling had handicapped them in the existing kind of examination.

I set to work and devised the first Northumberland Mental Test (still being sold by Harraps!). I could not standardize it before the event, nor validate it except by a later follow-up. But I standardized it on the candidates themselves, in a manner which has stood up wonderfully well, by confining my calculations of age allowance to those among the tested children who were neither advanced nor retarded in their position in the primary school classes. It was — had to be — a group test. By its aid we selected a few dozen of the children of highest score, and three of us toured the county giving these an individual Binet test. Finally about a dozen were given free places, as an experiment — for education authorities are cautious bodies. An account of the tests and the experiment was published in the *British Journal of Psychology* for 1921, and it received considerable publicity, especially in a book by Ballard.

We followed up the selected children and on the whole found that they justified the choice. Two, alas, died in an influenza epidemic, and two or three failed to complete a good secondary school course, though more I think for social and economic reasons than for lack of intelligence. Others, however, went on and did very well. Long afterwards I received a letter from one of them. "You will not remember my name," he wrote, "but I was one of the boys you tested in 1921. I have several times thought of writing to you but have not found courage to do so till now, when I have just won the gold medal at the end of my medical course and I felt you would like to know."

In 1922 in Northumberland we gave a second group test which I had made, this time to a complete age group, thus beginning a practice which I have since steadily recommended. The complete age group avoids sampling error, and socially it has the advantage that one is sure that if any intelligent children are missed, it will at least not be because they were not tested. Of course a "complete" age group is never perfectly complete. There are always some absentees through illness or accident or sometimes truancy. But in our complete samples we always exceed 90 per cent of the children, usually reaching 94 or 95 per cent, and the absentees are almost a random sampling, with only a slight bias to lower IQs.

In the year in which I was absent in America I advised Northumberland to ask Cyril Burt to make the tests, and he not only did so in "intelligence," but also made and standardized tests of attainment in English and arithmetic.

Those Northumberland tests of mine were the beginning of a lifelong task, which I have felt bound to persevere in for the sake of intelligent children. I began at once to receive requests from other counties and towns in England to make tests for them for their selective problems. For these they paid me fees such as they had been in the habit of paying to the examiners who previously had set questions for them in English, history, and what not. Soon after I went to Edinburgh in 1925 I decided that I would safeguard myself from the temptation to make money out of this activity, and I devised a committee to receive all these fees, and the University of London Press royalties from the publication of my tests (after 1925 called Moray House Tests), and apply them to research in education, particularly research into the making and standardizing of tests. After a few years I took legal advice and had a regular trust deed made and trustees appointed by the University of Edinburgh. This body of trustees has recently, among other activities, given a substantial grant to the University, and the promise of more, to begin the endowment of a lectureship in experimental education, to which Mr. W. G. Emmett, for long my right-hand assistant in research, has been appointed with the rank of Reader. Moray House Tests of intelligence, of English, and of arithmetic are now made with all the latest methods of item analysis and the like, and twenty-five generations of research students have investigated different aspects of their use. Most of the tests are for 11-year-old children, but a few are for other ages: 7, 9, 13, 16, Adult. Space Tests have been added in the last five years. Especially the 11-year-old tests are used very widely in Great Britain, some million and a quarter of them being administered by education committees in their selection work in 1949. The correspondence with these education committees and the preservation of the test records has enabled much research work to be done which would have been impossible without such widespread cooperation.

In Edinburgh I had greatly increased administrative duties as principal of Moray House. Moreover it must be remembered that my department was not the department of psychology, the head of which was Professor James Drever (Senior), but of education. Much, however, of our work at Moray House, under the name of "experimental education," was what would be called elsewhere educational psychology. Our two departments, Drever's and mine, ran in double harness, pulling together, and we had and have a joint honors degree, the Bachelor of Education, requiring two years' full time work after the M.A.

During the whole quarter century that I have been at Edinburgh the chief tendency in my work has been a steady endeavor to make experimental psychology and experimental education more rigorous in their methods and deductions by applying the devices of mathematical statistics in the form of tests of significance, the analysis of variance, etc. And as a school we have been greatly interested in, though somewhat sceptical about, factorial analysis. We have been called, with some justice perhaps, a school of statistical psychology. We have never been antagonistic to clinical psychology, nor have we lacked interest in the individual. But clinical psychology seemed to be more suitably the concern of the department of psychology proper, while the circumstance that we were necessarily concerned with the wholesale testing of many thousands of children naturally indicated the nature of the problems we had to face. Moray House has during my time trained many generations of advanced students of education in statistical methods. Some, who had already honors degrees in mathematics, could go far in this. Others had as a rule to be content with a general grasp of principles, and a careful training in the actual arithmetical methods. My own inclination towards these methods was powerfully stimulated by the presence in Edinburgh University of mathematical colleagues, especially Sir Edmund Whittaker and A. C. Aitken, who were making important fundamental contributions in this province. I was fortunate in being able to recruit on to my staff two very able young mathematicians, first Walter Ledermann and as his successor Derrick N. Lawley, who is now the university lecturer in statistics with his own department, but still gives assistance in our work.

The year 1937–38 was for me a sabbatical year made possible in part by the University regulations about such leave, in part by a large and generous grant from the Carnegie Corporation, and in part by the very broadminded action of the National Committee for the Training of Teachers in Scotland in also giving me leave, on full pay, from my duties as principal of Moray House, from which I drew half my salary. I was thus free both from my university chair and my administrative work, and spent the year in writing *The Factorial Analysis of Human Ability,* which is now (1950) in its fourth edition. I tried to make the body of the book readable by anyone with only school mathematics, but packed a lot of mathematics into a mathemathical appendix. I tried to do justice to all the different and sometimes conflicting ideas about "factors," including my own "sampling hypothesis." My own most original contributions in the book were probably that "sampling theory," and the two chapters on "selection" and its influence in modifying and even creating factors.

Especially in the second and later editions, *Factorial Analysis* reflects clearly the interest I had in the work of L. L. Thurstone of Chicago, for whom I have a great admiration. His contributions to the methods of multiple factor analysis found in me an interested and appreciative reader, and in later years I was more than once privileged to see MSS. of his before publication.   I was, I think, the first, and am almost the only psychologist on our side of the Atlantic to teach his methods regularly and commend them to students, for his school has by no means won the acceptance here which it enjoys in America.   I must not be misunderstood as saying that I am a convert and adherent, for I am as doubtful of the real existence of his factors as of any others.   But I admit that it is possible that he is right, and I have tried to give my students an appreciation both of his mathematical devices and of his experimental acumen.

I must now, I think, again return to 1922 and my second year of testing in Northumberland.   On that occasion we began a line of social research to which I have repeatedly returned.   We ascertained for each tested child the occupation of his father; and James Duff, who was at that time on my staff but is now Vice-Chancellor of the University of Durham, investigated the connection between the intelligence of the child and the occupational status of the father, while I analyzed the data geographically, finding the distribution of intelligence, or rather of test-score, in the area around the city of Newcastle, in the coalfield, in the coastal fringe, and in the valleys of the Cheviots.   We published our results in a joint paper in the *British Journal of Psychology* in 1923.   The average IQ was high near the city, sank in the coalfield, and then rose until it was again high in the hills at a distance from the city.   This I suggested (though this is a hypothesis admittedly almost incapable of proof) might be due to a natural selection, the attraction of the city sucking out of the near hinterland a number of the more intelligent, but not reaching to such an extent the more remote parts of the county.   Among the occupations, we found a steady drop of average IQ among the children as we proceeded from the families of the professional classes, through the ranks of first skilled and then semiskilled classes, to the unskilled and casual laborers.   Again it is difficult to know which is cause and which is effect.   I have spent a considerable part of my life in trying, for the sake of my own philosophy of education, to decide whether heredity or environment has more to do with the scatter of intelligence among children, and even now all I can venture as a scientist to say is that both are certainly concerned, but in what proportion I do not know.

Since it was generally reported that the average size of the family rose as one came down the occupational scale from professional class to unskilled workers, it seemed almost certain that there would be a negative relation between intelligence and family size.   I determined to check this directly and obtained data on a large scale from the West Riding of Yorkshire, and from the Isle of Wight.   There was no doubt about the correlation, which was about −.25. But of course the cause might be either heredity — the more intelligent parents both marrying later and restricting their families — or environment — the large family being handicapped, *ceteris paribus*, by the poverty resulting from its size. We (various of my research students and I) tried to find a crucial experiment. We restricted the parents to one occupation only, coal hewing, but the negative correlation persisted. We compared orphans, whose fathers had fallen in the war in the year of the child's birth and whose family size was therefore in part due to accident, not intention, with a control group. The negative correlation was less marked in the former group, as was to be expected on the heredity hypothesis, but not significantly so in a statistical sense. We "partialled out" a number of social factors without finding any reduction in the negative association, but again the probable errors of the result made the conclusion mathematically dubious. We did learn, however, that it is extremely difficult to abolish the negative condition. It persisted.

It seemed to us that this negative correlation between family size and intelligence was in any case an important fact, whether the cause was social or genetic, but particularly if its cause was heredity, for in that case there seemed reason to fear that it would lead to a fall in average national intelligence if it persisted. As we could find no conclusive evidence of the hereditary nature of the cause, however, we made no assertions and no calculation of the possible loss of intelligence which might be going on. For a number of years I made no further endeavor to elucidate the question.

Then in 1944 I was asked by the Royal Commission on Population to write for them a memorandum on the matter, and I gave an account, more detailed than the above, of my work along these lines. This led to an invitation from the Eugenics Society to deliver the Galton Lecture in 1946, a lecture given annually on Galton's birthday in February. My lecture, "The Trend of National Intelligence," was published in the *Eugenics Review* for April, 1946. (The occasion of my lecture was one of the last public appearances of Lord Keynes, himself a former Galton lecturer, who came to present in the name of the Society the Galton gold medal to Sir Alexander Carr-Saunders, who has now succeeded Lord Horder as its president.)

In that lecture I referred to the calculations which had been made by some writers, first I think by Theodore Lenz in the *Journal of Educational Psychology* (1927), and very confidently and with dramatic emphasis by Raymond B. Cattell in his book *The Fight for Our National Intelligence* (1936). I illustrated the calculation in question on my own Isle of Wight data which gave much the same answer as had been found by others, including Fraser-Roberts and his coworkers at Bath, namely a decline of about two points of IQ per generation. But the calculation is only valid if the cause is heredity and not enviroment. Moreover, as I said in my lecture, the commonsense of the man in the street rebels against a deduction about the difference of intelligence of two generations when the actual measures of intelligence have been obtained from one generation only, schoolchildren. He demands (before he will believe) that two sets of measurements be made, a generation apart. I sympathized with this, and was very ready to support a suggestion by Fraser-Roberts that such a straightforward test of the feared decline of intelligence could be made in Scotland. We began to carry this out, and when, a year and a half after my Galton Lecture, a sort of postmortem on it was held by the Eugenics Society, under Lord Horder's chairmanship, at which Carr-Saunders, Penrose, Burt, and others spoke, I was able to give some of the earliest results of the experiments to which I now turn.

In Scotland in 1932 the Scottish Council for Research in Education had tested, with one of my group tests, the complete age group of those born in 1921, numbering nearly 90,000, of which some 80,000 were actually tested on one day in June. One thousand of them, meant to be a random sample (and this could be tested by the group test scores and any bias corrected for) were also given an individual Stanford-Binet test. The thousand turned out in fact to be slightly superior, but only slightly.

The Population Investigation Committee of London now suggested to the Scottish Council that this survey should be repeated in 1947 on those born in 1936, and despite some doubts because of the comparatively short gap of 15 years, this was done by a joint Mental Survey Committee under my chairmanship. Moreover a great deal of sociological information was collected about the 75,000 or so children, and even more about some 7,500 of them, being those born on the first three days of any month in 1936. Those born on the first day of the even months of that year, numbering 1,215, were tested by an individual Terman-Merrill test.

The first results of this experiment were that the strong negative association of test-score with size of family was fully confirmed, but there had been no decline since the previous survey, either in individual or in group test average scores. Indeed the group test average had gone up a little. The committee published the details in a first volume *The Trend of Scottish Intelligence* (1949) and further volumes are planned (one of which will probably have appeared before this does) on some of the social correlations.

The simplest explanation of the apparently paradoxical result is of course that the whole phenomenon, including both the negative association of family size with test-score and the absence of a decline in average intelligence, is due to environmental influences. Some persons, however, fear that perhaps a real decline is going on but is being temporarily masked by increasing test sophistication. A purely genetic explanation has been suggested by Penrose, namely that the total absence of offspring from the lowest forms of intelligence just balances the differential birthrate of the ordinary levels of intelligence. We hope in Scotland to endeavor to elucidate the various possibilities by continued analysis of the results of our survey. One doubt our data seem to have set at rest: There is no evidence of a steady influence on intelligence of the position in the family, though the first born *and* the last born were, in every size of family, with a trivial exception, slightly more intelligent than those between, though only very slightly. An environmental explanation certainly seems the most likely one here.

We are planning to follow up the 1,215 specially tested children for twenty years (and I have every intention of doing my best to last long enough to see this through. Ninety is quite young nowadays!). They differ from Terman's follow-up group in being a random section of Scotland, covering the whole range of intelligence and hailing from every social level and every county.

A similar comparison of two nation-wide age groups separated by fifteen years was not possible in England, but we were able from Moray House to conduct a smaller experiment on complete age groups in a number of districts in England, numbering together about 40 per cent of the Scottish year group. The time between the two tests, however, was only about ten years. Even this was only possible owing to the fact that Moray House tests had been used so widely and so long in England, and that we had preserved the records in Moray House. We obtained the cooperation of a number of Education Committees, who undertook to administer again the same test as they had used ten years earlier. The details were planned and superintended by Mr. Emmett, whom I have already mentioned, and who has published the results in *Population Studies*. They are not very different from those of Scotland.

As a by-product, however, the English repetition confirmed a suspicion which had been growing during the war years, that girls were beginning to excel boys in intelligence test scores, of a verbal type, in which the two sexes had, up to the war, been equal. We had the earlier records of the tests used, in which girls and boys had been equally good. In the newer application of identically the same set of tests the girls were superior by a statistically significant amount. This superiority is now, three years later, apparently disappearing. It would seem to have been somehow due to war conditions, perhaps to the absence of the disciplinary influence of the father (away on war service) in so many homes.

It is certain that the whole of this problem of the differential birthrate, and its influence on the intelligence of a nation, is one of great importance, though also of great difficulty. Our valiant effort to make a decision, in our Scottish surveys, has left the matter undecided for those who fear that the conditions, as regards familiarity with tests, were different in 1932 and 1947; or it may be claimed as supporting an environmental explanation of the persistent relation between size of family and intelligence test score. For myself, as a man of scientific training, I recognize that the evidence is either against selection, or at most is inconclusive.

But I still cannot prevent my mind returning to the thoughts which I expressed in the opening paragraphs of my Galton Lecture. Speaking of the selection of children and young people in Great Britain, for higher forms of education, I said: "The children chosen at 11 or 12 to enter on a longer and more difficult course of education are likely, on the average, to marry later (if at all) and to have fewer children (if any) than those who are not chosen. This is still more the case with those chosen later to enter colleges and universities. The men will marry later than they otherwise would have done, and a large proportion of the women will not marry at all. In short, the educational system of the country acts as a sieve to sift out the more intelligent and destroy their posterity. It is a selection which ensures that their like shall not endure." I still feel the force of those observations and of that fear. Time will show.

In 1944 I became a member of the Colonial Social Science Research Council and am now the chairman of its committee on sociology and anthropology. The application in the colonies of some of the educational and vocational selection methods used in Great Britain was one of the matters which came under our purview.

Supported by the Colonial Development and Welfare Fund researches were carried out in Jamaica and in Trinidad by two workers (trained in Moray House), and other researches have been going on in the Gold Coast and Nigeria. It is possible that this movement will develop as it has in Great Britain, both for educational and for vocational guidance.

In India there is quite a group of my old students (Indians), based on Delhi, engaged in intelligence testing, and others are working from Bombay. Much more than translation into the various languages is required, of course, for the whole background of customs and material surroundings has to be considered, and test-making has to begin from the very beginning.

In 1940 it had been intended to hold the 12th International Congress of Psychologists at Edinburgh, with Professor James Drever (Senior) as president and myself as general secretary, and before war broke out in September, 1939 a good deal of preliminary work had been done. War, of course, made the Congress impossible then, but in 1948 it was held, with the same officers, though Drever was now Professor Emeritus. I took little part in the scientific side, being fully occupied by the administrative details. The Congress was, I think, a success. Certainly it was successful in a social and friendly sense, and financially; and what I heard about the papers read was favorable in the main. One thing which caused me much distress and annoyance was the long delay in getting the Report printed, owing first to paper shortage and later to shortage of skilled printers.

When in 1949 I was president of Section J (psychology) of the British Association for the Advancement of Science, I determined to devote my presidential address to the problem which, even more than that of heredity, had occupied my mind since that summer of 1911 when Charles Myers talked with me in Cambridge about mental measurement. I gave my presidential address the title *The Nature of the Mind's "Factors,"* putting "Factors" in quotation marks. I wanted to call attention once more especially to two points I had for thirty years kept returning to in papers and chapters, without gaining much attention or, I fear, being often understood. These two points are (1) that ordinary methods of factor analysis create very large specific factors, found in one test only, and then conveniently forget all about them, and (2) that a hurly-burly of many small influences creates correlations which are interrelated in exactly the same way as would be the case if a small number of common factors — plus very large specifics — were the cause. My address (published in *The Advancement of Science*) gives my reasons for scepticism about such large specific factors at greater length than would be suitable here. The procedure which by using communalities reduces the rank of the matrix of correlation coefficients to a minimum, at the same time maximizes the specific factors, without any psychological consideration whether such large specific factors are present. The suggestion that the specific factors are only specific because no partner is present in the battery means — for they are all orthogonal and uncorrelated — that an analysis with minimum communalities implies the existence somewhere of more common factors than there are tests in the battery, yet the procedure is actually defended on the score of parsimony.

As for my second point, that random samples of a large number of small influences will give correlation coefficients identical with those produced by a few common factors diluted by specifics, only a handful of people have understood it. A common form of misunderstanding is to suppose that all it means is that "g" is not simple but complex or composite. It means a great deal more than that; it means that the whole underlying complex of causes of what are called "factors" is an inextricable tangle. If the tests are completely random chunks of this tangle, the rank of the matrix of correlation coefficients, off the diagonal, will approximate to rank one, although links between the tests are of every possible extent, and the links common to all may be very few; and it will in any case approximate to a low rank. This is a mathematical, not a psychological phenomenon, and it is very dangerous to base psychological hypotheses on it.

When I look back on my career I realize, and the reader of this autobiography will already have realized, that my connection with psychology has been unusual and almost despite myself. I never had any teaching in psychology worth mentioning. I had the inestimable advantage of the influence and inspiration of Charles Myers during that summer of 1911, and of subsequent correspondence, but cannot call myself his pupil, only his admirer and disciple. I learned a great deal from Charles Spearman, but only by crossing swords with him, not as a pupil. And I have learned from many others by their correspondence and their friendship. But I never had a course in psychology, though I took a D.Sc. degree in it in 1913 on presentation of my publications, and an oral examination by Myers and Bainbridge.

What I have enjoyed most — I enjoy any kind of teaching — has been trying to clarify in students' minds the applications of mathematics to psychology. That, with my Sampling Hypothesis, my work on the influence of selection on factors, and the fact that I have had rather a flair for inspiring and conducting big surveys, seem to have been my main contributions.

L. L. THURSTONE

THE biography of an individual scientist cannot be expected to be of general interest except when there has been a spectacular achievement or a colorful personality or both. The present case has no claim to either. Some students may find encouragement in knowing that something can be accomplished in spite of much floundering with objectives that do not seem as clear as they will in retrospect.

Both of my parents were born in Sweden. In order to get some education my father joined the Swedish army and became an instructor in mathematics and fortifications. In later life he was a Lutheran minister, a newspaper editor, and a publisher. My mother, born Sophie Stråth, had a very good voice and a strong interest in music. My sister, Adele, is two years younger than I. Both of us were started at the piano when we were quite young. My sister was the better student, both in high school and at the piano. She finished a Bachelor of Music degree.

My parents changed the family name, which was Thunström, because it was so frequently mispronounced and misspelled. I have never joined any Swedish clubs and I have had very few contacts with Swedes until recently when I have become acquainted with Swedish psychologists.

I was born in Chicago on May 29, 1887, but my elementary education was in many scattered places, including Berwyn in Illinois, Centerville in Mississippi, a public school in Stockholm, Sweden, a boys' school in Stockholm, a grade school and a high school in Jamestown, New York.

At the age of fourteen it was expected that I would be confirmed in the Lutheran church. This was a problem because I declined to learn the catechism. When it became evident that this was really awkward, there was a conference with my father and another Lutheran minister and myself. I was offered the proposition that if I would select any three questions in the catechism to which I was willing to learn the answers, then I would be confirmed. I accepted this proposal and thus I was officially confirmed in the Lutheran church. When I accepted this proposal, my seniors really won the case because I read the catechism voluntarily in order to select the three questions to which I would be willing to memorize the answers.

The only honor that I received in high school was a first prize of thirty dollars in the Prendergast competition in geometry. With the prize money I bought a second-hand bicycle and a box Kodak which was the starting point for my work in photography. This is still my principal hobby. When I was a high school sophomore I had my first publication. It was a short letter to the *Scientific American,* published in June, 1905. At that time there was a good deal of discussion about the hydroelectric power companies at Niagara Falls. The power companies were accused of diverting so much water to their power plants that the beauty of Niagara Falls was being ruined. I proposed a very simple solution for the conflict between the power companies and the tourist interests. This is what I wrote:

"How to Save Niagara"

"To the Editor of the *Scientific American:*

"There has lately been much discussion on how to save Niagara Falls. I take here the liberty to describe a method for utilizing the greater part of the energy in the falls without injuring in the least the beauty of the falls and without necessitating any engineering structures in the vicinity of the falls.

"Suppose a dam, constructed across Niagara River, a few miles above the falls or at the beginning of the river. Let the gates of the dam be closed half of the time and opened half of the time, making the river flow, say, twelve hours in daytime. There would be no danger of overflow when the gates are shut, with the large area of Lake Erie above the dam. It is evident that twice the regular flow of the river could be extracted from Lake Erie in the daytime. Let the regular flow pass over the falls and take a quantity equal to half the regular flow continually for power purposes. This would give about 3,500,000 horsepower without injuring in the least the beauty of the falls. The gates of the dam could be open, say, nine hours in the day and three hours in the night, in order to make it possible to see the falls also at night. It seems to me that if these arrangements were possible, it would give a great amount of power and at the same time save the destruction of the falls.

Louis L. Thunstrom.

Jamestown, N. Y., June 20, 1905."[1]

There was a comment in one of the national magazines that I was proposing a way in which we could eat our cake and have it, too.

Engineering

Every high school student has probably puzzled at some time about the old problem of trisecting an angle. As a high school sophomore I worked

[1] L. L. Thunström, How to save Niagara, *Sci. Amer.*, 1905, 93, 27.

out a French curve which could be used with a straight edge for trisecting any angle but, of course, the solution was not within the restrictions of Euclidian geometry.   In a freshman class in analytical geometry at Cornell, I learned how to write the equation for that curve and I showed the solution to my instructor.   Professor Hutchinson told me that he knew over twenty solutions to that old problem but that he had never seen this particular one before.   The solution was published in the *Scientific American,* and this was my second publication.[2]   I also learned a good deal of physics in high school by puzzling about the old problem of perpetual motion.

At Cornell I started in civil engineering but changed to electrical engineering.   Perhaps I should have majored in physics, instead.   In the basement of Rockefeller Hall I worked with one of the physics instructors, Dr. Nasmith, who was studying the singing arc.   I set up some experiments in the transmission of sound through a light beam by projecting the sound into an arc and receiving the light beam on a selenium cell.   The idea was eventually to record the variations in light intensity on the edge of a motion-picture film by means of a cylindrical lens, but we never got that far.   At the same time I was playing with a new design for a motion-picture camera and projector.   In this design every point on the screen is continually lighted so that there is no dark interval or flicker.   The film moves uniformly through the projector without any intermittent motion.   These two effects are accomplished by means of two rotating sets of mirrors which keep the distance from the film to the objective constant, even though the film is moving continuously.   This machine was actually built and demonstrated.   But it was not until several years later that I demonstrated it in New York.

In the engineering school I had great admiration for Professor Dexter Kimball.   His course on machine design was probably the best arranged instruction that I have even seen.   For example, when several hundred students were working on the design of a shaper, he had the problems so arranged that no two students were working on exactly the same problem.   In his lectures on machine design I acquired many ideas that have been useful in other contexts.   He pointed out, for example, that in a design problem one starts at the cutting edge and that the frame is the last thing to be designed.   The uninitiated probably sees the frame first and his impulse might be to design the frame and then to hook the mechanism onto the frame, which is the most ineffective way to proceed.   Kimball's admonition that one should start to solve a problem at the cutting edge is a useful idea in many other contexts.   In a committee session one can sometimes be helped by formulating as precisely as possible what is to be accomplished.   That is the cutting edge of the problem.   An organizational outline might then correspond to the frame of a machine.

[2] L L. Thurstone, Curve which trisects any angle, *Sci Amer Suppl*, 1912, 73, 259.

In one of his lectures Professor Kimball described some psychological characteristics in the history of a machine such as the sewing machine or the lathe. In the early stages in the development of a machine the designer introduces decorative effects which have nothing to do with function. It is as if the designer were trying to compensate for the inadequacy of the design even though he may not be aware of it. In the more mature stages of a machine its beauty is found in the close relation between design and function. These ideas were well illustrated with lantern slides of the history of mechanical devices. I remember thinking at the time that the curlicues on automobiles were certainly examples of nonfunctional additions. If we look at the automobile designs today (1950), we must admit evidence of immaturity even now. The useless and expensive shapes of automobile bodies and the distracting decorations on the automobile dashboard are evidence of the immaturity of present automobile design, and this is forty years after Professor Kimball's lectures on that subject.

Ever since my undergraduate days I have been interested in the psychological aspects of machine design, especially as regards human limitations in visual-motor coordination in the controls. During the Second World War a lot of military equipment was designed under pressure of time with inadequate consideration for this problem. The results were often serious. One does not have to go far to see examples of design defective because of psychological factors.

While in the engineering school, I became interested in the possibility of studying the learning function as a scientific problem. Partly in this connection I visited several lectures in psychology. One of these was a lecture by Professor Bentley on the higher thought processes, and I heard a lecture by Titchener. I remember being interested in his lecture but curious about his extremely formal and pompous manner. I certainly had no idea that I would myself be lecturing in the same subject. Boring finished his engineering degree at Cornell several years ahead of me, but I did not know him at that time. In the senior year I was elected a member of the electrical engineering fraternity, Eta Kappa Nu, an honor that I appreciated all the more because I did not earn it on scholarship.

The motion-picture machine problem had interested me off and on for several years during high school and college. Since Thomas Edison was manufacturing one of the best known motion-picture projectors at that time, I arranged to demonstrate my model in his laboratory in East Orange, New Jersey. A demonstration was arranged in 1912 and I went there with my working model. I met Mr. Edison and his chief engineer, Bliss, and several other men who expressed considerable interest in the model. They spent a good deal of time on it and they were evidently considering the possibilities of marketing this type of projector. They told me finally that it would be necessary to retool their whole plant for the manufacture of a machine of such radical design and that they were unwilling to do so; they said they had no doubt that the new type of projection would eventually be generally used, because it entirely eliminated the flicker. At that time the flicker was much more of a problem than it is in present machines. It was then that Mr. Edison offered me an assistantship in his laboratory. Immediately after being graduated with a mechanical engineer's degree, I went to work in Mr. Edison's laboratory in East Orange. I saw him daily and I had a very good chance to observe his work habits.

Thomas Edison was a man of strong convictions and he did not have much admiration for university education. For every experimental failure he seemed to produce three more experiments to try. In this sense he seemed to be tireless. The cot in his office was probably used for lying down to think about his problems as often as it was used for sleep. Thomas Edison seemed to have a startling fluency of ideas, which often ranged far from the immediate problem. He seemed to have an absolutely endless array of stories; very few of them were fit for publication. If problem-solving ability is to be studied scientifically and experimentally, it will be advisable to include studies of different kinds of fluency. Edison was interested in educational motion pictures but he had rather inadequate ideas on that subject. Even now, nearly forty years later, motion pictures have not found their proper place in the teaching process. When motion pictures are used in teaching, they usually cover so many ideas for each minute of the film that they are intelligible only to those who already know the subject. Effective teaching must be much more deliberate and it must include judicious repetition and summary. I have seen few motion pictures that satisfy this fundamental criterion for teaching effectiveness.

In the fall of 1912 I decided to return to a university with a good graduate school, and I accepted an instructorship in descriptive geometry and drafting in the engineering college at the University of Minnesota in Minneapolis. In my freshman classes I had two students who have won distinction in their respective fields and who are now on the University of Chicago faculty. They were Karl Holzinger, who is professor of Education, and Thorfin Hogness, who is now professor of chemistry and director of the Institute of Radiobiology.

While teaching in the engineering college for two years, I had my first instruction in psychology from Professor Herbert Woodrow and from Professor J. B. Miner. Woodrow taught experimental psychology and he was very generous with the engineering instructor who became interested in the experimental study of the learning function.

Graduate Study at Chicago

In the summer of 1914 I started graduate study in psychology with Professor Angell at Chicago. I recall one of my first impressions of graduate students of psychology. When they were asked a question, they would start to talk fluently, even when they obviously knew nothing about the subject. I was sure that engineers had higher standards of intellectual honesty. One of my first courses was called advanced educational psychology and it was taught by Professor Judd. I used to wonder what the elementary course could be like if the course that I was taking was called "advanced." I soon became accustomed to the fact that prerequisites did not mean anything and that there was no real sequence of courses in psychology, even though they were listed by number and title to give the appearance of a sequence, in which one course was supposed to build on another. I never had an elementary course in psychology or in statistics. My first degree was M.E., and I was never flattered when it was interpreted at Chicago as a master's degree in Education!

One of my accomplishments during that year was to learn how to carry five soup plates over my head through the swinging doors at the University Commons where I worked as a waiter. The alumni waiters from the University Commons include a very large group of professional men.

One of the most interesting among the graduate students in psychology was Beardsley Ruml, who has earned more distinction than any of the rest of us. He left psychology to do it. Even as a graduate student he was very much interested in economic theory. I recall one evening at the Midway Gardens when the discussion turned to economics. Ruml, armed with a stein of beer, declared emphatically that we would be just as well off if we dumped all the gold in the ocean. It was prophetic of later times.

Carnegie Institute of Technology

In 1915 Walter Bingham interviewed graduate students at Chicago to find assistants for the newly established Division of Applied Psychology at Carnegie Institute of Technology in Pittsburgh. He was assembling his staff for that important and interesting new development. He asked me about psychological research. I told him about my interest in the galvanic reflex and its possibilities for experimental psychology. With some hesitation I also told him about my interest in the psychological problems concerned with melody. At that time I was considering writing a master's thesis on the Hindu ragas, in which the melody covers a very small pitch excursion so that occidental standards of tonality are not involved. The psychological problem is then to determine, if possible, what constitutes the perceptual unity of such a melody. I had no idea at the time that Bingham was himself interested in such problems, that he had worked with Stumpf and von Horn-bostel, and that he was interested in collections of phonograph records of exotic music. When I received a telegram from Bingham appointing me to an assistantship with an annual stipend of one thousand dollars, I was prob-ably more pleased than I was twenty-three years later when I was promoted to a distinguished service professorship at Chicago.

Bingham's venture was to establish the first department of applied psy-chology in this country. The work was challenging at every turn and, while the orientation was always toward practical applications of psychology, there was a generous interest in theoretical problems. It was a privilege for a graduate student to be closely associated with the staff which included, be-sides Bingham, Walter Dill Scott, Clarence Yoakum, G. M. Whipple, E. K. Strong, Kate Gordon, W. W. Charters, and J. B. Miner. Bingham once told me that I was a good assistant but that I was not dependable in looking after details. He was right. After the first year as assistant, I was told about President Hamerschlag's comment that I had not made enough of an im-pression. Nevertheless, I received a reappointment for a second year as assistant in 1916. In 1917 I received a doctorate in psychology at Chicago and, after that, promotions in rank and salary came annually. Before I left Carnegie, I had a full professorship and was chairman of the department of psychology. It has often seemed strange that I did not undertake any funda-mental theoretical problems during the seven years at Carnegie. Such interests must have been incubating without my realizing it because, when I later came to Chicago in 1924, such work seemed to get under way with a great deal of pressure.

All of our objective psychological test material at Carnegie was made available for the Army in the First World War. My own assignment was to work in the trade-test division in Newark, New Jersey, in the design of objective methods of appraising the oral trade tests. My main contribution in that assignment was the key-word principle for scoring oral trade tests. I wrote a memorandum[3] on the key-word principle for Beardsley Ruml, who was director of the Newark trade-test office. There was a lot of discussion in our staff in Newark as to whether the key-word principle would be feasi-ble, but it was given a field trial with favorable results. A large number of oral trade tests for army use were then designed on the key-word principle.[4] In the application of this principle, the examiner asks a question which he reads from the manual. If the respondent uses any of the specified words

[3] Thurstone, *Oral trade tests*, Committee on Classification of Personnel in the Army, Trade Test Division, 1918.
[4] Thurstone, *Aid for interviewers*, Issued by the Adjutant General of the Army for use of personnel officers, Trade Test Division of the Committee of Classification of Personnel, Orange, N. J., 1918.

that are listed as key-words, then the respondent is given credit for the question. In this manner the examiner can give a preliminary screening of the candidates without himself knowing anything about the trades involved. The same principle was applied to picture tests in which the respondent answered questions concerning the numbered or lettered parts in pictures of trade equipment and processes.

One publication, written at Carnegie, was a short monograph on *The Nature of Intelligence* (1924). It was published in the International Library of Psychology, Philosophy, and Scientific Method in London. The monograph was the result of ideas initiated by Professor Mead's lectures at Chicago. Professor Mead's lectures in social psychology probably had a greater influence on my psychological thinking than any other course. It certainly had nothing to do with the social psychology of 1950. I became interested in focal consciousness as representative of the incomplete act. I tried to relate the concepts of the incomplete act with the concepts of intelligence. I tried to show that the degree of intelligence is associated with the degree of incompleteness of the act at which it becomes focal in consciousness. The more incomplete the act, the greater is the range of possible overt expression. If the act becomes focal in consciousness at a very incomplete and abstract stage of development, then the conscious choices control a wide range of overt resolution. The less intelligent act approaches completion before it becomes focal in consciousness and therefore it controls a very narrow range of possible overt expression. This interpretation of intelligence is sometimes listed in the textbooks as one of the numbered theories that students are expected to memorize. I have never seen a textbook summary of this theory which is intelligible to me.

The department of applied psychology flourished for eight years at Carnegie, but in 1923 it was no longer in favor and the research activities in applied psychology were discontinued. In these early days of applied psychology, Walter Bingham's group at Carnegie made substantial contributions towards the eventual acceptance of applied psychological research.

Washington in 1923

In January, 1923, I went to Washington to help initiate some studies in civil service personnel methods in the Institute for Government Research which was supported by a foundation grant. The purpose was to assist civil service commissions throughout the country to write better civil service examinations. My assignment was to prepare materials and manuals from which civil service commissions might prepare improved examinations with the new objective methods. Some of the commissions were very receptive to the idea of having a central agency prepare materials for use in different commissions with a considerable saving in expense and time. At that time very few commissions had psychologists and qualified examiners who were familiar with the objective methods. Much has been accomplished since that time and many of the civil service commissions now have technically trained psychologists and examiners on their staffs.

While in Washington, in 1923, I discussed with some friends in the Navy the possibility of investigating experimentally the problem of learning during sleep. This was evidently a new idea and I was invited to carry out a preliminary experiment on learning the telegraphic code. The first experiment was made with the Navy in Washington. An instructor gave code practice at night when students were asleep. The practice was given in half-hour periods with alternate half hours free from practice. The speed was adjusted each night to about two words a minute faster than the average speed of the class during the previous day. It was found that the class completed the course in three weeks less time than was expected, and, as a consequence, there was great interest in the idea. I was invited to set up a more complete and controlled experiment at Hampton Roads, and that was done. I made only occasional visits to Hampton Roads, so that I was not there to supervise the work which was carried out by noncommissioned officers. After the experiment was under way, I received a letter from Captain Smith at Hampton Roads explaining that the experiment had probably failed because of the lack of comparability of the control group and the experimental group. The instructors of the control group were afraid that they would be judged as to their teaching efficiency if their class did not keep up with the experimental group which was getting code practice during sleep. In order to overcome such a supposed handicap, they gave several hours' additional practice daily to the control group in the hope of keeping up with the experimental group. That was about the time when I left Washington so that I could not be at Hampton Roads to set up a new experiment and to explain the procedures more adequately to the instructors.

Return to Chicago

It was in the summer of 1924 that Thelma Gwinn and I were married and we returned to Chicago where I had been appointed an associate professor of psychology. (At that time, and several years later, we had the opportunity to go to Berkeley, California.) Both Thelma and I had been graduate students at Chicago and we were thrilled to return there. Since I had been teaching statistics at Carnegie, I volunteered to give such a course at Chicago. Professor Carr was willing for students in psychology to take a one-quarter course in descriptive statistics if they wanted it. Although this course was a novelty in the department at Chicago, it was not important work. My main attention went to the teaching of mental test theory. In all of the American colleges this subject was taught mainly from the various authors' manuals, and practically all such courses were confined to detail of the Stanford-Binet test. Neither instructors nor students seemed to have any interest in the theory of this subject, and this circumstance was probably responsible for the low prestige of mental test work. I decided to make some contribution toward improving this situation, and I now had the definite objective to start work on fundamental problems in psychological measurement. Most of my previous work had been concerned with descriptive and applied aspects of psychological measurement.

There was general discussion about the normality of the distribution of intelligence at point age and I investigated the application of this assumption to various educational scales that had been constructed. In the early educational scales it was assumed, in effect, that the distribution of any educational test was the same for young children as for educated adults and that they differed only in the mean. Turning to the description of general intelligence, I assumed two parameters for each age-group, namely, the mean and a measure of dispersion. Applying this idea, a scaling method for psychological tests was developed and this was my first paper on the theory of psychological measurement.[5] I regard that paper as one of my best.

The next problem was to examine the mental-age concept which had previously been criticized by Otis and others. In another paper[6] I described the logical difficulties of the mental-age concept. In scoring the test performance of a child there is always some uncertainty as to whether the child is failing in a test item or whether he is merely distracted. In an attempt to minimize this source of error in the total score, I wrote a paper proposing that the score should be a scale value which is exceeded by as many successes as there are failures below it.[7] Interesting things are often discovered accidentally. At one time I asked my research assistant, Annette McBroom (Wiley), to plot two curves for some psychological test data, namely, the relations between mean-test performance against age and the dispersion against age. Both of these were determined first by scaling. Although I had not asked for it, she also plotted the relation between the mean-test performance and the standard deviation for each age after these values had been obtained by scaling. I then noticed that the relation was linear for the successive ages. Capitalizing on this simple relation, I located a rational origin for the scale of intelligence. This was done by extrapolating the linear relation until it reached a base line of zero dispersion. I reasoned that if we locate a point on a scale at which variability of test performance vanishes,

[5] Thurstone, A method of scaling psychological and educational tests, *J. educ. Psychol*, 1925, 16, 433–451.

[6] Thurstone, The mental age concept, *Psychol. Rev.*, 1926, 33, 268–278.

[7] Thurstone, The scoring of individual performance, *J. educ. Psychol.*, 1926, 17, 446–457.

then such a point ought to represent a rational origin because the dispersion cannot be negative. This idea is perhaps remotely analogous to some ideas in the kinetic theory of gases. I tried this procedure on a number of psychological tests that had been scaled, and I found that the age at which the rational origin is located turns out to be several months before birth. My neurological friends assured me that such a finding could be justified and a paper on this subject was published in 1928.[8] Next we turned attention to the problem of the mental growth curve. The special difficulty with this problem, in contrast with similar curves for physical growth, is that in psychology we had no metric for appraising intelligence. Since the scaling method provides such a metric and a test for its internal consistency, we decided to construct a mental growth curve by a scaling method and with a method of locating a rational origin. That material was published in 1929.[9]

Shortly after coming to the University of Chicago, I had an opportunity to join the staff of Dr. Herman Adler at the Institute for Juvenile Research on a part-time basis. That experience was profitable in many ways. My work with Dr. Adler was largely advisory on problems of personnel and research. It was at that time I discovered Richard Jenkins, a medical student, in one of my classes. I offered him a research assistantship at the Institute for Juvenile Research and he started to work on the problem of intelligence in relation to family size and birth order. His work was so outstanding that I made him a co-author of a monograph on that problem.[10] Dr. Jenkins was later director of the Institute. At that time I met Andrew W. Brown who joined the Institute staff. My work at the Institute was terminated when I was offered, through Professor Charles Merriam, a promotion to a full professorship at the University of Chicago. It was a curious circumstance that the promotion to a professorship at Chicago did not come through the department of psychology. Ever since my promotion to a professorship, our work has been in the Social Science building and we have had the friendly interest of our colleagues in sociology, political science, and economics. The Social Science Research Committee has given us several research grants and some space. I have especially appreciated that in all these relations Dean Ralph Tyler of the Social Science Division has been helpful and friendly to our research projects.

Since there was no textbook on the theory of mental tests, I assembled a lithoprinted booklet on the reliability and validity of tests,[11] which was useful for teaching. Most of the material was drawn from journal articles on statistics, including Spearman's early work on reliability. The pamphlet was

[8] Thurstone, The absolute zero in intelligence measurement, *Psychol. Rev*, 1928, 35, 175–197.
[9] Thurstone and L. Ackerson, The mental growth curve for the Binet tests, *J educ. Psychol*, 1929, 20, 569–583
[10] Thurstone and R L. Jenkins, *Order of birth, parent-age, and intelligence*, 1931.
[11] Thurstone, *The reliability and validity of tests*, 1931.

prepared for temporary use in teaching because of the complete absence of any textbook on mental test theory. Today, twenty years later, although that pamphlet has been out of print for many years, we have frequent inquiries for it. The reason for this circumstance is that until now there has not been any textbook on this important subject. It is difficult to understand why this should be the case, because all departments of psychology give instruction in psychological tests. I am rewriting that old pamphlet in the form of an elementary book on test theory, and fortunately Gulliksen of Princeton has written a rather complete treatise on this subject which has just been published.[12] The absence of any suitable teaching material for elementary courses in test theory may indicate a continued lack of interest in the principles of this subject. The curricula of psychology departments still have many courses of instruction in test theory, but I fear that most of them teach the student only how to give particular tests, especially the Rorschach which is now so much in vogue.

In 1925 I had some evening discussions with Dr. David Levy in regard to the Rorschach test which he was introducing in this country. We discussed the possibility of objectifying the scoring and the interpretation. I was interested by the proposal to undertake this study, but I decided to gamble my time on other problems in psychological measurement because I had in mind the scaling methods for tests and the rewriting of psychophysical logic. The original monograph by Rorschach is well worth reading, but few of his enthusiastic followers seem to have contributed anything of consequence to psychological theory and science. In psychological science there is now no group that is more cultish and superficial than the Rorschach followers, and yet they dominate a large section of clinical psychology.

Psychophysics

Now we turn to psychophysics which is psychological measurement proper. It is another line of development that was started soon after our arrival at the University of Chicago. When I started to teach psychological measurement in 1924, it was natural that I should encourage the students to learn something about psychophysical methods. The standard reference was, of course, the two big volumes on quantitative psychology by Titchener. The determination of a limen was the basic problem in old-fashioned psychophysics. In order to be scholarly in this field, one was supposed to know about the old debates on how to compute the limen for lifted weights to two decimal places with a standard stimulus of one hundred grams. One could hardly worry about anything more trivial. Who cares for the exact determination of anybody's limen for lifted weights? In teaching this subject I felt

---

[12] H. Gulliksen, *Theory of Mental Tests*, 1950.

that we must do something about this absurdity by introducing more interesting stimuli. Instead of lifted weights we used a list of offenses presented in pairs with the instruction that they should be judged as to their relative seriousness. The subject checked one of each pair of offenses to indicate which he thought was the more serious. Instead of selecting one of the offenses as a standard, we asked the subjects to compare every stimulus with every other stimulus. It was now apparent that the classical method of constant stimuli is a special case of the more complete psychophysical method of paired comparison. We followed this same procedure with a list of nationalities that were also presented in pairs. For each pair of nationalities the subject was asked to check the one which he would prefer to associate with. I did not realize at the time that it was going to be necessary to rewrite the fundamental theory of psychophysics in order to cope with data of this type.

The starting point for our work in psychophysical theory was a square table with rows j and columns k. In examining this square table of proportions for any experiment, I set myself this theoretical problem, namely, that if some of the entries were erased, then it should be possible in an overdetermined experiment to fill in the missing entries so as to be consistent with the given entries. The first impulse might have been to solve this problem in the statistical manner by plotting one column against some other column, or perhaps against the sum of the rows. A linear or non-linear regression might then be fitted and one might be able to make an estimate about the missing entries. A statistical procedure of this kind is useful, especially when one has no theory or idea about the underlying order. In this case my ambition was to formulate a theory about comparative judgments, so that the missing entries could be supplied on a more rational basis. This problem haunted me for a time because it implied a subjective metric which required, of course, a subjective unit of measurement. No solution was acceptable unless it could be operationally defined with checks for internal consistency. I wrote a solution to this problem in a paper on psychophysical analysis, which I regard as the best paper that I have produced. The resulting equation was called a law of comparative judgment. The principal difficulty was not in the mathematics which turned out to be extremely simple, but rather with the psychological concepts. By the method of paired comparison we were able to allocate each stimulus to a point on the subjective continuum. In addition to a mean scale value on this continuum, each stimulus was also characterized by a dispersion which was called the discriminal dispersion. This dispersion was in the subjective or experienced quality of a stimulus and the standard deviation of this dispersion for a standard stimulus could be chosen as a subjective unit of measurement. Subjective scaling of this kind is completely defined operationally and tests for internal consistency were readily available. For example, the sum of the subjective separations between the stimulus pairs AB and BC must be equal to the experimentally independent determination of the separation AC. If the continuum was undimensional, then this simple type of check would establish the fact. Five papers in 1927[13] describe my efforts to establish some law and order in psychophysics, but I should never claim that they are more than a beginning in the development of psychophysical theory.

The next problem was to investigate the relations of these new psychophysical formulations to Fechner's law and Weber's law. Fechner's law states that the subjective allocations of the stimuli are a logarithmic function of the physical stimulus magnitudes. The law of comparative judgment enables one to allocate each stimulus to the subjective continuum, even when the stimuli vary in ambiguity or discriminal dispersion. Perhaps its most important feature is that a subjective metric can be established even when there exists no physical stimulus magnitude for the attribute that is judged. The law of comparative judgment enables us to measure social, moral, and aesthetic values where we have no corresponding physical stimulus magnitudes. Weber's law does not involve the subjective continuum, because it states a relation between two physical magnitudes, namely, the stimulus magnitude and the physically measured error. This relation is stated statistically in terms of the relative frequency with which a given error magnitude is to be expected. A customary statement of Weber's law contains a number of ambiguities which make it indeterminate as to how it should be experimentally verified. I attempted to state Weber's law symbolically in such a manner that its experimental verification became operationally defined. It also became apparent that equally often noticed differences are not equal unless the discriminal dispersions are equal. The reason why this circumstance had not previously been found was no doubt the fact that experimental work was confined to simple stimuli whose ambiguities were all equally small. An experimental demonstration of the separation between Fechner's law and Weber's law could be easily set up by varying the stimulus ambiguities. These should markedly affect Weber's law, but theoretically they should have no effect on Fechner's law. At the same time I questioned the Phi-Gamma hypothesis,[14] which was demonstrated on logical grounds to be necessarily false. It was demonstrated to be false if one assumed Weber's law or any other law in which the observational errors are any monotonic increasing function of the stimulus magnitudes. The method of rank order

[13] Thurstone, Psychophysical analysis, *Amer. J Psychol.*, 1927, 38, 368–389, The method of paired comparisons for social values, *J. abnorm. soc Psychol.*, 1927, 21, 384–400; Equally often noticed differences, *J. educ. Psychol.*, 1927, 18, 289–293; A law of comparative judgment, *Psychol. Rev.*, 1927, 34, 273–286; Three psychophysical laws, *Psychol. Rev.*, 1927, 34, 424–432.

[14] Thurstone, The Phi-Gamma hypothesis, *J. exp. Psychol.*, 1928, 11, 293–305.

was brought in to the same theoretical structure and it was shown to be consistent with the method of paired comparison.[15]

Subsequent developments in psychophysical theory were concerned largely with the measurement of social values. Two of the later studies will be considered here because they are concerned with psychophysical theory. One of these deals with the number of dimensions in a psychophysical domain, a problem that was frequently discussed in our seminars. The initial attempt to rewrite psychophysical theory assumed a unidimensional subjective continuum with adequate tests for unidimensionality. Since some psychophysical problems deal frankly with a multidimensional domain, there was necessity for setting up a suitable experimental procedure to establish a multidimensional subjective metric. Methodologically this problem , was solved by Marion Richardson,[16] who introduced the method of triads as a psychophysical method. The subject is presented with sets of three stimuli and he is asked to indicate which two are more similar and which is, therefore, the odd stimulus. The subject does this for each presented triad and the proportions of paired comparison can then be inferred. It should be carefully noted that the subject's task is not to say that one stimulus is x'er than another as to some specified attribute x. Such a question implies unidimensionally. In the method of triads the subject is merely asked to indicate which pair of stimuli are more nearly alike. This gives him freedom to make his judgments in a multidimensional subjective domain. The analytical problem of determining the dimensionality for a set of data by the triad method was solved by Young and Householder[17] who contributed an ingenious matrix solution. Therefore we are no longer limited to a unidimensional domain in dealing with psychophysical problems. Psychological measurement can be carried out with a multidimensional subjective psychophysical metric.

About twenty years later I returned to a different type of psychophysical problem. In psychophysical analysis that has been discussed here so far, the problem has been to allocate each stimulus to a point in the subjective continuum whether it be unidimensional or multidimensional. If we assume that this job has been done, then we can ask whether any predictions can be made as to how people will behave in relation to the objects or ideas that they have been judging. This is, in a sense, an obverse psychophysical problem because, instead of allocating the physical stimulus to the subjective continuum, we now want to use the subjective allocations in order to predict overt conduct. A simple examination of this problem leads to some rather

[15] Thurstone, Rank order as a psychophysical method, *J. exp Psychol.*, 1931, 14, 187–201.

[16] M. Richardson, Multidimensional psychophysics, *Psychol. Bull*, 1938, 35, 659–660. (Abstract.)

[17] G. Young and A. S. Householder, Discussion of a set of points in terms of their mutual distance, *Psychometrika*, 1938, 3, 19–22, 126.

startling and interesting conjectures which can probably be experimentally verified. This is what I have called the prediction of choice.[13]

These inferences seem to have immediate practical application in a variety of problems, such as the prediction of elections, the study of consumer preferences, and the prediction of relative consumption of competing objects. Consider two political candidates who have the same average popularity. Their subjective scale values are, therefore, the same. Let one of these candidates have a much more variable dispersion in the sense that some people are enthusiastic about him while others hate him. The other candidate may be assumed to have a smaller dispersion so that there are not such wide differences of opinion about him. In an election these two candidates would split the vote. The more variable of the two candidates can insure a plurality by introducing a third candidate, even with lower average popularity, on the assumption that the correlations in popular estimates of the three candidates are not very high. The less variable of the two principal candidates has no such leverage on this situation. The same logic applies in the prediction of choice among competing commodities. Lately it has been found that the extremely simple psychophysical method of successive intervals can be used for survey purposes in the prediction of choice. The method of successive intervals is essentially a variant of the method of single stimuli with multiple categories of judgment. It seems almost certain that psychophysical theories and methods will invade an increasing territory of practical application. By these methods we can honestly say that we are measuring moral and social values.

Social Psychology

Although I have not attempted to gain competence in the general field of social psychology, our work in psychological measurement has naturally turned to the measurement of social values. This was largely due to our attempt to introduce some life and interest in psychophysics, which was dominated for a long time by the trivial problems of lifted weights and limen determinations. The extension of psychophysical methods to the measurement of social values was especially tempting when it turned out that the law of comparative judgment is entirely independent of the physical stimulus magnitudes. This circumstance enables one to use the law in the measurement of social and aesthetic values where physical stimulus measurement is entirely irrelevant. Our work on attitudes was started when I had some correspondence with Floyd Allport about the appraisal of political opinions, and there was discussion here at that time about the concept of social distance which was introduced by Bogardus. It was in such a setting that I speculated about the possible use of the new psychophysical toys. I wrote

[13] Thurstone, The prediction of choice, *Psychometrika*, 1945, 10, 237–253.

a paper entitled "Attitudes can be measured."[19] Instead of gaining some approval for this effort, I found myself in a storm of criticism and controversy. The critics assumed that the essence of social attitudes was by definition something unmeasurable. There followed a number of other papers on the construction of particular attitude scales and on methodology, including a little monograph on *The Measurement of Attitude* by Professor E. J. Chave and myself (1929). There was a good deal of interest in the subject and a lot of attitude scales were constructed for particular issues. These included attitude scales on the treatment of criminals, patriotism, Sunday observance, the church, war, the Negro, prohibition, unions, communism, public office, constitution of the United States, social position of women, immigration, birth control, the Chinese, the Germans, the law, censorship, evolution, capital punishment, economic position of women, and others.

Our best work in this field was a study, supported by the Payne Fund, on the effect of motion pictures on the social attitudes of high school children. The only adequate description of that work and the principal findings was in a lithoprinted monograph[20] which has long since been out of print. About thirty experiments were carried out on a large number of films. The procedure was to arrange with a local theater to run a particular film on a particular evening. The films were selected by special previews here in Chicago. Those films were selected which might have some effect on the social attitudes of high-school children on some debatable issue. Free tickets were distributed in the local high school and students were told that they must write their names on the tickets to validate them. In this way we had a record of the students who saw the film. A few days before and a few days after the film was shown, we gave attitude schedules in the high school on the issue which might be affected by the film. In this way we demonstrated, for example, that the film "The Birth of a Nation" has a very strong effect in making high school children less friendly toward the Negro. Similar studies were made with other films on other issues. At Mooseheart we succeeded in demonstrating by experiments the summation effect on social attitudes. When a single film did not give a statistically significant effect, and when two films a week apart gave a barely noticeable effect, we demonstrated that three films showed a significant effect. The summation effect is an important principle in a propaganda program with material in which a single film may not be adequate to demonstrate a significant shift in attitude.

There was heavy correspondence with people who were interested in attitude measurement, but they were concerned mostly with the selection of attitude scales on particular issues to be used on particular groups of people.

[19] Thurstone, Attitudes can be measured, *Amer. J. Sociol.*, 1928, 33, 529–554.
[20] Thurstone and Ruth C Peterson, *The Effect of Motion Pictures on the Social Attitudes of High School Children,* 1932 (obtainable on microfilm from the Univ. of Chicago Library, Dept. of Photographic Reproduction, Film No. 1696).

There seemed to be very little interest in developing the theory of the subject. The construction of more and more attitude scales seemed to be unproductive, and I decided to stop any further work of this kind. Incomplete material for a dozen more attitude scales was thrown in the wastebasket and I discouraged any further work of that kind in my laboratory. I wanted to clear the place for work in developing multiple factor analysis.

Our social psychological studies have been opportunistic in a sense, because they have consisted in applications of new psychophysical methods on suitable occasions. Rarely have we set out to devise a measurement method for an existing social psychological problem. The question can be raised to what extent the development of a young science should be under pressure of the major problems of the day. Perhaps the principal reason why social psychology has very low prestige is that many authors in that field reveal that they have an axe to grind. It is doubtful whether one can be a propagandist and a scientist in the same field and at the same time. Similar comments can be made about many social studies. The excuse is often made that social phenomena are so complex that the relatively simple methods of the older sciences do not apply. This argument is probably false. The analytical study of social phenomena is probably not so difficult as is commonly believed. The principal difficulty is that the experts in social studies are frequently hostile to science. They try to describe the totality of a situation and their orientation is often to the market place or the election next week. They do not understand the thrill of discovering an invariance of some kind which never covers the totality of any situation. Social studies will not become science until students of social phenomena learn to appreciate this essential aspect of science.

Learning

Although the field of learning was my first interest in psychology, I have not been productive in that field. It has always seemed to me that we have missed something essential in learning which is not represented by the ordinary studies of rote learning. My doctor's dissertation on the learning curve equation[21] was a very simple study, and a paper on variability in learning[22] related to a current controversy at that time. Something more elaborate was developed in a paper on the learning function,[23] in which it seemed that the learning curve for rote learning should be S-shaped. Some of these ideas were incorporated in a study of the relation between learning time and length of task,[24] in which I was pleased to find that nine experimental studies

[21] Thurstone, The learning curve equation, *Psychol. Monogr.*, 1919, 26, No. 114.
[22] Thurstone, Variability in learning, *Psychol. Bull.*, 1918, 15, 210–212.
[23] Thurstone, The learning function, *J. gen. Psychol.*, 1930, 3, 469–493.
[24] Thurstone, The relation between learning time and length of task, *Psychol Rev*, 1930, 37, 44–53.

in the literature fitted the theoretical expectations according to which the learning time varies as the 3/2 power of the number of rote items in the list. Another study of the error function in maze learning[25] was an elaboration of the same theme in another setting.

Multiple Factor Analysis

The work on multiple factor analysis was started in 1929, but it did not get under way seriously for another year until completion of other commitments. The original observation equation for multiple factor analysis was written in Pittsburgh before 1922, but it was ten years before I started serious work on the problem. Much has been written on multiple factor analysis, so that this discussion will be limited to some of the incidents and accidents concerned with the development of the main ideas. Our early work was supported by annual grants from the Social Science Research Committee at the University of Chicago. We had a number of research grants from the Carnegie Corporation for research assistants and for the purchase of calculating machines. One of the Carnegie grants was specifically for the development of a matrix multiplying machine. We investigated some of the new calculating equipment that was being designed at Cambridge, but we finally decided to use a modified form of IBM scoring machine which could be adapted for matrix multiplication. The machine was built by the IBM Company in Endicott, and it has been in daily use in our laboratory for many years. As far as I know, that is the only matrix multiplier of this type that has been built. The machine was designed largely by Dr. Ledyard Tucker, and we had the interest and assistance of Professor Eckert of our Physics Department at that time.

When it became evident that the development of multiple factor analysis would require special research grants, I decided to consult Dr. Keppel on one of my trips to New York. I explained to Dr. Keppel that I needed some research funds to develop what I called multiple factor analysis and that it was a big gamble. I told him that I could give him no assurance that this gamble would be successful but that I expected to give my major time to this problem, perhaps for several years. He gave me an initial grant of $5,000, which was a great help. Subsequently we had several grants from the Carnegie Corporation for this work. I did not realize at that time that I would be giving major effort to this problem and its application in identifying primary mental abilities during the next twenty years.

Many of the turning points in the solution of the multiple-factor problem depended on minor incidents. On one occasion, when I was having lunch with Professor Bliss, chairman of the Mathematics Department, and with

[25] Thurstone, Error function in maze learning, *J gen Psychol.*, 1933, 9, 288–301.

the astronomer Bartky, I asked them about some arithmetical operations that I was doing on rectangular tables of numbers. I asked them if there was any kind of mathematics that could be useful in operations of that kind. They both laughed and told me that I was extracting the root of a matrix. When I asked what was meant by a matrix, they suggested that I talk with Professor Barnard, who was teaching three courses in this subject. Professor Barnard took a friendly interest in the problem and helped us a great deal. I appointed Patrick Youtz as a research assistant, and he tutored me in the elements of matrix algebra. Youtz was then a graduate student of mathematics, and he is now on the staff at M.I.T. At a later time Bartky gave valuable assistance when I was working on the principal axis solution. I was trying to solve a problem in least squares with a conditional equation, although I had not at that time put the matter in so simple and direct a manner. He told me that this was an old problem in celestial mechanics and he gave me the solution. Then I discovered that I had myself studied that solution in theoretical mechanics, but I did not think of the solution in connection with my own problem. I described the principal axes solution at an A.A.A.S. meeting in Syracuse in 1932. These incidents illustrate the erratic way in which research can be done, in spite of the limitations of the investigator.

Beginning with Spearman's famous paper in 1904, there was a quarter of a century of debate about Spearman's single factor method and his postulated general intellective factor g. Throughout that debate over several decades, the orientation was to Spearman's general factor, and secondary attention was given to the group factors and specific factors which were frankly called "the disturbers of g." Even now much British writing and some American writing on factor analysis are oriented toward the general factor and the group factors which constantly disturb the general factor g. The development of multiple-factor analysis consisted essentially in asking the fundamental question in a different way. Starting with an experimentally given table of correlation coefficients for a set of variables, we did not ask whether it supported any one general factor. We asked instead how many factors must be postulated in order to account for the observed correlations. At the very start of an analysis we faced very frankly the question as to how many factors must be postulated, and it should then be left as a question of fact in each inquiry whether one of these factors should be regarded as general.

In 1931 and 1932 some of the present writers on multiple-factor analysis were still concerned with the problem of this general factor and with such related problems as the standard error of the tetrad difference. At one time I decided to relate the work on multiple-factor analysis to the earlier work of Spearman, and for this purpose I wrote the tetrad difference equation on a piece of paper. I expected to spend a good deal of time on this problem. As I looked at the tetrad difference equation, it dawned on me that it was nothing but the expansion of a second-order minor. If all of the second-order minors vanish, the rank is, of course, unity, and immediately one can then ask the corresponding question about the vanishing of third-order minors, fourth-order minors, and so on. If the question had been asked in that manner, multiple-factor analysis would probably have developed many years earlier. The work in multiple-factor analysis introduced several ideas which extend the earlier work of Spearman. These ideas include the interpretation of Spearman's single factor theorems as a special case of unit rank, the matrix formulation of the factor problem, the communalities, the simple structure concept, the rotation of the reference frame for scientific interpretation, the desirability of interpreting primary factors as meaningful parameters, the use of oblique reference axes, and the principles of configurational invariance. Later work introduced the second-order factors and studies in the effects of selection on the factorial structure. All of these ideas are concerned with methodology.

Throughout this work, the emphasis has been on factor analysis as a scientific method distinguished from problems of statistical condensation of data, which we have considered to be of secondary importance for most scientific work. There are, of course, entirely legitimate problems in which statistical condensation is the essential purpose of a factorial analysis. But this is not the type of problem to which we have given principal attention in the Psychometric Laboratory at Chicago. My first paper on multiple-factor analysis was published in 1931[26] and a multiple-factor analysis of vocational interests was published in the same year.[27] The principal publications in this field from our laboratory have been *The Theory of Multiple Factors* (1933), *The Vectors of Mind* (1935), and my APA presidential address of the same title.[28] The first volume was rewritten in more extended form with the title *Multiple-Factor Analysis* which was published in 1947. In the last fifteen years multiple-factor analysis has attracted the attention of many competent students, so that there are now available a number of texts on this subject. For some reason that I have never been able to understand, the principal concepts of multiple-factors analysis have met severe criticism. Among these the greatest surprise was the criticism and ridicule of the introduction of communalities, the simple structure concept, and the oblique reference frame. These concepts and methods were introduced to resolve troublesome problems of factorial indeterminacy. The striking results that have been obtained in a large number of scientific studies with these methods have reduced the severity of criticism, but these concepts are by no means generally accepted. A curious type of criticism has been made of my attempt to give meaningful

---

[26] Thurstone, Multiple factor analysis, *Psychol. Rev.*, 1931, **38**, 406–427.
[27] Thurstone, A multiple factor study of vocational interest, *Person. J.*, 1931, **10**, 198–205.
[28] Thurstone, The vectors of mind, *Psychol. Rev.*, 1934, **41**, 1–32.

interpretation to the factorial parameters. I can hardly imagine a more absurd type of criticism and yet it is very commonly made.

Primary Mental Abilities

As soon as the methods of multiple-factor analysis had been developed to the point where practical application seemed feasible, we started work on such a project. The development of a large battery of fifty-seven tests for various aspects of intelligence was a large undertaking. When this job had been done, the whole battery was given to a group of 240 volunteers in the spring of 1934. Analysis of these records constituted our first attempt to identify primary mental abilities. A short paper on this experiment was published in *Psychometrika*[29] and a more complete report constituted the first issue in the *Psychometric Monograph Series*.[30] Although my first text on multiple-factor analysis, *The Vectors of Mind*, had previously been published (1935), with a development of the concepts of communality, the rotation of axes, and the use of oblique axes, I hesitated to introduce all of these things in the first experimental study. In particular, there was strong advice from Thorndike, Kelly, and other men for whom I had respect, that an oblique reference frame would be completely unacceptable. Instead of proceeding according to my convictions, that first factor study was published with the best fitting orthogonal frame, although we knew about more complete methods. This was an effort to avoid the storm of controversy that we feared in the introduction of so many different procedures in the first experimental study.

In the last fifteen years the identification of primary abilities and traits has proceeded at an entirely unexpected pace. Fortunately the problem has attracted the attention of some mathematicians and mathematical statisticians. A number of the papers are so technical that they are beyond the comprehension of some of the rest of us who were concerned with the development of these methods in their primitive stage.

The correlations of the primary factors can be factored, just like the correlations among tests. When this is done we find several second-order factors. One of these seems to agree very well with Spearman's general intellective factor g. The critics feature our support of Spearman's g, but they ignore the fact that this work represents at least a modest gain in unraveling the complexities of mental organization.

When a number of the primary factors had been identified with some degree of assurance, it was challenging to develop some tests of primary abilities for use in the public schools. We hope that it will be possible to

---

[29] Thurstone, The factorial isolation of primary abilities, *Psychometrika*, 1936, 1, 175–182.
[30] Thurstone, Primary mental abilities, *Psychometric Monogr*, 1938, No. 1.

get teachers and psychologists to describe children in terms of their mental profiles instead of the single intelligence quotient. To develop tests of primary abilities for use in the schools introduces new problems. As usual there is always the limitation of time for psychological testing. The practical question is, then, how many of the primary abilities can be appraised in the amount of time that is allowable for psychological testing in the schools. The pressure is always to reduce to a minimum the time limit for each test so as to cover as many abilities as possible within one or two class periods. We have tried to make practical compromises in this regard in order to make available in the schools our findings about primary mental abilities. The results of these efforts, issued first in a set of tests of primary mental abilities, were distributed by the American Council on Education in 1938. Subsequently the procedures were simplified with various scoring devices and the tests were shortened considerably. The distribution of this test series was taken over by Science Research Associates where Lyle Spencer and Robert Burns are directors. It has been a pleasure to work with these men in the distribution of psychological test material because they have a genuine interest in the scientific values involved and also a realistic recognition of the practical demands in the schools. It was Robert Burns who was largely responsible for initiating the three-year research project on mechanical aptitude which was supported by the Office of Naval Research. In that study we verified rather clearly that the second space factor, identified by Guilford in his factor studies for the Air Force during the war, was the main component in the complex that is called mechanical aptitude.[31]

In all of our studies in psychological measurement and especially in the theoretical and experimental work on the primary mental abilities, I have been very fortunate in having my wife as a partner because she is a genius in test construction and related problems. With the assistance of Katherine Byrne and Katherine Vitato, she assembled a set of seventy games that could be given to five-year-old children who have not yet learned how to read. These game-tests were given to an experimental population of five- and six-year-old children and a multiple-factor analysis was made of the scores. That unpublished study showed essentially the same primary factors at the kindergarten age which we have found in other studies for adults. A new set of tests was constructed for kindergarten children.

Examination in the College

Before the reorganization of the college at the University of Chicago, Dean Ernest H. Wilkins had several committees at work on the problem of cur-

---

[31] Thurstone, *An analysis of mechanical aptitude*, Psychometric Laboratory Report, No 62, 1951, also in *Psychometrika* (in press).

riculum construction. When Mr. Hutchins came to the university, he developed aggressively a revised curriculum for the college and many other new arrangements. When it was proposed to introduce comprehensive examinations for the determination of grades, I wrote a memorandum to Dean Works, in which I suggested certain principles that should be adopted in writing those examinations. I was asked if I would help to start the new examination procedure as chief examiner for the college. I accepted with the idea that I would help to get the system started, but I did not leave this assignment until Professor Ralph Tyler came to Chicago seven years later. I proposed some new principles to be used in the construction of college examinations, and these were accepted. One principle was that the examinations should become public property as soon as they had been given. The purpose of this system was to eliminate bootlegging of examinations in fraternity houses and elsewhere. One of the consequences was that a new examination had to be written each time, and here several novel ideas were introduced. No question was used in a comprehensive examination if the instructors did not know the answer. If the instructors started to argue about the answer to a question, it was either eliminated or revised until the instructors agreed about the answer. The identity of the student was not known by the person who assigned the grades. The grades were determined by the distribution of scores before the identities of the students were known. Some departments objected that new examinations could not be written each time that a course was given. Our response was that if a new examination could not be written at the end of each course, then there was no justification for the course.

In the initial work of the Board of Examinations we were fortunate in having an exceptionally good staff of examiners. On the staff we had Wolfle, Richardson, Gulliksen, Kuder, Adkins, Stalnaker, and Russell. I have always been proud of the fact that I collected this group of examiners when they were graduate students and recent post-doctorates. All of them have arrived professionally. The standards of workmanship were exceptionally high, and I believe that we had the good will of the faculty.

Studies of Personality

One of my principal interests in psychology to which I have returned several times has been the study of personality. Soon after completing the doctorate, I turned my attention seriously to the study of abnormal psychology, and I read Freud and a good deal of the psychoanalytical literature. My conflict here was that, on the one hand, the center of psychology probably was the study of personality, but, on the other hand, I was unable to invent any experimental leverage in this field. That was the reason why I turned to other problems that seemed to lend themselves to more rigorous analysis.

During my first year at the University of Chicago, Beardsley Ruml asked me to spend a quarter in Philadelphia to work with Elton Mayo. My assignment was to work with him daily and to try to decipher his psychological system. I found it an extremely profitable experience to spend the mornings with him at the Philadelphia General Hospital and the afternoons at Ardmore when he went there to work with patients. I became convinced that no one should ever receive a doctorate in psychology without such an experience, no matter what his major field might be. As to the assignment, I had to report that to systematize Elton Mayo was an impossible job. By that I did not mean to depreciate Elton Mayo for whom I had the very highest regard, but I did not see the possibility of any textbook exposition of his ideas.

Teaching

In 1948 we had an unusual experience when both Thelma and I were appointed as visiting professors at the University of Frankfurt in Germany. Our group was the first one to go from the University of Chicago to Frankfurt. Our principal motivation for that enterprise was the opportunity to help, even in a very small way, to repair what is left after the physical and moral destruction in Europe. Our lectures and seminars in Frankfurt were scheduled on the first three days of each week so that we had every week end for visiting lectures at Marburg, Heidelberg, Munster, and other places. We have never had more grateful students and colleagues. We brought American books and we were informed that these were the first books from outside Germany to reach their laboratories since before the war. We admired the efforts in reconstruction against terrific odds, including hunger, lack of supplies, and living quarters built by hand in the rubble.

We have had a number of foreign students in our laboratory. These included Charles Wang and E. H. Hsü from China, who have been productive. Mariano Yela from the University of Madrid, Spain, who spent two years here, was one of our best students. From South Africa we have had three superior students. John Karlin remained in this country and is now on the staff of the Bell Telephone Company laboratories in Murray Hill, New Jersey. Mrs. Melany Baehr was sent here from South Africa by the National Bureau of Personnel Research. Mrs. Baehr's dissertation was written here for a doctor's degree that was awarded in South Africa. We have had similar cooperative arrangements about several other dissertations for degrees that were awarded in other universities. Mrs. Carol Pemberton came here from South Africa and is now completing work for the doctorate with a dissertation on the closure factors in relation to personality traits. According to our last information several years ago, Nicholas Margineau was still a political prisoner in Rumania.

At the present time we have an exceptionally promising group in the Psychometric Laboratory. Among the advanced students are Thomas Jeffrey, who is in immediate charge of the Laboratory, Andrew Baggaley, Fred Damarin, Robert Fantz, William Harris, Ray Hartley, Thomas Johnson, Father Lawlor, John Mellinger, and Jonathan Wegener. In addition to these advanced students we have an exceptional group of Fellows: Professor Allen Edwards for the Social Science Research Council, Dr. Lyle Jones on a National Research Council fellowship, Dr. J. E. Birren on a Public Health Service fellowship, Jean Cardinet from Professor Piéron's laboratory in Paris, and Per Saugstad on a fellowship from Norway. As this manuscript is being written, Dr. Horacio Rimoldi is preparing to go to Uruguay on a new professorship.

The graduate students of psychology who have a major interest in research will probably find it advantageous now, as in the past, to serve an apprenticeship in teaching. To teach is probably still the best way to master one's subject and to recognize its major research possibilities. When I was promoted to a professorship at Chicago in 1927, I was offered the opportunity to devote full time to research without teaching obligations. I chose instead a program that implied the teaching of one course each quarter, and I still believe that was a wise decision, partly because it has enabled me to keep in touch with promising talent among graduate students and to select associates in my laboratory. The research men who are completely divorced from teaching are often isolated professionally unless they have served for some years in active teaching before withdrawing to their laboratories. Seldom is a young man destined to professional recognition if he withdraws from teaching immediately after the completion of the doctorate.

Psychological measurement is generally regarded as a field of specialization, but this is an unfortunate circumstance. Those who specialize in this field often regard mathematical statistics as their basic subject matter and the result is that they often forget psychological theory and problems. It would be more fortunate if the quantitative aspects of psychology were treated as integral parts of psychological theory and experimental procedure. Psychological measurement theory would not then be relegated to separate courses. It would be part of psychological subject matter in social psychology, the cognitive functions, personality theory, learning and forgetting, the sensory and perceptual functions, and the rest. It is a challenge to develop further the quantitative aspects of psychology itself. Mathematical statistics is a useful tool but it is an entirely different subject. It is in no sense a substitute for psychological measurement theory which is part of psychological science.

This biography has been concerned primarily with the development of psychological ideas that have guided my work. But all of my time has not been at the office and laboratory. Our family has lived in the same house for twenty-four years, and much of our interest has centered there. Our oldest son, Robert (23), has just been graduated in electrical engineering at Illinois Institute of Technology; Conrad (20) is completing the second year in medicine at the University of Chicago; and Fritz (18) is completing the sophomore year in physics at California Institute of Technology. Our policy has been to encourage their projects in a basement machine shop and electronics laboratory, the grinding of telescope reflectors, and the assembly of their own television set, a bedroom radio station that barely left room for a bed, and many other enterprises. For many years we have spent long vacations in a summer colony, Wabigama, on Elk Lake near Traverse City, Michigan. That unusual group of twenty families of scientists and professional men have individual cottages on the lake, and we have had an unusual experience in community living with one of the most friendly groups we have ever known. The boys have had the experience of knowing well these men and their families in the informal life of that summer colony, a privilege that they appreciate the more as they reach maturity. Summers have been more than vacations. They have been rich episodes in living, including fishing, fly-tying, rod-making, sailing, house construction, work in the woods and orchard, outboard motors, and help in all the emergencies. Outside of my own connection at the University, the associations in Wabigama have had the most important impact on our family.

Thelma has the outstanding achievement in our family in managing an active household at the same time that she was professionally active. She has been a partner in every research project in the Psychometric Laboratory. For many years she was in the laboratory daily, helping to plan the projects, supervising most of the test construction, and participating especially in the psychological interpretation of results. In 1948 she left this work to become director of the Division of Child Study in the Chicago Public Schools. This report should really have been written as a biography for both of us.

EDWARD CHACE TOLMAN

I WAS born in Newton, Massachusetts in 1886. I went to the Newton Public Schools, which were then, and still are, considered to be unusually good, and then went to the Massachusetts Institute of Technology, where I obtained a B.S. in electrochemistry in 1911. I went to M.I.T. not because I wanted to be an engineer, but because I had been good in mathematics and science in high school and because of family pressure. After graduating from Technology I became more certain of my own wants and transferred to Harvard for graduate work in philosophy and psychology.

My family was, I suppose, what now would be called "upper middle" or possibly "lower upper." My father was president of a manufacturing company and my maternal uncle president of a similar company. My brother, who was five years older, and I were, first one and then the other, expected to go into our father's business. Hence, we both went to M.I.T.; my father had been a member of the first graduating class and was a Trustee. My brother, however, escaped by becoming a theoretical chemist and physicist and I, having read some William James during my senior year at Technology, fancied that I wanted to become a philosopher. Upon graduating from M.I.T., I went to the Harvard summer school and took an introductory course in philosophy with Perry and one in psychology with Yerkes — both then young assistant professors in the combined department of philosophy and psychology. I decided then and there that I did not have brains enough to become a philosopher (that was still the day of great metaphysical systems), but that psychology was nearer my capacities and interests. It offered, at that date, what seemed a nice compromise between philosophy and science.

The fact that my brother and I both avoided family expectations and chose academic careers, instead of going into the factory, and the further fact that this led to no family quarrels and that we were even financially supported during the process, probably tells a good deal about the nature of the family setup and of the general cultural milieu in which we lived.

Our immediate family consisted of a warm, loving, but in some areas Puritanical mother and of a kindly, affectionate but very much occupied father — who was depressingly energetic and excited about his business, so much so that when he tried to get us boys interested in it he merely wore us out — and of a still older sister who, as far as I was concerned, was already leading a grown-up life outside my ken.   This seems the sort of setup which the recent studies of ethnocentrism suggest may be conducive to the developing of ambitious, but non-authoritarian personalities.   Although we lived in a well-to-do conventional suburb with stress on appearances, there still persisted in our family and in those of some of the neighbors the legacy of reformism, equal rights for Negroes, women's rights, Unitarianism and humanitarianism from the earlier days of the "Flowering of New England." These social tendencies were combined with the special Bostonian emphasis on "culture" together with, in our family, a special dose of moral uplift and pacifism.   Typical mottoes of my father were, on the one hand, "Tend to business" and, on the other, "Man does not live by bread alone."   There was relatively great freedom of discussion between children and parents and close ties to the wider family.   What I am trying to say is that the rebellion of my brother and of myself against parental domination was in directions which the parents themselves could not too greatly, or too consciously, disapprove.   We were choosing the professions.   We were set to increase the sum of human knowledge and presumably were to apply such an increase of knowledge to the betterment of mankind.   Furthermore, we would be living up to the Puritan tradition of hard work and to the Quaker tradition, on our mother's side, of plain living and high thinking.   This is not to say that our parents were not deeply and basically disappointed that we did not really adopt the other strain in their own natures and in the New England culture at large — that of making money and taking advantage of the expanding national economy.   But it *is* to say that, since in large measure we were merely following what they had preached, they could not show their disappointment too strongly either to themselves or to us.   Undoubtedly this typical parent-child tragedy of America was mitigated for them, as it is for so many American parents, because we, the children, were striving towards what, at least in New England, could be considered a form of upward social mobility.

Turn now to a more particular question.   Why did I, personally, go into psychology rather than choosing to follow my brother into physics or chemistry.   I suspect the following factors were involved.   First, during adolescence it seems to have been my brother with whom I identified and picked as my model rather than my father.   Thus, I was set to follow my brother into the academic world.   On the other hand, I did not dare compete with him in his own field.   An older brother is both a tremendous example and a very frightening rival who, because of his advantage in years, has one licked intellectually before one starts. Secondly, I suspect that, although I was considered by my teachers to be as good as my brother in mathematics and science, my mind was in fact less rigorous and less logical. Third, as the youngest in the family I had been over-babied and over-protected — being made into a shy adolescent — who had therefore been led, perhaps, to become especially sensitive to and interested in human relations. Further, at the age of seventeen I was taken out of school for two years because of a functional heart disorder which at that time was laid to too rapid physical growth; the more probable psychoanalytic explanation I leave to the reader. This left me much time to introspect, to become somewhat morbid and to imagine myself as a potential "writer," "humanitarian," or "saver-of-souls" — in, of course, a chaste, rationalistic, Unitarian sort of way. Again, as a late maturer and one who had always been poor at sports and one who, no doubt due to the influences of a mother of Quaker origin, was afraid of bodily competition and of masculinity in general, I probably had suffered a sufficient number of rejections from all but a small intimate group of boyhood friends to have had another reason for needing to "understand" human reactions. Although I had thought I wanted to be a philosopher, I can remember the excitement I felt in that first course in psychology with Yerkes in which we did little "experiments" on reaction time, mental images, and the like. I felt that here one was going to learn what made people tick. It would be much more successful than preaching at them. (I had gone through a phase of thinking that I wanted to be a Unitarian minister.)

In the fall of 1911, therefore, after only one summer session course in philosophy and one in psychology, I began at Harvard as a full graduate student (unthinkable in these days) in the joint department of philosophy and psychology. The courses I remember most vividly were: Perry's course in Ethics, which laid the basis for my later interest in motivation and, indeed, gave me the main concepts (reinforced by a reading of McDougall's *Social Psychology* as part of the requirement of the course) which I have retained ever since; Holt's course in Experimental (largely two-point thresholds and epicritic and protopathic sensations) which I took my first semester and which proved a terrible letdown from the really humanly important problems which I had supposed psychology was to be concerned with; Langfeld's course in Advanced General, using Titchener as a textbook, which almost sold me temporarily on structuralistic introspectionism; Holt's seminar in Epistemology in which I was introduced to, and excited by, the "New Realism"; and Yerkes' course in Comparative, using Watson's *Behavior — an Introduction to Comparative Psychology*, which was just out, as a text.

In addition to these more or less formal courses there was the graduate research done under Münsterberg with Langfeld doing most of the actual supervision. This, if I remember correctly, I began after one year only of graduate enrollment. It had, of course, a tremendous influence upon me. Münsterberg was then at the height of his interest in applied psychology. And most of the research projects which were being carried out in the laboratory involved primarily objective measurements of sensory-motor skills. And even my own research dissertation, which was assigned to me, and which involved the learning and relearning of nonsense syllables under pleasant and unpleasant odors, according to Ebbinghaus's Learning and Savings Method, was primarily objective in nature. I used the then up-to-date *"Rupp-Lippmann Gedächtnis Apparat"* and all I had to do was to sit and count revolutions. Yet in spite of this objective character of practically all of the research being carried out and reported in the weekly laboratory meetings, Münsterberg several times made little opening speeches to the effect that *the* method of psychology was *introspection.* We were expected to ask our subjects, the other graduate students in the group, for introspections, and we took these introspections down in our protocols. But, as far as I remember, none of us was able to make much use of them in his final write-up. And this troubled my theoretical mind. If introspection were "the" method of psychology and we weren't doing it, shouldn't I really go to Cornell where Titchener taught one to do it properly? This worry about introspection is perhaps one reason why my introduction in Yerkes' course to Watson's behaviorism came as a tremendous stimulus and relief. If objective measurement of behavior and not introspection was the true method of psychology I didn't have to worry any longer that we were not doing the latter, or, at least, not doing it in any consistent and approved way.

I say that this was a great relief to my "theoretical mind." As to just when and why this theoretical orientation developed I am not clear. It may be in part constitutional, whatever that may mean. But I am more inclined to believe that it developed from my early fear of, and awkwardness in, manipulatory activities; I had never been especially good in the laboratory at M.I.T. Such fear and awkwardness were perhaps induced as a reaction against my father's extreme interest and proficiency in such matters and also against my brother's slightly greater identification with our father's pattern.

Whatever the explanation, I have always wanted simple and wide-reaching, if not too precise, explanations and have always bogged down in the face of a multiplicity of facts. I can learn facts if I have to, but I forget them equally easily. And in any argument, academic or otherwise, I always find myself handicapped by having forgotten the factual details which alone would buttress my stand. I can make a parade of scholarship, but I find it tiresome and the parade is, I suspect, usually a phony. All the necessary facts are just too many for me to keep in mind. I suspect that I also have some weakness, innate or acquired, in verbal imagery. This is the reason

I feel comfortable only when I have translated my explanatory arguments into diagrams. I always did like curves better than equations. Analytical geometry was a lot more fun than advanced algebra. (They used to be separate courses in my day.) I am very unhappy whenever I do not have a blackboard in my office.

At the end of my first graduate year at Harvard I went to Germany for the summer to help me prepare for the required Ph.D. examination in German. I have always been enormously intrigued by foreign languages although I have no natural talent for them. For I have a poor ear and always have to learn phrases and vocabulary by seeing the words and not just by hearing them. At Langfeld's suggestion I spent a month in Giessen with Koffka, who had been a fellow student of Langfeld's in Berlin and who was then a young *Privatdozent* in psychology at the University of Giessen, and so got my first introduction to Gestalt psychology — although at that time I sensed only vaguely what it was all about. Nevertheless it prepared me to be receptive to Gestalt concepts when after the first World War we began hearing about them more fully in this country through the writings of Wertheimer, Kohler and Koffka. And in the fall of 1923 I went back to Giessen for a couple of months to learn more.

After getting my doctor's degree at Harvard in 1915 I was instructor for three years at Northwestern. I had a compulsive drive from the beginning to do research and to write. I think this was due in part to my brother's example, who was already hell-bent on research and academic success. This compulsion for research and writing, although it did not result in a very large output at the time, interfered with my learning to become much of a teacher. I was still relatively self-conscious and inarticulate, and was afraid of my classes. Also my difficulty in — or dislike for — organizing and remembering a large array of facts was already a handicap. Further, this was just before we got into the first World War and my pacifist training, plus my own problems about aggression, kept me in a terrific emotional turmoil so that I did a still poorer job. I was called before the Dean sometime during the winter of 1917–18 because I had given my name to a student publication, circulated in the Middle West, that was concerned with "war aims," and which had, no doubt, something of a pacifist tinge. The Dean, in leafing through an issue in my presence did not feel any less hostile because the leading article turned out to be by no less eminent a person than David Starr Jordon. In any event, I was dismissed at the end of that academic year on the grounds of war retrenchment and my not too successful teaching. But I have always thought that my near pacifism had something to do with it. I escaped the first draft by being a couple of months too old. But the second draft came along and my pacifist principles and my doubts about the war did not prevent me from signing up and trying to get a commission.

But I was already too late to get into the psychological testing service organized by Yerkes. In the early fall of 1918 I was offered a commission to work with Dunlap and Stratton on the screening of air force candidates. But by that time everyone knew that the Armistice was on its way. So I did not accept.

In the meantime, during the summer of 1918, I was without a job but by luck plus Langfeld's good offices I was offered in the fall an instructorship at California. And here in Berkeley I have stayed extremely happy ever since until very recently. From the very first California symbolized for me some sort of a final freeing from my overwhelmingly too Puritanical and too Bostonian upbringing. The "Freedom of the West," whether real or fancied, at once captured my imagination and my loyalty and has claimed them ever since — although with the years I have, of course, become aware that all is not gold that glitters — even in California. In any case, there are features about the climate and the landscape which seem to me better as a steady diet than those provided by any other place in the world. Particularly the Bay Area (although it produces its share of tonsils, allergies, and influenzas) seems absolutely ideal as an all-year-round working climate. Whatever my early psychological instabilities, they have all but disappeared. Whatever my increasing psychological maturity — and there has been some — I like to credit most of it to the social, intellectual, and physical virtues of Berkeley plus an extraordinarily happy marriage.

I have never been comfortable or efficient in administrative or committee activities and have in large part managed to escape them. My drive has gone into trying to be creative and in my earlier years whenever I was feeling inept on some social or academic occasion, I can remember going home and talking to myself in some such words as: "Well, I'll show them, I will be better known in my field than they will be in theirs." And then I would return to the laboratory, or the study, with an enhanced drive. This compulsive academic ambition, which has, of course, lessened with the years — this self-ideal of somone going to be truly successful in the academic world — came, I suppose, from the fact that in childhood and boyhood I was always successful in school, but never on the playground, and from the fact that, as already indicated, I identified with my older brother. Furthermore, Academe was for me a protected haven in which one could release one's aggressions, of which I undoubtedly have my share, and stick one's neck out on paper without its being too obvious either to oneself or to the other fellow.

Having thus tried to think out, as a very amateur clinical psychologist, what kind of a person I think I am and how I think I got that way, let me try to present a brief history of my psychological interests and concepts. Presumably these have been affected by the structure of my personality;

but whatever the interconnections, these are beyond my ability to unravel. I shall present now, therefore, merely as objective and straightforward an account of my ideas as I can.

In my three beginning years as instructor at Northwestern I was still think-ing largely in terms of classical introspective and associationistic problems. For, although I had been, as I said, tremendously excited by Yerkes' intro-duction to and criticism of Watson's behaviorism, the behavioristic point of view had not yet really got into my blood. Thus the first papers I turned out were concerned with such pre-behavioristic problems as retroactive in-hibition, imageless thought, and association times for pleasant, unpleasant and neutral words.[1]

When, however, I joined the department at Berkeley as instructor in 1918, I found it was up to me to suggest a new course. Remembering Yerkes' course and Watson's textbook I proposed "comparative psychology." And it was this that finally launched me down the behavioristic slope. Only a few students enrolled and at first a lot of time was spent in arguing against anthropomorphism and the Clever Hans error. But, before too long, I ac-tually acquired some rats from the Long-Evans strain which had been developed in the Anatomy Department. And I and a few graduate, or advanced undergraduate, students began trying out minor experiments in learning. (Even though I had been clumsy in the physical and chemical laboratories at M.I.T., I *could* build mazes.)

It was Watson's denial of the Law of Effect and his emphasis on Fre-quency and Recency as the prime determiners of animal learning which first attracted our attention. In this we were on Watson's side. But we got ourselves — or at least I got myself — into a sort of in-between position. On the one hand I sided with Watson in not liking the Law of Effect. But, on the other hand, I also did not like Watson's over-simplified notions of stimu-lus and of response. Nor did I like his treatment of each single stimulus and each single response as a quite insulated phenomenon which has prac-tically no relation to any other stimuli or any other responses. That is, I was already becoming influenced by Gestalt psychology and conceived that a rat in running a maze must be learning a lay-out or pattern and not just having connections between atom-like stimuli and atom-like responses "stamped in" or "stamped out," whether by exercise *or* by effect. In fact, my objection to Thorndike's Law of Effect was not to the importance of motivation as a factor in learning, but rather to his wholly mechanical notion as to its operation by way of effect. According to Thorndike, an animal learned, not because it achieved a wanted goal by a certain series of re-

[1] E. C. Tolman, Retroactive inhibition as affected by conditions of learning, *Psychol Monogr.*, 1918, 25, No. 1; More concerning the temporal relations of meaning and imagery, *Psychol Rev*, 1917, 24, 114–138; (with I. Johnson), A note on association-time and feeling, *Amer J. Psychol*, 1918, 29, 187–195.

sponses, but merely because a quite irrelevant "pleasantness" or "unpleasant-ness" was, so to speak, shot at it, as from a squirt gun, after it had reached the given goal-box or gone into the given *cul de sac*. And it is this same quite mechanical and irrelevant notion as to the operation of the modern successor of Effect — "Reinforcement" — which underlies, I believe, my main objection to *it*. I have, that is, always found difficulty in conceiving how a completely post and divorced "pleasantness," or a completely post and divorced "need-reduction" (*i.e.*, reinforcement), can act back upon and selectively strengthen the appropriate synaptic connections merely because these synapses happen, quite irrelevantly, to have been the ones which have functioned most recently in time.

It was also during this early period at California that I began developing certain more basic theoretical concepts. These were initiated by a growing belief that a really useful behaviorism would not be a mere "muscle-twitchism" such as Watson's. It soon appeared to me that "responses," as significant for psychology, are defined not by their physiological, muscular or glandular, details but rather by the sort of rearrangements between organism and environment or between the organism and its own internal states which they achieve. It also seemed to me that "stimuli" as actually used by psychologists are defined in most cases not in terms of the details of sense organ stimulation but in terms of environmental "objects" and "situations" identifiable only in relatively gross, often merely commonsense, terms. That is, I was beginning to have the as yet rather vague notion that there was something which I wanted to call "behavior *qua* behavior." This would be something other than and different from the mere muscle contractions and gland secretions and the mere punctiform sense-organ stimuli underlying such behavior.

The further notion that purpose and cognition are essential descriptive ingredients of any such non-physiologically defined "behavior *qua* behavior" I borrowed from Perry.[2] He pointed out that behavior as such is both persistent and docile. (Thorndike's cat exhibited persistence and docility relative to getting out of the box.) The cat's behavior has to be described and identified in terms of these purposive and cognitive features — but in a quite non-metaphysical and non-teleological sense.[3]

During this period I also spent considerable effort in trying to translate some of the familiar pre-behavioral concepts, such as "sensation," "emotion," "ideas" and "consciousness," into these new, non-physiological behavioral terms.[4] And in the course of so doing I came to use the term "molar" to

---

[2] R. B. Perry, Docility and purpose, *Psychol Rev*, 1918, 25, 1–20; The cognitive interest and its refinements, *J Philos.*, 1921, 18, 365–375.

[3] E. C. Tolman, A new formula for behaviorism, *Psychol. Rev.*, 1922, 29, 44–53.

[4] Tolman, Concerning the sensation quality. A behavioristic account, *Psychol Rev*, 1922, 29, 140–145, A behavioristic account of the emotions, *ibid*, 1923, 30, 217–227, A behavioristic theory of ideas, *ibid*, 1926, 33, 352–369; A behaviorist's definition of consciousness, *ibid.*, 1927, 34, 433–439.

designate "behavior *qua* behavior," as contrasted with the term "molecular" to designate the underlying physiological units of sense-organ stimulation, central neural activity and final muscle contraction or gland secretion. This pair of terms — "molar" vs. "molecular" — was suggested to me by Professor Donald C. Williams, then a graduate student in philosophy and psychology in Berkeley.

The above ideas, expanded and elaborated, were finally brought together in the book, *Purposive Behavior in Animals and Men* (1932). As I survey now ambivalently that extensive tome, I find a number of features in it which strike me as probably still worth calling attention to.

First, it is to be noted that I spent what would now seem an unconscionable amount of space and effort in attacking "mentalism" and in defending an objective approach to psychology. Bridgman's book[5] had, to be sure, appeared in 1927. But I had not as yet read it, so I did not use the term operational; but it was obviously an operational set of concepts for a non-physiological behaviorism which I was groping for. Today, however, the operational battle has so largely been won that to the average psychologist it no longer seems worth arguing about. In other words, today we are practically all behaviorists. In some loose sense we practically all subscribe to the doctrine that the only psychological statements that can be scientifically validated are statements about the organism's behavior, about stimulus situations or about inferred, but objectively definable, intervening variables.

Secondly, I am still amused and bemused by my neologisms. They have, of course, never been as offensive to me as to others. Further, I would point out that a number of them have gained some currency in the literature. Thus "*discriminanda*" and "*manipulanda*," appear here and there in the writings of others. Further, the more basic central term of "sign-gestalt-expectations," while seldom picked up in its entirety, seems to have been the source, through the agency of the Hilgard and Marquis book,[6] of the now widely current term, "expectancy." It should be pointed out, however, that "expectancy" as used by others is probably a more atomistic concept than was intended in my original meaning of "sign-gestalt-expectation." Finally, the term "means-end-readiness" seems also to have found favor among some rat runners and even among some personality psychologists.

Thirdly, I still would want to emphasize the distinction to which I was trying to draw attention by the use of the two concepts "means-end-readiness" and "sign-gestalt-expectation." This was a distinction which few readers, if any, seem to have understood or, at any rate, to have remarked upon. By the introduction of these two concepts I was trying to say that what the organism acquires in a given *concrete* situation is *first* an "expecta-

[5] P. W. Bridgman, *The Logic of Modern Physics*, 1927.
[6] E. R. Hilgard and D. G. Marquis, *Conditioning and Learning*, 1940.

tion" that by responding to this spatially and temporally located *concrete* sign (or means) by a given behavior it will arrive at a further concrete "significate" (or goal) and, *secondly*, that the organism is also acquiring a general "readiness" thereafter to accept this same general *type* of sign or means as leading to the same general type of significate or goal.   The sign-gestalt-expectation is limited to, and goes off in, the particular concrete situation. The means-end-readiness is a more universalized disposition which, once acquired, the organism carries about with him to new situations.   I today would still hold to this basic distinction, although I would now phrase it somewhat differently.   Instead, that is, of now talking about concrete sign-gestalt-expectations and correlated, governing, means-end-readinesses, I would speak, rather, of concrete "behavior-spaces" of the moment and of governing, controlling "belief-value matrices."[7]   These new terms seem to me to emphasize better another essential point of the doctrine which is that each single sign-gestalt-expectation is always part of a larger *field* of expectations and that any single means-end-readiness — belief-value unit — is also part of a larger field or *matrix* of such units.

Fourth, another feature involved in the concept of sign-gestalt-expectations, which seems not to have been understood by most readers was that a sign-gestalt-expectation is not to be conceived as just an S-S association.[8] It is to be thought of rather as a single interconnected and interacting whole — hence the term gestalt — such that the discriminated character of the sign will within limits affect that of the significate and vice versa.   Thus, I was postulating, for example, that a perceived door, which, it has been learned led to food, probably has, in some degree, different immediate discriminable properties from a perceived door, which, it has been learned, leads to electric shock.   Further, I was emphasizing in contrast to classical Gestalt theory, that, even from a phenomenological point of view, the smallest unit of experience is not just a mere sensory-perceptual pattern but such a pattern suffused with instrumental meaning.[9]

Fifth, in connection with my new notions of the "behavior-space" and of the "belief-value matrix," I would now find a certain further defect in the book in that the concepts "sign-gestalt-expectation" and "means-end-readiness" did not allow for the "self" as an object within such an expectation or such a readiness.   It is probably the influence of Lewin, with his concept of the "Life-Space" and of the "Psychological Person" *as in* the Life Space, and

---

[7] I am amused that I can't seem to get away from neologisms and hyphens even today. One reason is, I suspect, the tremendous impact of the German language on me in the summer of 1912 when I went to Giessen in preparation for my language examinations.   Good psychology and compounded nouns, as used in German, somehow became synonymous for me.

[8] Thus, for example, Spence, who otherwise presented a very fair and illuminating account of my theory, seems to have missed this point   See K. W. Spence, Theoretical interpretations of learning, Chap. 11 in *Comparative Psychology*, 1942 (rev. ed.).

[9] E. C. Tolman, Gestalt and sign-gestalt, *Psychol. Rev.*, 1933, 40, 391–411.

the influence of psychologists and sociologists, who have been investigating group phenomena, which have led me now to substitute a behavior space, which contains both a behaving self and goal-selfs and a belief-value matrix, which may also contain universalized self-images.

A sixth feature of the book which still fascinates me is that it attempted to provide a theoretical scheme for summarizing and interrelating a great many types of learning experiment. It was hoped at the time the book was published that it might be used as a textbook in courses in animal psychology. And a few hardy individuals did so use it. I myself never was able to. It always turned my stomach. I had just torn out my vitals and exposed them to the world. I was therefore unable to look upon those vitals without suffering either extreme shame or unseemly pride. I wanted to vomit at it and often still feel so inclined. There was too much self-consciousness and affectation of style. However, I still think that the book provided what was at the time a stimulating organization of empirical data on animal motivation and animal learning.

Finally, the last feature in the book, which I now wish to draw attention to, is the fact that it was also an attempt to lay out a scheme for the lines of interaction between all the various variables determinative of behavior. Among these variables were what I then called the "immanent determinants." These were my first step toward what later I conceived of as "intervening variables." I felt vaguely at that time that the cognitive and purposive features of behavior, which I was postulating, were somehow statements about the shapes of the functions connecting the final dependent behavior to its various independent determiners of environmental stimuli and physiological drive states. Therefore I said the cognitive and purpose features were "immanent" *in* these connections or functions It was only later that I hit upon the notion of breaking up the total functions into two or more successive steps and inserting "intervening variables" as intervening events or processes or states between such successive steps or functions. So much for the book.

Let me consider now the development of this concept of intervening variables as I attempted to elaborate it in several articles which succeeded the book. Intervening variables I conceived as hypothesized states or processes between the variables of stimulus situations, physiological drive conditions, heredity, age, past training, etc., on the one hand, and the final dependent variable of behavior, on the other hand. This notion of "intervening variables" as constructs defined in part in terms of their postulated functional relationships either to the independent variables, on the one side, or to the dependent variable of behavior, on the other, was presented in three articles. In the first of these articles, "Psychology versus immediate experience,"[10] the emphasis was upon finally laying the ghost of a subjective,

---

[10] *Philos. Sci*, 1935, 2, 356–380.

primarily introspective, definition of the intervening variable. The second article, "Operational behaviorism and current trends in psychology,"[11] was further concerned with the functional, mathematical, dependencies of the intervening variables upon the independent variables and with operational ways of measuring these intervening variables. It also raised the further problem of the functions by which such intervening variables were to be conceived to interact with each other and to produce the final dependent behavior. Finally, in the third article, "The determiners of behavior at a choice point,"[12] an attempt was made to use this sort of an analysis for bringing together all the more important rat experiments to that date (1937). The attempt was made to show which functions — those between independent and intervening variables or those between different intervening variables or those between these and the final dependent behavior — the various individual rat experiments were respectively concerned with.

More recently, it has been argued by MacCorquodale and Meehl[13] that a distinction is to be drawn between "intervening variables," defined solely in terms of functional relationships to the independent or dependent variables, and "hypothetical constructs," defined in terms of constitutive properties attributed to the intervening states or processes as such. It is claimed by these writers that Hull,[14] who has borrowed and also found useful the notion of intervening variables, and I myself have both built our theories primarily on "intervening variables" in their sense and not upon "hypothetical constructs." It is my present contention, however,[15] that all theories really use "hypothetical constructs." We theorists have differed merely in the explicitness with which we have indicated either to ourselves or to others just what the assumed constitutive properties of our hypothetical constructs are. In other words, I do not agree that there are two separate kinds of theoretical concept — intervening variables, on the one hand, and hypothetical constructs, on the other. I accept the importance of the distinction between the assumed functional relationships of the intervening variables, or, if you will, hypothetical constructs, and their assumed constitutive properties. And MacCorquodale and Meehl did us a great service in emphasizing this distinction. Yet I do not believe one can fruitfully argue about the one feature, of functional relationships, without also arguing, or at least implying, something about the other feature, of constitutive properties. Thus the constitutive properties which, my type of theory as-

[11] *Proc 25th Anniv Inauguration Graduate Studies University of Southern California*, Los Angeles: USC, 1936, 89–103.
[12] *Psychol Rev.*, 1938, 45, 1–41.
[13] K. MacCorquodale and P. E. Meehl, On a distinction between hypothetical constructs and intervening variables, *Psychol Rev*, 1948, 55, 95–107.
[14] C. L. Hull, *Principles of Behavior*, 1943.
[15] See "A Psychological Model," in the book by Talcott Parsons, Edward A. Shils, *et al.*, *Toward a Theory of Action*, 1951.

sumes, are those implicit in a topological, electromechanical model. I have called it elsewhere a pseudo-brain model.[16] But it is far more "pseudo" than it is "brain," even though it is full of hypothetical constructs in the narrow MacCorquodale and Meehl sense. A more extended discussion of this model will be presented below.

I would like to turn now to some of the kinds of experiments on rat learning done in the Berkeley laboratory which seem to have influenced, or been influenced by, my theoretical position. Theory is viable and to be justified only in so far as it stimulates, or is stimulated by, research. My theoretical pronouncements have, to be sure, usually been phrased merely loosely and programmatically. And so they have seldom made possible any precise theoretical deductions which could then be specifically subjected to experimental test. Nevertheless, these theoretical meanderings have conditioned me and my students to be interested in certain *kinds* of *experiment*. The theory though loose, has been fertile; perhaps fertile primarily because loose.

Now, for the experiments themselves. In trying some two years ago to summarize the major directions of research in the Berkeley laboratory it seemed to me that a majority of the experiments could be grouped under five main headings:[17] (1) "latent learning" (2) "vicarious trial and error" (VTE), (3) "searching for the stimulus," (4) "hypotheses in rats" and (5) "spatial orientation." I shall not attempt to catalogue these experiments here nor shall I attempt to give the credit which is due to the individual students and research workers who actually had most of the specific ideas, developed the experimental designs, and did the actual work. Rather, I wish to suggest merely that all of the experiments were in one way or another supportive, on the one hand, of a field theory of rat learning, and, on the other hand, of a theory which asserts that the animal brings to the stimulus situation certain cognitive sets — "hypotheses," means-end-readiness; needs to solve — VTE's and searching for the stimulus — as well as specific states of motivation. These cognitive sets and motivational states cause him to react selectively and actively to the then and there presented stimulus array and determine the behavior space which he comes to perceive and the new means-end-readiness (belief-value matrices) which he will carry away. All of these experiments from my point of view, if not from that of their authors, have reinforced the general notion of the essentially cognitive character of learning. The original crucial experiments in this doctrine of the cognitive character of learning were those on "latent learning" initiated by Blodgett.[18]

[16] E. C. Tolman, Interrelations between perception and personality. a symposium. Part I. Discussion, *J. Personal*, 1949, 18, 48–50.

[17] Tolman, Cognitive maps in rats and men, *Psychol Rev*, 1948, 55, 189–208.

[18] H. C. Blodgett, The effect of the introduction of reward upon the maze performance of rats, *Univ. Calif. Publ. Psychol.*, 1929, 4, 113–134.

Turn now to a quite different problem. I have always been obsessed by a need for a single comprehensive theory or scheme for the whole of psychology. And I have also always wanted to be something more than a mere learning or rat psychologist. I have wanted a scheme which would cover not only rat learning but also one which would be pertinent to the problems of human thought and of human motivation. In *Purposive Behavior in Animals and Men* I was already tempted into pronunciamentos concerning primary and secondary drives, demands, insight and ideation as well as concerning learning *per se*. And under the impetus of a general human concern for social events and of a need to discover how man is ever to achieve a stable, or even a merely satisfying, society I have a number of times been tempted into relatively *ad hoc* assertions concerning drives or needs and concerning complex motivational dynamisms both in individuals and in society.[19]

All of these pronouncements have been somewhat abortive because of lack of training on my part in the other social sciences and even in personality psychology and in social psychology. Yet I do not wish to disown them. The pronouncements may have been naïve; but I do not think that any of them has been basically wrong or mischievous. They constituted my first steps towards a more complete conceptual scheme — a scheme which would allow me to handle not only simple learning but also problems such as the operation of innate or socially acquired secondary and tertiary needs, the operation of the psychoanalytical and other dynamisms, and finally, the explanation and prevention of individual and social maladjustments. I have been concerned throughout with man's basic needs, biological or social, and with the question of how these needs become modified through social learning as a result of given cultures and given training procedures within a family. Why is it that individuals and cultures go astray? Why is it that a social system seems so seldom to allow for reasonable satisfactions in most of the individuals involved in it? Can we arrive at some naturalistic definitions of the good life or of different kinds of good life? And, having arrived at such definitions, can psychology and the social sciences eventually agree upon ways to produce such lives? These are the sort of questions which I would seek to raise and would like answers for.

Very recently[20] I have attempted a new theoretical statement, more com-

[19] See, for example, Physiology, psychology and sociology, *Psychol. Rev.*, 1938, 45, 228–241; Psychological man, *J. soc. Psychol.*, 1941, 13, 205–218; Motivation, learning and adjustment, *Proc. Amer. Philos. Soc*, 1941, 84, 543–563; *Drives Toward War*, 1942; Identification and the postwar world, *J. abnorm. soc. Psychol.*, 1943, 38, 141–148; A drive-conversion diagram, *Psychol. Rev.*, 1943, 50, 503–513; The nature and functioning of wants, *ibid.*, 1949, 357–369; The psychology of social learning, *J. of Social Issues*, Special Issue, December 1949, 5–18.
[20] See again "A Psychological Model" in the book by Talcott Parsons, Edward A. Shils, *et al., Toward a Theory of Action*, 1951.

prehensive, I believe, than that presented in *Purposive Behavior in Animals and Men* (1932) which I hope eventually may allow for the putting and answering of such questions in a fruitful way. Let me give a brief résumé of this new scheme. I now find it useful to postulate three main systems of intervening variables: a need-system, a belief-value-matrix or matrices, and concrete behavior spaces. This is not the place for an extended exposition of these constructs. I wish merely to indicate their general character.

The *need-system*. This construct is patterned on Lewin's concept of the inner core of the psychological person as composed of intercommunicating need and quasi-need compartments. Instead of postulating, as I have formerly, two different kinds of needs — positive needs and negative needs — I now assume that each need has both its positive and its negative side. I assume, for example, that food-hunger, when aroused, is operationally definable both as a readiness to approach and eat foods and as a readiness to avoid and to get away from non-foods. And, likewise, I assume that fear, when aroused, is operationally definable both as a readiness to avoid and/or get away from painful situations and as a readiness to get to and to remain in "safe" "secure" situations. To define operationally the magnitude of the arousal of any given need at a given time one will have to agree upon a "standard" defining, positive or negative, situation in which the magnitudes of the approach, or avoidance, responses can be quantitatively measured. Such defining experiments will not be easy ones to decide upon; nor will they be technically easy to carry out. But the notion of such possible experiments is, I believe, implicit in almost everyone's thinking about needs.

This construct of a need system is accompanied also by an assertion that a distinction is to be drawn between such *needs*, as measurable behaviorial propensities, to go to or away from such and such types of goal objects and the *physiological drive states* which are often determinative of these needs. Physiological drive states are an independent variable; needs are an intervening variable. This distinction between physiological drive states and needs allows for such facts, for example, as that food-hunger, as *drive state*, defined as a condition of physiological deprivation, and food hunger, as *need*, defined as a behavioral readiness to approach and consume food, are not necessarily related in linear fashion. The concept of need compartments also allows for the assumption that some of the tension in a compartment may under some conditions be aroused directly by an environmental stimulus situation in some degree independently of the presence, or absence, of a correlated physiological drive state. Finally, the construct of a system of intercommunicating compartments suggests the possibility of hierarchies of superordination and subordination among needs and of mutual facilitations or inhibitions between needs.

Belief-value matrices. This construct, as has been indicated, is a development of the earlier concept of means-end-readiness. Belief-value matrices are thought of as chains of beliefs (means-end-readinesses) which connect successive banks of types of objects to one another in means-end, instrumental, fashion. Such means-end beliefs include also the characters of the "types of behavior" to be performed if the given type of means is to lead to the given type of end. And each categorized bank of objects, whether functioning as means or as end, is to be conceived as constituting a kind of generalization dimension along which are located functionally similar subtypes of object. Any given matrix may thus be thought of as in the nature of a pattern of "platonic ideas" (*i.e.*, object type differentiations, behavior-type differentiations and generalizations plus means-end relationships). Finally, there are also present in a matrix positive or negative values (deriving from the aroused needs), deposited on types of ends and relayed back to the means and which will be distributed along the generalization dimensions.

Finally, any matrix with its differentiations, generalizations, beliefs and values is activated by the aroused needs and the present stimulus situation and serves along with the presented environmental stimuli, to determine the character of the specific concrete "behavior space" which will be "perceived" at the moment.

The *behavior space*. This third construct is very similar to Lewin's Life Space save that the "insides" of Lewin's "psychological person" have been elaborated and placed outside as the need system and the governing belief-value matrix. The behavior space contains a "behaving self" which is perceived as located in time and place relative to the perceived array of objects and possible locomotions. The behaving self contains within itself merely one or more negative "need-pushes" (not complete needs). These need-pushes are derived from the needs and functions in that, as negative, they cause the behaving person to be attracted to positive valences and repelled by negative valences. The valences themselves are derived from the values in the governing belief-value matrix. Values are for given *types* of object. Valences are for concrete *instances* of such types of object. Lastly, it may be emphasized that, in the case of human organisms, the self, both as behaving self and as possible goal selfs, will appear in practically any behavior space.

The just preceding paragraphs are, I realize, too condensed and the model itself is too complicated for such a brief account to have much intelligibility. I have introduced it, partly, to indicate that I am still up to my old trick of trying to talk about too many facts and findings at once, but also because I believe that the concept of belief-value matrices will provide a schema which will prove helpful to the other social sciences. I would suggest, in short, that such concepts as "attitude," "culture pattern," "need-disposition," etc., as used by various social scientists, will all be translatable into, and be illuminated by, the concept of belief-value matrices.

In conclusion it would seem meet to indicate the main sources from which I think my ideas have come. First of all most of the credit, if it be credit, should go to all the students whose ideas I have shamefully and consistently adopted and exploited throughout the years, and ended up by believing to be my own. Secondly, it should go to my teachers at Harvard who taught me to think, to be critical, to be complicated but to remain naturalistic. Thirdly, it should go to all the members of the department of psychology at Berkeley who have always given me untold moral and intellectual support in spite of considerable tolerant skepticism as to the worth of my final outpourings. Next, it should go to the Gestalt psychologists, but especially to Kurt Lewin whose ideas I have borrowed time and again and absorbed into my very blood. Again, it should go to my year's stay in Vienna and especially to Egon Brunswik, who opened my eyes to the meaning and the viability of the European psychological tradition, both academic and psychoanalytical, and who gave me new insight into the essentially "achievement" character of behavior. Still further, it should go to all my colleagues, old and young, in the Assessment Program of the Office of Strategic Services. There once and for all I finally became addicted to PSYCHOLOGY and no longer content to think merely of rats and of learning. I there acquired an aspiration level relative to personality psychology which I have since been striving for but have, of course, not achieved. And, finally, my thanks must go to the Department of Social Relations at Harvard University, which during the year 1949–50 taught me something of sociology and of anthropology and of personality and of social psychology, and set me wondering about ways in which my rat concepts might eventually become amalgamated with those of the scientists in these other fields. For, if we are to advance, we must first understand, and then attempt to incorporate into our own, the perspectives of our sister sciences — not merely of those sciences which pertain to physiology but also and even more of those which pertain to social living.

INDEX

°The name in parenthesis indicates the autobiographer who has mentioned the subject

341